John Lydgate and the Making of Public Culture

Inspired by the example of his predecessors Chaucer and Gower, John Lydgate articulated in his poetry, prose, and translations many of the most serious political questions of his day. In the fifteenth century Lydgate was the most famous poet in England, filling commissions for the court, the aristocracy, and the guilds. He wrote for an elite London readership that was historically very small, but that saw itself as dominating the cultural life of the nation. Thus the new literary forms and modes developed by Lydgate and his contemporaries helped to shape the development of English public culture in the fifteenth century. Maura Nolan offers a major reinterpretation of Lydgate's work and of his central role in the developing literary culture of his time. Moreover, she provides a wholly new perspective on Lydgate's relationship to Chaucer, as he followed Chaucerian traditions while creating innovative new ways of addressing the public.

MAURA NOLAN is Assistant Professor of English at the University of Notre Dame.

CAMBRIDGE STUDIES IN MEDIEVAL LITERATURE

This series of critical books seeks to cover the whole area of literature written in the major medieval languages – the main European vernaculars and medieval Latin and Greek – during the period *c.* 1100–1500. Its chief aim is to publish and stimulate fresh scholarship and criticism on medieval literature, special emphasis being placed on understanding major works of poetry, prose, and drama in relation to the contemporary culture and learning which fostered them.

A complete list of titles in the series can be found at the end of the volume.

John Lydgate and the Making of Public Culture

MAURA NOLAN

CAMBRIDGE
UNIVERSITY PRESS

CAMBRIDGE UNIVERSITY PRESS
Cambridge, New York, Melbourne, Madrid, Cape Town, Singapore, São Paulo

CAMBRIDGE UNIVERSITY PRESS
The Edinburgh Building, Cambridge CB2 2RU, UK

Published in the United States of America by Cambridge University Press, New York

www.cambridge.org
Information on this title: www.cambridge.org/9780521852982

© Maura Nolan 2005

First published 2005

Printed in the United Kingdom at the University Press, Cambridge

A catalogue record for this book is available from the British Library

ISBN-13 978-0-521-85298-2 hardback
ISBN-10 0-521-85298-6 hardback

For my parents
Jack and Carolyn Nolan

Contents

vii

Acknowledgments

I have many people to thank for their help in the making of this book. I was introduced to medieval literature by Kevin Brownlee, Alan Gaylord, and Peter Travis, and to being a medievalist by the singular example of Aranye Fradenburg. I had the good fortune of studying with David Aers, Sarah Beckwith, and Lee Patterson, and have been aided by each in innumerable intellectual and personal ways over the years. Michael Moses helped me at several critical junctures. At Notre Dame, Katherine O'Brien O'Keeffe has been a sage adviser and friend since the very beginning. To Jill Mann I owe a special debt of gratitude for much material assistance and inspiration, both Latin and vernacular. Other colleagues have been supportive throughout, including Jim Dougherty, Steve Fredman, Sandra Gustafson, Greg Kucich, Jesse Lander, Don Sniegowski, Chris Vanden Bossche, Ewa and Krys Ziarek, and particularly Graham Hammill and Michael Lapidge. Tom Noble of the Medieval Institute kindly made a research trip possible at a crucial moment. Sarah Beckwith, Larry Scanlon, and James Simpson read portions of the manuscript and made many helpful suggestions and comments. With typical generosity, Paul Strohm challenged me to think through my assumptions and define my terms. Alastair Minnis supported the project at an early stage and never wavered. The anonymous readers for the press gave considered and constructive advice, and Linda Bree shepherded me through the publication process with patience and energy. Andrew Cole has been my most faithful and severe critic; his belief in the project sustained me throughout. With a thoughtfulness on which I have come to rely, Lisa Lampert sent me a postcard that made me see mumming in a new way. Conversations and exchanges with friends have strengthened and deepened my thinking about medieval literature; many thanks to Chris Chism, Bruce Holsinger, and Emily Steiner, as well as to David Benson, Charles Blyth, Chris Cannon, Patricia DeMarco, Robert Epstein, Frank Grady, Barbara Hanrahan, Paul Hyams, Ethan Knapp, Katie Little, Bobby Meyer-Lee, Liz Scala, George Shuffleton, Gabrielle Spiegel, and Vance Smith. I owe special thanks to Tim Collins. The graduate students at Notre Dame questioned and tested my thinking about the fifteenth century and renewed my pleasure in the project. Audiences at Rutgers and Carleton College gave me warm receptions and asked incisive questions, as did the participants in the Vagantes conference at Cornell. Michael Wood welcomed me to Princeton for a year, and Rita Copeland and David Wallace extended their characteristic hospitality to an occasional visitor at Penn. No one writing a book about Lydgate can fail to thank Derek Pearsall, who led the way for all of us.

I completed the book while at the National Humanities Center, with the generous support of the Carl and Lily Pforzheimer Foundation. I was greatly aided by support from the Institute for Scholarship in the Liberal Arts and the Kobayashi Travel Fund at Notre Dame. The librarians at the Hesburgh Library at Notre Dame and the Firestone Library at Princeton cheerfully fulfilled every request. John Pollack of the Annenberg Rare Book and Manuscript Library at the University of Pennsylvania and Joanna Ball of Trinity College Library at Cambridge gave valuable and timely aid. My research assistants, Rebecca Davis, Ben Fischer, and Kathleen Tonry, helped me inestimably. Lynn McCormack was always generous with her time and assistance. An earlier version of chapter one appeared in *Speculum*, volume 78, 2003; I am grateful for permission to reprint it here.

Dan Blanton read the entire manuscript with his usual acumen and insight, and insisted that I finish it properly; thanks are not enough for these and other kindnesses great and small. I am lucky that my sister and brothers, Kate, John, Tim, and Dan, were always ready to come to my aid. This book is dedicated to my parents: to my father, who taught me to read poetry, and my mother, who showed me how to write about it.

Introduction: the forms of public culture

In a world governed by Fortune, kings are especially at risk. On August 31, 1422 Henry V died at Vincennes, south of Paris, at the age of thirty-five, only nine years after he had ascended to the throne. Those years had been marked by a string of military successes, culminating in the Treaty of Troyes, which established Henry as the heir to the French throne and placed France under English rule. His premature death punctured the illusion of invincibility he had perpetuated throughout his reign, reminding his subjects of the vulnerability of the great and creating a void at the very center of the realm. Henry V's legacy to his nine-month-old son was either a curse or a blessing; the years of the minority were either the finest hour of the Lancastrian regime – proof positive of its legitimacy and authority – or a prelude to the dark days of civil war and internecine strife to come. Whatever the ultimate verdict on the success or failure of the minority, it cannot be disputed that the death of Henry V produced an extreme challenge to Lancastrian authority, one that would have to be met in the arena of culture as well as politics if the reign of Henry VI was to succeed. This book begins with a very basic question: what happened to forms of cultural expression after the death of Henry V and the accession of his infant son?

It might be said, quite simply, that what happened was John Lydgate. Already known as an able promoter of English and regnal interests from his work for Henry V, especially the massive *Troy Book*, Lydgate produced during the years of the minority – what Derek Pearsall has called his "laureate" period – a whole series of texts designed to bolster and support the authority of the child on the throne.[1] These texts have typically been read as expressions of the Lancastrian penchant for self-promotion; the regime during the minority experimented with a wide variety of forms of propaganda, including coins, pictorial images, royal spectacles, and written texts.[2] Indeed, some of them are quite straight-forward advertisements for Henrican kingship. But not all. This book focuses centrally on a series of Lydgate's works that defy attempts to categorize (and thus dismiss) them as superficial and occasional, ranging from a tract written immediately after the death of Henry V, *Serpent of Division*, to performance texts – a series of mummings and disguisings – to verses written to memorialize a lavish royal entry, Henry VI's return to London from France in 1432. Each of the texts I discuss here simultaneously demands to be read in topical terms, as a meditation on or negotiation of the problem of sovereignty during the minority, and resists topicality by asserting its status as a distinctively literary object, characterized by excess, ambiguity, and an overt concern for its own status as part of a poetic tradition.

Readers of medieval English poetry will find the latter characteristics familiar. Chaucer has long been recognized as a poet whose texts resist simple contextual readings by countering the topical with such tactics as dialogism, polysemy, irony, and the like. Even Lydgate has been increasingly acknowledged as a complex and skilful practitioner of Chaucerian poetics in such works as *Troy Book*, the *Siege of Thebes*, and the *Fall of Princes*. But the works under consideration here, each of which was written for a particular occasion or commission, do not at first glance appear to fit the Chaucerian model; each wears its topicality on its sleeve, proclaiming first and foremost that it is an instrumental text, written to perform a function and to respond to the particular historical conditions of the minority. *Serpent of Division* directly addresses the problems of conciliar government and the dangers of "division" among "lordes and prynces of renowne." The mummings and disguisings are all specifically crafted for performance before audiences comprised of England's ruling elites, both aristocratic and mercantile; all address questions of governance, right rule, and sovereignty. Lydgate's verses memorializing the 1432 entry of Henry VI seem on the surface simply to report on what happened as a way of glorifying both the king and the patron of the piece, the Mayor of London. Overall, the immediate impression given by these texts is one of simplicity, directness, and didacticism; each seems like a tissue of late medieval convention and platitude rendered interesting to the critic only by the unique circumstances of minority rule.

But what is striking about the texts I consider here is the degree to which, even as they proclaim their instrumentality, they indulge in literary practices that seem inimical to the ends of propaganda. To take one example, in the "Disguising at London" Lydgate presents his audience with a moralized allegory of Fortune and the four cardinal virtues. The lesson seems obvious: resist the vagaries of Fortune by embracing virtue. On closer examination, however, it becomes clear that the text is both a very complex meditation on the philosophical problem of contingency, and a multilayered response to both Latin and vernacular source texts. Were Lydgate a pure propagandist, he would eschew this kind of intertextuality in favor of didacticism. But he does not, nor is the "Disguising at London" the only example of his embrace of formal complexity in a purportedly instrumental text; it is in fact *more* likely that Lydgatean propaganda will challenge its consumers by invoking literary traditions and exploring philosophical problems than otherwise. The question is not (as it so often has been in Lydgate criticism) one of poetic quality or competence. Rather, we must ask why, at a moment of distinct historical crisis, Lydgate turned to complex forms of literary discourse rather than to purely functional modes such as consolation, exhortation, or exaltation.

It is the argument of this book that Lydgate, spurred on by a strong sense of crisis, remade the forms of public culture available to him, and did so in a counterintuitive way that challenges our assumptions about propaganda – not only the Lancastrian propaganda of the minority, but also instrumental texts more generally. As I have suggested, Lydgate's occasional texts are distinctly literary – by which I mean semantically dense, self-referential, allusive, and above all, Chaucerian – and in making them so, he systematically undermines their ability to exalt or console in any straightforward way. By translating the poetic and literary techniques he has learned from Chaucer into new media, especially spectacle, Lydgate creates uniquely hybrid texts, part reassuring moralisms or praise, part literary works in search of educated and savvy readers. These readers find densely layered texts seeking imaginary and symbolic resolutions to critical cultural problems and contradictions.

In identifying these works as "public" texts, I am making a double reference, first to their external status as representations of

3

performances or spectacles – a simple reference to the fact that these texts commemorate public occasions – and second, and more importantly, to the imaginary public that each text constructs and solicits. There is a good argument to be made that the publicness of Lydgate's performance texts is fundamentally in doubt; after all, no corroborating record exists to prove that his mummings and disguisings were performed, and it is not even clear that Lydgate witnessed the royal entry of 1432 before writing his verses. *Serpent of Division*, moreover, is written for a single patron and specifically designed to be read, not enacted. But whether or not concrete evidence of performance can be found, what is most important to recognize about all of the texts I describe here is their distinctive consciousness of their own public status, and their powerful tendency to *imagine* their audience as a public rather than as an inchoate group of readers or viewers. This sense of what a "public" might be emerges in part out of the work of Lydgate's vernacular predecessors, especially Chaucer and Gower. In the late fourteenth century, Anne Middleton has argued, "public poetry" developed as a special kind of discourse, "experientially based, vernacular, simple, pious but practical, active ... [an] essentially high-minded secularism."[3] This idea of the "public" is essentially bound up with notions like "common profit," notions expressed by poets such as Chaucer and Gower, "interpreter[s] of the common world."[4] The "public culture" I am describing here is intimately related to this "public poetry" – as I will show, Lydgate returns again and again to both Gower and Chaucer – but it is also quite different, produced by a dramatically different historical situation and responding to a changed political landscape. Paradoxically, though I am arguing that Lydgate ultimately sought to expand the audience for Chaucerian writing, the "public" imagined by the texts described in this book is quite small, comprised of the king and his household, nobles, and the London elite.[5] What transforms this group of readers and viewers into a "public," however, is the way in which these texts combine didacticism – moral exhortation and pedagogical instruction – with a clear sense that their audience *represents* the only public that matters: the ruling elite. Instead of broad notions of "common profit," we find exercises in persuasion, designed to assert the sovereignty of the youthful king, as well as attempts at consolation for those still mourning his father's death.

This change in the definition of the "public" marks an important historical shift, a turn away from a Chaucerian vision of the social whole as variegated, multiple, and inclusive, and toward an understanding of the social totality as hierarchical and exclusive, organized around a notion of "representativeness" that starts with the king as the head of the body of the realm. This shift produces the paradoxical effect of a simultaneous narrowing and broadening of the audience; Lydgate seems at times to be introducing Chaucerian poetics to new groups of readers and listeners, while at other moments it becomes clear that the "public" he addresses is in fact very small. This paradox requires that we distinguish between historical audiences (readers and viewers) and imaginary audiences, those to whom texts are fictionally addressed. For the most part, Lydgate's fictional audiences are limited to aristocrats and the London elite; there is nothing in his occasional works resembling the diverse social whole of the *Canterbury Tales*. In this sense, his poetry is narrower and more limited than Chaucer's. At the same time, however, Chaucer wrote for the court or a small circle of readers, while Lydgate was actively fulfilling commissions from both inside and outside the court, using Chaucerian tropes, characters, and rhyme schemes to provide poetry for Mercers, Goldsmiths, mayor, and citizens.[6] Understanding the public culture of the minority, then, means understanding precisely what "public" means at any given moment; it may be the London crowds in 1432, or it may be a tiny group of lords and princes understood by Lydgate to represent the realm in its totality.

LYDGATE'S PUBLIC

David Lawton has argued that the fifteenth century saw the construction of a "public sphere," which was "parallel to and connected with the structures of power," one in which modes of discourse were developed that expressed common notions of the social good.[7] Such a public sphere was, like Lydgate's imaginary audiences, fictional rather than real, a distinction also made by John Watts; as he suggests, "a public that is literally and actually in communication with a wide group of people is surely a different beast from a public that is simply idealised as collective."[8] In fact, over the course of the fourteenth and early fifteenth centuries the "real" public was growing, coming to include more people with a "common stock of political expectations and languages."⁹ As this growth occurred, it inevitably created circumstances in which the lower social orders sought to gain access to a public voice and public status; the Rising of 1381 bears strong witness to this process. Watts suggests that after an initial – and shocked – period of openness at the end of Richard II's reign and at the beginning of the Lancastrian regime, lay authorities sought to redefine the "common" voice to exclude precisely those groups that had laid claim to the term in the first place. As he states, "The public permeated medieval elites; indeed, the communitarian aspects of its diction troubled the very distinctions that enabled their public power."¹⁰ Here we see precisely that process of narrowing and broadening that is the legacy of the Chaucer tradition: more people are inexorably drawn into the public, even as those in power seek to restrict and limit the membership of that group, paradoxically by producing a discourse of openness, "common profit" and representativeness. This paradox creates a very deep, very difficult cultural contradiction that we see Lydgate attempting to negotiate and articulate as he moves from persuading "wyse governours" in *Serpent of Division* to addressing mayor and city in his 1432 verses.

The key to grasping how this contradiction works during the minority, particularly in relation to the death of Henry V, is the idea of "representation," the notion that a person or a group can stand in for the realm and for everyone in it. In his history of the public sphere, Jürgen Habermas describes how, in feudal culture

> it was no accident that the attributes of lordship, such as the ducal seal, were called "public"; not by accident did the English king enjoy "publicness" – for lordship was something publicly represented. This *publicness* (or *publicity*) *of representation* was not constituted as a social realm, that is, as a public sphere; rather it was something like a status attribute . . . representation pretended to make something invisible visible through the public presence of the person of the lord."

The idea of *representation*, the notion that the king literally embodied the realm, was a crucial one during the minority, when it was deployed precisely to compensate for the absence of an adult king. What Watts's analysis shows is that in England this idea is historically specific; it was very deliberately embraced by the ruling elite as a counter to a more participatory idea of governance shared between king and people that was beginning to emerge.[12] In Habermas's terms, that is, the "public sphere" had begun to emerge as a meaningful category, so much so that it met with powerful resistance by elites committed to the "representativeness" of the king. Lydgate's writing during the minority is thus caught between conflicting historical imperatives. On the one hand, the inexorable emergence of a broader public sphere resulted in a wider audience for elite forms of cultural expression like Chaucerian poetry. The Lancastrian regime, afflicted with the Achilles heel of a child-king, had to surrender to this broader notion of the public in order to make sure that the representativeness of the king remained intact – hence, its enormous commitment to propaganda. At the same time, the Lancastrians were especially devoted to the hierarchical idea of the king as the embodiment of the realm, an idea that insisted that "publicness" be limited and representative rather than expansive and inclusive. As a result, when we see Lydgate simultaneously addressing new audiences and limiting his address to a tiny elite, we see a poet caught up in a larger historical shift and its local and specific manifestations. Lydgate's mummings, disguisings, and the 1432 verses confirm that this notion of representation permeated the culture of the minority; what they also reveal is the extent to which Lydgate's redeployment of traditional forms worked to undermine its efficacy. In the mercantile mummings, for example, what we find is the substitution of the mayor for the king: the aura that Habermas describes as surrounding the king in a structure of representation is granted by Lydgate to another figure of authority. Such a displacement is necessarily a very delicate operation, something even more evident in the 1432 verses, in which king and mayor compete for aura. Judging from the final stanzas of the poem, which address Mayor John Wells, the young king lost the battle.

What enables Lydgate to make this change is the manipulation of form: the cultural form of the mumming, the poetic form of the envoy, the social and political form of the royal entry, even the generic form of the exemplum, all of which he adopts, transforms, and invests with new meaning. This use of form both asserts and shatters what Habermas calls "the publicness of representation." The rift between real and imaginary publics described by Watts is continually traversed and crossed in this process, as Lydgate both reaches outward – to merchants, for example – and retrenches, here embodying the aura of representation in the king, there investing in the mayor, but never allowing it to stand still. He cannot, for that aura is itself a shifting and mobile category during the minority, embodied by the child-king, but also, and inevitably, still vested in the spectral presence of his father.

One of the most important features of form – including ritual form, dramatic form, and literary form, all elements of the set of texts I discuss in this book – is its resistance to linear chronology, its tendency to persist over time in relatively stable fashion, and to forge links between radically different historical moments. Form itself, then, is always already anachronistic by its very nature, investing it with a paradoxical freedom; it escapes the straightjacket of strict topicality and one-to-one causality. Of course, at the same time an essential feature of form is precisely its confining quality, the way in which it limits the range of possible actions and interpretations in relation to history and experience. As a result, those moments at which forms are altered, invested with new content and thereby reshaped, become extremely significant. In relation to the texts considered in this book, historical change – typically understood as the operation of contingency in time – provokes a response in which form (compilation, for example, or an exemplum, or the generic form of tragedy, or even the ritual of mumming before the king) is activated as a way of providing generic stability in the face of historical uncertainty. In the process, it is subjected to the intense pressure of radical contingency and thereby remade, sometimes with surprising results. Understanding those results depends upon reading the texts at hand very carefully, looking for those moments at which "function" becomes inadequate as a category of explanation, those instances of critical breakdown in the face of textual excess.

Let me emphasize, however, that the "excess" I am describing is not the sheer deconstructive excess of some forms of poststructuralism; it is not a principle of generalized linguistic indeterminacy or multivalence. Nor is it the willed effect of a poet *intending* to obfuscate, to equivocate, or to otherwise veil his texts from interpretation. And finally, it is not a side effect of repression, intolerance, or censorship. All of these are factors to be considered, and indeed have some part to play in an analysis of the texts in question, as my readings will show. But none

8

of these factors taken singly (or even together) can account for the complex interplay of history, textuality, and form that distinguishes the writing of the minority, especially when the question of periodization, or diachrony, is raised. It is a curious effect of all of the works I consider here that each poses some challenge to literary history as written. Each carries with it a certain futurity, an anticipation of aesthetic developments to come, even as every text declares its conventionality and "medievalism." *Serpent of Division* is unusual among Middle English texts for its focus on Rome and Caesar. Lydgate's mummings anticipate the interludes and masques of the sixteenth and seventeenth centuries. His disguisings forge a link between the categories of "tragedy" and "comedy" and dramatic performance that would not be fully articulated until much later. When Lydgate identified a royal entry as a "triumph" in 1432, he made a link between medieval processions and Roman practice that was nearly unprecedented in English writing, but that would become standard in Renaissance civic display. All of these instances disrupt strictly periodizing rationales, making the future seem to be present in artifacts of the past. Nor is it satisfactory to see this body of writing as a moment of origination, an embryonic version of later developments. Paul Strohm has called this phenomenon "unruly diachrony," a moment at which the residual and the emergent collide to produce oddly asynchronous texts, both ancient and modern at once.[13] It is "unruly diachrony" that governs the ambiguous status of the "public," "publicness," and the "public sphere" during the minority. Such ambiguities constitute the epicenter of historicity, the place where history itself – subject, of course, to form – is forged and transmitted. It should be clear by now that when I use the term "*historicity*," I do not mean "facts" or "events" (names, dates, battles, trials), though the nuts and bolts of history are critical to my reading. Rather, I mean to signal a temporal phenomenon that becomes legible only at certain moments and under certain conditions, one in which the forms that structure experience (both individual and collective) are subjected to intense stresses by catastrophe or crisis. The death of Henry V constituted one such crisis, and it is my argument here that in responding to that catastrophe, Lydgate (largely unintentionally) began to construct new forms out of old. These moments of change, these instances in which contingency rends diachronic narratives of development (both literary history and the history of the public) by exposing their falsities, form the subject of this book in the broadest sense.

THE LANCASTRIAN THESIS

Whatever the differences among critics regarding specific texts and their implications, historicist readings of early fifteenth-century poetry are almost universally driven by what might be called the "Lancastrian thesis." In its mildest form, this thesis simply asserts, in good historicist fashion, that context matters – and that an historical event of the magnitude of Richard II's deposition must necessarily be reflected in the kind and nature of poetic representations of events. This turn to political history accounts for the "remedievalizing" of poetry after Chaucer by asserting the power of the social, broadly speaking, in relation to the cultural. As a result, much of the work on Lydgate, and a dominant strain in fifteenth-century studies, is historicism of a specific kind. It focuses on politics in an old-fashioned sense, on the activities of those in power and the major events that affected the kingdom. It is right to do so. As Lawton has argued, fifteenth-century poets used the trope of "dullness" to engage in serious social critique, whose goal was the production of "continuity and unity" at the very center of the realm, in the face of "instability and 'dyuisioun.' "[14] The major literary productions of the early fifteenth century were thus devoted to articulating and defending a notion of sovereign power as uniform, monolithic, and hegemonic; poetry was understood to be precisely the medium through which the powerful should seek self-representation. At the same time, the particular context for this poetry – provided by the Lancastrian usurpation and subsequent need to consolidate and legitimate monarchical power – necessarily thwarted the attempts of poets to erase difference in favor of unity, to substitute an idealized portrait of kingship and the realm for the divided and fractured reality.

One of the most powerful versions of this thesis has been articulated by Paul Strohm. In tracing the effects of the deposition of Richard II on the cultural productions of the reigns of Henry IV and Henry V, Strohm argues that the usurpation created a dangerous absence at the heart of the realm, an "empty throne" that the Lancastrians continually sought to fill. In particular, Henry IV and Henry V, "with varying but unceasing intensity over a period of twenty-three years ... sought a symbolic enactment of their legitimacy persuasive enough to control the field of imaginative possibility."[15] These "symbolic enactments" include a huge variety of texts and practices, ranging from chronicle reports, petitions, prophecies, coronations, and trials to the work of Lydgate and Hoccleve. Strohm's vision of the Lancastrian world is founded on a theory of culture in which access to the symbolic is controlled by the powerful and serves as a means of suppressing the imaginary – the utopian, the unruly, the motile.[16] It depends explicitly on a notion of the textual unconscious, that which the text cannot say but cannot help but reveal: "All texts are selective, diversionary, and amnesia-prone, forgetting or repressing crucial things about their own origins and those of the events with which they deal."[17] Lancastrian rule was thus repressive, obsessed with its own legitimation, and prone to enact its power by constructing opposition groups (such as the Lollards). As a result, the workings of that rule may best be understood through close attention to textuality, its gaps and inconsistencies, its absences and evasions.

A slightly different, though related view of the Lancastrian period has been formulated by Lee Patterson via a thorough mapping of the relationship between the self-fashioning of Henry V and Lydgate's poetic "making." The tension between literary art and political efficacy appears here in terms of identity and difference; Lydgate, Patterson argues, ceaselessly worked to produce unity and sameness in the face of historical realities that undermined and fractured both his and Henry V's attempts to present Lancastrian rule over England and France as legitimate, unitary, and imperial.[18] This argument is cast in the light of broader questions of methodology in medieval studies; Patterson raises the question of the relation of historicism to poststructuralism, suggesting that deconstructive technologies of reading provide historicism with an important way of articulating how "'reality' is put into place by discursive means."[19] This metacommentary on the practices of historicism posits first a *self-conscious* connection between a poet like Lydgate and the modes of discourse he adopts; Lancastrianism appears here as the product of an intentional, though not always successful or fully self-aware, relationship between cultural agents and history. Second, it suggests that historicism provides a counterpoint to universalizing narratives and discourses, both medieval and modern; just as Lydgate can be seen to resist (even as he buttresses) the imperial scope of Henry's ambitions, so too the historicist must resist (even as she deploys) the colonizing capacity of poststructuralist reading techniques. For Patterson, the "Lancastrian thesis" works only so long as the polysemy and multivalence of the literary text – its capacity to lay claim to unitary discourse even as it undermines its authority – are acknowledged.

The difference between this formulation and that of Strohm, who also asserts that the danger of fragmentation produces Lancastrian anxiety about authority, lies in the degree of autonomy and self-consciousness each critic is willing to grant the author of a text. Patterson's historicism reserves a place for the agency of the subject within the larger symbolic arena. For Strohm, texts disclose themselves against their will, operating according to a logic of repression that makes the operation of the reader, analyst, literary critic necessary to the production of meaning.[20] This methodological difference is a very serious one, with important implications for work on fifteenth-century writing and cultural practice. Most work done on this period has granted a certain agency to its historical actors; to take but one example, James Simpson has argued powerfully that Lydgate's *Siege of Thebes* represents a deliberately bleak vision of the possibility for "constructive human activity" in the world after the death of Henry V.[21] For Simpson, though Lydgate might describe a world in which humans are trapped by circumstance, the poet himself is fully capable of intention, of self-consciously responding to Chaucer's *Knight's Tale* in order to "shape a powerful, prudential admonition concerning the treacherousness of history."[22] But intention, as I understand it to operate here, is a far more complex phenomenon than any of these formulations suggests. To read Lydgate's writing during the minority in formal terms means to explore very specific ways in which he makes self-conscious alterations to his source texts, changes which imply a degree of intentionality at work and require a certain notion of agency within a broader understanding of the period as a whole. But this intentionality is necessarily limited; the twin forces of history and tradition work as boundaries within which certain forms of representation are made possible and outside of which discourse becomes unthinkable. As I argue above, there are critical moments in Lydgate's writing during this period at which we see emergent forms lurking beneath the medieval conventions of which it is comprised. These moments cannot usefully be understood within a structure of intention. Rather, they illustrate what happens to a certain kind of elite representation when a severe challenge is posed to the ideologies and forms through which the social is constructed and the political is ordered. Lydgate's texts proclaim their own status as self-conscious literary artifacts over and over. What they cannot say – but what they cannot help but reveal – is the extent to which that self-consciousness is a product of larger historical forces, an effect of changes beyond the capacity of a single poet to acknowledge, control, or grasp.

The use of the term *Lancastrian* itself constitutes a claim about historical agency. To call Lydgate a Lancastrian poet, or to describe a Lancastrian mode of rulership, means to relocate agency, moving it out of the realm of the individual poet or king and into some more abstract and bureaucratic notion of the state.[23] In this model, various forms of official culture are produced and a variety of other cultural modes are proscribed or excluded in a process that directs attention away from particular historical actors and toward more generalized understandings of the workings of power in history.[24] As it has evolved, the Lancastrian thesis has come to herald a particular kind of historicist work on power of a particular kind: state power. And while it is hardly worth denying the very real manifestations of that power in the early years of the fifteenth century (the burning of heretics, persecution of the Lollards, suppression of rebellion), it is also worth noting how convenient a category a centralized regime proves to be for historians and critics. Such a category collects what would otherwise be disparate shreds of culture into broad categories (orthodox and heterodox, official and unofficial) that inevitably avail themselves to analysis and deconstruction. The Lancastrian thesis makes the salutary point that no text can be understood in isolation from other forms of cultural production, or from the historically recognizable signifying systems within which they were created and comprehended. But it is important to recognize the very real danger of mistaking one strategy of state power for the state itself, particularly when the "state" is fragmented and diffuse. It is all too easy to reify the Lancastrian in the process of naming and analyzing its political technologies and cultural manifestations. At the same time, it would be simply wrong to ignore the distinctive patterns into which the evidence for a Lancastrian state falls – the alliance between church and king, the construction and stigmatization of heresy, the very real sense in which forms of culture were deployed and censored in order to buttress that state. Most work on Lancastrianism has focused on the reigns of Henry IV and Henry V, and on the effects of the deposition; it is my argument here that the death of Henry V created a void that demanded a certain kind of cultural response, one markedly different from earlier forms of Lancastrian cultural production. How the loss of the king in 1422 remapped the political and aesthetic landscapes is a question that can be answered in two ways, the first by examining the events of the minority and their effects on the realm as a whole, and the second by turning to the texts themselves. The majority of this book is taken up with the latter project; it is to the former – to "history" – that we must now turn.

MINORITY RULE

Despite the fact that Henry VI was a particularly ineffective king in many ways, his reign is of pivotal interest to the analysis of state formation and the development of the monarchy in England. In particular, a group of historians has made the reign of Henry VI the subject of what they term "new constitutional history," a reconsideration of the legacy of K. B. McFarlane – for many years the preeminent historian of the Lancastrian period – to the historiographical project more generally. Edward Powell has argued that the effect of McFarlane's rejection of old-style constitutional history (as defined by William Stubbs in the nineteenth century) was a focus on patronage, on the "ties of lordship which bound political society together and enabled it to function."[25] This focus, in Powell's view, has directed attention toward the informal workings of self-interest among members of the ruling elite, and away from broader considerations of the "machinery of law and government," which would include "the values, ideals and conventions governing political life and the exercise of authority."[26] In particular, Powell points to "advice to princes" literature as a useful index to the political culture of the fifteenth century – a suggestion taken up, as we will see, by John Watts, the most recent biographer of

Henry VI. A related view (though with a slightly different assessment of McFarlane) is that of Christine Carpenter, who sees the focus on patronage and noble self-interest after McFarlane as a distortion of his "central belief in the normal coincidence of royal and monarchical interests" and insists upon the importance of understanding the "framework of government and power within which ... events were occurring."[27] Watts similarly argues that, "What is needed now is ... an investigation of the patterns and principles governing public life; and, in fact, a reinterpretation of what 'public life' involved."[28] In practice, what these calls for "new constitutional history" have meant is a reevaluation and reassessment of the role of kingship and the status of the monarchy, particularly during the reign of Henry VI, whose various incapacities posed serious challenges to a monarchical system of government. Both Watts and Carpenter use the phrase "political society" to designate "the people with a stake in the world of governance and politics"; in Watts's understanding, the constitution itself is the "shared dialectic – in a sense, the common language – of a political society."[29] Crucially, "political society" is a *public* category, one in which the king plays a special and distinct role as the embodiment of the realm; as Watts argues, "in the last resort, [kings] enjoyed a monopoly of legitimate power ... the king was the representative and embodiment of the realm."[30]

This latter formulation, as Watts notes, differs from traditional formulations of English monarchy as a shared power between king and people, and it is most explicitly described in the "advice to princes" genre of writing that flourished in the fifteenth century.[31] In particular, Watts cites the Egidian tradition, emerging from Giles of Rome's *De Regimine Principum*, as a crucial source for fifteenth-century understandings of the power and extent of kingship; in this tradition, the will of the king supersedes all counsel or intervention from below because it alone can "express [the] common good." The purpose of "advice to princes," in this reading, is to promote virtue as an internal restraint that would enable the king to exercise his will prudently and "according to the common interest."[32] Watts's turn to the arena of the literary – he explicitly discusses Hoccleve's *Regiment of Princes* and the ownership of other literary works, such as the *Fall of Princes* – reveals a critical assumption about fifteenth-century politics undergirding the "new constitutional history," which is that the realm of culture can function as an accurate index of common understandings of the political, including monarchy, law and governance.[33] And indeed, literary critics have asserted for some time the centrality of culture – of forms of representation, be they textual, visual, or spectacular – to the project of writing and understanding history; it is a central premise of this book that it is primarily through such forms that history is made available to us at all. In the case of the "advice to princes" tradition, we find, as Larry Scanlon has argued, a fully rhetorical, contradictory, and inconsistent genre that nevertheless sought to articulate a utopian model for rule.[34]

Like Watts, Scanlon critiques the tradition of "old" constitutional thought that sees in the "mirrors for princes" a movement away from hierarchy and toward "secular, human centered" ideas of the polity.[35] In contrast, he argues, the *Fürstenspiegel* presents the prince as "concretizing in a single subject-position the moral values the audience shares."[36] In the case of Giles of Rome, we see the monarch "above everyone else" with "unlimited authority," a notion of kingship as representation, in Habermas's terms, in which the king stands in for everyone in the realm.[37] Of course, as Watts notes, medieval theorists knew that "individual kings came in all shapes and sizes, and that few indeed would fit the ideal model of a king who innately knew the common weal and ordained for it."[38] But as both his and Carpenter's visions of the minority show, the "new constitutional" model of fifteenth-century kingship is distinctly optimistic; it suggests that even though the absence of an adult king created insurmountable difficulties in a polity organized around the royal will, "political society" as a whole was so committed to maintaining the authority of the monarch that it continued to function as if the king were fully capable of exercising his power. The process of representation, that is, continued to function as if the disruption of Henry V's death had not happened; by vesting all authority – indeed, all "publicness" – in the person of Henry VI, the lords of the realm were, in this reading, able to gloss over and conceal the absence of an adult king.

But Lydgate's writing during the minority, from *Serpent* to the 1432 verses, repeatedly suggests that this concealment did not, in fact, work in the realm of culture. How are we to reconcile these very different visions of the minority, one produced by reading records and documents and attending to consequences – to the actual functioning of the state – and the other arising from a close examination of literary texts and social forms? When I suggest that the textual evidence adduced in this book implies a very different vision of the minority than that articulated by Watts and Carpenter, I do not mean to substitute my own account of cultural production for their narratives of governmental and political function; such an attempt would be fruitless, a diminution of the historical complexities at work during this decade. Indeed, their image of kingship during the minority, complete with its ideological contradictions, fundamentally accords with the picture that emerges from Lydgate's texts of a supreme monarch upon whose sovereignty the fate of the realm rests. The difference lies in the contrast between the utopianism of Watts's understanding of "advice to princes" and the fundamentally tragic sensibility that pervades the works discussed here. An acknowledgment of that sensibility leads, in my view, to a shift in emphasis in accounting for the minority and its effects.

The traditional view of Henry V's legacy to Henry VI has been that it was a *damnosa hereditas*, the dual monarchy an impossible burden to sustain, and the provisions for minority rule unsustainable in the long term.[39] Carpenter argues, in contrast, that Henry V "did not leave his son an impossible inheritance. On the contrary, he left him a legacy that was the main reason for his survival for so many years of incompetent rule."[40] This is an important point, and one that echoes an earlier statement by Bertram Wolffe, that "The long minority of Henry VI revealed the inherent political maturity of fifteenth-century England."[41] But neither Wolffe nor Carpenter suggests that the minority was untroubled, nor would the evidence support them if they did. As Watts argues, there was a fundamental ideological contradiction at work in the establishment of conciliar government; if the king truly embodied the realm, if the king's will constituted the only means of acting for and representing the body politic, then no council could adequately govern in the king's stead:

> In an important sense, Henry VI's "personal rule" began at the moment of his accession. This was more than just a legal nicety, it was a conceptual political necessity. If there was no royal *persona publica*, there could be no body politic. So it was that the lords of 1422 set out not only to provide counsel, but also to establish an artificial

royal authority as the basis of the governmental will which they needed to be able to exercise.[42]

But this "artificial royal authority" was necessarily an ambivalent one, perpetually in danger of usurping the king's authority or being disrupted by divisions within the council or among the lords. Conciliar government itself was an innovation, expressly contradicting the deathbed provisions made by Henry V for the minority, which had assigned the regency of England to one of his brothers, Humphrey, duke of Gloucester, and the stewardship of France to another, John, duke of Bedford.[43] But when Humphrey attempted to assert his claim, the lords rejected him as regent and substituted the council in his place; Gloucester was named "Defensor of this Reme and chief counseiler of the kyng" in Parliament in December 1422, and the principle of conciliar government was set in place.[44] As Watts argues, this solution came about as a means of preventing rival claimants to the regency – Gloucester and Bedford – from creating division within the realm and undermining the authority that resided in the infant king.[45]

But division was precisely what Humphrey of Gloucester proceeded to create. He provided serious challenges to conciliar government in 1422, in 1425–26, and in 1428, all occasions upon which he sought greater powers in relation to the king than the council was willing to provide. In 1425 Gloucester's quarrel with his main rival, the chancellor, Bishop Henry Beaufort of Winchester (Henry V's uncle), became so acute that the two factions met armed on London Bridge.[46] Not until Bedford himself returned to England from France to mediate were the two reconciled. As Watts notes, Bedford's intervention constituted a momentary breach in the principle of conciliar government, a point at which Bedford's "personal and intrinsic" authority superseded that of the council, much as would the king's when he came of age.[47] In other words, faced with internal division, the need for a sovereign became so acute that the king's authority was abrogated temporarily in order to preserve the peace. In the very next year, Gloucester once again demanded from Parliament a clarification of his position as protector and defender; he received his response early the next year, when Parliament strongly affirmed the principles established in 1422 and asserted the very limited nature of his authority.[48]

But this powerful articulation of the king's personal authority proved to be one of the last actions of the protectorate. As Ralph Griffiths has described, in 1428–29 the fiction of stability came to an end: "the strains of conflicting personal ambitions, disputed foreign ventures, and . . . a shattering military defeat in France produced such a crisis in government that the protectorate was brought to an end in November 1429."[49] The English were defeated at Orléans by the French, led by Joan of Arc, in June 1429; on July 18, Charles VII was crowned king of France at Rheims.[50] In a letter written in April of that year, having seen the likelihood of defeat, Bedford had suggested to the council that Henry VI be crowned in France as a means of reasserting English legitimacy and countering the rival claim of the Dauphin.[51] This tactic was embraced, and Henry VI was crowned at Westminster on November 6, 1429, preparatory to leaving for an extended stay in France; he would be crowned at Paris two years later, on December 16, 1431. The historical narrative with which this book is concerned ends in 1432, at the moment of Henry VI's return to London as king of both England and France. Not coincidentally, Lydgate soon after retired from his priorate at Hatfield – where he had resided while writing most of the texts discussed here – and returned to Bury St. Edmunds, where he continued writing *Fall of Princes*, commissioned by Gloucester in 1431.[52] His career as a propagandist was largely over. The uncertainty of minority rule had also come to an end, though the future was anything but certain (and as we know with hindsight, not a bright one for Henry VI).

I suggested above that the texts I am describing in this book betray a deep level of anxiety about sovereignty and are characterized by a sense of profound loss at the death of Henry V. It should be clear by now that I am not making a topical argument, which would imply that Lydgate's writing reflects, in a simple way, the particular events and crises of the minority. Rather, understanding the history of the minority – which, despite its overall success, was characterized by periodic crises brought about by the constitutive instability of conciliar government – forms the necessary precondition for explaining the particular cultural phenomena under consideration here. Once it has been established, for example, that the king constituted the literal embodiment of the realm, that his will was coterminous with and identical to the will of the people, and that without a functional king the ideology of kingship simply could not be sustained, then it becomes clear precisely how devastating the loss of Henry V was bound to be.

EXCESS, ELITISM, AND LITERARY FORM

In my focus in this book on what appear to be highly instrumental texts, rather than on the more obviously "poetic" works through which Lydgate's aesthetic is typically defined – *Troy Book* and *Siege of Thebes* – I am deliberately turning away from conventional narratives of post-Chaucerian aesthetic development and Lydgatean aureation. Derek Pearsall usefully summarizes what have become critical commonplaces:

> What we witness in the fifteenth century is not a decline, but a change of temper, or, to be more precise, a reassertion of orthodoxy. Moral earnestness, love of platitude and generalisation, a sober preoccupation with practical and ethical issues (often combined with a taste for the extravagantly picturesque and decorative) – these are the characteristic marks of fifteenth-century literature, and it is in these terms that Chaucer is absorbed and redefined. Lydgate is the pattern of the new orthodoxy, though as symptom rather than cause.[53]

Pearsall's parenthetical aside – concerning the "extravagantly picturesque and decorative" qualities of fifteenth-century literature – strikes at the heart of what has been seen as the "Lydgatean aesthetic": it is excessive, visual, ornamented, and amplified. In contrast to Chaucer, who shows a gratifying restraint, a sense of irony, Lydgate's poetics are extravagantly unwieldy, reflecting (so the argument goes) the taste for spectacle indulged by courtly and mercantile audiences alike. Indeed, Lydgate developed an entire lexicon of terms that articulate this taste: *enlumyne, adourne, enbelissche, aureate, goldyn, sugrid, rhetorik,* and *eloquence*.[54] It is not precisely this version of the "Lydgatean aesthetic" that interests me here, though almost any of his texts can be read – indeed, on occasion must be read – within this interpretive frame.[55] Nor am I strictly concerned with the related narrative described by Richard Firth Green, in which literature as such emerges from the court as part of an emergent system of patronage and reward, rather than as fodder for a "new reading public" – though this narrative is critical to the historical understanding of Lydgate's poetry.[56] Certainly, Lydgate's

poetry confirms various hypotheses about aureate style and the dominance of aristocratic taste in the cultural productions of the fifteenth
century; it further suggests, as I will argue, the desire of groups outside
the court to acquire and exercise that taste for themselves. But the
argument cannot end here. Its focus is at once too narrow (on
Lydgate as self-conscious poet) and too broad (on his poetry as an
index of a certain trajectory of historical development). Lydgate's writing demands a critical practice that refuses to jettison the old (traditional modes of scholarship, for example, or residual understandings of
the social whole) while simultaneously embracing the newness of the
past, its capacity to surprise, to cast up the unexpected – in short, to
remain, despite all attempts to fix it, contingent and unpredictable.
Simpson has recently called for just such a revision of our understanding of Lydgate, one that recognizes him as the agile and creative poet
that he was by refusing to categorize him as simply "medieval" or
"propagandistic"; as he argues, "Lydgate produced texts that jointly
form a heterogeneous collage of differently figured histories."[57] Such
histories are precisely what I am concerned with here.

Each of the texts I describe in this book challenges topical readings
even as it betrays its historical origin. Chapter 1 focuses on Lydgate's
Serpent of Division, a prose tract written in 1422, which recounts the life
of Caesar as a way of warning of the dangers of political and social
division in the wake of Henry V's death and the establishment of
conciliar government. In using Caesar as an example of a "fallen
prince," Lydgate follows Chaucer's precedent in the *Monk's Tale*. But
his Caesar is a more complex and opaque figure, both a power-hungry
tyrant and a tragic hero, both the cause of division in Rome and a
murder victim. This ambiguity, I argue, has a double origin. On the one
hand, it is produced by the deep political and cultural ambiguities at
hand when Lydgate wrote the text shortly after the death of Henry V.
On the other, it is an effect of Lydgate's own writerly practices, his
obsessive attention to his multiple source texts and his complex relationship to the literary authority of both his Latin and vernacular
predecessors. *Serpent of Division* is a short tract with a strong narrative
drive; it begins with the abolition of kingship in Rome after Tarquin's
rape of Lucrece, and ends with Caesar's death. But even in the small
amount of space he has allotted himself, Lydgate manages to create an

impressive compilation of sources and authorities. Some of these he cites explicitly – Lucan and Chaucer are two examples – and others he silently translates, especially his main source for the text, Jean de Thuin's *Li Hystore de Julius Cesar*. The result of this mixing of sources, especially when combined with the extreme delicacy of the historical situation to which Lydgate was responding, is a text that strongly resists attempts to pigeonhole it as a propagandistic exemplum. I begin the book with *Serpent of Division* not only because it is one of the first, if not the first, written texts we have from the minority, but also because its status as a prose exemplum means that it lacks the protective coloration of verse embellishment and ornamentation and thus aptly illustrates the point that even Lydgate's seemingly simple texts are far from being monologic and straightforward. In fact, *Serpent of Division* introduces two crucial and complex themes that will prove central to Lydgate's work during the minority as a whole: the philosophical problem of contingency in the world, and the fundamentally poetic issue of form, both social and artistic.

These themes become especially central in the following two chapters, both of which deal with Lydgate's dramatic texts. It has long been recognized that among Lydgate's most original contributions to literary history were his "mummings," short pieces written to be performed in a variety of settings, from the royal household to guild halls. These texts date from the middle years of the decade to the end of the minority, with most clustering during the intense years of 1428–30, when Henry VI was being prepared for his coronation and crowned, and they are in many ways typically medieval, using personified figures to exalt and praise both the mayor and the king. I have divided my discussion of these texts – six in total – into two chapters, based on what I see as a fundamental formal distinction between two types, the mumming and the disguising. In chapter 2 I address the mummings, a series of four dramatic texts that thematize succession, sovereignty, and right rule, all concerns clearly related to the end of the protectorate and the coronations of Henry VI. Two of these mummings – the most topical texts I address here – were performed before the king; the remaining two, the "Mumming for the Mercers" and the "Mumming for the Goldsmiths," address a mercantile audience, with the mayor at the center of the performance. The royal mummings are short, simple, and direct. The first, performed at Eltham, stages the bringing of gifts from Bacchus, Juno, and Ceres to the king by merchants; the second, staged at Windsor, retells the French coronation myth and was clearly designed to bolster the court's confidence as it prepared for Henry's crowning in France. These two texts form a marked contrast with the mercantile mummings, both of which are distinguished by layers of textual complexity and ambiguity, and particularly by poetic and dramatic self-referentiality. The "Mumming for the Goldsmiths" describes the bringing of Christmas gifts to the mayor as a procession of David with the ark of the covenant; inside the mayor finds a document with suggestions for good governance and right rule. The use of an Old Testament scenario allows Lydgate to make a whole series of exegetical allusions and references that not only raise the question of sovereignty – through David's relationship to Saul – but also seek to justify performance itself, rendered here as David's dancing before the ark. In similar fashion, the "Mumming for the Mercers" is filled with literary and classical allusions, so much so that John Shirley, the copyist and compiler of the manuscript, felt compelled to provide elaborate glosses. The Mercers' mumming narrates the appearance of a herald traveling from the East with a letter for the mayor, who passes three ships with inscriptions in French before arriving at London, where he finds vessels at anchor with merchants aboard, waiting to visit the mayor, presumably with gifts. This simple premise is elaborated with references to figures such as Petrarch and Boccaccio, Circe and Bacchus, and to exotic places such as Jerusalem, Mount Parnassus, and Egypt. I argue that such references show Lydgate responding to the desire of mercantile elites to participate in aristocratic and royal forms of cultural expression, and doing so in didactic fashion, teaching his audience the basics of literary and interpretive traditions familiar from the vernacular poetic tradition. In both of the mercantile mummings, Lydgate expands the Chaucerian audience he inherited to include new consumers – and what they are consuming is not merely Lancastrian propaganda, but dense and complex poetic fare in which serious questions of sovereignty and rulership could be represented and negotiated.

Two other dramatic texts – Lydgate's "Disguising at London" and his "Disguising at Hertford," most likely performed in 1426–27, form the subject of chapter 3. These two poems are usually classed as mummings, but they are distinctly different from the four texts discussed in chapter 2; much longer, these poems are in rhyming couplets rather than rhyme royal, and seem designed for a somewhat more elaborate kind of performance. They are also explicitly concerned with genre, specifically the genres of tragedy and comedy, and represent extremely sophisticated attempts by Lydgate to come to terms with – and in some ways supersede – Chaucer's understanding of these modes. The "Disguising at London" is an allegory of Fortune and the four cardinal virtues, Prudence, Rightwysnesse, Fortitudo, and Attemperance; Fortune is first described and her powers elaborated, after which the virtues are introduced as the remedies for her instability and changeability. Like the "Mumming for the Mercers," the London performance is distinctly literary; Lydgate cites not only Chaucer but also the *Romance of the Rose* and Boethius as he builds his picture of Fortune and the virtues – references that might not be obvious to a viewing and listening audience but that invited sustained and careful interpretation by readers. One of the aspects of the text such readers would be asked to interpret was its gesture to tragedy: not only does Lydgate explicitly encourage his audience to read "comedyes" and "tragedyes," but he also describes Henry V in distinctly tragic terms. On the one hand, Henry V was an example of a king who embraced virtue, an illustration of Fortitude. On the other, as *Serpent of Division* shows, he was a victim of Fortune whose virtue did not, in the end, save him from her wheel. The philosophical contradictions that Lydgate elucidates in the "Disguising at London" are not resolved, nor can they be; his solution to the impasse he reaches is simply to counterpose another mode of discourse, this time comedy. That solution, the "Disguising at Hertford," is Lydgate's best-known dramatic work. It stages a comic debate between six husbands and their wives, in which the husbands complain to the king that they are dominated and abused by their wives. The wives respond with the claim that women, not men, have the law on their side, citing statutes and the right of succession "frome wyff to wyff" as their justification. The king is forced to concede that the women are right, and agrees that they should rule their husbands for one year, while a search is made for legal remedy for the men. The impotence of the king in the face of the law, I argue, stands in for what Lydgate sees as the ultimate failure of the Chaucerian comic mode in the face of the tragic world that Henry V left in his wake. Like the "Disguising at London," the Hertford text is highly allusive, replete with explicit references to the Wife of Bath and Griselda as well as more subtle gestures toward figures such as Goodlief, Harry Bailley's wife; it is a deeply serious answer to Chaucer's use of the comic as a response to the tragic after the *Monk's Tale*.

The very fact that Lydgate would choose a public performance for such an elaborate poetic endeavor testifies to the extent of his desire to bring Chaucerian poetics into a broader sphere. In no way can the disguisings be described as "propaganda"; they are imaginary negotiations of serious social and aesthetic questions, designed to be staged for an elite audience and to be read by sophisticated readers. In the last chapter of the book I turn to the most public of Lydgate's writing during the minority – which, paradoxically, is primarily a private text, designed for reading rather than listening. In 1432 Henry VI returned from France in an elaborate entry procession through London, which was recorded by John Carpenter, town clerk, in a Latin letter. Lydgate adapted this letter and rendered it in verse in what was later titled "Henry VI's Triumphal Entry into London." In this poem, commissioned by the mayor, Lydgate imagines a wide audience of spectators for the pageants, placing vernacular speeches into the mouths of allegorical figures that Carpenter describes as adorned with rolls or placards with "scriptures," or Latin phrases from the Bible and liturgy. Lydgate ends this poem and his writing during the minority just as he began it: with a reference to Caesar, in which he describes the entry as like one of Caesar's "triumphs" – a cultural practice he had described at length in *Serpent of Division*. Lydgate's gesture to the Roman triumph in this description of an actual royal entry is unprecedented; medieval kings had entered cities in state from the earliest times, but they were not described as Roman triumphators. There was a medieval tradition of Roman triumphs, but it was a learned and Latin tradition, an exemplum used in sermons and commentaries that gradually made its way into vernacular writing in the works of Gower and Lydgate. In this chapter I shift focus slightly, taking a broadly diachronic view of the triumph tradition as it leads through writers such as Hugutio of Pisa, Robert Holcot, John Bromyard, and Ranulph Higden and texts such as the *Gesta Romanorum* and *Fasciculus Morum*. Tracing the fortunes of the triumph exemplum through the work of these writers reveals a new kind of historical discourse emerging, a conception of the classical past as distinctively different from the present rather than assimilable to it by means of allegory. This mode of discourse comes to the fore in Gower and Lydgate's versions of the triumph, as they struggle to create a kind of secular exemplarity for princes while remaining safely in the realm of political abstraction. When Lydgate, in his verses on Henry's return to London, combines that secular exemplarity, with its historical understanding of the Roman past, with medieval spectacle, he sutures together a specifically literary tradition with the social and cultural practice of a king's entry, and in so doing forges a crucial link between the poetic and the public.

The premise of this book is an historical one: all of the texts I describe fall within a specific time frame, and can be understood as responses to a particular social formation. At the same time, the very notion of textual "response" is one which the works considered here consistently challenge; with a few exceptions, each text undermines its own status as propaganda, consolation, exhortation, or exaltation by embodying a principle of formal excess and interpretive ambiguity. In so doing, they each, in one way or another, invoke transhistorical or diachronic narratives of development, particularly because each functions as an anticipation of contents and forms typically associated with the Renaissance – classical imitation, the genres of tragedy and comedy, the performance of interludes and masques. Thus, a tension emerges between the principle of historical specificity – the idea that these texts are distinct to the minority of Henry VI – and a broader notion of literary and dramatic history that implies that the formal logic at work in Lydgate's writing during this period transcends the localities of time and place. That tension is itself historically specific, produced by a particular set of events and circumstances that call it into being; it is manufactured out of the unique deployment of residual forms with unexpectedly new contents. This "newness" is typically understood by Lydgate as historical contingency, what he describes in *Serpent of Division* as the "unware strook," and it functions dialectically in relation to both textual and social forms, being contained by them and warping them *at the same time*. Just as the traditional form of kingship was vigorously asserted in the face of the necessity of conciliar government, so too the conventionality of Lydgate's writing appears at first to be its most salient feature. The turn to traditional form, in this reading, is an attempt to appropriate its stability, its resistance to temporality and change, as a way of compensating for the radical uncertainty brought about by the loss of Henry V. As a close look at these texts shows, however, matters are not that simple. When Lydgate uses the triumph exemplum, for example, he invokes the authority of a long textual tradition in order to compliment the young king. At the same time, however, his invocation transforms that tradition by moving it from the abstract realm of ideas (moral didacticism) and into the concrete world of events (an actual royal entry). Both entry and exemplum – both forms of organizing and stabilizing experience – are profoundly altered by this recontextualization. As each chapter will show, this transformative process repeats itself over and over again in the texts under consideration here; literary and dramatic forms are continually deployed as a means of creating unity and stability, only to mutate as they are placed in new contexts or filled with new content. The process works in reverse as well; each form carries with it a sedimented content that itself makes meaning in relation to the particular events or occasions being represented. Thus, for example, when Lydgate uses the form of the mumming – a mode of expression specifically designed as an address to the king – in a mercantile performance, he calls upon its authority as a monarchical form even as he inserts it in a new context. In a slightly different way, but according to the same principle, when Lydgate invokes the generic form of the tragedy in both *Serpent of Division* and the "Disguising at London," he calls up a whole chain of associations with Chaucer, Jean de Meun, and Boethius that insert Henry V into a narrative of tragic causality that fundamentally warps the simple model of moral exemplarity subtending those texts.

These twin processes – the dialectical way in which forms shape contents and vice versa – raise serious methodological questions in relation to historicist reading practices more generally. In turning away from (though not abandoning) historical particularity, and toward an investigation of form, it becomes possible to see that the complex ways in which history becomes legible over time are fundamentally formal procedures. This book argues, in various ways and through a variety of examples, that form – meaning those conventions through which experience is rendered legible and lent a significance that transcends the local (particular times and places) – constitutes the only genuinely historical category of analysis for the cultural critic, that it is only through grasping how form works in culture that we may come to understand the historicity of the past.[58] I further argue that certain modes of discourse pose the problem of form more insistently than others. Though there is no denying that history is always already textualized, and that texts themselves, whether chronicle accounts or love poetry, behave in similarly ambiguous and rhetorical fashion, my argument here depends on the idea that certain discourses, both literary and dramatic, are specialized modes with particular relations to history and to form. Thus, I have restricted my readings to works that are clearly identifiable as "literary" texts, written by a poet who clearly saw himself responding to other "literary" texts, within an identifiable tradition of such writing. It is extremely significant that this specialized mode of discourse emerged during a specific period of crisis as a means of publicly negotiating historical conflicts. What had previously been a mode restricted to small groups of readers was in the process of becoming not a *common* (as in commonly available) form of represent-ation, but rather a *privileged* mode of secular and public political expression. Characteristics such as excessiveness, ambiguity, and multi-valence are specifically valued as indices of the seriousness and adequacy of this kind of expression to the highest realms of political life.

It must be acknowledged that the forms and genres deployed by Lydgate during the minority as privileged modes of expression were available only to a tiny portion of England's actual population. Other kinds of writing and performance also flourished during the fifteenth century, many of which had a far larger and more diverse audience (romances or cycle plays, for example), and perhaps a better claim to be "public culture." Other modes of discourse, especially those having to do with the self and subjectivity (in Hoccleve's poetry, or in the *Book of Margery Kempe*), perhaps make more powerfully universalizing claims, and thus have a clearer relationship to modernity. The idea of a literary aesthetic that is both elite and representative, that asserts both its exclusivity and its applicability – its right to speak *for* a public or *for* the realm – emerges during the minority as part of a broader insistence upon the representative nature of kingship. That is, the form of sovereignty is imitated by, as well as constructed by, certain forms of cultural expression. And because those modes of expression are firmly linked to the ruling elite, because they are transmitted and reproduced by those with the power to do so, they acquire a certain durability and longevity. That is why, though none of Lydgate's actual writing during the minority became widely known, the principles subtending his use of form – its relation to sovereignty, its exclusivity, its representativeness – were to last. In the end, to make a claim, as I do, for the centrality of these neglected works is to make the slightly contrarian assertion that in their elitism lies their significance, then and now. It is in the forms at work in these particularly functional texts that historicity declares itself, as that which solicits and demands not simply an instrumental response – pure propaganda – but also an aesthetic surplus, something extra. Historical accounts of the social meaning of such texts, however subtle and nuanced, fail if they cannot take into account this surplus as itself an historical phenomenon. To argue for the initial embrace of the "literary" – for attention to the forms and techniques by which meaning is made and feeling structured – is *not* to reject history. It is rather to assert that history as we know it is a formal matter, that through forms we come to apprehend and to know the past. Such a critical practice allows Lydgate to emerge from the shadows of Chaucer, appearing finally as the complex and innovative poet that he was – and prompts, in the end, a serious rethinking of the place of the fifteenth century in literary history.

NOTES

1 Pearsall, *John Lydgate*, 160–91. Lydgate worked for a wide variety of patrons. Pearsall lists a series including Humphrey of Gloucester, the earl of Salisbury, his wife Alice and her second husband, William de la Pole, earl of Suffolk. He also lauded a number of notable women, including Katherine, queen mother and widow of Henry V; Elizabeth, first wife of the earl of Warwick and her daughter Margaret; Warwick's third wife, Isabella; and countess Anne of Stafford and her daughter Ann Mortimer (wife of the fifth earl of March).

2 For a comprehensive description of this propaganda, see McKenna, "Henry VI of England and the Dual Monarchy."

3 Middleton, "Idea of Public Poetry," 112. Emily Steiner takes up Middleton's suggestion and argues astutely that Langland "invents public poetry from the matter of documentary culture" in her *Documentary Culture and the Making of Medieval English Literature*, chapter 4, "Writing Public: Documents in the *Piers Plowman* Tradition," 143–90.

4 Middleton, "Idea of Public Poetry," 113.
5 In her book, *Clerical Discourse and Lay Audience in Late Medieval England,* Fiona Somerset gives a number of examples of precisely this phenomenon in various controversial texts of the late fourteenth and early fifteenth centuries. John Trevisa's translation of *De Regimine Principum,* she argues, claims to be "aimed at the common profit," but in fact is aimed at a tiny audience of lords (78). Roger Dymmock's response to the Lollard *Twelve Conclusions* identifies a narrow category of "public persons" that includes kings, dukes, bishops, and scholastic doctors (106), even as he claims to be providing a "universal antidote" (110) to Lollard thought. Somerset is describing a particular phenomenon that is clearly related to the "public" I am discussing here, but is also distinct from it, in that she focuses on the relationship between clerical discourse and ideas about the "public," rather than on texts whose purpose is largely secular – that is, largely devoted to the monarchy and its legitimacy to the exclusion of clerical concerns.
6 Paul Strohm has noted this simultaneous narrowing and broadening in his "Chaucer's Fifteenth-Century Audience and the Narrowing of the 'Chaucer Tradition,'" 18. He notes that while Chaucer originally seems to have written for a circle of readers that included knights and bureaucrats, after his death an "altered public" emerged that was "more widely distributed geographically and more disparate socially."
7 Lawton, "Dullness and the Fifteenth Century." Following Lawton and Middleton, but in the service of a much different argument about public reading and aurality, Joyce Coleman notes the emergence of a "public sphere" in fourteenth- and fifteenth-century vernacular writing; see *Public Reading and the Reading Public in Late Medieval England and France,* 93–97.
8 Watts, "Pressure of the Public," 159–80, 165.
9 Ibid., 161.
10 Ibid., 179.
11 Habermas, *Structural Transformation of the Public Sphere,* 7.
12 Watts, "Pressure of the Public," 178–79.
13 Strohm, *Theory and the Premodern Text,* 93, and 80–96 more generally.
14 Lawton, "Dullness and the Fifteenth Century," 793.
15 Strohm, *England's Empty Throne,* 2.
16 Ibid., 30.
17 Ibid., xii.
18 Patterson, "Making Identities in Fifteenth-Century England."
19 Ibid., 71. For a contrary view of the relation between medievalist scholarship and deconstruction, see Aers, "Medievalists and Deconstruction."
20 For a methodological statement by Strohm, see his *Theory and the Premodern Text,* xi–xvi.
21 Simpson, "'Dysemol Daies and Fatal Houres,'" 33.
22 Ibid., 16.
23 Ethan Knapp's important discussion of Hoccleve illustrates very well the extent to which individual poets could exceed the limiting label "Lancastrian"; see *The Bureaucratic Muse: Thomas Hoccleve and the Literature of Late Medieval England,* especially his discussion of Hoccleve's "Address to Sir John Oldcastle," 137–46.
24 An excellent example of the "Lancastrian thesis" at work may be found in Nicholas Watson's influential "Censorship and Cultural Change in Late-Medieval England."
25 Powell, "After 'After McFarlane,'" 1.
26 Ibid., 10.

27 Carpenter, *Wars of the Roses*, 21, 23.

28 Watts, *Henry VI and the Politics of Kingship*, 8.

29 The first quotation comes from Carpenter, *Wars of the Roses*, 34, the second from Watts, *Henry VI and the Politics of Kingship*, 13. Watts turns to the work of Quentin Skinner and J. G. Pocock as a way of redefining "constitutional history" in the fifteenth century; see Skinner, *Foundations of Modern Political Thought*, and Pocock, *Ancient Constitution and Feudal Law* and *Politics, Language and Time*.

30 Watts, *Henry VI and the Politics of kinship*, 17.

31 Ibid., 19.

32 For the preceding two quotations, see ibid., 27, 25. The importance of such "mirrors for princes" can be illustrated by the Privy Council records of June 1428, which explicitly concern the education of King Henry VI by the Earl of Warwick and encourage him to use "mirrours and examples" of virtuous kings (who receive good fortune) and kings of the "contrairie disposicion" (who experience "contrair fortune"). See *Proceedings and Ordinances of the Privy Council of England*, vol. III, 299, and generally 296–300.

33 Watts, *Henry VI and the Politics of Kingship*, 52–56.

34 Scanlon, *Narrative, Authority and Power*, 82–84, and chapter 5, "The Public Exemplum," 81–134, more generally.

35 Ibid., 84.

36 Ibid., 82.

37 Ibid., 111.

38 Watts, *Henry VI and the Politics of Kingship*, 30.

39 Bertram Wolffe, *Henry VI* uses the phrase "*damnosa hereditas*," 27; Griffiths, *Reign of King Henry VI*, 20 describes the failures of Henry V's provision for minority rule.

40 Carpenter, *Wars of the Roses*, 75.

41 Wolffe, *Henry VI*, 27.

42 Watts, *Henry VI and the Politics of Kingship*, 112.

43 See Griffiths, *Reign of Henry VI*, 15–19, and Wolffe, *Henry VI*, 28–31.

44 Griffiths, *Reign of Henry VI*, 22.

45 Watts, *Henry VI and the Politics of Kingship*, 115.

46 For the fullest account of this crisis, see Griffiths, *Reign of Henry VI*, 73–81. Carpenter sees this episode, and Gloucester's other challenges, as evidence for the stability of conciliar government overall, for the voluntary restraint exercised by the nobility for the good of the realm. See *Wars of the Roses*, 80–84.

47 Watts, *Henry VI and the Politics of Kingship*, 116.

48 See Wolffe, *Henry VI*, 44–45.

49 Griffiths, *Reign of Henry VI*, 38.

50 Wolffe, *Henry VI*, 55.

51 Ibid., 54.

52 Pearsall, *John Lydgate (1377–1449)*, 32–34.

53 Pearsall, *John Lydgate*, 68.

54 This list is taken from Ebin, *Illuminator, Makar, Vates*, 20, 58.

55 In *Chaucer and his Readers: Imagining the Author in Late Medieval England*, Seth Lerer has insightfully described the formation of the Chaucer canon and its relationship to laureate poetry and laureation; see especially chapter 2, "Writing Like the Clerk: Laureate Poets and the Aureate World," 20–56, for discussion of Lydgate's occasional poetry and his "laureate" period.

56 Green, *Poets and Princepleasers*, 211.

57 Simpson, *Reform and Cultural Revolution*, 55. See his chapter, "The Energies of John Lydgate," 34–67 more generally for the fullest articulation of his compelling argument about "reformist" culture and Lydgate's place in it.

58 My thinking about form has been shaped by my reading of Fredric Jameson (*Marxism and Form*, *The Political Unconscious*) and Raymond Williams (*Marxism and Literature*).

Tragic history: Lydgate's *Serpent of Division*

> This is the final and insurmountable limit of literary invention. A writer can and should invent a great deal. He cannot invent the realistic core of a tragic action. We can weep for Hecuba. One can weep for many things. Many things are sad and melancholy. But tragedy originates only from a given circumstance which exists for all concerned – an incontrovertible reality for the author, the actors and the audience. An invented fate is no fate at all. (Carl Schmitt, "The Source of the Tragic"[1])

One of the most puzzling of Lydgate's works is *Serpent of Division*, a short prose tract written in 1422, recounting the life of Caesar and describing the terrible consequences of political and social division.[2] At first glance, the text appears to be an ideal object for historical analysis; written at a critical moment in Lancastrian history just after the death of Henry V, it narrates the rise and fall of a brilliant military leader as a warning to "lordes and prynces of renowne" of the "irrecuperable harmes" (66, line 19, line 2) of political and social division. The allegorical logic of the text is difficult to ignore, as is Lydgate's insistence on a resolutely moral reading of both "division" and Caesar himself. Indeed, a simple historical reading arguing that Lydgate uses the exemplum as a means of negotiating the crisis produced by the death of the monarch seems to be what the text itself demands.[3] Yet by virtue of this very modesty, perhaps, *Serpent of Division* pushes against the generic boundaries of the tragic exemplum, ultimately exposing its limitations in such a way that the fundamental ideological and epistemological assumptions that subtend the writing of moralized history are shown to be inadequate to the task of representing both past and present. Another way of making this point might simply be to say that

Lydgate tries and fails to accomplish a task made impossible by the pressure of the real – of present events – on the forms through which the historical is mediated and made safe for consumption. Considered in relation to the *Canterbury Tales,* or even Lydgate's own *Siege of Thebes,* the failure of *Serpent of Division* seems to condemn it to a rightful obscurity as a literary curio. But just as curios may function in near synecdochal fashion as nodal points for the analysis of cultures and their histories, so too *Serpent of Division* reveals the obsessions and impasses of its own fifteenth-century moment. In so doing, it reveals as well the limitations and blindnesses of the very interpretive practices that it appears most earnestly to solicit: the use of history and the study of sources. This chapter engages in both of these modes of analysis, taking *Serpent* seriously as both historical commentary and learned compilation. But it seeks as well to grasp more fully than historicism or formalism can allow the implications of this odd text for our understanding of how – and why – literary art should seem to be the appropriate response to the state of crisis brought about by the death of a king.

The quotation from Carl Schmitt that forms my epigraph here proposes a relation among the real, the tragic, and dramatic invention that begins to suggest how the category of form might be factored into an historical analysis of the literary text. For Schmitt, the tragic provides for its audience and its makers a zone in which to encounter – in an almost ontological sense – the obdurate facticity of history itself. The essential tragic action – exemplified by *Hamlet* – is the transformation of a given reality into myth; thus Shakespeare's singular achievement lies in "extracting from his contemporary political situation the form capable of being raised to the level of myth."[4] This relation between "reality" and "myth" – denominated here by the term "tragic" – can only obtain in special circumstances. "Reality" does not refer to the quotidian; not any given moment in time can qualify as the "reality" that produces the tragic. Nor is "myth" simply a code word for a set of traditional beliefs, oriented to the past, that function as supplements to an inchoate historicity. Rather, the tragic is produced by the transformation of a specific kind of reality into a myth that transcends quotidian temporality and projects itself into the future as a hermeneutic for unimaginable new realities (Caesar for future rulers, for example).

This myth-making reality is fundamentally unpleasant; as Schmitt argues, myth emerges from "present and inescapable realities from which one shrinks out of timidity, out of moral and political considerations, out of a sense of tact and natural respect."[5] Thus, certain historical conditions – "realities from which one shrinks" – solicit a form that can *enact* history in such a way that myth is both remade and made anew, both called out of the political unconscious and called upon to invent a new consciousness.

When Lydgate chooses Caesar as the exemplary figure through which to explore the nature of "division," he both embraces the reality of Caesarian history and engages in a traditional mode of literary invention, compilation. *Serpent of Division* simultaneously makes a truth claim – that the story of Caesar is relevant precisely because it is real – and repeatedly betrays the extent to which "reality" is created out of conflicting and contradictory source texts. On the one hand Lydgate's goal is to write an exemplary narrative in which Caesar serves as a warning to "lordes and prynces of renowne"; to this end, he invokes an economy of sin and punishment drawn from Gower's *Confessio Amantis* as a way of inserting Caesar in a moralized tragic narrative. On the other hand he persists in representing the unfolding of history as a Chaucerian drama of contingencies in which catastrophe proceeds not from sin but from chance. The fundamental philosophical conflict between these notions of causality produces a deep structural tension in the text that must be understood as the product of both Lydgate's formal practice – his insistence on synthesizing conflicting sources – and of the intense pressure his present reality has on the version of the past he has chosen to narrate. The myth of Caesar and the reality of Henry V mingle uneasily in a nexus of competing and complementary textualities held together by the powerful capacity of form to contain as well as sustain the forces of historical contradiction. *Serpent of Division* is an antiquotidian text; its world is a world in which the extremity of events must be digested and remade in mythical terms. But how that digestion works – how, that is, form creates a zone in which to encounter the historical – cannot be understood by theoretical means alone. Lydgate constructed *Serpent of Division* detail by detail, source by source; grasping the complexity of that construction requires first engaging the text on its own ground.

THE TEXT: SOURCES

In all but one manuscript, *Serpent of Division* ends with an envoy that draws out the moral implications of the story, encapsulating the narrative in three short stanzas:

> This litill prose declarith in figure
> The grete damage and distruccion
> That whilome fill, bi fatell auenture,
> Vnto Rome, þe myȝti riall towne,
> Caused onely bi false devision
> Amonge hem selfe, þe storie tellith þis,
> Thorowe covetise and veyne Ambicion
> Of Pompey and Cesar Iulius.
>
> Criste hymselfe recordith in scripture
> That euery londe and euery region
> Whiche is devided may no while endure,
> But turne in haste to desolacion;
> For whiche, ȝe lordes and prynces of renowne,
> So wyse, so manly, and so vertuous,
> Maketh a merowre toforne in youre resoun
> Of Pompey and Cesar Iulius.
>
> Harme don bi deþe no man may recure,
> Aȝeins whose stroke is no redempcion,
> Hit is full hard in fortune to assure,
> Here whele so ofte turnith vp and downe.
> And for teschewe stryf and dissencion
> Within yowreself beth not contrarious,
> Remembring ay in yowre discrecion
> Of Pompey and Cesar Iulius.
> (66, lines 7–26)

The import of the story is clear: "lordes and prynces of renowne" are warned of the dangers of division and the inevitable workings of Fortune in the world, urged to make "a merowre toforne in youre resoun" of the past as a means of preventing disaster in the present. These are conventional fifteenth-century sentiments and prescriptions, typically Lydgatean in both content and form. But *Serpent of Division* is unusual both for Lydgate and for English writing at this time; not only is it Lydgate's only prose work, but it is also one of the earliest English biographies of a secular historical figure.[6] Further, it is the only lengthy treatment of Caesar's life in Middle English; though Chaucer, Hoccleve, and Gower all mention Caesar, none attempts an account on the scale of *Serpent*.[7] Although Lydgate himself refers to the text as "this litill and this compendious translacion" (66, lines 4–5), *Serpent* is a compilation of a wide range of vernacular sources. For his account of Caesar's rise to power and defeat of Pompey, he relies on Jean de Thuin's *Li Hystore de Julius Cesar*, a French prose biography written in the later thirteenth century and primarily based on Lucan's *De Bello Civili*, as well as on *Les Faits des Romains*, an anonymous Old French prose text of the early thirteenth century based on Lucan, Sallust, and Suetonius.[8] Jean's text had one great deficiency for Lydgate's didactic purpose: it ends with Caesar at the height of his power, giving no account of his betrayal and death (which are, however, included in *Les Faits des Romains*). For the downswing of Fortune's wheel, Lydgate turns to Vincent de Beauvais's *Speculum Historiale*. Other texts are incorporated at moments throughout *Serpent* – Higden's *Polychronicon* (and possibly Trevisa's translation), Isidore of Seville's *Etymologiae*, Walter Map's *De Nugis Curialium*, Chaucer's *Monk's Tale*, and possibly the *Brut*.

Lydgate himself cites as his sources Lucan, Vincent de Beauvais, Eusebius, Valerius Maximus, and Chaucer. Of these five, he can be shown to have used Vincent, Valerius, and Chaucer; his citations of Lucan and Eusebius suggest familiarity with the names, rather than the texts, of those authorities. Although Henry Noble MacCracken, editor of *Serpent*, argues that Lydgate did use a copy of *De Bello Civili* available to him in the Bury Library, a close examination of the text suggests otherwise. Much like his "maistere Chaucer," whose own citation of Lucan in the *Monk's Tale* appears to be gestural rather than substantive, Lydgate relies on medieval rather than classical texts, often invoking a classical authority he knows only by reputation.[9] In describing the causes of the war between Caesar and Pompey, he explicitly claims to be translating Lucan:

> But so as Lucan likith to reherse & specyfie in his boke toforeseide amongis oþer causes þat he put he in especiall writeth of þre, whiche were chiefe begynnyng and rote of devision amonge hem-selfe

preuynge bi reson in þilke þre þat hit muste nedes bene þat þe felicite and þe prosperite of Rome muste abate and drawe to declyne, þe which þre that Lucan put bene þese.

Firste he seithe hit was necessarie and hit was consuetudinarie, and þe þirde was voluntarie. (55, lines 1–7)

MacCracken argues that "Lydgate took his text straight from a manuscript of Lucan, embroidering upon it the rhetoric of his own conventional style of poetry," citing the following lines from *De Bello Civili*:[10]

> Fert animus causas tantarum expromere rerum,
> Inmensumque aperitur opus, quid in arma furentem
> Inpulerit populum, quid pacem excusserit orbi.
> Invida fatorum series summisque negatum
> Stare diu nimioque graves sub pondere lapsus
> Nec se Roma ferens.

> My mind moves me to set forth the causes of these great events. Huge is the task that opens before me – to show what cause drove peace from earth and forced a frenzied nation to take up arms. It was the chain of jealous fate, and the speedy fall which no eminence can escape; it was the grievous collapse of excessive weight, and Rome unable to support her own greatness.[11]

Nothing in Lucan, in this passage or elsewhere, refers to the three causes Lydgate elucidates. And there is no reason for MacCracken to insist that Lydgate's ultimate source was *De Bello Civili*; as the editor himself points out, Jean de Thuin's elaboration of the causes of the war bears a far greater resemblance to this portion of *Serpent of Division*.[12] Certainly, the general notion that fate or Fortune caused the downfall of Rome ultimately derives from Lucan, but Lydgate nowhere uses language or deploys details from *De Bello Civili* that cannot be found in a later translation or redaction of the classical source.

Lydgate's secondary (or even tertiary) relation to Lucan can be further illustrated by examining his claim to be translating Eusebius, the other unsupported citation in *Serpent*. In his account of Caesar's conquest of Britain, Lydgate ascribes to Eusebius the story of King Cassibolan's brother, who repelled the Romans until struck down by Fortune: "liche as hit is specially remembrid & recordid by writynge of the worthi clerke Eusebius" (51, lines 8–9). The episode is retold in

Lydgate's *Life of St. Alban and St. Amphibal*, written between 1434 and 1440 (most likely in 1439), in language distinctly reminiscent of *Serpent of Division*:

> Twies put off bi record of lucan,
> At his arryvail, bi verray force & myht,
> Bi the prowesse of Cassibalan.
> Touchyng the titil, wer it wrong or riht,
> Off seid Cesar, deme euery maner wiht
> What that hem list; for in conclusion,
> Cause of his entre was fals division.[13]

In this version, Lydgate's classical source has become Lucan instead of Eusebius; neither ascription is correct. Lydgate's nearest source for his summary of Caesar's conquest is the anonymous *Tractatus de Nobilitate, Vita et Martirio Albani et Amphibali*, found in a St. Alban's manuscript datable to the late fourteenth century.[14] The *Tractatus* version is quite brief and lacks such details as the conflict between Cassibolan and Androgenes, and the heroics of Cassibolan's brother – details which, however, were readily available to Lydgate in a version of the *Brut*.[15] Lydgate's source for the citation of Eusebius would seem to be Vincent de Beauvais, who acknowledges Eusebius in his version of Caesar's life in the *Speculum Historiale*.[16]

In sum, Lydgate's citations of such figures as Lucan and Eusebius, at least in *Serpent*, refer not to specific texts, but rather to a generalized notion of classical authority synecdochally embodied in the names of its authors. The practice is less citation than invocation; authorities are called up, not referenced. Indeed, Lydgate nowhere acknowledges the vernacular sources to which he owes the greater part of his narrative, *Li Hystore de Julius Cesar* and *Les Faits des Romains*, nor does he mention Gower's *Confessio Amantis*, to which he is particularly indebted for the notion of division itself. His five invocations – Lucan, Eusebius, Vincent, Valerius, and Chaucer – reveal far less about the background of *Serpent of Division* and more about Lydgate's vision of cultural authority; readers are expected to trust his text, not to seek out his sources.

This citational practice has led to a critical commonplace: Lydgate is typically understood as both being slavishly devoted to authority and as an incompetent compiler, afflicted with debilitating hero worship, especially of Chaucer, and unable to treat his masters' texts with the care they deserve. Indeed, Lydgate's own description of *Serpent* as "þis litill and þis compendious translacion" (66, line 4) suggests precisely this view. Editors like MacCracken have willingly believed Lydgate's citations (of Lucan, for example), while refusing to believe he might have consciously revised or manipulated his sources for literary effect. In *Serpent*, Lydgate's use of Jean's *Li Hystore* is modified in several places by details available in *Les Faits des Romains*, based on his low estimation of Lydgate's capacities, MacCracken posits an intermediary French redaction of Jean, corrected with reference to *Les Faits*, as Lydgate's source.[17] Though he does acknowledge that Lydgate is capable of a certain editorial freedom, he cannot imagine that the synthesis of the two French texts is within the monk's abilities, though his own analysis of the text confirms that it relies upon both versions of the story.[18] In fact, Lydgate's use of sources is both simpler and more complex than MacCracken indicates, as an examination of three unusual instances from *Serpent* will show. On the one hand, we find Lydgate simply deploying the material he has immediately available, using seemingly irrelevant details as a means of dilating the moral he wishes to emphasize, a familiar Lydgatean practice. But on the other hand, it becomes clear that Lydgate negotiates the relationships among his various authorities with some care; he is neither slavish nor whimsical.

The first instance occurs at the very end of the tract; as one of the signs of Caesar's impending death, a poor man brings him letters warning of the conspiracy.

> Also, þe same daye of his mordir as he wente most riall in his imperiall araye towarde þe consistorie a pore man called Tongilius toke him lettirs of all þe purposid conspiracie bi þe Senat vpon his deþe, but for he was neccligent to rede þe lettris and vnclos hem þe vengeable mordre was execute vpon him bi whiche example lete no man be slowe nor neccligente to make delaye to rede his lettirs leste aftir for his necclygence hit turne hym to grete damage which aftir may not liȝtly be recured. (64, lines 36–38; 65, lines 1–5)

The incident with the letters occurs in Vincent, in Higden, in Laurent, and is repeated in the *Fall of Princes*.

A poore man callid Tongilius
Whiche secreli the tresoun dede espie,
Leet write a lettre, took it Iulius
The caas declaryng of the conspiracie,
Which to reede Cesar list nat applie.
But, o alas ! ambicious necligence
Caused his mordre bi vnwar violence.
(*Fall of Princes*, book 6, lines 2857–63)

Lydgate's versions are unique, however, in naming the messenger "Tongilius"; he has added this detail from Walter Map's *De Nugis Curialium*, where Tongilius appears as a type of the humble but wise man ("Tongilio humili quidem sed divino"), ignored by Caesar at his peril.[19] Here it would seem that Lydgate has simply supplemented his sources (Vincent, Higden, Laurent) with a version that emphasizes the failure of Caesar to heed the warning, his "ambicious necligence." This move – along with his seeming suggestion that the moral of the Caesar story is that men should read their letters – is almost parodically Lydgatean.

But moralizing is not Lydgate's only mode of thought. Two contrasting examples illustrate the delicacy with which he approaches his sources, particularly when Chaucer is involved, and suggest that in his use of these texts he exercises a greater capacity for discrimination than is usually admitted by his critics. The first of these comes early in the narrative; Lydgate corrects an error made by both Chaucer and Higden, who wrongly identify Julia as Caesar's wife:[20]

> And as þe stori rehersith also, as for a lamentable kalendes of more infortune þat aftir schulde folowe, Iulia þe noble wife of Pompeye, and dowȝter to Cesar, deied of a childe berynge. (52, lines 9–11)

MacCracken argues that the error originated with Suetonius, who has Caesar propose to Pompey's daughter and records no refusal.[21] Lydgate, however, has Jean's *Li Hystore* at hand, in which Julia's relation to Caesar is correctly given, and he adopts the French version over Chaucer's. This decision would have been made solely on the basis of Lydgate's judgment of the reliability of the texts in question; there is no evidence that he knew any classical authority that rightly identified the relationship of Caesar and Julia. Nor is there any narrative justification for the choice; the moral import of this "litill translacion" is hardly altered by the correction. Lydgate has simply left Chaucer behind in favor of what he considers the better source.

The second example seems at first to be more characteristically Lydgatean. In the final episode of the narrative, Lydgate identifies the murderer of Caesar as "Brutus Cassius":

> so þat towchynge þe vengeable maner of his piteous mordre I may conclude with hym þat was flowre of poetis in owre englisshe tonge & þe firste þat euer enluminede owre langage with flowres of Rethorike and of elloquence, I mene my maistere Chaucere which compendiously wrote þe deþe of þis my3ti Emperour seyenge in þis wise:

> 'with boidekyns was Cesar Iulius
> mordered at Rome of Brutus Cassius,
> whan many land and regne he had brow3te ful lowe;
> loo who may triste fortune any throwe?'
> (65, lines 11–19)

The error of "Brutus Cassius" for "Brutus and Cassius" was common in medieval texts; MacCracken suggests that it may have arisen from a misreading of Vincent's "Bruti *et* Cassii" as "Bruti Cassii," noting an early printed version of the *Speculum Historiale* in which the "et" was abbreviated by a mark that may have faded over time.[22] However, Lydgate's source for the mistake is clearly Chaucer, as he takes pains to tell us, and he selects "Brutus Cassius" from among several options. Higden refers to "duobus Brutis," while Laurent de Premierfait correctly identifies the killers as Brutus *and* Cassius.[23] Indeed, the editor of *Fall of Princes*, where Lydgate repeats the mistake, cannot quite believe that the poet would deliberately ignore his primary source: "It seems extraordinary that he should do so after having read Laurence. Perhaps he skipped that part of Laurence."[24] But Lydgate had no way of knowing that Laurent's was the "right" version; his best judgment led him to what he deemed the most authoritative source *in this instance:* Chaucer. And strikingly, despite his fulsome praise for his predecessor, the lines that Lydgate claims to be citing from the *Monk's Tale* are in fact badly misquoted, an error that suggests, along with his correction of Julia's status, that his relationship to his "maistere" is more complex than is customarily thought.[25]

These examples illustrate the critical consciousness at work in the making of *Serpent*, though they do not point clearly to the principle of selection that guides that consciousness. Some alterations Lydgate makes to his sources seem meaningful – that is, designed to adapt the story to an overriding moral purpose, as in his naming of Tongilius. Others bear no moral weight – the correct identification of Julia, the mistaken invocation of Brutus Cassius – but suggest that Lydgate conceives of his sources in relation to a notion of authority that depends on the value of names (Lucan, Chaucer) rather than on the accuracy of details. Further, his need to invoke those names varies according to the narrative significance of a given detail. Julia is a minor figure at best; Brutus Cassius is the villain of the piece. Lydgate follows Jean and *Les Faits* very closely in the early part of *Serpent*; the incident with Julia is simply not important enough to induce deviation from those texts. The murder of Caesar – the culmination of the story – is a different matter. The turn to Chaucer, then, is dictated not only by Lydgate's sense of Chaucer's greater authority than Laurent, but also by the demand of the narrative for a weighty (and well-attested) conclusion.

Lydgate's treatment of his sources in *Serpent* thus reveals twin aims; he seeks both to moralize the story of Caesar and to legitimize that moralized narrative by invoking a variety of authorities. To this end, he assembles the raw material of the story from several sources, and arrays the latter under a new set of rubrics, the names of figures who, in his opinion, will lend his story the proper air of historical *gravitas*. This compilation is on occasion clumsily done, but it cannot be dismissed as unselfconsciously incompetent. As we will see, Lydgate's raw material includes more than the direct sources for *Serpent*'s narrative detail and *exempla*; he has also turned to one of his most recent English predecessors for the controlling idea of division itself.

DIVISION: GOWER AND THE SERPENT

In choosing "division" as his theme, Lydgate has selected a relatively new word in English; the *Middle English Dictionary* gives its earliest appearance as 1382, in a citation from the *Wycliffite Bible*. The term has a variety of meanings, from the simplest "the act or processes of splitting" to the technical scholastic use for "the process of distinguishing, analyzing, defining" to the use that will concern us here, "dissension, discord, strife, schism."[26] "Division" is also a term with a vernacular poetic history, one that Lydgate deliberately suppresses but that provides the key to understanding the complex valence of the word and the concept. In the *Prologue* to the *Confessio Amantis*, Gower performs a thorough exegesis of division, its causes and its contemporary effects – an exegesis that, it is clear, Lydgate knew well but chose not to acknowledge.[27] The erasure of Gower from *Serpent of Division* is part of a more general trend in Lydgate's work of misattribution and deliberate forgetting of sources, manifested in *Serpent* not only by the substitution of classical for English vernacular authority (Chaucer excepted), but also by the complete suppression of the major French sources for the story of Caesar. But unlike his use of the French texts, Lydgate's major debt to Gower is a conceptual one; it is to Gower that he owes the association of "division" with epistemological inquiry into the origins and causes of strife and dissension. And unlike his elision of Jean and *Les Faits*, his refusal to cite Gower derives as much from an unwillingness to burden the narrative of *Serpent* with an unyielding hermeneutic system as from anxiety of influence.

For Gower, "division" is both a specific social or narrative problem and a condition of being. If in the *Knight's Tale* Chaucer had explored the sources of and consolations for misery in the world, providing an array of possible causes (the Furies, the gods, Providence, contingency itself) for the "wo" experienced by Palamon and Arcite, Gower in the *Confessio Amantis* reduces those possibilities to one, man himself: "The man is cause of alle wo, / Why this world is divided so" (*Prol.*, lines 965–66). The constitution of man as a fundamentally divided being has profound social and historical consequences:

> Division, the gospell seith,
> On hous upon another leith,
> Til that the Regne al overthrowe:
> And thus may every man wel knowe,
> Division aboven alle
> Is thing which makth the world to falle,
> And evere hath do sith it began.
> It may ferst proeve upon a man;
> The which, for his complexioun

44

Is mad upon divisioun
Of cold, of hot, of moist, of drye,
He mot be verray kynde dye:
For the contraire of his astat
Stant evermore in such debat,
Til that o part be overcome,
Ther may no final pes be nome.
(*Prol.*, lines 967–82)

Man is literally composed of division, always already constituted by the internal "debat" of warring elements, "of cold, of hot, of moist, of drye." In contrast, when Chaucer explicitly describes the relationship of the elements in *Parliament of Fowls*, we find a Boethian vision of natural balance: "Nature, the vicaire of the almyghty Lord, / That hot, cold, hevy, lyght, moyst and dreye / Hath kynt by evene noumbres of acord."[28] But Chaucer's delicate exploration of the implications and limits of the Boethian world – like his refusal to allow a singular causality to govern the *Knight's Tale* – has no place in Gower. Division has an unambiguous cause:

For Senne of his condicioun
Is moder of divisioun
And tokne whan the world schal faile.
(*Prol.*, lines 1029–31)

It also has a specific moment of origin:

He may that werre sore rewe,
Which ferst began in Paradis:
For ther was proeved what it is,
And what desese there it wroghte;
For thilke werre tho forth broghte
The vice of alle dedly Sinne,
Thurgh which division cam inne
Among the men in erthe hiere.
(*Prol.*, lines 1004–11)

Gower's account is powerfully syncretic: it assimilates classical texts and stories to an overarching Christian narrative of fall and redemption. By contrast, Chaucer never insists upon a simple moral reading; as the *Knight's Tale* makes clear, he is too interested in the complexities of causes and effects to subject them entirely to a narrative of sin and punishment. Over and over in Chaucer we find characters tossed on the seas of contingency and chance – Palamon, Arcite, Custance are just a few – and whether or not the story comes to a providential and ordered conclusion, those images of the unpredictability and randomness of human life remain. One has the sense that Chaucer enjoys this Boethian tension between chance and providence; the lapsarian logic of willed transgression and just punishment is consistently paired with images of cruel contingency. A fury rises up to unseat Arcite; Egeus counsels, "This world nys but a thurghfare ful of wo, / And we been pilgrymes, passynge to and fro" (lines 2847–48). Such images, of course, are always susceptible to a providential reading – the Prime Mover's "faire cheyne of love" (line 2991) can always be invoked – but they never go away. If Chaucer allowed contingency and chance to haunt his poetry, giving full expression to a vision of the world at the mercy of arbitrary gods while embedding that vision in a providential frame, Gower insists in simpler fashion that all of human history be understood as a gradual disintegration proceeding from an originary moment of sin.[29] The seemingly random workings of Fortune are in reality the fault of man: "That we fortune clepe so / Out of the man himself it groweth" (*Prol.*, lines 548–49). This fault is both immediate and world-historical; present ills are caused not only by the fallen nature of the world, but also by the present acts of fallen men. To illustrate this principle, Gower turns to what Russell Peck has called his "favorite emblem for dis-integration," Nebuchadnezzar's dream from the Book of Daniel, a vision of a figure with a golden head, a silver breast, a brass torso, steel legs, and feet of steel mingled with crumbling earth.[30]

Nebuchadnezzar's dream is both a thematic and a methodological starting point for the *Confessio Amantis* as a whole. By expounding on the image of the monster of time, Gower is able to narrate a history of the world utterly subject to the themes of division and decay. In so doing, he establishes a relation between narrative (a progression from event to event) and moral (immutable truth) familiar to any reader of exemplary history: events themselves may not be predictable, but their meaning always is. This hermeneutic of exemplarity allows Gower to shape multiple histories – classical, Old Testament, Christian, English – into a single narrative of successive reigns and progressive fall, beginning with Babylon and culminating with the fragmentation of Christendom in the present day. Each age is initiated by conquest: Cyrus and Cambises subdue Baltazar to end the age of gold; the world of silver is destroyed when Alexander defeats Darius; the age of brass is ruined when Alexander divides his realm among his knights, until Caesar subdues them and inaugurates the age of steel, which is still in the process of supersession by the age of earth. History moves relentlessly toward its end, figured in the dream by a great stone that falls upon the feet of the monster, breaking it in pieces and turning all to powder. This calamitous end is of course the Day of Judgment, when "every man schall thanne arise / To Joie or elles to Juise" (*Prol.*, lines 1041–42).

Rome occupies an anomalous place within this progression. Unlike his predecessors, Caesar does not rise up against an established ruler; his conquest reunifies the fragmented world, healing the division caused by Alexander and instituting the rule of steel, hardest and most durable of metals: "As Stiel is hardest in his kynde / Above all othre that men finde / Of Metals, such was Rome tho / The myhtieste" (*Prol.*, lines 733–36). It is in the destruction of this age and this empire that Gower locates the origin of present division; after narrating the recent (post-Constantinian) history of Rome, he tells us:

> Come is the laste tokne of alle;
> Upon the feet of Erthe and Stiel
> So stant this world now everydiel
> Departed; which began riht tho,
> Whan Rome was divided so:
> And that is forto rewe sore,
> For alway siththe more and more
> The world empeireth every day.
> (*Prol.*, lines 826–33)

The world of the present is saturated by division – in the Church, in Europe, in England – a division that seems in this account to be an effect of the fragmentation of Rome. But this simple version of historical causation cannot stand alone; its very logic implies a utopian reversability at odds with the eschatological import of the prophecy. Because the stone will fall and the Day of Judgment will come, division cannot be remedied in this world. It is not ultimately caused by rebellion or strife, but by the sinful nature of man himself, "a litel world," according to Gower:

> The man, as telleth the clergie,
> Is as a world in his partie,
> And whan this litel world mistorneth,
> The grete world al overtorneth.
> (*Prol.*, lines 955–58)

In many ways, *Serpent of Division* constitutes an elaboration and dilation upon a specific moment in the history described by Nebuchadnezzar's dream, the moment at which the "age of stiel" was inaugurated. It is a narrative designed to illustrate that division has always already been present; in it we find Caesar himself, founder of the empire that unified the descendants of Alexander, represented as an agent of division and strife. In this sense, though *Serpent* would seem to belie Gower's vision of the past supremacy of Rome, Lydgate confirms the darkest import of Nebuchadnezzar's dream: in a history of this postlapsarian world, any episode monadically replicates the master narrative of Fall and Judgment.

The brilliance of Gower's description of the monster of time lies in its symbolic capacity to articulate the whole of history in a single image; like all prophecy, it dissolves distinctions between past and present, present and future, arresting the inexorable movement of time and creating a space for interpretation in which temporal and historical differences can be ignored. The monster of time is no simple portent of things to come; the very density and difficulty of its imagery demands a hermeneutic free of local restrictions, an interpretive practice with a global scope. Such a practice depends on the articulation of similitudes: the age of gold is like the age of silver, is like the age of brass, and so on. Within this model the image functions both as the object of interpretation and as its governor; as history unfolds it is submitted to the rule of similitude by reference to the power of the prophetic image, authorized in this case by its biblical origin. The history that Gower seeks to subsume is not merely the series of events that have led to his fourteenth-century present, however; it is a textual history, a past landscape of competing and contradictory sources and authorities, classical and Christian. Gower finds in

Nebuchadnezzar's dream an image sufficiently variegated and singular to serve as the controlling referent for both this landscape and his own iteration of it in the succeeding books of the *Confessio Amantis*. Indeed, as Rita Copeland has argued, the dream is itself a scholastic exercise, "an iconographic *divisio* of *divisioun*" that exploits a tension inherent in the technique itself, between *divisio* as an ordering device (a cure for division) and as an effect of the *confusio linguarum* emerging from the myth of Babel – which Gower adduces in the *Prologue* as an emblem of sinful division. The *Confessio Amantis* is itself, as a vernacular text, a product of linguistic division – the solution to which can be found in a synthesis of vernacularity and scholastic ordering: in *divisio*.[31]

Lydgate never directly refers to Gower or to Nebuchadnezzar's dream. But it is clear, both textually and formally, that he has imbibed Gower's vision of a world divided. Not only do we find direct echoes of the *Confessio* in both *Serpent* and *Siege of Thebes*, but we also see in the image of the serpent an analogous use of a controlling symbol to produce and to guide interpretation of the past. In Lydgate's most elaborate description of the serpent – found not in *Serpent* but in *Siege* – we see Gower's description of division specifically linked to Leviathan and the Fall:

> And as the byble / trewly can devyse,
> Hegh in heuene / of Pryde and Surquedye
> Lucyfer, fader of Envie,
> The olde Serpent / ,he levyathan,
> Was the first / that euer werrë gan:
> Whan Michael / ,the heuenly Champioun
> with his Feerys / venqwisshyd the Dragoun,
> And to hellë / cast hym downe ful lowe.
> The whiche serpent hath the Cokkyl sowe
> Thorgh al erth / of envye and *debat*,
> That vnnethys / is ther non *estat*,
> withoutë stryf / can lyve in Charite
> (*Siege of Thebes*, lines 4660–71, emphasis added)

This language of "debat" is used by Gower to characterize man himself: "For the contraire of his *astat* / Stant evermore in such *debat* / Til that o part be overcome, / Ther may no final pes be nome" (*Prol.* lines 979–82, emphasis added). Lydgate too links the "debat" produced by Satan with conflict and war on earth:

> For euery man / of hegh and lough degrè
> Envyeth now / that other shulde thryve.
> And ground and causë / why that men so stryve,
> Is coveytise / and fals Ambicioun,
> That euerich wold han domynacioun
> Ouer other, and trede hym vndyr foote:
> which of al sorowe / gynnyng is and Roote.
> And Crist recordyth – red luk and ȝe may se –
> For lak of love / what meschief þer shal be.
> For O puple / as he doth devyse,
> Agayn anoþer / of hatë shal aryse.
> And after tellith what dyvisions
> Ther shal be / atwixë regyouns,
> Euerich bysy / other to oppresse.
> (*Siege of Thebes*, lines 4672–85)

For Lydgate, the cause of "debat" is lack of love, as Gower before him has made clear:

> The world is changed overal,
> And therof most in special
> That love is falle into discord
> And that I take to *record*
> Of *every lond* for his partie
> The comun vois, which mai noght lie;
> Noght upon on, bot upon alle
> It is that men now clepe and calle,
> And sein the regnes ben divided,
> In stede of love is hate guided.
> (*Prol.*, lines 119–28, emphasis added)

Using similar language, Lydgate elaborates this theme in the envoy to *Serpent of Division* with a reference to Luke 11.17:

> Criste hymselfe *recordith* in scripture
> That *euery londe* and euery region
> Whiche is devided may no while endure,
> But turne in haste to desolacion;
> (66, lines 15–19, emphasis added)

The idea of division emerges from Lydgate's deep investment in his English vernacular predecessors; no reading of his use of sources in *Serpent* can be complete without an examination of these conceptual debts. Indeed, *Serpent of Division* works as a kind of double palimpsest, with the direct borrowings that constitute the narrative itself (Jean, Vincent, *et al.*) overlaying a bedrock of English writing from which Lydgate derives his most basic notions of how to represent and recreate the past. These include specific techniques – the blending of classical and Christian texts in Chaucer and the moralizing of those texts found in Gower – as well as a general commitment to a formal rendering of the historical, to declaring "in figure."

Lydgate's primary "figure" here is the serpent, an image that is both allegorical and historical; it is simultaneously a figure for division and the actual serpent that tempted Eve. Although Lydgate, like Chaucer and unlike Gower, never takes an explicitly polemical stand in relation to the present, his use of a biblical figure invokes the prophetic herme-neutic described by Nebuchadnezzar's dream, inserting the Roman past into Christian lapsarian history and suggesting that the dangers of that past are contiguous with problems in the present. In this sense, *Serpent of Division* is fully invested in the exemplary mode of historical repre-sentation articulated by Gower in the *Confessio Amantis*. Indeed, Lydgate's citation of the *Monk's Tale* suggests that he understands the story as a type of "tragedie," an example of the great brought low, designed to edify and instruct his audience about the dangers of Fortune and prosperity. His later use of the Caesar story in the *Fall of Princes*, a text explicitly identified as a set of "tragedies," firmly embeds Caesar in this tradition.[32] But a Chaucerian interest in the complexity of historical causation – in the potential operation of contingency in history – haunts *Serpent* as well. This tension between exemplarity and contin-gency is in part produced by the contradictory ambitions of the text itself: it both aims to be a prophetic warning for readers in the present, an illustrative instance of an immediate danger (division), and seeks to recount the life of Caesar in full, adhering in some way to a notion of accuracy and completion in historical retelling. Put another way, Lydgate attempts to write an exemplar in Gowerian fashion even as he gives in to the desire to amplify and correct the historical authorities that provide him with the story itself. As the next section will show, these additions necessarily undermine the simple model of causation – sin causes division, Caesar's sin caused Rome's destruction – derived from the generic model of the exemplar found in *Confessio Amantis*.

MYTH AND REALITY: HISTORY WRITING

As we have seen, Lydgate's identification of *Serpent of Division* as a "translacion" refers not to a classical source, but primarily to the French *Li Hystore de Julius Cesar* of Jean de Thuin, modified with reference to some version of *Les Faits des Romains*. Unlike the *Confessio Amantis* or the *Monk's Tale*, these prose texts purport to record the life of Caesar on its own terms, not as an exemplar but as a history. As Gabrielle Spiegel has argued, both French texts strive to accommodate the classical past to the thirteenth-century present, albeit in different ways; both seek to establish a continuity between past and present that reassuringly aligns the contemporary world with an idealized Rome.[33] Spiegel establishes as a method for reading these texts the notion of "deformation," arguing that the inconsistency with which medieval translators deployed anachronism can serve as a guide to points of cultural stability and instability: "the deformed aspects of the past ... point most clearly to the issues that medieval authors and audiences sensed as problematic."[34] Both *Les Faits* and *Li Hystore* perform this kind of historical operation on the life of Caesar, shaping the story in specific ways that reveal particular ideological concerns.

Les Faits des Romains, an anonymous prose history dateable to 1213–14, is compiled from several classical sources – Suetonius's *Life of Caesar*, Sallust's *Catiline Conspiracy*, Caesar's *Commentaries on the War of the Gauls*, and Lucan's *De Bello Civili*, among others.[35] The Caesar of *Les Faits*, while imbued with the martial ideals of this chivalric world, is a cautionary figure for absolutist ambition; as Spiegel puts it, the author, "seems to have wavered constantly between a half-hearted attempt to vindicate the reputation of Caesar and a desire to demonstrate, with Lucan, the socially pernicious consequences of intemperate ambition."[36] But in his focus on Caesar's life, rather than on the more abstract history of Rome itself, the author makes a critical alteration to Lucan's text: he personalizes the story, subjecting Caesar to evaluation according to standards for individual behavior. This move to the personal is far more pronounced in the text that forms Lydgate's major source for the first half of *Serpent*, Jean de Thuin's *Li Hystore de Julius Cesar*, dating from the mid-thirteenth century.[37] Unlike *Les Faits*, Jean's version is an unapologetically positive rendition of Caesar's life; by removing all of the negative aspects of Lucan's portrayal of Caesar, Jean simplifies the complexities found in *Les Faits* and produces a version of history as moral allegory.[38] Jean's version, like Nebuchadnezzar's dream in the *Confessio Amantis*, absorbs the raw material of history and assimilates it to a dramatically simplified model of historical causation. And Lydgate's translation of Jean seems from the outset to faithfully reproduce this theological historicity; sin destroys Rome:

> For the surqvidous pride [on the party] of Iulius, and the contagius Covetise entremelled with envye on the party of Pompye, made the famous Citie of Rome ful waste and wilde. (50, lines 3–5)

Lydgate clearly intends this simple structure of causation – individual sin causes political and social destruction – to serve as an interpretive guide for the narrative that is to follow; the moral of the story is proleptically given in order that the story itself make sense. But for a narrative to work as an effective moral exemplar, it ought to be short or simple and preferably both. Thus Chaucer in the *Monk's Tale* and *Legend of Good Women* and Lydgate himself in the *Fall of Princes* – not to mention their "auctor," Boccaccio, in his exemplary texts – streamline the stories they tell in order to subordinate them to an ultimate meaning: the goodness of women, or the inevitable downfall of the mighty.

But *Serpent of Division* is neither particularly short nor especially simple. At times, Lydgate seems strangely compelled to recount events that challenge his didactic aims; his Caesar is at once the prideful tyrant of *Les Faits*, the chivalric hero of *Li Hystore*, and the tragic figure of the *Monk's Tale*. On the one hand he is filled with "surqvidous pride"; on the other he is the "manly man" who acts prudently, "mekely and humbely" in the face of Pompey's envious plotting. This tension emerges out of the constitutive conflicts entailed in writing a history while committed both to a moral vision of the past and to the idea that the past can be comprehensively and completely represented in the light of such a vision. An older Lydgate articulates these twin aims in the Prologue to the *Fall of*

Princes, arguing that his *auctor*, Laurent de Premierfait, has rightfully modified Boccaccio's tragic vision of the past:

> This said auctour [Boccaccio], auise and riht sad,
> Hath gadred out, with rethoriques sueete,
> In dyuers bookes which that he hath rad,
> Off philisophres and many an old poete,
> Besied hym bothe in cold and hete
> Out to compile and writen as he fond
> The fall of nobles in many dyuers lond.
> Vpon whos book in his translacioun
> This seid Laurence rehersith in certyn,
> And holdith this in his opynyoun,
> Such language as open is and pleyn
> Is more acceptid, as it is offte syen,
> Than straunge termys which be nat vndirstande,
> Namly to folkis that duellyn vp-on lande.
>
> And he seith eek, that his entencioun
> Is to a-menden, correcten and declare;
> Nat to condempne off no presumpcioun,
> But to supporte, pleynli, and to spare
> Thyng touchid shortly off the story bare,
> Vndir a stile breeff and compendious,
> Hem to prolonge whan thei be vertuous.
> (lines 71–91)

This aesthetic of virtuous prolongation – of amplification – allows both Laurent and Lydgate to incorporate more and more historical material under the rubrics established by Boccaccio, justifying the alteration of an authoritative source by establishing a principle of moral emendation. Poets may "make and vnmake in many sondry wyse, / As potteres, which to that craft entende / Breke and renewe ther vesselis to a-mende" (lines 12–14). They must do so with the proper intention, "afforn prouydid that no presumpcioun / In ther chaungyng haue noon auctorite" (lines 29–30). And they make such changes with the edification of their audience in mind:

> For a story which is nat pleynli told,
> But constreynyd vndir woordes fewe
> For lak off trouthe, wher thei be newe or old,

Men bi report kan nat the mater shewe;
(lines 92–95)

In this model, men understand "trouthe" more fully when given more information, "pleynli told"; the profusion of words seems for Lydgate to be a guarantee of the truth value of the text as well as of its ultimate didactic efficacy. Indeed, his poetry in general confirms this belief in the value of amplification; as many scholars have noted, Lydgate never uses a single word where four will do.

In this light, *Serpent of Division*'s compression of its sources appears distinctly anomalous, particularly since its subject – the history of Rome – seems as worthy of dilation as the histories of Troy and Thebes. And given Lydgate's unusual practice of condensation in the text, those moments at which he interpolates episodes and commentary become especially significant. If the purpose of amplification may be defined, as in *Fall of Princes*, as virtuous prolongation – the addition of materials with a specifically moral intent – then we might expect to find in *Serpent*'s interpolations an index to the particular didactic goals of the text. At two decisive junctures Lydgate adds material to his sources: he interpolates the conquest of Britain into Jean's account of Caesar's victories, and he inserts a meditation on causality into Vincent's version of Caesar's downfall. Both additions are designed to moralize the narrative, the first by making it relevant to English readers, and the second by providing a learned hermeneutic through which to understand the text as a whole. But unsurprisingly, perhaps, these instances of "deformation" also represent moments of profound historical and philosophical contradiction – and as such, they become precisely those moments at which "myth" and "reality" intersect to produce the uneasy encounter between the formal and the historical that so distinctively marks this text.

In the first interpolation, Lydgate describes the conquest of Britain as a signal instance of the dangers of division; it is not Caesar's prowess alone that yields his victory, but the inability of the Britons to remain unified while under threat. Cassibolan, the British king, is betrayed by Androgius, the duke of Cornwall, who allows Caesar to land in Britain; it is a textbook picture of Lydgate's theme:

> whiles vnite & acorde stode vndefowled and vndividid in the bondis
> of Bretayne, þe myȝti conquerowre Iulius was vnable and impotente

to venqvische hem. By whiche example 3e may evidently consideren & seen þat devision, liche as is specified toforne, is originall cause in prouynces & regions of all destruciovn. (51, lines 1–5)

By constructing the conquest of the Britons as an illustration of division, Lydgate would seem to be inserting the history of England into the narrative of Nebuchadnezzar's dream; England itself is always already divided, always subject to conquest and decay. But division is not the only reason for England's defeat. Fortune intervenes to kill the best English knight, Cassibolan's brother:

> But O, alas, when he was weried of fi3t, hit befille casuelly of Fortvne, whiche is ay contrary and peruers, þat he of aventure mette with þis manly man Iulius; and both twoo, liche as made is mencioun, ferden as Tigres and lions, eueryche wowndinge other full [mortally]; tille sodeynely, bi disposicion of fate, Iulius with an vnware stroke of his dredefull swerde rofe him evyn atweyne. (51, lines 15–20)

The demands of exemplarity here yield to an historical imperative: the events of the narrative must be understood in a way that preserves the glory of the English past. The true consequence of division – English defeat – is ignored in favor of a causality in which events are determined by "aventure," the "vnware stroke." The English episode is a signal instance of what Spiegel calls "deformation," a moment at which the ideological anxieties underpinning the text are revealed, an index to the particular historical contradictions in which Lydgate and his audience (imagined or real) are embedded. These anxieties and contradictions are both generically and locally produced. For any medieval English writer, the enterprise of English history writing is subtended by the paradox of conquest: to insert England into the genealogy of Rome means both to participate in its glory and to narrate the supersession of the English themselves. For Lydgate, this paradox is also manifested in a very particular way: to write a history that iterates and reiterates the downfall of rulers (Tarquin, Cassibolan, Caesar), no matter what the moral content, is in 1422 a fraught endeavor.

It is clear that Lydgate intends *Serpent* to have a contemporary resonance and to function as a warning to present-day readers; he ends the text in the imperative mood: "lete þe wise gouernours of euery londe and region make a merowre in here mynde of þis manly man Iulius, and consideren in þer hertis þe contagious damages & þe importable harmes of devision" (65, lines 25–27). Indeed, the interpolation of an English instance of division seems designed to enforce this demand for a connection between present and past. Further, considered in the light of the events of 1422, the plot of *Serpent* would appear to be both a remarkably straightforward "merowre" of contemporary conditions and a distinctly complex consideration of their causes. When in the opening paragraphs of the text Lydgate narrates the elimination of monarchy in favor of conciliar government, an historical reading becomes not only possible but inevitable. The premature death Henry V in August 1422 had produced precisely the situation outlined by *Serpent* upon Tarquin's exile: the replacement (however temporary) of the king by a council, the sharing of a singular power among competing authorities.

To a Lancastrian regime perpetually anxious about its own capacity to retain and exercise its power, the loss of Henry V and the prospect of an extended minority would have seemed nearly catastrophic. The need for effective governance was acute; the Treaty of Troyes had extended the reach of the English monarchy across the Channel, creating a realm both geographically divided and politically unstable. Henry's will had provided that his younger brother, Humphrey of Gloucester, act as regent, while either the Duke of Burgundy or the Duke of Bedford should govern France, an allocation of power that set the stage for a series of complex negotiations over the extent and nature of the authority of the regency.[39] In particular, Lydgate's "moste worschipfull maistere and souereyne," Humphrey of Gloucester, sought to define the protectorship in such a way as to garner for himself extensive powers over the realm. He argued that a codicil to Henry V's will granted him *tutelam et defensionem principales*, and further cited the precedent of William Marshal's protectorship, in which the title *rector regis et regni* was granted. In essence, what Humphrey wanted – and to which the lords strenuously objected – was the right to administer his ward's possessions (including the realm) while being accountable only to the king upon his majority.[40] What he was granted, in the end, was a far more restricted role, "subordinate to the council and [lacking] the prerogatival powers which the council had claimed to exercise on behalf of the king during the minority."[41] While ultimate authority over the realm always resided in the will of the infant king, the monarchy had effectively become a site for continual negotiation and compromise; the unavailability of an ultimate arbiter in the person of the king meant that conditions in the realm as of 1422 were perpetually on the edge of instability and disruption.[42]

In this light, *Serpent of Division* would seem to be a relatively simple historical allegory, a warning, safely clothed in the garments of the past, of the dangers arising from the division of power. But such a warning could easily have been delivered in a more suitable form; Lydgate might have written an occasional poem, a series of short exemplars, or a far more direct prose tract.[43] Instead we find an elaborately constructed historical narrative, with layer upon layer of borrowings and amplifications that frequently serve to confuse or obscure the overt message that frames the story. A text whose sole purpose is to caution its readers at a moment of political crisis cannot afford to raise fundamental epistemological or historical questions. Yet *Serpent of Division* consistently does precisely this. In part the complexities of the text are due to Lydgate's formal ambitions, his desire to synthesize fundamentally contradictory sources; his Caesar is inconsistent because his sources conflict. But like Chaucer and Gower before him, Lydgate is also concerned to account for history itself, to engage in a practice of history writing not limited to the simple recounting of events or the accretion of exempla.

Lydgate's second major interpolation seems designed to resolve just those difficulties produced by his desire to write a history faithful to both past and present. Immediately after describing Pompey's refusal to grant Caesar a triumph for his victories, Lydgate attempts to define and classify a set of philosophical categories through which to understand Caesar's fall. As was stated earlier, he claims that Lucan has adduced three causes for the destruction of Rome, the "necessarie, the consuetudinarie and the voluntarie." The necessary cause is quite elaborately described with Chaucerian comparisons to nature:

> For liche as þe rage of [þe] haboundant flode whan hit haþe rawȝt his stordi wawes to þe hieste sodeynely þer folwith an ebbe and makith hym resorte ageyne, and In þe same wise whan eny temperall prosperite is moste flowenge in felicite þan is a sodeyne ebbe of aduersite moste to be dradde. (55, lines 18–22)

The sense of inevitability evoked here is reinforced by the "consuetu-dinarie," or customary cause, a subset of the "necessarie": "euer of custome hit fallith þat when þe blynde goddesse of variawnce Dam[e] fortvne haþe enhansed a man hieste vpon hir whele, with a sodeyne sweihe sche plungeth hym downe" (55, line 37; 56, lines 1–3). Historical causation appears here as the operation of providence in time, working upon both nature and man in predictable fashion; in this model contingency – the "vnware stroke" – is merely untheorized necessity. The third cause, in contrast, eliminates contingency altogether by assigning responsibility for events to man:

> And towchynge þe þirde cause of distruccion of þe Cite lucan likith to call hit in his poeticall mvses voluntarie, which is as mochell to seyne as cause rotid vpon wilfulnes withowte eny grownde fowndid vpon reson, for onely of volunte þei were so blyndid in þer hiȝe prosperite þat them liste not to knowe hem selfe but þowȝte hem so assured in here felicite þat þei myȝte not bi no collaterall occasion of aduersite be perturbed. (56, lines 4–9)

The contradiction between the "necessarie" and "voluntarie" causes – between necessity and will – is nowhere acknowledged by Lydgate.[44] Yet it represents a tension fundamental to the kind of history writing that *Serpent* attempts, a tension sustained by Chaucer as an invigorating ambiguity and subsumed by Gower in a rigidly linear account of the origin of sin. Lydgate's compulsion to articulate and taxonomize causes is an effect both of his literary ambition and of the historical conditions that structure and shape that ambition.[45] As the self-proclaimed successor to Chaucer, he cannot be satisfied with a simple exemplum or tract. As a poet embedded within and produced by a particular moment in history, a moment distinguished by profound uncertainty and the unpredictability of change, he seeks in literary models a means through which to account for history itself, for the "vnware stroke" that defeats the English both past and present.

The chance unfolding of historical events – the fact of contingency in history – both threatens and sustains the formal enterprise of *Serpent of Division*. To return to the vocabulary of "myth" and "reality" with which this chapter opened, the "vnware stroke" that felled Henry V constitutes precisely that "reality from which one shrinks" and which, in Schmitt's formulation, demands to be transformed by the tragic into the mythical. Lydgate's choice of a narrative both tragic and mythical is thus ultimately demanded by the central historical questions raised by the "incontrovertible reality" of the death of the sovereign. *Serpent of Division*'s version of Caesar's life and death, with its complicated causality and layered textuality, contains an urge to transcend (though it cannot be said to have transcended) its origin in the moral exemplum, reaching toward the genuinely tragic as a means of grasping the historical. Thus, when Lydgate imagines a Caesar caught between the "voluntarie" and the "necessarie," able to subject reality to his will but subject to contingency, he exceeds the limits of the genre of tragedy in such a way that its logic breaks down and the text seems mired within an irreconcilable contradiction. When Lydgate elects to retell the life of Caesar, when Schmitt fastens on to Hamlet as the paradigmatic tragic hero, what compels these choices is fundamentally the same desire to assimilate that which is by definition unassimilable: the loss of the sovereign. The untimely death of Henry V, Hamlet's father's murder, the execution of Caesar, indeed the exile of Tarquin are all instances in which the transfer of power is disrupted and the normalcy of sovereignty undermined. And both Lydgate and Schmitt recognize that such losses demand aesthetic as well as political responses if sovereignty is to be reconstituted and maintained.

If the death of Henry V produced a condition of danger, what might be called, following Schmitt's most famous formulation, a state of emergency, in so doing it also created a perspectival point from which to consider the possibility of a world without a king – indeed, without kings. The whole of the Caesar story can in this light be seen as a narrative anatomy of a floating sovereignty, now embodied in the dictators, now in Caesar, now nowhere. Schmitt's definition of sovereignty is useful here because it attaches the sovereign firmly to a particular kind of power, power over the exception:

> [The sovereign] decides whether there is an extreme emergency as well as what must be done to eliminate it. Although he stands outside the normally valid legal system, he nevertheless belongs to it, for it is he who must decide whether the constitution needs to be suspended in its entirety. [46]

One of the reasons Caesar begins as an exemplar of overweening pride and ends as a tragic figure is because he gradually achieves precisely this power over the exception. When he is one of three dictators and subject to the laws of Rome he may be defined as a threat to the interest of the state; as soon as he defeats Pompey and enters Rome he himself defines the public interest. In this light we can see that *Serpent of Division* is not merely a collection of instances of division strung on the thread of a well-known narrative. It is a story of sovereignty lost, found, and lost again. The concern of the text with the nature of sovereign power is encapsulated in a single detail added by Lydgate to the account of the subjection of Rome: when Caesar enters the city, he breaks down the walls:

> liche as some Autours expresse whan þe Romeyns for drede were redy to haue resseyved him bi þe gatis he of indignacioun and disdeyne made breke þe wallys & prowdely entered as a conquerowere & Iustefied þe Romeynes at his liste, and hoolly vndevided toke on him þe gouernaunce not onely of þe Cite but of all þe hole Empire. (62, lines 4–8)

The source for this part of the narrative is Vincent de Beauvais, who merely states "tandem romam intravit"; the manner of Caesar's entry is Lydgate's addition.[47] It is a crucial detail because Caesar's destruction of the walls of the city claims sovereignty over them; by entering as a conqueror, he refuses the assent of the people and establishes rule by force. Unlike the dictatorship, which was instituted by the Senate, Caesar's governance depends upon his capacity to destroy that which he governs – to determine, and to produce, the "state of emergency" described by Schmitt. It is he, not the citizens or the Senate, who determines the boundaries of Rome, who makes and unmakes distinctions between outside and inside. These distinctions represent the very foundation of sovereign power. Not only does Caesar fashion himself as the sovereign, then, but he also quite literally makes Rome a space in which his sovereignty can exist, a place in which the doubleness of his position, as both "rebell and traitour" and "emperour," becomes that which validates the order he has imposed. He himself embodies the distinction between inside and outside, between Roman and not-Roman, outlaw and ruler, necessary to the construction of the state itself. As such, the Rome that Caesar makes is entirely a projection outward from his being, from his own status as sovereign exception. What Lydgate recognizes, though he would not express it in this way, is that the murder of Caesar represents the death of the particular Rome that he signifies.

The narrative of *Serpent of Division* ends at precisely this moment. Caesar has become a tragic figure not because of his great heroism but because his death represents the loss of sovereignty itself, a loss that leaves Rome "bare and bareyne ... destitute and desolate" (65, lines 33–34). To return for a moment to the admittedly impoverished terms of political allegory, the death of Caesar inevitably recalls the death not of Henry V but of the particular England that *he* had signified; simply put, *Serpent of Division* warns of the dangers of division during an extended minority, of the threat to the state posed by competing claims upon sovereignty. When Lydgate calls upon "ʒe lordes and prynces of renowne" to make "a merowre toforne in youre resoun / Of Pompey and Cesar Iulius," he both interpolates his audience in this narrative of sovereignty lost and found, and reconstitutes in England the very order destroyed by division in Rome. Paradoxically, the death of Caesar – the loss of sovereignty – becomes a future possibility, an event whose potentiality can be foreclosed by "lordes and prynces" properly apprised of the threat.

As a mode of history writing, then, *Serpent of Division* seeks to shape the present by inserting it safely into the past, to control potential division by mapping its contours within a structured and objectified history of a figure long dead and buried. But of course history writing is a kind of animation, a remembering of the corpses divided by time; Caesar is remade from textual pieces, each with an afterlife of its own, none of which fits precisely with any other. If in a performative sense the text makes and unmakes sovereignty, it does so by means of an operation that may appear historiographical but is in fact literary and formal. An elucidation of the historical conditions in which *Serpent of Division* is embedded can account for its specific and abstract contents – the minority and sovereignty – but it cannot ultimately explain its form. Lydgate's layering of text upon text, source upon source, his commitment to amplification, necessarily impede the simple moral or allegorical meanings the text seems designed to divulge. As such, the critical question to ask of *Serpent of Division* is not "How is this text historically produced?" but "Why does this text insist upon producing history through literary form?"

An answer to these questions may lie in the problem of contingency, the "vnware stroke" that both subjected England to Caesar and killed Henry V. It is precisely contingency for which, it would seem, *Serpent of Division* strives to account; it is contingency that disrupts the Gowerian model of exemplary causation otherwise so central to Lydgate's notion of division. True to form, Lydgate articulates the problem of contingency in conventional terms; at the end of the narrative he warns his audience of the fickleness of "Dame Fortune"

> þe frowarde and þe contrarious ladye Dame Fortune þe blynde and þe peruerse goddes with hir gery and vnware violence sparith noþer Emperour nor kynge to plonge him downe sodeynely fro þe hiest prikke of hir vnstable whele. Alas lete euery man lifte vp his hertis eye and prudently aduerten þe mutabilite and þe sodeyne change of þis false worlde. (65, lines 20–24)

Despite this vision of a mutable and changing world, "wise governours" must still "considre þe irrecuperable harmes of division" (65, lines 25–27) – must, in other words, still act as if it were possible to remedy those harms, to combat division by wisely meditating on the example of Caesar. Nothing in Lydgate's conclusions is in any way unusual or unconventional; indeed, they are rather heavy-handed expressions of typical fifteenth-century sentiments regarding Fortune and the responsibilities of princes. But their typicality cannot conceal the fact that they represent fundamentally incompatible visions of historical causation and the role of human agency in history. "Wise governours" are given an impossible task: to accept the inevitability of the "sodeyne change of þis false worlde" (65, lines 24–25) while simultaneously behaving as if such change could be prudently foreseen and prevented. If *Serpent of Division* is fundamentally a text about crisis – the crisis of Henry V's death, the crisis of sovereignty it provoked – then the impasse to which it brings these "wise governours" constitutes the foundation of that crisis. Contingency, the "vnware stroke," the "vnware violence" of Fortune, perpetually waits on the verge of irrupting into even the most prudently arranged history. Lydgate does not tell his readers how to prevent division or defend against that contingency; he merely insists that they "make a merowre toforne in youre resoun / Of Pompey and Cesar Julius." In other words, by reading *Serpent of Division* "wise governours" can engage in a formal practice of remembering the past that in itself can compensate for the fractured and contingent present.

To understand *Serpent of Division* as a kind of consolation or remedy for the "false worlde" of Lydgate's own present is, however, to grasp it only partially. Consolation may be provided by texts far simpler, remedy sought in more obvious places. The inadequacy of a merely functional reading of *Serpent* as compensation for loss, or as a warning to princes, is suggested by Lydgate himself, when he describes his "entente":

> and for þis skille moste especially bi commaundemente of my moste worschipfull maistere & souereyne, I toke vpon me þis litill and þis compendious translacion, & of entente to don him plesaunce after my litill connyng I haue hit put in remembrawnce. (66, lines 3–6)

To place *Serpent of Division* in "remembraunce" is to give pleasure, not simply to articulate the ideological contradictions of sovereignty, not merely to gloomily describe a false and fleeting world. Indeed, this kind of remembering *finds* a certain pleasure in the contingent, for it is chance that makes history – and its representation – possible at all. The ephemeral moment of the "vnware stroke" is precisely that which calls that pleasure into being; terrifying as such a moment may be, it contains a kernel of excitement at the possibility of change. Certainly, *Serpent of Division* is a deeply conservative and traditional text. But to read it simply as a response to a set of historical conditions, even in highly sophisticated and abstract terms, is to ignore its investment in form, in its own status as literary art, and in the contingent pleasure that calls art out of history.

NOTES

1 Schmitt, "Source of the Tragic," 143.
2 *Serpent of Division* exists in four fifteenth-century manuscripts and three early printed editions. The MSS are: Cambridge, Fitzwilliam Museum MS McClean 182; Cambridge, Magdalene College MS Pepys 2006; Cambridge, MA, Harvard University, Houghton

Library MS English 530; London, British Library MS Additional 48031 (formerly Baron Calthorpe, Yelverton MS 35). The text was printed by P. Treverys (1521–35?), R. Redman (*c.* 1535), Owen Rogers 1559, E. Allde 1590. From Pearsall, *John Lydgate (1371–1449)*, 77. For a description of the Harvard MS, see Voigts, "Handlist of Middle English." For a description of each manuscript and of the Treverys, Allde, and Rogers prints, see *Serpent*, ed. MacCracken, 45–47. For a discussion of the Rogers print as the possible work of John Stow, see Ringler, "Lydgate's *Serpent of Division*." The only modern edition of *Serpent of Division* is MacCracken's 1911 text, which is marred, as Lister Matheson notes, by typographical and transcription errors. See Matheson, "Historical Prose."

The attribution of *Serpent of Division* to Lydgate is based upon both external and internal evidence from manuscript and text; a colophon appears in one manuscript stating: "Here endeth the cronycule of Julius Cesar Emperoure of Rome tyme [toune?], specifying cause of the ruyne and destruccion of the same, and translated by me, Danne John Lidgate, Monke of Bury seint Edmund, the yere of our lord god MCCCC" (British Library MS Additional 48031; quoted from MacCracken, *Serpent*, 3). MacCracken points out the links to *Siege* and *Troy Book*, 4–7, as well as *St. Alban and St. Amphibal*, 16–17. Hammond, *English Verse between Chaucer and Surrey*, 176–77 notes the similarity in vocabulary to the life of Caesar in *Fall of Princes*, as well as the distinctive use of "Tongilius" to denote the bearer of letters to Caesar, which does not appear elsewhere. Pearsall also notes the similarity to *Siege, John Lydgate (1371–1449)*, 24.

Some controversy has arisen over the date of the text. The colophon to British Library MS Additional 48031 gives a date of 1400, but the manuscript ends with a clear reference to the reign of Henry VI: "The forseide division so to schewe I have remembred this forseid litill translacion. The moneth of Decembre the ffirst yere of oure souvereigne lorde that now ys king henry vj^{te}" (quoted in MacCracken, 4). In the introduction to his edition and in a 1913 note MacCracken defends the later date, arguing that "the reference to Chaucer in the text speaks of him as some one long dead, and as Chaucer did not die until December, 1399, the two dates cannot be reconciled" (MacCracken, 4). MacCracken defends this date in a response to a review of his edition by J. W. H. Atkins; see Atkins, *Modern Language Review* 7 (1912): 253–54 and MacCracken, *Modern Language Review* 8 (1913): 103–04. The safest position is probably that of Eleanor Hammond, who regards the dating question with determined skepticism: "But that the Serpent was translated in 1422, or antedated the Fall [*Fall of Princes*], is not proved by resemblances in vocabulary or phrasing ... the entire question is unsolved" (*English Verse between Chaucer and Surrey*, 177). More recently, scholars have been bolder in turning to internal evidence to support MacCracken's date, arguing that the theme of division reflects the confusion that attended Henry V's death; in Derek Pearsall's words, "the subject of 'division' is appropriate to 1422 (and is directly picked up from *Thebes*, lines 4661–88) in a way that it was not in 1400, when the theme was rebellion, not division" (*John Lydgate (1371–1449)*, 24). The most compelling internal evidence for the 1422 date lies in Lydgate's dedication of the text to his "maistere & souereyne"; placed alongside the mention of "oure souvereigne lorde that now ys king henry vj^{te}," the reference to two "souereynes" points inevitably to the moment in 1422 when Humphrey, lord of Gloucester and uncle to the infant king, was made protector and thus "spoke in England with the sovereign's voice" (Pearsall, *John Lydgate (1371–1449)*, 23). Two recent treatments have attempted to redate the text; I find both unconvincing. Both rely on evidence from two manuscripts – British Library MS Additional 48031A and Cambridge, Magdalene College MS Pepys 2006 – that end with the initials "J. V." or "J. B." and "J. de V." or "J. de B.," respectively. Anne Sutton and Livia Visser-Fuchs

("Provenance of the Manuscript") speculate that the initials could refer to John Baret of Bury St. Edmunds, arguing that *Serpent* might then be dated to the 1430s and 1440s, when Lydgate had retired to Bury. Susanne Saygin, *Humphrey, Duke of Gloucester (1390–1447) and the Italian Humanists*, 41–47, rejects this interpretation and date, but proposes that the initials stand for "Jean duc de Bedford" and redates the manuscript to 1425–26, when Humphrey left England to join Bedford in France, leaving Henry Beaufort, bishop of Winchester, in charge of the realm. Saygin suggests that the establishment of the triumvirate in *Serpent* thus fits the topical situation in 1425–26 far better than the political circumstances of 1422, and argues that *Serpent* was commissioned by Gloucester for the edification of Bedford. However, given that one of the manuscripts in question – British Library MS Additional 48031A – was copied by John Vale, the simplest explanation for the initials is simply that they belong to Vale himself. Further, both Saygin and Sutton and Visser-Fuchs depend on a too rigid notion of topicality, in which each detail in *Serpent* must allegorize a specific element of the political situation at hand; Lydgate's text depends on a much more complex understanding of the function of literature in relation to history than either of these critics allows. In the absence of convincing evidence to the contrary, then, I accept the 1422 date.

3 V. J. Scattergood briefly sketches an historical reading of *Serpent* in his *Politics and Poetry in the Fifteenth Century*, 138–41. Other readings of the text have focused on its contribution to the development of prose style; for a detailed discussion of Lydgate's prose, see Schlauch, "Stylistic Attributes of John Lydgate's Prose." For a brief mention of *Serpent of Division* that places it in the broader context of English prose, see Burnley, "Curial Prose in England," 612–13. For a discussion of *Serpent* as a possible influence on Spenser's *Ruines of Time*, see Orwen, "Spenser and the Serpent of Division."

4 Schmitt, "Source of the Tragic," 146.

5 Ibid., 145.

6 As Lister Matheson points out in his discussion of *Serpent*, biography was in its infancy in the fifteenth century; the other biographies he cites date from the later fifteenth century and include the English Warwick Roll, the *Pageant of the Birth, Life and Death of Richard Beauchamp, Earl of Warwick*, and two English biographies of Henry V (Matheson, 229–30).

7 Chaucer's Caesar appears of course in the *Monk's Tale* and is cited by Lydgate. Gower mentions Caesar twice in book 7 of the *Confessio Amantis*, first as an example of largesse and second to illustrate wisdom; in both cases he is presented as an ideal king (*Complete Works of John Gower*, vol. III, *The English Works*, ed. G. C. Macaulay, book 7, lines 2061–114; lines 2449–90, hereafter cited by book and line number in the text). Caesar appears briefly three times in the *Regiment of Princes*: twice as an example of kingly pity, and once as an illustration of patience. See *The Regiment of Princes*, ed. Blyth, lines 3246–48; lines 3270–311; lines 3513–28. A further vernacularization of Caesar's life may be found in Trevisa's translation of Higden, which narrates Caesar's rule and fall as part of a broader world history; see *Polychronicon* vol. II, 181–223.

8 *Li Hystore de Julius Cesar*, ed. Settegast; *Li Fet des Romains*, ed. L.-F. Flutre and K. Sneyders de Vogel.

9 Chaucer's invocation reads, "Lucan, to thee this storie I recomende, / And to Swetoun, and to Valerius also" (lines 2719–20). Though there has been critical disagreement on Chaucer's use or non-use of Lucan, the view of Robert Root (Bryan and Dempster, eds., *Sources and Analogues of Chaucer's Canterbury Tales*, 642), that "I can find no grounds for believing that Lucan was ... an immediate source," has been generally accepted. Further, it has been suggested that, like Lydgate, Chaucer used Jean, Vincent, and

Higden, all secondary recountings of the Caesar story. See the note to lines 2671–726 of the *Monk's Tale*, *Riverside Chaucer*, ed. Benson, 934; all references to Chaucer hereafter are cited by text and line number in the text.

10 MacCracken, *Serpent*, 23.

11 Lucan, *The Civil War (Pharsalia)*, trans. J. D. Duff, book 1, lines 67–72, 6–9.

12 MacCracken, *Serpent*, 24–25. Jean's text reads:

> "Nampourquant tout ausi comme Fortune fait l'oume joiant, tout ausi tost le refait elle dolant, quant la roee tourne; et d'autre part on ne voit mie souvent avenir que orgius et grans signourie puissent ensanle durer lonc tans, mais de tant com li hom amonte plus haut en poissance, de tant chiet il plus tost, ausi comme li pesans fais ki trop est grans. Tout ausi est il de Ponpee: il estoit si couvoiteus d'ounour tenir k'il ne voiloit ke nus fust a lui pers de seignourie et voloit ke si commandement fuissent gardet sour tous autre et tenut; et cou est une chose que on ne voit mie souvent avenir, que doi chevalier ki tenant soient d'une tiere soient ensamble concordant." (*Li Hystore de Julius Cesar*), 12–13.

MacCracken points to "words like 'Nampourquant' and phrases like 'on ne voit mie souvent'" as Lydgate's source for the "consuetudinary" cause, and to the phrase "Ponpee *voloit*" as the source for the "voluntary" cause.

13 *Life of St. Alban and St. Amphibal*, ed. Van Der Westhuizen, lines 120–26.

14 The manuscript is MS Cotton Claudius E.IV., which also includes two other sources for the poem, *Interpretatio Guilielmi* (William's *Vita*) and the *Vita Secundi Offae* (Westhuizen, *Life of Saint Alban and Saint Amphibal*, 45). The relevant passage follows:

> Iulius Caesar primus Romanorum imperator, postquam Gallias subiugavit, Britannie, que nunc appelatur Anglia, arma intulit, temporibus regis Cassibelanni; et post conflictus varios licet cum difficultate victor extitit, et terram posuit sub tributo edi ditque statua quae postea longo tempore fuerunt in insula observata. (89)

15 MacCracken's claim that Lydgate turns to the *Brut* for the details of the Britain episode is a likely one, though based on the erroneous assumption that Lydgate himself contributed to the chronicle. In what Lister Matheson in *The Prose Brut: The Development of a Middle English Chronicle*, 257–259 terms a "Peculiar Version" of the *Brut*, Harvard University MS Eng. 530 (1), John Shirley attributes the 1377 to 1419 continuation to Lydgate: "nowe translated by daun Johan Lydegate the munk of Bury." Not coincidentally, the MS also contains several other works by Lydgate, including *Serpent of Division*; Matheson suggests that Shirley's attribution "may be [an] error, but it could also be a deliberate promotional ploy" (258–59). It would be very surprising if Lydgate did not know some version of the popular *Brut*, though his assertion in *Serpent* that he can find the name of Cassibolan's brother nowhere in his source is odd. Nennius is a well-known figure, appearing in Geoffrey of Monmouth and in the *Brut*, including the version attributed to Lydgate.

16 Vincent de Beauvais, *Speculum Historiale*, Liber Sextus, cap. 1.

17 MacCracken, *Serpent*, 34–35. There is no reason to assume that Lydgate used Trevisa's translation, rather than Higden's original; indeed, as I show in chapter 4, Lydgate would have been more likely to use the Latin text.

18 The two passages at issue for MacCracken are the crossing of the Rubicon and the prophecies before the war. In both cases, Jean has excised all of the supernatural elements of the story from Lucan (and perhaps from his own reading of *Les Faits*). Lydgate's

version of each incident is clearly based upon *Les Faits*, with two exceptions, both from the prophecies before the war. The first is Lydgate's comparison of the divided flame in the temple of Vesta to the division of the smoke on the funeral pyres of Polynices and Etiocles, which he clearly derives from his source for *Siege of Thebes*, a prose version of the *Roman de Thebes* entitled *Le Roman de edipus*. See *Roman de edipus*, ed. August Veinant, Kii verso. The passage is also printed in the notes to Axel Erdmann and Eilert Ekwall's edition of the *Siege* (135, notes to lines 4562–87). Surprisingly, Lydgate does not use the image in *Siege*. Perhaps the image of division persisting even after the restoration of order by Theseus did not fit Lydgate's vision of the end of his poem, or of the beginning of Chaucer's *Knight's Tale*. The second exception concerns Lydgate's use of the riddle of the Sybil, which does not occur in Lucan or *Les Faits*, but which ultimately comes from Laurent de Premierfait's translation of Boccaccio's *De Casibus Illustrium Virorum*, Lydgate's source for his account of Caesar in the *Fall of Princes*. Lydgate's use of it here further argues for a date of 1422 for *Serpent*, as the date of Laurent's redaction is 1409. The story of Caesar may be found in Bergen, ed., *Fall of Princes*, book 6, lines 2234–919; for Laurent's version, see the notes to line 2341, vol. IV, 260.

19 Walter Map, *De Nugis Curialium: Courtier's Trifles*, ed. and trans. M. R. James, 298–99. Eleanor Hammond identifies this source in her notes to the *Fall of Princes* in *English Poetry from Chaucer to Surrey*, 450, n. 43.

20 The passage from the *Monk's Tale* reads: "O myghty Cesar, that in Thessalie / Agayn Pompeus, fader thyn in lawe" (lines 2679–80). In Trevisa's translation of Higden we find, "ßanne in his comynge to Rome ward, whanne he come to Alpes, he sente to Pompeus, whos douȝter he hadde i-wedded" (*Polychronicon*, vol. III, 193).

21 MacCracken, *Serpent*, 43. See also Suetonius, book I, XXVII (*Lives of the Caesars*, ed. Rolfe, 69).

22 MacCracken, *Serpent*, 39; see also the notes to the *Monk's Tale*, line 2697 in the *Riverside Chaucer*, 935.

23 *Polychronicon*, vol. III, 206. MacCracken also notes that the two "Bruti" appear in Petrarch's *Triunfo di Fama* (*Serpent*, 39).

24 *Fall of Princes*, vol. IV, notes to lines 2871 ff., 265.

25 Lydgate is clearly working from memory, recalling "Brutus Cassius" and "boidekins." The relevant passage from the *Monk's Tale* reads:

> To Rome agayn repaireth Julius
> With his triumphe, lauriat ful hye
> But on a tyme Brutus Cassius,
> That evere hadde of his hye estaat envye,
> Ful prively hath maad conspiracye
> Agayns this Julius in subtil wise,
> And caste the place in which he sholde dye
> With boydekyns, as I shal yow devyse.
> (lines 2695–702)

As James Simpson has recently argued in *Reform and Cultural Revolution*, the idea that Lydgate is obsequiously subservient to Chaucer is largely a figment of twentieth-century critics' imaginations: "almost none of Lydgate's works is directly imitative of Chaucer; those poems that do relate to Chaucer's do so with more powerful strategies in mind than slavish imitation" (50).

26 *Middle English Dictionary (MED)*, 1a, 4a, 6a.

27 A. J. Minnis discusses the *Prologue* as a form of "extrinsic" prologue, found in medieval commentaries on the Sapiential Books, drawing comparisons between Gower and Robert Holcot. See "John Gower: *Sapiens* in Ethics and Politics," 169–74.

28 *Parliament of Fowls*, lines 379–81. The passage ultimately derives from Boethius; see *Boece*, book 3, m. 9, lines 18–24.

29 Chaucer, of course, repeatedly articulates the Boethian vision of a world bound up by love, in which contigency must be understood as an illusion produced by the inadequacy of human vision; see the "Prime Mover" speech from the *Knight's Tale* and in the "Canticus Troili" in *Troilus and Criseyde*, both ultimately derived from Boethius, book 2, m. 8. In *Boece*, love constrains heaven, earth, and sea, "al this accordaunce [and] ordenaunce of thynges is bounde with love, that governeth erthe and see, and hath also comandement to the hevene" (book 2, m. 8, 13–16). Compare Gower's vision, in which the very heavens are divided by man's sin: "A mannes Senne is forto hate, / Which makth the welkne to debate" (*Prol.*, lines 927–28).

30 Peck, ed., *Confessio Amantis*, xvii.

31 Copeland, *Rhetoric, Hermeneutics*, 212, 202–20.

32 Lydgate's prologue to the *Fall of Princes* outlines his debts to Boccaccio, Laurent, and Chaucer, each of whom he identifies as a writer of tragedy. He identifies himself as a compendious translator, following his sources "pleynly": "Hauyng no colours but onli whit & blak, / To the tragedies which that I shal write. / And for I can my-silff no bet acquite, / Vndir support off all that shal it reede, / Vpon Bochas riht thus I will proceede" (lines 465–69). But the prologue also contains a defense of Laurent's amendment of Boccaccio, which is done without "presumpcioun." For an important discussion of Lydgate's posture here see Copeland, "Lydgate, Hawes, and the Science of Rhetoric," 70–75.

33 Spiegel, *Romancing the Past*, 105–06.

34 Ibid., 106.

35 Ibid., 124. The text is variously named *Li Fet des Romains, Les Fais des Rommains, Le livre de Julius César, Le vraie histoire de Julius César. Li Fet* typically refers to manuscript V3; this MS is the one used by Jeanette Beer in her book on the text, *A Medieval Caesar*. In his partial edition of the text, Thomas J. McCormick, Jr. uses manuscript L3, *Les Fais des Rommains*. See McCormick, *A Partial Edition of* Les Fais Des Rommains, for a recent study of the text.

36 Spiegel, *Romancing the Past*, 160. Beer's interpretation of *Les Faits des Romains* is quite different; she sees the text as an apology for imperial ambition, arguing that "the translator is using Roman Gaul as a historical justification for Philip Augustus' dream of a larger, unified France" (74). Spiegel's analysis of the negative presentation of Caesar in *Les Faits*, however, clearly shows that the text's portrayal of such ambitions is highly critical.

37 Spiegel shows that, although he calls his text a translation of Lucan, Jean uses a variety of classical sources for *Li Hystore*, including Caesar, Suetonius, Ovid, Plutarch, Cassius Dio, Appian and Isidore of Seville, the *Roman d'Enéas* and the *Roman de la Rose* (183). He also knew and indeed may have written the *Roumanz de Jules César*, attributed to Jacos de Forest (184–85).

38 See Spiegel, *Romancing the Past*, 195–96.

39 Griffiths, *Reign of King Henry VI*, 20.

40 I have relied here on Ernest Jacob's discussion of the terms of the minority in *The Fifteenth Century: 1399–1485*, 211–18.

41 Jacob, *Fifteenth Century*, 211.

42 For a somewhat controversial but ultimately compelling argument about the nature of conciliar government in Henry VI's reign, see Watts, *Henry VI and the Politics of Kingship*, particularly pages 111–18. For a more traditional account, see Wolffe, *Henry VI*, 27–35.

43 Walter Schirmer has argued that the *Serpent*'s seemingly disorganized form and layering of sources and interpolations conform to the structure of a sermon; while this claim convincingly elucidates one aspect of Lydgate's formal practice (the combination of theme and exempla), it cannot account for the tensions and contradictions that mark the text's attitude to historical causation. *John Lydgate: A Study in the Culture of the XVth Century*, 82–88.

44 Though it is explored in Chaucer's translation of Boethius; see *Boece*, book 5, pr. 6, lines 144–61. Indeed, the phrase "unware stroke," used by Lydgate to indicate the working of Fortune, comes from *Boece*, book 2, pr. 2, lines 67–70: "What other thynge bywaylen the cryinges of tragedyes but oonly the dedes of Fortune, that with an unwar strook overturneth the realmes of greet nobleye?" The phrase appears at the very end of the *Monk's Tale* as well: "Tragediës noon oother maner thyng / Ne kan in syngyng crie ne biwaille / But that Fortune alwey wole assaille / With unwar strook the regnes that been proude" (lines 2761–64).

45 Here Copeland's account of Gower's use of scholastic *divisio* suggests that Lydgate is similarly using the techniques of academic, Latin discourse in order to counter the division instantiated by the fall of Rome, healing the fragmentation of the past by taxonomizing and ordering it. For a reading of the *Prologue* that deemphasizes its authority within the *Confessio* as a whole, see Robins, "Romance, Exemplum."

46 Schmitt, *Political Theology*, 6–7.

47 Vincent de Beauvais, *Speculum Historiale*, Liber Sextus, cap. 35.

2

Social forms, literary contents: Lydgate's mummings

In Trinity College Cambridge MS R. 3. 20 may be found a series of short poems by Lydgate that its compiler, John Shirley, introduced with variations of the term "mumming" – "the devyse of a momyng," "in wyse of mommers desguysed."[1] These include two performances before King Henry VI, at Eltham and at Windsor, and two spectacles in honor of Mayor William Eastfield of London, commissioned by the Mercers' and Goldsmiths' guilds. In his 1934 edition, *The Minor Poems of John Lydgate*, Henry Noble MacCracken added to these four a further three "mummings" – those at Bishopswood, London, and Hertford – creating a minor canon of Lydgate's dramatic works, all of which can be dated between the years 1424 and 1430.[2] These texts have been little discussed, despite (or perhaps because of) the fact that they occupy an anomalous place within both literary and dramatic histories of late medieval England; lacking detailed performance records, historians of the theatre find the mummings intriguing but ultimately unrevealing, while literary critics have typically eschewed them in favor of Lydgate's more poetically ambitious texts, such as *Siege of Thebes* or *Troy Book*. But there is good reason for examining these poems more carefully. The very fact that they are performance pieces with an identifiable author makes the mummings stand out among medieval English dramatic texts. Further, because they exist at the intersection of genres and media – not quite "poetry," nor yet "drama" – Lydgate's mummings challenge the assumptions from which both literary and dramatic criticism proceed. They tempt critics to speculate, to experiment with possible performance details and to reconstruct audience responses, even as the dearth of evidence for such performances enforces its own relentless logic of absence. Critical speculation about the mummings has tended to

71

extrapolate in two ways, either drawing conclusions about the genre of "mumming" and its history, or supplying details of performance that have no basis in textual evidence.[3] To note the latter is not to say that I do not recognize the need for what Paul Strohm has called "rememorative reconstruction" – the reassembly of the past in the present from the shards and bits of history, the defragmentation of what are necessarily disconnected and disparate shreds of medieval texts and textuality.[4] But it is precisely the *textuality* of Lydgate's mummings that is at issue here. These are poems that insist upon their status as parts of a vernacular poetic tradition emerging – in large part due to Lydgate – as a privileged form of social commentary and political reflection. It thus becomes crucial to heed the cues that the texts themselves provide. In the case of Lydgate's mummings, those cues tell us to look first at the words on the page.

"Writtenness" is particularly evident in Lydgate's dramatic texts.[5] It would certainly be futile to argue (and I am not doing so here) that literary texts and dramatic performances had not been linked before Lydgate's mummings. As any basic history of drama in England will show, scripted performances were occurring throughout the Middle Ages.[6] But the mummings are peculiarly literary documents. Lydgate deploys all of his usual poetic devices – the citation of authoritative sources, personification, and amplification, to name a few – to produce what can only be called a mixed form, part didactic poetry, part allegorical procession, part Christmastime household entertainment. In their display of Lydgate's signal skill as a "maker" – his capacity for synthesis and syncretism – the mummings bear more than a passing resemblance to *Serpent of Division*, itself a text, as we have seen, that foregrounds its status as a palimpsest of classical and medieval sources. Similarly, the mummings insistently recall to the reader the textual field in which they are embedded, both as poems designed to be read and as scripts made for performance. The resemblance to *Serpent* is not merely a formal one, however. If Lydgate's 1422 tract staked a claim for the literary as a privileged site for political discourse, particularly the discourse of sovereignty, the mummings extend that claim beyond the genre of advice to princes, bringing the ideological and methodological tactics of the earlier text to bear on a larger and more variegated audience. In *Serpent*, Lydgate warned Humphrey and the lords of the realm about the dangers of "divysioun," a warning both prescient and predictable; in the mummings we see the skillful work of a master propagandist, honed by several years of writing poetry in a highly charged and delicately balanced political environment in which the potential for "divysioun" has repeatedly been realized.

The need to iterate and reiterate Henry VI's claim to the dual monarchy was at one level a simple one; France was never totally in the grip of English rule during the minority, and over the course of the 1420s matters became steadily more uncertain, culminating with Joan of Arc's victories and the crowning of the Dauphin, Charles VII, at Rheims in 1429.[7] Lydgate responded to these uncertainties with a variety of texts, including two poems written to bolster the Lancastrian claim to the French throne, "The Kings of England sithen William Conqueror" and "The Title and Pedigree of Henry VI"; Pearsall describes the latter commission as the "decisive moment in [Lydgate's] new career."[8] Written in 1426, "Title and Pedigree" was commissioned by the Earl of Warwick and translated a French poem by Lawrence Calot that had been posted, along with a pictorial genealogy, on the wall of Notre-Dame in 1423 as a way of reinforcing Henry VI's title for his new subjects.[9] Calot's poem is an obvious instance of Lancastrian propaganda, revealing the felt need of the English to promote the claim of its child-king in the traditional terms of succession and right rule, and Lydgate's translation clearly aims to make the same claims for English sovereignty for a native audience.[10] Lee Patterson has argued that "Title and Pedigree" reveals contradictions internal to the dual monarchy in a realm characterized by an almost obsessive concern for identity and singularity; the poem "bespeaks by the very ardor of its commitment the tenacity of the doubts it means to remove."[11] Those doubts are structurally produced by the very existence of two crowns – a fundamental "divysioun" – that metaphorically stand in for other profound English anxieties about the problem of France, including what Patterson calls the difference between "the imperial ambitions of the chivalric class and the local concerns of the nation at large," as well as the continuing danger of faction within the king's council itself.[12]

The rule of the council, with Gloucester as Protector and the Duke of Bedford as regent in France, was marred by precisely the kind of division against which Lydgate had warned; Gloucester continually sought greater autonomy in relation to the king, and repeatedly encountered the resistance of the council to his attempts to act with singular authority.[13] These tensions came to a head in 1425, when Gloucester and his uncle, Bishop Henry Beaufort, openly clashed in London; they were reconciled only by the direct intervention of Bedford, who returned from France in order to make peace.[14] The solution to both the erosion of English rule in France and the division at home was, as John Watts has argued, "a vigorous assertion of the rule of Henry VI" – not the prospective or awaited rule of the child-king, but the immediate personal rule of the monarch.[15] Such assertions produced what Watts calls "a certain paradox": "Bedford, Gloucester and the lords of the council served the infant sovereign, but they also represented him. He ruled, but the lords executed his rule. They counselled him, but equally, they, not he, were the recipients of this counsel."[16] It was Gloucester's powerful sense of the illogicality of attributing personal rule to a child under the tutelage of a council that produced his repeated attempts to be named regent – and it was the council's awareness of the danger of usurping the king's personal authority that resulted in such legitimating propaganda as Lydgate's "Pedigree." Indeed, when in 1429 the English found themselves facing severe losses in France and confronted with the coronation of Charles VII, the solution devised by the Duke of Bedford reveals the extreme symbolic and real significance of the person of the king: Henry VI would be crowned in France and in England, and would assume the personal rule that the council had so zealously safeguarded.[17] The coronations produced a flurry of propaganda, both textual and dramatic, much of which Lydgate produced or was involved in producing. These include two poems in honor of the English coronation at Westminster in November 1429 ("Roundel at the Coronation of Henry VI" and "Ballade to King Henry VI upon his Coronation") as well as verses to accompany the *soteltes*, or sugar sculptures, at the coronation banquet.[18] All three texts emphasize the lineage of the young king – "descendid frome twoo lynes / Of Saynt Edward and of Saynt Lowys" ("Ballade," lines 9–10) – and express hope that he will reign in wisdom and virtue. Similar sentiments were expressed, though not by Lydgate, in France; just prior to his coronation in December 1431, Henry ceremonially entered Paris and was greeted with elaborate pageantry, including symbolic tableaux replete with images of the

Passion of Christ, St. Denis, and the two crowns of England and France.[19] Not to be outdone (and perhaps because the French response to their new king was disappointing), the city of London staged a spectacular entry upon Henry's return in February 1432; Lydgate recorded its details in a series of verses that trace the progress of the king through the city and describe the pageants and their significance.[20] A giant, antelopes, allegorical figures, virgins, the seven liberal arts, historical and biblical characters, the familiar Sts. Edward and Louis, a Jesse tree, and the Trinity combined with ritual gift-giving and the conferral of the scepter of St. Edward to create one of the most splendid productions of monarchical power and authority recorded in medieval England; hope for a stalwart king in the image of Henry V reveals itself in every line of Lydgate's verses.

It was during this period of intense political and cultural activity – 1428–32 – that Lydgate wrote the four poems described by Shirley as "mummings."[21] Two ("Eltham" and "Windsor") are simple royal entertainments written in the same register and using some of the same imagery as the coronation poems, revealing both formal and thematic contiguities between public forms of spectacle and private entertainments for the king and his household. These mummings illustrate the seriousness of royal entertainment; both are streamlined vignettes of royal power, much like the pageants witnessed by Henry in 1432, and both are permeated with the aura of the king's majesty. This similarity between public and private forms of cultural expression emerges from a notion of kingship as personal and intimate; as John Watts has remarked, "in a world where the ruler 'si geret personam civitatis,' the private disposition of the king determined the public disposition of the realm."[22] Propaganda, in such circumstances, always has a double function, as an address to both king and people that seeks to affirm monarchical power at the same time as it directs and shapes the exercise of that power. Both the royal mummings function in this dual way, making them typical examples of fifteenth-century political discourse; were it not for Shirley's label, "mumming," little would distinguish them from Lydgate's other efforts to assert the hegemony of Lancastrian rule. But Shirley has placed these poems in a category with two others – "The Mumming for the Mercers" and "The Mumming for the Goldsmiths" – neither of which was performed for the king, and both of which focus in an overt way on civic rather than monarchical themes and images. As a result, the question of genre emerges particularly strongly for these four texts, demanding an analysis that begins not from historical contiguity (though they were all written within a few years of each other), but rather from their generic identity as "mummings." The turn to genre removes these poems from the chain of causes and effects that usually constitutes "history" (losses in France cause English propaganda) and enables one to examine them first as exercises in form.

Such a focus allows the poems to emerge as texts embedded within a cultural field partly constituted by royal and national politics, partly by social and ritual practices, and partly by their links to a whole series of authoritative texts, tropes, narratives, and images that they reproduce and "deform." John Shirley, as a medieval witness, gives testimony that allows us to see that the genre of "mumming" itself made meaning in specific and predictable ways, as a form of behavior associated with the kind of personal rule Henry VI's coronations were designed to reinforce. Though Lydgate himself did not use the term "mumming," it is clear from the texts that he was engaging with the form of the mumming as it was transmitted from the late fourteenth century. Not only did he invest a familiar practice with new content, he also manipulated the very form itself, transforming what had been a relatively simple and symbolic act into an occasion for the kind of heightened, excessive, and multivalent discourse that can only be called "literary."

Throughout this chapter my contention will be that the mummings, much like *Serpent of Division*, constitute a formal response to an historical moment *and* that it is within that form that historicity must be sought. Though the events of 1422 and 1428–32 necessarily condition these texts at a very deep level, producing the cultural crises to which they seek to provide imaginary resolution, it remains fundamentally reductive to limit their meaning to the topical. That is not to say that historical topicality cannot account for certain literary texts; as I will show, the mummings at Eltham and Windsor are constrained by audience and theme such that Lydgate's intention becomes very clear – and his intention was precisely to produce a simple historical interpretation. But the emergence of unmistakably self-conscious poetic discourse in the two mercantile mummings demands a literary as well as an historical view. To be sure, historical causes can be adduced for this phenomenon – the development of mercantile culture, the power of elite London guilds, Lydgate's own need for patronage – but they cannot account for the very basic fact that it was to poetry that Lydgate and his patrons turned for propaganda, edification, and pleasure at a moment of political instability and social anxiety.

In his mummings, Lydgate took up a traditional social form and invested it with a new, and distinctly poetic, content. Mumming typically functions as an address to the king, as a mode of subordination and a means of reproducing the proper relation between sovereign and subject. *Serpent of Division*, too, is a medium for the address of a subordinate to a superior; Lydgate's assertion in that text that what history provides and demands is "plesaunce" and "remembrawnce" is meant as both admonition and consolation. *Serpent* simultaneously fills an aesthetic need and creates aesthetic desire within a readership of "wise gouernours" and Lydgate's "maistere & souereyne," Humphrey of Gloucester, and it does so in a literary form that is both complex and contradictory – characteristics, I have suggested, solicited by the text's structuring preoccupation with the nature and limits of sovereignty, for kings and for councils. If the mumming was indeed a mode of addressing the sovereign, then the performances at Eltham and Windsor would by their very simplicity appear to confirm this reading; the king, once an infant, is now fully present and the need for discursive complexity – for the negotiation of contradiction – has passed. What, then, of the mummings for the Mercers and Goldsmiths, poems as layered and intertextual as the most allusive of Lydgate's literary efforts? The complexity Lydgate found so necessary in *Serpent* has reappeared and been magnified, revealing, I will argue, the desire of a new audience for the kind of literary erudition directed at "wise gouernours." That desire is an historical one; Lydgate helps to make it just as it makes him. It is further a formal desire, which is to say that it is channeled and structured through cultural forms that are both traditional and emergent. In what follows I begin by exploring the medieval parameters of "mumming" as form and practice. I argue, in brief, that common assumptions about dramatic practice (the status of mumming as a popular genre, for example) must be rethought in light of a dispassionate look at the records – which suggest that, at least in England, "mumming" had an historically specific and elite form and function. Finally, I turn to the texts themselves and to a reading of the four mummings that examines precisely how the obsession with sovereignty, the desire for cultural capital, and the emergence of the literary come together to produce dense and alien poems.

ÞEY ÞAT NOȝT SPEKE: THE FORM OF THE MUMMING

The late medieval word list, *Promptorium Parvulorum*, defines "mummyn" as "þey þat noȝt speke," a frustratingly simple definition that sheds little light on the diverse mentions of mumming to be found in late Middle English chronicles, ordinances, and literary manuscripts.[23] Mumming can appear as a festive, aristocratic holiday game, as in a well-known 1377 Christmas celebration for the young prince Richard.[24] On this occasion, the mummers entered the castle and invited the prince to play at (loaded) dice; he made three casts and won a gold ball, a gold cup, and a gold ring. After his mother and the other lords in the household had cast and won gold rings, the prince called for wine and the evening ended with dancing, mummers on one side and the royal household on the other. Because the 1377 mumming is the first extended description of the practice, its elements – disguise, gift-giving, game-playing, and dancing – have long been identified as the standard characteristics of a common and familiar Christmas scenario.[25] Beginning with E. K. Chambers's *The Mediaeval Stage*, with its narrative of the folk origins of medieval drama, mumming has traditionally been understood as a folk custom that appears in the records at the moment it is appropriated by aristocrats and denied to the very persons with whom it originated.[26] But the association of mumming with some kind of long-standing popular festive practice can only be speculative. No records for such performances survive. Records that use the term "mumming" are almost nonexistent before the reign of Richard II; Ian Lancashire's *Dramatic Texts and Records of Britain* cites only one, an incident in 1224 in which five Franciscans were confused with "mummers" – a record Lancashire classifies as "doubtful."[27] Indeed, the *MED* cites no use of the words "mumming" or "mummer" before 1417. During Richard's reign, however, behaviors associated with mumming begin to appear in the records, both in reference to royal occasions and in prohibitions.[28] Shortly after Christmas 1377 (at Kennington, January 25), in 1393 (at Eltham, January 6) and in 1394 (at Westminster) the citizens of London presented entertainments and brought gifts to Richard II,[29] while in 1387 a proclamation was recorded in the *Guildhall Letter-Book* using the term "mumming."[30] It is clear that practices like wearing visors or masks and dice-playing – the most commonly forbidden activities – did not suddenly arise during Richard II's reign. As even a cursory glance at the records shows, people in England had been disguising themselves on festive occasions since at least the thirteenth century and probably long before.[31] But in the latter half of the fourteenth century and the first part of the fifteenth century prohibitions against such disguisings multiply to a surprising extent. Beginning with a proclamation in 1334, Ian Lancashire records prohibitions that specifically mention mumming practices (masking and playing at dice in the earlier records, "mumming" itself in the later) in 1352, 1372, 1376, 1380, 1387 (January and December), 1393, 1404, 1405, 1417, and 1418.[32] All of the proclamations are dated November, December, or January, making it clear that the activity being outlawed is associated with Christmas. The term "mumming" appears for the first time in English in the 1417 proclamation; the word would appear to have entered the language from the French.[33] Excluding the doubtful 1224 reference, the two earliest records in England that refer to "mumming" are dated 1387 and 1393 – from the *Guildhall Letter-Book* and Gilbert Maghfeld's account book, respectively – and are written in French.[34] By 1418, the prohibition of mumming has become both detailed and specific:

> No manere persone, of what astate, degre, or condicioun þat euere he be, duryng þis holy tyme of Cristemes be so hardy in eny wyse to walk by nyght in eny manere mommyng, pleyes, enterludes, or eny oþer disgisynges with eny feynyd berdis, peyntid visers, diffourmyd or colourid visages in eny wyse, up peyne of emprisonement of her bodyes.[35]

After the January 1387 proclamation, playing at dice is not mentioned. All of the proclamations are issued in London.[36]

What is to be made of this cluster of proclamations? It would seem that mumming was considered a behavior in need of regulation; that it comprised disguising oneself by altering one's "visage" and walking about at night, possibly playing dice; that it was a London practice, or at least a particular problem in London; and that mumming functioned as a means of address to the king. Glynne Wickham noted long ago this perplexing disjunction between the "known continuance of mumming" and the repeated prohibitions against it, arguing that the folk mumming was gradually refined by the noble classes and transformed from a custom with a high potential for disorder and misrule into civilized entertainment.[37] What cannot be ascertained, of course, is whether or not such a folk custom existed prior to its appearance as a practice associated with the nobility. Meg Twycross and Sarah Carpenter have suggested that it did, adducing evidence from the Continent and from "modern survivals" of the practice in places such as Newfoundland, as well as noting the series of proclamations cited above.[38] The net effect of their argument – though they do caution against extrapolating from Continental or modern sources – is to suggest that mumming was a *popular* and common form of Christmastime entertainment, so much so that it required regulation and social control.

Taking the existing records as they stand, however, a somewhat different picture of mumming emerges. Mumming seemingly appears first as an elite behavior, an entertainment specifically linked to the king. Further, sanctioned mumming involves the relation of nonnoble persons – in particular, the London oligarchy – to the king; mummers, however disguised, are Londoners paying homage to royalty. If the royal entry symbolically enacts the relationship of the king to the city, both signifying its submission to him and displaying its wealth and power, the mumming functions as a more private intrusion by the city into the king's household. The prohibitions that appear with such frequency during Richard's reign, and that typically issue from the mayor and aldermen, would seem not to be attempts to forbid the practice entirely, but (like sumptuary laws) restrictions upon who might be authorized to behave in a particular way. Mumming seems to have been a London practice that the London elite were determined to keep for themselves. And while it would surely be rash to suggest that the only mumming that occurred in England was that for which we have textual evidence, it remains the case that the practice emerged as a named activity at an historically specific moment, and can be analyzed within quite particular parameters, without recourse to "folk custom" or popular tradition.[39]

These conclusions are borne out by the evidence for mummings themselves. Three times during Richard's reign we find records of elaborate Christmastime entertainments performed by London citizens for the king – in 1377, 1393, and 1394 – and at Christmas 1400 / 01 a mumming was performed by the men of London for the emperor of Constantinople, Manuel II, at Eltham.[40] All but the 1394 performance are identified by a source using the term "mumming," although for the 1377 occasion the reference comes from a chronicle of a later date.[41] In the *Westminster Chronicle* it is reported that at Christmas 1393 and 1394 Londoners visited the king at Eltham and Westminster; though on both occasions there was music, dancing, costumes (in 1393 the Londoners came with "glorioso apparatu" and in 1394 with "diverso apparatu"), and gifts (in 1393 a dromedary and a great bird, in 1394 a ship filled with offerings for the king and queen), the 1393 visit provided the occasion for a complicated negotiation of fines owed by the city to the king.[42] In every instance, mumming involves the appearance at court of Londoners at Christmastime, reenacting, in however attenuated a fashion, the visit of the Magi to the infant Christ before their earthly king. As the 1393 visit makes clear, these occasions created a space for festive resolutions to political problems; the powerful symbolism of the Epiphany visit lifted king and citizens out of the narrow world of city politics and into a more abstract and pleasing realm of serious play.

This portrait of mumming may seem far too narrowly drawn given such evidence as the 1334 prohibition, which seems to imply that the Christmastime house visit was extant rather earlier than 1387. But it has the advantage of delimiting a field of inquiry according to a vocabulary for which there is distinctive historical evidence. If it cannot be said that mumming was *always* a practice restricted to London and involving the king in some way, it must be noted that the reign of Richard II saw the development of a form of entertainment dedicated on *most occasions* to staging the relationship between the king and the London oligarchy. It required legislation not only because of the intrinsic potential of disguise to erase critical identity markers of class and status, but also because it was a recognizably privileged form within which subordinates could negotiate, enact, and engage power relations, a form easily appropriable by groups less interested in gift-giving and social order.

The dangerous potential of mumming came to the fore in 1400 and 1414, when rebels disguised as Christmas mummers plotted against both Henry IV and Henry V. John Capgrave's *Abbreuacioun of Cronicles* records an assassination attempt on Henry IV by mummers in 1400:

> In þe secund ȝere of þis kyng þe erlis of Kent, Salesbury, and Huntingdon, onkende onto þe kyng, risin ageyn him – vnkynde were þei, for þe puple wold haue hem ded, and þe king spared hem. These men, þus gadered, purposed to falle on þe kyng sodeynly at Wyndesore vndir þe colour of mummeres in Cristmasse tyme. The kyng was warned of þis, and fled to London.[43]

And the chronicle of William Gregory describes a similar use of mumming in 1414:

> And that same yere, on the Twelfe the nyght, were a-restyd certayne personys, called Lollers, atte the sygne of the Ax, whithe owte Byschoppe ys gate, the whyche Lollers hadde caste to have made a mommynge at Eltham, and undyr coloure of the mommynge to have dystryte the kyng and Hooly Chyrche.[44]

In these instances, rebellious lords and Lollards have pretended to be mummers in order to obtain the access to the king necessary for the destructive action they intended (according to the chronicles) to take. Because mumming fundamentally depended on an intimate and personal notion of kingship, in which contact with the sovereign himself constituted the highest form of politics, it should not be surprising that it appealed to those seeking to alter radically their political world; or, if the chronicle accounts are viewed more skeptically, that fears about the safety of the king at moments of historical conflict should be manifested in relation to a practice that stages the relationship between king and subject by inviting the subject into the king's household. Though the mumming presents itself as a form of play, with "fauuisages" and props (in 1394, for example, the mummers bring a "navi[s] conficta", a pretend ship), it is also a very real engagement between the sovereign and his people. Its artifice in part consists of the pretense that such an engagement is merely a form of holiday play, an imitation of the homage paid to the infant Christ by the three kings; its efficacy depends upon its concealment of the rawer lineaments of the power relation at work between the king and the mummers. Mumming thus stands at the intersection between representation and the real; it is both a performance for an audience (the king) and a very literal exchange in which both king and subject have roles to play. The king is simultaneously very distant, an observer, uncostumed, and set apart from the mummers, and very near, a crucial participant in the action. The giving of gifts effectively costumes the king, adorning him with objects that dissolve the distance between supplicant and superior, performer and watcher. The relation that the mumming articulates between artifice and reality, between the "fauuisage" and the genuine gift, reassuringly insists that what is being "played" – an ideal and loving relationship between sovereign and subject – is in fact truly present. And indeed, as the 1393 mumming shows, what is pretended may indeed become real *by means of* the performance itself: the breach between Londoners and the king is healed when each side behaves as if it does not exist. The gift-giving of the Londoners makes possible the king's generosity, not merely as a simple matter of exchange – gift for gift – but because the Londoners have enacted their submission and called forth the generous king that the very idea of mumming presumes.

It can never be sufficient, however, to describe any social practice in its ideal form. As many scholars have commented, modes of behavior designed to promote social cohesion not only conceal deep divisions within a culture but are also subject to inversion and subversion.[45] Whether the misuses of mumming in 1400 and 1414 actually took place or were products of chroniclers' imaginations and fears, it is clear that mumming seemed dangerously available to agents of unrest and rebellion. The fact that mumming comes to the fore as a potential means of destruction rather than resolution and affirmation at these two critical junctures in the Lancastrian kingships of Henry IV and V (in the first year after the usurpation and the year of the Oldcastle uprising) suggests strongly that mumming was a practice deeply linked to kingship and sovereignty. It is no coincidence that at the moments of greatest threat to Lancastrian rule, the very form of festive resolution favored by Richard II should be deployed (actually or textually) against the usurper and his son. Indeed, neither Lancastrian king seems to have welcomed mumming; there is only one record of mumming during Henry IV's reign (and it took place almost immediately after the usurpation, in 1400), and none during the reign of Henry V, though there were prohibitions in 1404, 1405, 1417, and 1418.[46]

It is not until the reign of Henry VI that evidence for the performance of mummings resumes. As in the case of the 1377 mumming before the young prince Richard, these performances take place before a youthful sovereign – and indeed, as soon as Henry VI is crowned records of mummings cease. There are also comparatively few prohibitions of mumming during his reign; Lancashire records only two between 1419 and 1451, and none during the 1420s, when Lydgate's mummings were written.[47] Of course, had Trinity College Cambridge R. 3. 20 not been collected and copied by John Shirley, there would be no record of any such performance during the 1420s, and a discussion of mumming during Henry VI's reign would look very different.[48] Since the mummings of the 1420s share a number of characteristics with the mummings of Richard II's reign – Christmas or Epiphany performance, costume, gift-giving – one might expect to find that they similarly provide a structured and formal but intimate and private venue for the articulation of the relationship between king and London oligarchy. And indeed, two of Lydgate's mummings thematize the relation between sovereign and subject quite explicitly; for example, the "Mumming at Windsor" retells the French coronation myth, while the "Mumming at Eltham" stages the giving of gifts to the king and his mother. But neither the "Mumming for the Mercers" nor the "Mumming for the Goldsmiths" explicitly involves an address to the king, nor were they performed in a royal context. In these two cases, the Ricardian mumming has been redeployed within the context of mercantile acquisition and London politics; the king has been replaced by the mayor. The overt message of the mummings has also changed. While Eltham and Windsor communicate sentiments such as "Pees with youre lieges, plente and gladnesse," the mercantile mummings contain aphorisms such as "grande peyne / grande gayne." That the recognizably royal form of address that constituted mumming in the late fourteenth century should become in the fifteenth century a mode of mercantile self-aggrandizement and local politicking is obvious from even a cursory look at the two texts. But what remains surprising about the "Mumming for the Mercers" and the "Mumming for the Goldsmiths" – and what is their most crucial aspect – is their insistence upon the legitimacy of poetic and dramatic tradition, not in relation to cultural rituals or practices, but to a corpus of authorized texts. I will now examine the Eltham and Windsor mummings briefly as illustrations of the conventional use of the form (albeit with the innovation of a dramatic script). I then turn to the mercantile mummings, finding in those texts a challenge to purely "functional" or "historical" readings and returning ultimately to the question of form, both social and poetic.

DRAMA ON PARNASSUS: POETRY AND PERFORMANCE

The mummings at Eltham and Windsor are very short, very simple, and very direct. Both can be reasonably accurately dated, both took place at Christmas, and both are thematically appropriate for performance before the young sovereign. The mumming at Eltham consists of twelve rhyme-royal stanzas describing the bringing of gifts (wine, wheat, and oil) from Bacchus, Juno, and Ceres by "marchandes þat here be" (line 5).[49] The first seven stanzas culminate in the refrain, "Pees with youre lieges, plente and gladnesse" and are addressed to the king; the remaining five are addressed to his mother, Queen Katherine, with the refrain, "Ay by encreese ioye and gladnesse of hert."[50] These conventional themes are elaborated in general terms, though the poem does contain topical references to the "rebelles, wheeche beon now reklesse" (line 24) and to the joining of the "hertes of England and of Fraunce" (line 33). The mumming was likely performed in 1425 or 1428, when Henry was at Eltham for Christmas; the reference to "rebelles" favors the later date, when the Dauphin and the French army had seriously threatened the English and the stability of the "two reavmes" (line 27) was in great doubt.[51] If the mumming form had provided Richard II and the London oligarchy with a means to negotiate and articulate the relationship between royal and civic authority, in the late 1420s the most pressing political question was not the role of London but the status of France. Despite the fact that merchants play a role in the Eltham mumming as mediators between the divinities Bacchus, Juno, and Ceres and the king – perhaps a gesture toward the civic origin of the form – the real issue addressed by the poem is the problem of double-sovereignty, "two reavmes."

In its similar concern with the dual monarchy, the mumming at Windsor is a companion piece to the mumming at Eltham.[52] It is an extremely simple retelling in rhyme-royal stanzas of the conversion of King Clovis through his wife, St. Clotilde, his baptism by St. Remigius, and the miraculous appearance of the golden ampoule and fleur-de-lis. Its topicality is made perfectly clear; Lydgate describes how the ampoule and chrism are preserved at Rheims for the anointing of French kings, and how "right soon" Henry VI will "resceyve his coroune." The date for the Windsor mumming is surely Christmas 1429; Henry VI was crowned at Westminster on November 6 of that year, and crowned at Paris December 16, 1431.[53] The vision of the monarchy presented at Windsor asserts the divine right of Henry to rule by "just succession" (Lydgate refers to "succession" three times in eight lines); it is an openly propagandistic use of French traditions in order to buttress English claims.[54] Indeed, it is typical of the kind of propaganda that the English were producing during the latter years of the minority, which exploited French history to solidify Henry VI's position.[55] This propagandizing extended to the king's household itself; at Christmas 1430 Henry VI received from Anne, wife of the Duke of Bedford, a book of hours with a miniature of Clovis receiving the fleur-de-lis from St. Clotilde.[56]

The Eltham and Windsor mummings respond directly to the exigencies of the political situation in the late 1420s; their simplicity and brevity make clear that the question of the dual monarchy was the dominant issue at the English court. Lydgate more than earns his reputation as Lancastrian apologist in these poems; by adopting a form of court entertainment typically devoted to the negotiation of relations between the king and his subjects, he asserts the fundamental subordination of the French. The felt need for such an assertion, even at the English court, testifies to the degree of uncertainty caused by the changing fortunes of the war in France and by the youth of the king – and the mummings may be seen in this light as a combination of propaganda (directed outward) and flattery (directed to the king himself). This combination was designed to entertain and to reassure its audience; it takes up the familiar mumming form as a means of identifying the proper role for the king as receiver of gifts and sovereign lord. Thus, Eltham and Windsor ultimately must be seen as instrumental texts, whose existence serves a specific purpose; they are illuminated by an historical understanding of the mumming form and its sedimented meaning, but they do not break away from or reshape either that form or its content.

By contrast, the "Mumming for the Goldsmiths" and the "Mumming for the Mercers" present their audiences with the old form in a new context. In very different ways, the two performances stage the appropriation of multiple cultural traditions, forging a synthesis of practice and textuality that ultimately exceeds the limit of the form.[57] The "Mumming for the Goldsmiths" is a performance similar to the Ricardian mumming in almost every way; it includes a procession of costumed folk bearing gifts, singing, and making music. A group of mummers carrying the ark of the covenant, led by David, processes toward the mayor, the central focus of the poem. The gifts in this mumming, rather than being for the king, are for another figure of authority – and betray not only an ambivalence about mayoral authority and a concern for such problems as legitimacy and succession, but also a deep structural interest in the authority of dramatic representation. The "Mumming for the Goldsmiths" can be precisely dated to February 2, 1430, Candlemas Day, the Feast of the Purification of Mary.[58] The kinds of political anxieties that provoked the propagandistic mummings at Windsor and Eltham are here displaced both temporally and figurally; instead of being a straightforward delivery of gifts, the mumming presents an elaborate and densely layered Old Testament scenario susceptible to both the simplest and the most exegetical of readings. By combining a royal form, a biblical theme, and a mercantile setting, Lydgate manages to produce a conservative document (and no doubt performance) with radical implications.

From the very beginning, the mumming is characterized by a mixture of registers. Shirley's headnote states that a herald called Fortune brings the mumming in the form of a letter. The use of a herald and the figuration of Fortune lend to the occasion a chivalric air that fits oddly with the Old Testament note immediately sounded in the first stanza:

> Þat worþy Dauid, which þat sloughe Golye,
> Þe first kyng þat sprang out of Iesse,
> Of God echosen, þe bookes specefye,

87

> By Samuel sette in his royal see,
> With twelve trybus is comen to þis citee,
> Brought royal gyfftes, kyngly him taquyte,
> Þe noble Mayre to seen and to vysyte.
> (lines 1–7)

The sheer density of references in this stanza is belied by the simple visual image of the gift-bearing procession that it is designed to illustrate. Several themes are introduced here that will be woven together and elaborated over the course of the performance. First, the reference to Jesse, particularly in a mumming performed on the Feast of the Purification of Mary, recalls a series of well-known biblical texts that were associated with the Jesse tree image and the lineages of Mary and Christ. Isaiah 11.1 – "et egredietur virga de radice Iesse et flos de radice eius ascendet" (Vulgate) – and Matthew 1.1–14 (which traces the lineage of Christ) were linked by commentators as prophecy and fulfillment. The flowering rod (virga) of Jesse became the pregnant virgin (virgo) in a powerful synthesis of Old Testament and New Testament, a synthesis exploited here to link the Feast of the Purification with secular homage to the mayor.[59] Secondly, the image of Samuel anointing David, from 1 Samuel 16, links succession to divine election, asserting that kingship must be ratified by anointment even when God has handpicked his candidate. This nexus of texts and images of divine lineage and succession is carried forward into the present by the action of the tribes carrying gifts to the mayor; the mayor acquires "royal gyfftes" just as David sits in his "royal see."

But the reference to Samuel necessarily recalls a moment of great doubt, the failure of Saul and the transfer of succession to the lineage of Jesse. Divine election covers a disruption in lineal descent caused by the inadequacy of Saul as king; Samuel's anointment represents the compensating earthly gesture necessary to accomplish the divine will. The mumming for the Goldsmiths thus shares with the mummings at Eltham and Windsor an obsessive concern with lineage, succession, and hereditary right. But while the royal mummings were straightforward assertions of the legitimacy of Henry VI's rule in France, this mumming more subtly explores the parameters of such claims. Not only does Lydgate introduce a frame of reference – biblical exegesis – far more complex than the simple parade of pagan deities at Eltham or

Windsor's miraculous story of conversion, he also inserts a royal theme into a mercantile context. The idea of lineal succession is here applied to the mayor, an appropriation that allows the Goldsmiths to flatter their mayor extravagantly while also presenting the right to rule as an acquired and negotiable status. In the first three stanzas of the mumming, the lineal relation of Christ and David is emphasized in order to suggest the mayor's place in the hereditary chain: like Christ, who "lyneally ... came adowne" (line 11), the David figure in the mumming "is nowe descended" (line 16) to bring "gyfftes þat beon boþe hevenly and moral / Apperteyning vn-to good gouuernaunce" (lines 19–20). As the recipient of these gifts, the mayor is both positioned within this divine succession and made to recognize the contingency of his power and authority; the gift confers both honor and obligation.

Thus far it seems clear that the substitution of the mayor for the king produces a different gift-giving dynamic. Gifts of gold (as in the 1377 mumming) or wine, wheat, and oil, even read allegorically, remain fundamentally simple homages and bespeak a simple relationship of obligation between lord and servant. What the mayor is given, however, is the ark of the covenant, and what he finds in it is writing – a "wrytt" – with instructions for governing the city, suggesting a far more nuanced and complicated interaction between subordinate and superior. Lydgate brings to the traditional mumming a notion of literary patronage that implies that such cultural productions function both as vehicles for praise and honor and as serious engagements with questions of good governance and right rule. In the Goldsmiths' mumming, this dual purpose is present from the beginning. The gift of the ark depends upon the capacity of the recipient to use it well:

> Þe arke of God, bright as þe sonne beeme,
> In-to þis tovne he haþe goodely brought,
> Which designeþe, *if hit be wel sought*,
> Grace and good eure and long prosperitee
> Perpetually to byde in þis cytee.
> (lines 24–28; emphasis added)

The ark of God can only signify grace, good fortune, and prosperity if it is sought *properly*; it is a conditional gift that demands an active and engaged response. The nature of such a response is suggested by the next few stanzas, which outline and gloss David's behavior, both in the Old Testament and in the action of the mumming itself. First the Levites, the tribe specially designated as caretakers of the ark and its bearers here, are given a stage direction to "dooþe youre devoyre" and sing in honor of the Lord. Lydgate then turns to 2 Samuel 6, which describes David dancing before the ark as he enters Jerusalem, using the biblical text as theatrical scenario:

> Whylome þis arke, abyding in þe hous
> Of Ebdomadon, brought in ful gret ioye;
> For in effect it was more gracyous
> Þanne euer was Palladyone of Troye.
> Hit did gret gladnesse and hit did accoye
> Thinges contrarye and al aduersytee.
> Þeffect þer-of, whane Dauid did see,
>
> And fully knewe, howe God list for to blesse
> Thorughe his vertu and his mighty grace,
> Þat of gladdnesse þey might nothing mysse –
> Wher hit aboode any maner spaace,
> God of His might halowed so þe place –
> Wherfore Kynge Dauid, by gret deuocion,
> Maade of þis ark a feyre translacion.
>
> In-to his hous and his palays royal,
> Brought by þe Levytes with gret solempnytee;
> And he him-self in especyal
> Daunsed and sang of gret humylyte,
> And ful deuoutely lefft his ryaltee,
> With Ephod gyrt, lyche preestis of þe lawe,
> To gyf ensaumple howe pryde shoulde be withdrawe.
> (lines 36–56)

The exemplary lesson to be drawn from David's behavior is that a humble demeanor is appropriate to those in power; pride must be "withdrawe" in order that the ark may be properly honored. Lest the mayor find the point too direct, Lydgate suggests in the next stanza that the lesson is particularly meant for "mynistres of þe Chirche" (line 59), though he makes sure to note that it applies as well to "yche estate" (line 57). This simple exegetical reading of the passage from Samuel, however, belies the complexity of Lydgate's choice of biblical text. Not only is the incident of David dancing before the ark particularly fitting for the Feast of the Purification, but it also constitutes a justification for dramatic representation itself.

The very presence of the ark in the Goldsmiths' mumming would have signified its Marian focus to an educated audience. In typological terms, the ark of the covenant was understood to prefigure Mary as a vessel with precious cargo; the contemporaneous *Mirour of Mans Saluacioune*, a Middle English translation of the immensely popular typological handbook, *Speculum Humanae Salvationis*, makes the connection between the ark and the Feast of the Purification explicit:

> Oure Ladie the fourtied day of Cristis natiuitee
> Of hire purificacioune did the solempnitee;
> Bot sho ne had nothing nede of purificacioune,
>
> . . .
>
> The Arke of Gods Testament prefigured hire þarefore,
> In whilk the preceptis of his Lawe warre shette, both lesse & more.
> (lines 1207–09, 1215–16)[60]

Thus, the procession of the ark toward the mayor recalls the visit of Mary to the temple, a typological link that further strengthens the connection between the visual imagery of the mumming and the verses that accompany the action. The text chosen by Lydgate – David dancing before the ark – can also be understood in typological and Marian terms. The *Mirour of Mans Saluacioune* glosses the passage as a prefiguration of Mary's Assumption:

> And this assumpcioune of Marie was sometyme figurid
> When in the Kyng Dauid house Gods Arc was translatid.
> Dauid harped and daunced tofore thilk Archa Domini.
> (lines 3837–39)

David here is a figure for Christ, who brings his mother to his house in a festive procession just as David translates the ark to his Jerusalem palace. But David's dancing references Christ in yet another way. The account in Samuel concludes with David's wife Michol, daughter of Saul, angrily reproving the king for his exuberant and undignified behavior:

> reversusque est et David ut benediceret domui suae et egressa Michol filia Saul in occursum David ait quam gloriosus fuit hodie rex Israhel discoperiens se ante ancillas servorum suorum et nudatus est quasi si nudetur unus de scurris

> (And David returned to bless his own house: and Michol the daughter of Saul coming out to meet David, said: How glorious was the king of Israel to day, uncovering himself before the handmaids of his servants, and was naked, as if one of the buffoons should be naked.)
> (2 Samuel 6.20, Vulgate and Douay-Rheims translation)

In the *Mirour* this passage is identified as a prefiguration of Christ's humiliation on the cross; David is scorned by Michol as Christ is scorned by the Jews. In a striking image, the anonymous translator compares Christ's crucified body to the strings on David's harp:[61]

> Dauid in his harping prefigured Crist in this thinges,
> For Crist was stendid on the Crosse als in ane harpe ere the stringes.
> O Lord, how this faire harpe gaf a swete melody
> When Crist with doelfulle teres for vs cried myghtylye.
> (lines 2719–22)

The figure of David dancing before the ark, scorned by Michol, thus produced a powerful synthesis of earthly degradation and heavenly music, of bodily humility and the performance of devotion. In this reading, David's use of his body for worship is ratified and authorized by Christ's suffering; in both cases, the alienation of the worldly – the scorn of Michol, the act of crucifixion – from the divine authenticates the act of worship as genuine. But this authentication could work in reverse. For example, when Bernard of Clairvaux cites David's response to Michol, "I will play and make myself more vile," in a letter in which he provocatively compares monks to *joculatores,* he not only suggests that worldly scorn constitutes the measure of the success of devotional practice, he also links David's dancing and playing with the behavior of medieval performers:

> In fact, what else do seculars think we are doing but playing when what they desire most on earth, we fly from; and what they fly from, we desire? Like acrobats and dancers (*joculatores et saltatores*), who with heads down and feet up, stand or walk on their hands, and thus draw all eyes to themselves. But this is not a game for children or the theater where lust is excited by the effeminate and indecent contortions of the actors, it is a joyous game, decent, grave and admirable, delighting the gaze of the heavenly onlookers.[62]

Like performers, monks are ridiculed and humbled by people in the world; the monks, at least, will ultimately be exalted by God for their humiliation. Other commentators made this connection as well. Bernard's association of worship with performance similarly characterizes the discussion of 2 Samuel 6 in *Dives and Pauper*. In a chapter immediately following the well-known defense of "steraclis, pleyys & dauncis þat arn don principaly for deuocioun" (com. 3, cap. 17, lines 13–14), Pauper cites David's dancing in order to legitimate "dauncis and songis" on holidays and feast days:

> We fyndyn also in þe secunde book of Kyngis, þe sextie chapitle [14–23], þat whan Dauyd schulde fettyn Goddis hoche into Ierusalem Dauyd & al þe peple of Israel wentyn þerwith and pleyydyn in al maner menstrasie & songyn & daunsedyn & sckepedyn for ioye and so preysedyn & worschepedyn God.[63]

In *Dives and Pauper*, Michol's reproof provides the necessary counterpoint against which a defense of festivity can be mounted; David's dancing is truly devotional because it elicits scorn, unlike "vnhonest dauncis and pleyys" that "steryn folc to lecherie & to oþer synnys" (com. 3, cap. 17, lines 40–42). It is a commonplace that festive behavior exists on the border of the licit and illicit; what Bernard and the authors of *Mirour* and *Dives and Pauper* assert is that it also rests uneasily between the worldly and the divine.[64]

Like Bernard and the *Dives and Pauper* author, Lydgate recognizes the fit between the story of David's dancing and contemporary medieval performing practices. He fully exploits the dramatic potential of the scene by restaging the translation of the ark; in this way the mumming becomes a performance that contains its own authorization. Oddly, however, Lydgate truncates the episode, eliminating the critical role of Michol and her reproof and turning instead to generalized commentary on humility. Lydgate's omission of Michol's scorn effects a substitution of exegesis for acting, replacing the biblical dialogue – which reveals that David's true audience is God – with a didactic gesture toward the "mynistres of þe Chirche." In the simplest terms, Lydgate is merely being delicate in regard to the mayor, backing away from a direct suggestion that he should cast aside his mayoral robes and embrace Davidian humility. And it is surely right to see this mumming as an illustrative example of the muted and conventional quality of fifteenth-century political discourse; the mayor is given advice on good governance in the most flattering and favorable way possible. Yet the very layering of references, the subtlety of Lydgate's rhetorical maneuvering, demands a more nuanced reading. The mumming for the Goldsmiths is patently meant to be read as well as performed; if in a crude way it simply represents an extravagant compliment to a man in power, it also presents itself to its audience as a text awaiting interpretation – awaiting the reader who will notice the absence of Michol's reproof. His substitution of generalizing platitudes for that reproof must ultimately be attributed to a desire to subdue the tension between earthly authority and divine power evoked by the conclusion to the biblical episode. Michol, daughter of Saul, the king whom David superseded, taxes David with his kingly responsibility to maintain dignity *in the world*; David responds with a world-rejecting claim that he can only be interpreted by a higher power:

> dixitque David ad Michol ante Dominum qui elegit me potius
> quam patrem tuum et quam omnem domum eius et praecepit mihi ut
> essem dux super populum Domini Israhel
> et ludam et vilior fiam plus quam factus sum et ero humilis
> in oculis meis et cum ancillis de quibus locuta es gloriosior
> apparebo

> (And David said to Michol: Before the Lord, who chose me rather
> than thy father, and than all his house, and commanded me to be
> ruler over the people of the Lord in Israel,
> I will both play and make myself meaner than I have done: and I will
> be little in my own eyes: and with the handmaid of whom thou
> speakest, I shall appear more glorious.)(2 Samuel 6.22, 23, Vulgate
> and Douay-Rheims translation)

What Bernard gleans from this passage is that David's performance is directed to God and interpretable only by God; similarly, he asserts, what appears to the world as ridiculous behavior in the monks is understood by God as worship. In *Dives and Pauper*, David's embrace of a "lowir degre" (com. 3, cap. 18, line 42) is misread by Michol as the behavior of a "knaue" (line 38); what David explains is that his perform-ance is not directed to the people, but to God, to whom it is utterly legible. But when Lydgate invokes the episode, he refuses the possibility of worldly misreading; David's dance for the Goldsmiths is glossed and

unambiguous. And although David is described as having "ful deuou-
tely lefft his ryaltee ... To gyf ensaumple howe pryde shoulde be
withdrawe," the absence of Michol's critique erases the possibility of
conflict between devotion (represented by dancing) and kingship.

Lydgate's portrayal of David functions differently from the mummings performed before Richard II. If in the earlier performances the
distinction between representation and the real was blurred until it
nearly vanished – the king himself "playing" the role of king – here the
artificiality of the procession stands out in relief. King David's humility
extends to his bringing gifts to the Mayor of London, "for þat meeknesse is a vertu feyre"; his figural status is clearly marked and indeed
highlighted. This insistence on figural interpretation is further exaggerated by Lydgate's use of Psalm 131 (Vulgate) as a linking device between
the description of David's dancing and the proffering of the gifts. In a
remarkable enjambment, Lydgate combines secular and sacred history,
chronicle-writing and the singing of Psalms in a heavily overdetermined
prayer for the prosperity of London:

> Nowe ryse vp, Lord, in-to Þy resting place,
> Aark of Þyne hooly halowed mansyoun,
> Þou aark of wisdome, of vertu and of grace,
> Keepe and defende in Þy proteccion
> Þe Meyre, þe citeseyns, þe comunes of þis tovne,
> Called in cronycles whylome Nuwe Troye,
> Graunte hem plente, vertu, honnour and ioye.

Lest readers fail to note the translation, the manuscript includes a gloss
to the appropriate lines in the Vulgate: "Surge domino in requiem
tuam. Tu est archa sanctificacionis tue." Lydgate's use of these lines
evokes not only the psalm itself, but also the broader context of Marian
devotion in which it was embedded. As one of the fifteen gradual
psalms, Psalm 131 appeared in Books of Hours or primers as part of
the Hours of the Blessed Virgin, making it familiar to both a lay and a
clerical audience as a distinctively Marian text.[65] But as Eamon Duffy
points out, even though "there is abundant evidence of very wide use of
the primers among the laity," very few English translations of the text
survive, a phenomenon he attributes to the "panic over Lollardy."[66]
Paradoxically, then, it would seem that the Latin text of the psalm,

which would have been recited by lay people at worship, may have been more familiar than the English translation that appears in the mumming. In this light, the Latin gloss to the passage would seem to address not merely a clerical audience but an educated lay readership as well.

As a performed text, the "Mumming for the Goldsmiths" is a complexly layered and stratified literary object, dense with allusion, that functions according to a logic all its own. The simplest narrative account of the action – a procession that retells the story of the translation of the ark by way of extravagantly complimenting the mayor – serves as a dominant hermeneutic that obviates more difficult (or dangerous) readings of the text and occasion. These alternative readings depend upon a sophisticated reading practice with its roots in biblical exegesis and secular poetics; they uneasily lurk just behind the screen provided by the ritualized gift-giving that structures the occasion and delimits its meaning. In the passage quoted above, Lydgate truncates the psalm in order to insert references to the mayor, the citizens, and the commoners of London, interpellating a secular audience as sacerdotal subjects. The psalm reads:

> Surge Domine in requiem tuam tu et arca santificationis tuae
> Sacerdotes tui induentur iustitia et sancti tui exultabunt.
>
> (Arise, O Lord, into thy resting place: thou and the ark, which
> thou has sanctified. Let thy priests be clothed with justice: and let
> thy saints rejoice.)(Psalm 131, lines 8–9, Vulgate and Douay-Rheims
> translation)

Lydgate replaces "priests and saints" with "Mayor, citizens and communes," effecting what appears to be a secularization of the psalm as well as of the ark and its contents. But while "secularization" may suffice as a description of the *means* by which the work of the text is accomplished, it cannot stand as an adequate explanation of what that work might be. Not only does the mumming consistently imply that the secular world of the city may be comprehended as part of the sacred world of the psalm – thus, the ark is "more gracyous" than the "Palladyone of Troye" (lines 38–39) and "Nuwe Troye" is recast by David's entry as a kind of "New Jerusalem"[67] (line 69) – but it also uses that sacred world as a means of diminishing the standing of the mayor by invoking a higher authority. Lydgate's insistence on David's humility, his abdication of his "ryaltee," appears at first simply as a compliment to the mayor:

> And for þat meeknesse is a vertu feyre,
> Worþy Dauid, with kyngly excellence,
> In goodely wyse haþe made his repayre,
> O noble Mayre, vn-to youre presence.
> (lines 71–74)

Here the mumming would seem to stage the submission of "kyngly excellence" to mayoral authority; just as David's dancing before the ark symbolically suggested the mayor's superior position (in performance, after all, David dances before the mayor), so too David's presentation of the gifts places the mayor in the traditional role of the king. But unlike the gifts that the Londoners brought for Richard II – gold balls and cups – David's present pointedly subordinates the mayor to the higher power of God:

> Of purpoos put þis aark to youre depoos,
> With good entent, to make youre hert light;
> And þoo three thinges, which þer inne beo cloos,
> Shal gif to yowe konnyng, grace and might,
> For to gouuerne with wisdome, pees and right
> Þ is noble cytee, and lawes such ordeyne,
> Þ at no man shal haue cause for to compleyne.
> (lines 78–84)

"Konnyng, grace and might" are the traditional attributes of the Son, the Holy Ghost, and the Father, mapped here on to the values of good governance, "wisdome, pees and right."[68] David's humility, which had seemed so fulsomely flattering to the mayor, is recoded here as meekness before the ark and its sacred cargo, a cargo that trumps the mayor's authority and places him in his proper relation both to God and to the Goldsmiths. The subsequent stanzas specify the imperative of the gift; the mayor will receive a writ – analogous to the Ten Commandments – that reveals "Where yee shal punysshe and where as yee shal spare, / And how þat Mercy shal Rygour modefye" (lines 85–86). The purpose of the entire performance, it would seem, has been to deliver what Claire Sponsler calls the "not-so-hidden message … that the goldsmiths expect the mayor to exercise his office effectively and fairly."[69] Indeed, the narrative arc of the mumming – minimal as it is – functions as a form of seduction; through flattery, it lures the mayor to accept, even if only ritually, advice and counsel from his subordinates. Such flattery, however, hardly needs the elaborate textual apparatus Lydgate has given it here. The detailed biblical scenario, with its exegetical links to the Purification of Mary and Marian devotion, might be understood as simply a pleasurable exercise in playmaking – as Lydgate's demonstration of what a literary monk could make of the traditional form of the mumming – but the particular themes that he chooses suggest a more complex motivation. The problem of succession that the reference to Samuel poses, the doubly significant "meeknesse" of David (as both exemplary humility before the Lord and symbolic submission to the mayor), as well as the embedded justification for performance contained in David's dance before the ark, all gesture outward to the broader cultural context in which the Goldsmiths produced their performance. Lydgate has appropriated the mumming both *for* and *from* the guild: on the one hand, he has produced a self-conscious imitation of royal occasions that bespeaks the ambitions of the mercantile class; on the other, he has used the mumming as a means of exploring the relationship of such occasions to a nexus of concerns characteristic of elite culture in the late 1420s.

It might be argued, in fact, that the appearance of such concerns – questions of succession and right rulership – hardly testifies to Lydgate's intentions, so dominant were these themes during the entire Lancastrian period. But the self-referentiality of this particular mumming, its interest in justifying not only the authority of God and kings, but also the very mode of representation through which that justification was accomplished – performance – suggests that this text functions as more than an index to fifteenth-century Zeitgeist. By producing an image of King David dancing before the ark and the mayor, Lydgate acknowledges precisely that need for the performance of power that the Duke of Bedford exploited in arranging Henry VI's double coronations. It is fundamentally a need for forms through which power can be represented and reproduced – a need that every medieval king recognized and sought to satisfy. But the density of the referential field in which the "Mumming for the Goldsmiths" is embedded belies the seeming simplicity of its status as propaganda. What the mumming reveals, in the end, is the degree to which representational forms – tropes, stories, images – contain deeply embedded contents that cannot be erased or excluded once they have been invoked. David always recalls Samuel; his dancing always summons Michol's reproof. The sheer excessiveness of meaning created by Lydgate's choice of images and his manipulation of authoritative texts exposes the limits of topical readings; the mumming cannot be neatly explained as the effect of an historical or cultural cause. Just as *Serpent*'s intertextual layering ultimately belied the static exemplarity of its base narrative, so, too, the exegetical referentiality of the "Mumming for the Goldsmiths" constitutes a refusal of the seeming simplicity of the mumming form and an insistence upon the value of interpretive density. As I will show in my discussion of the "Mumming for the Mercers," that value is both historical and social; it enables not only the exploration of such categories as sovereignty and authority, but also the analysis of the historicity – the life and afterlife – of the textual excess that such density inevitably produces.

– – –

Even upon a cursory examination of Trinity College Cambridge MS R. 3. 20, the "Mumming for the Mercers" stands out from the surrounding texts and from Lydgate's other dramatic works. It is heavily glossed in Shirley's cramped hand; the annotations cover the margins of the poem and indeed rival it for the attention of the reader.[70] A closer look at the mumming reveals that it is rife with dense and difficult images drawn from classical mythology, contemporary geography, and the vernacular poetic tradition; figures such as Circe and Bacchus, places such as Parnassus, and such poets as Ovid, Virgil, Petrarch, and Boccaccio are duly explained and contextualized by Shirley, who clearly feels that his audience will require a crib sheet in order to understand the text. The premise of the mumming is simple. Jupiter has sent a "poursuyant" from the East with letters for the mayor; having passed through Jerusalem, Libya, Ethiopia, "Inde," Mount Parnassus, Syria, and Egypt, the herald encounters three ships on his passage through the Mediterranean to England, each with an inscription in French. The first, which appears as he enters the great sea, is labeled "Grande travayle / Nulle avayle" and contains a fisherman with empty nets. The second and third boats come into view as the herald arrives at the Thames; their labels comment further on the relationship between work and prosperity. The second states "Taunt haut e bas que homme soyt, / Touz ioures regracyer dieux doyt," retrospectively couching the fruitless labors of the first fishermen in a context of general thankfulness to God, while the third ship, filled with fish, reads "grande payne / grande gayne." The ships signal that the herald is nearing London, where he finds several vessels waiting, "hem to refresshe and to taken ayr," aboard which are "certein estates, wheche purveye and provyde" waiting to visit the "noble Mayr." Unlike the "Mumming for the Goldsmiths," which animates the well-known narrative of David and the ark, the "Mumming for the Mercers" invokes a far less familiar set of allusions with which to engage its audience; the poem maps, along a spatial axis from East to West, a series of references to authorities and figures ("Petrark," "Jupiter") that represented the cultural capital of the aristocratic and royal elites. As Shirley's elaborate glosses show, Lydgate's mercantile audience would have approached these authoritative literary references as desirable but intimidatingly learned elements of aristocratic knowledge they wished to share.[71] The mumming dramatizes the assimilation of a messenger from a foreign land, the incorporation of the seemingly alien into the domestic structure of power relations with the mayor.[72] But the "alien" here is in fact precisely that knowledge – of classical mythology and vernacular poetry – which a London mercantile elite might wish to learn and display.

Thus, the "Mumming for the Mercers" can in part be understood as the attempt of a socially elite but nonnoble group to identify itself as consumers of aristocratic cultural capital – and Shirley's glosses reflect an uncertainty about *his* audience's capacity to assimilate such material without aid. Richard Firth Green has argued that the tastes of this elite can only be understood in relation to aristocratic and courtly culture, suggesting that "it is the aristocracy, not the bourgeoisie, who are the *Kulturträger* of the fifteenth century."[73] The intimate relationship between the cultures of the merchant classes and the aristocracy can be seen in mercantile book ownership; far from revealing a "middle class" with literary productions specifically aimed at a middlebrow audience, records of book ownership show that London merchants were reading such fare as romances, Chaucer's *Canterbury Tales*, Gower's *Confessio Amantis*, and a variety of works by Lydgate – including courtly texts such as *The Complaint of the Black Knight*, *Troy Book*, and *Siege of Thebes*.[74] In part, this interest in aristocratic literature was due to the mobility and variability of merchants and mercantile status; the famous example of Thomas Chaucer's rise to nobility provides only one instance of the fluidity that existed between the aristocracy and the merchant elite.[75] But an emphasis on the permeability of the boundary between noble and nonnoble should not be taken to imply that London merchants lacked identity in the early fifteenth century. Sheila Lindenbaum has described the way in which, after the turbulent years of Richard II's reign in London, which included not only the Rising of 1381 but also the factional disputes of Nicholas Brembre and John of Northampton as well as the Good and Merciless Parliaments, the merchant elites reasserted both political and cultural control of the city.[76] The elaborately glossed display of erudition that constitutes the "Mumming for the Mercers" appears in this light as a synthesis of mercantile, aristocratic, and clerical discursive fields; not only does it present the Mercers to themselves and to the mayor in the visual and linguistic codes of vernacular poetics and clerical learning, it also interpellates its audience as educated consumers and practitioners of elite courtly culture.[77] The Mercers' ambitions are made quite clear by Shirley, who states that the mumming was "ordeyned *ryallych* by þe worthy merciers."[78]

Lydgate's extended mapping of allusions along an East–West trajectory lends to the mumming an air of the exotic and the strange, a geographic sense of distance and difference. It is, however, a distinctly *literary* geography, and any aura of strangeness it produces must be attributed to the determinedly didactic mission of the text, to the way in which it both verbally and visually educates its audience in the tropes and figures of poetic culture. This literariness is evident from the beginning; as the herald travels through "Ethyope and Ynde," rather than encountering some exotic or strange person or object, he sees various dwelling places of the pagan gods and goddesses:

> Conveyed dovne, where Mars in Cyrrea
> Haþe bylt his paleys vpon þe sondes rede,
> And she, Venus, called Cytherrea,
> On Parnaso, with Pallas ful of drede;
> Smote on þe roche where þe Muses dwelle,
> Til þer sprange vp al sodeynly a welle,
>
> Called þe welle of Calyope,
> Mooste auctorysed amonges þees Cyryens –;

> Of which þe poetes þat dwelle in þat cuntree,
> And oþer famous rethorycyens,
> And þey þat cleped beon musycyens,
> Ar wont to drynk of þat hoolsome welle,
> Which þat alle oþer in vertu dooþe excelle –

The seeming split between "real" places – Ethiopia, India – and the mythological geography of "Cyrrea" and "Parnaso" is produced largely by the modern cartographic imagination. Lydgate deploys a notion of place derived not from mercantile encounter with the other, but from a set of unimpeachable medieval authorities whose map of the world is here deliberately substituted for whatever "real" experience of travelers and traders he might have known. Both Isidore's *Etymologiae* (which elaborates Servius's commentary on Virgil) and Persius's *Satires* describe the geography of Parnassus and its relation to the "hoolsome welle" of the Muses; Lydgate would appear to have followed these authorities – as well as Chaucer's *Anelida and Arcite* – not only in the "Mumming for the Mercers," but also in the "Mumming at Bishopswood" and *Troy Book*.[79] Details in each account vary, but the association of this particular landscape ("Cyrrea" and "Parnaso") with the origins of poetry remains standard throughout.

What is remarkable about the use of place and topography in the "Mumming for the Mercers," then, is less its evocation of the East than its mapping of a poetic genealogy across place and time. The invocation of Parnassus instantiates a literary travelogue from classical rhetoricians to vernacular poets, beginning with Tullius and Macrobius, moving through Ovid and Virgil, and culminating in Petrarch and Boccaccio. Lydgate presents the Mercers with an authorizing narrative that links the origins of poetry itself with the practice and performance of mumming, clearly implying that just as Petrarch and Boccaccio "Thoroughe þat sugred bawme aureate / . . . called weren poetes laureate" (lines 34–35), so too the maker of this mumming has drunk from the "hoolsome welle" of Calliope. Judging from Shirley's detailed gloss, readers and viewers were not expected to be instantly familiar with these names:

> Tulius a poete and a rethorisyen of Rome. Macrobye an olde philo-
> sofre. Ovyde and Virgilius weren olde poetes, þat oon of Rome, þat

oþer of Naples afore þe tyme of Cryst. Fraunceys Petrark was a poete
of Florence. So were Bochas and Dante withinne þis hundreþe yeere;
and þey were called laureate for þey were coroned with laurer in token
þat þey excelled oþer in poetrye.

What is alien and in need of familiarization to Lydgate's audience is
ultimately the store of cultural knowledge that authorizes and affirms
elite identity in fifteenth-century England, a form of cultural capital both
displayed as a marker of the Mercers' status and deployed as a didactic
tool, part of a process of acculturation by which merchants may be
integrated into the codes and practices that distinguish the elite.[80]
Contrary to Lydgate's usual habit when authorizing himself as vernacular
maker, he makes no mention of Chaucer or of English poetry more
generally, suggesting that it is precisely the relation between a foreign –
classical or European – tradition of eloquence and a native cultural
practice – mumming – that this performance stages.[81] Indeed, Lydgate
particularly seems to have avoided making a link between Chaucer and
the classical tradition of eloquence, a connection that he himself had
quite forcefully articulated a few years earlier, in *Troy Book*:[82]

> And Chaucer now, allas, is nat alyve
> Me to reforme or to be my rede
> (For lak of whom slougher is my spede),
> The noble rethor that alle dide excelle;
> For in makyng he drank of the welle
> Undir Pernaso that the Musis kepe,
> On whiche hil I myghte never slepe –
> Onnethe slombre – for which, allas, I pleyne.
> (book 3, lines 550–57)

The elision of Chaucer from the "Mumming for the Mercers" represents
both an insistence by Lydgate on his unmediated relation to classical and
European lines of poetic influence and an assertion of his own centrality
to the didactic project of the text and performance. Chaucer may have
"enlumined" the English language, but it is Lydgate who can effect a kind
of *translatio* from European high culture to the mercantile sensibility
embodied in the label "grande peyne / grande gayne."

This need for *translatio* produces the mode of excess and overdetermin-
ation in the "Mumming for the Mercers" that is revealed by Shirley's

glosses. In contrast to the relatively simple "Mumming at Windsor," for example, whose subject matter – the coronation of the king in uncertain times and in a foreign land – would seem far more likely to produce cultural anxiety and an excessive text, the "Mumming for the Mercers" is marked by repeated invocations of multiple authorizing narratives and modes of signification. Upon finishing his genealogical list of classical and European poets, Lydgate immediately turns to the Old Testament; leaving Parnassus behind, his herald passes through the Christian topography of Egypt, the Red Sea, and the River Jordan:

> And thorughe Egypte his poursuyant is comme,
> Dovne descendid by þe Rede See,
> And haþe also his right wey ynomme
> Thoroughe valeye of þe Drye Tree
> By Flomme Jordan, coosteying þe cuntree,
> Where Iacob passed whylome with his staff,
> Taking his shippe, to seylen at poort Iaff.
> (lines 43–49)

Significantly, Shirley feels no need to annotate this stanza; its Old Testament reference is clearly legible to all. Lydgate has moved his audience through the alien landscape of poetic laureation to the landscape of the Christian past, a juxtaposition that acquires continuity through the fiction of the traveling "poursuyant" but remains jarring nonetheless.[83] The effect Lydgate is aiming for, however, is a seamless integration of cultural systems; the appearance of the landmark River Jordan in the midst of this otherwise strange mythical world represents a performative attempt to absorb the markers of aristocratic culture – classical figures and places, laureate poets and rhetors – into the mode of representation most familiar to a Christian mercantile audience, with biblical geography serving as a kind of gateway to Europe. This tactic is familiar to us from the "Mumming for the Goldsmiths," in which the authorized secular narrative of London's Trojan origins is subordinated to and assimilated by the story of King David and the sacred ark, and it suggests a felt need on the part of both Lydgate and his audience for the synthesis of authorizing narratives and tropes – a need that reflects the uneasy fit between the classicizing drive of much vernacular poetry and the Christianizing impulse at the center of English medieval culture.

In this sense, the "Mumming for the Mercers" does work as a means of assimilation, a way of enacting the movement from classical to Christian to English, in which a contiguous map is drawn that leads inexorably to the Mercers' own city. It is through this movement inward that Lydgate asserts on behalf of the Mercers the right of the merchant elite to appropriate the central literary tropes of courtly vernacular culture. And by didactically displaying such cultural knowledge in a visual form designed for ease of consumption, Lydgate teaches his audience how to effect that appropriation themselves. In much the same way, Shirley's glosses substitute words for the ephemeral props and costumes that would have made legible the literary travelogue of the mumming, the movement from Parnassus to London, while his rubric – his invocation of the mumming as genre – operates in a similar fashion, making clear to the reader what would have been obvious to an audience: that this performance constitutes a redeployment of the practice of mumming, substituting for the king (its usual object of address) a figure from within the mercantile world itself, the mayor.

Lydgate's *translatio*, then, occurs on the level of both content (literary geography) and form (the mumming genre). What the "Mumming for the Mercers" reveals is not merely the *function* of cultural performances (their response to crisis, their negotiation of difference, their ordering of a disordered world), but also the *work* of a specific literary text in relation to an authorized landscape of such artifacts and texts – one that, for English merchants in 1429, bore marks of class status and privilege both alien and deeply desirable. To articulate the historicity of such a text requires us to embrace its form, to understand that our engagement with its "writtenness" or "literariness" does not undermine its status as an artifact of practice. It is not enough simply to note that Lydgate appropriates a form of address to the king in order to glorify the mayor; this merely illustrates the pride of the Mercers in their political and economic clout. That pride is important, to be sure, as are the anxieties of such a group as they negotiate the demands of daily life in a mercantile world. But neither pride nor anxiety can fully explain the need for poetry. And it is that need – for Parnassus, for Ovid, for Petrarch and Boccaccio – that the genre of the mumming translates and transforms. The literary world evoked by both the mercantile mummings, that is, constitutes their most genuinely historical element, its logic of excess revealing not the mere effect of an historical cause, not a simple social function, but a particular form hard at work to make and remake its own facticity – its own place in the past. As the next chapter will show, the need for such work emerges even more powerfully when the historical stakes are raised, when the audience for Lydgatean performance is not merely a status-conscious mercantile elite, or a royal court anxious to assert monarchical authority, but rather a "public" mourning the loss of its sovereign and confronting the bleakness of tragedy, both fictive and real.

NOTES

1 These lines are quoted from Shirley's rubrics for the "Mumming at Windsor" and the "Mumming for the Mercers"; see *Minor Poems of John Lydgate*, part 2, ed. MacCracken, 691, 695. For a complete treatment of this manuscript, see Connolly, *John Shirley*, particularly chapter 4, "MS Trinity College Cambridge R. 3. 20, its Partners and Progeny," 69–102. Seth Lerer discusses John Shirley, and Trinity College Cambridge R. 3. 20, in *Chaucer and his Readers*, though he does not address the mummings; see pages 119–46 (chapter 4) for Shirley, and pages 128–46 for a treatment of the manuscript. I am grateful to the Masters and Fellows of Trinity College for permission to examine the manuscript.

2 *Minor Poems of John Lydgate*, part 2, vol. 2, ed. MacCracken, 668–701. The only poem described by MacCracken as a mumming that does not appear in Trinity College Cambridge MS R. 3. 20 is the "Mumming at Bishopswood," which can be found in MS Bodley Ashmole 59, another Shirley manuscript. For discussion of MS Bodley Ashmole 59, see Connolly, *John Shirley*, 145–69. One other poem is described by Shirley as a "mumming," but not identified as such by MacCracken: "Bycorne and Chichevache," which also appears in Trinity College Cambridge MS R. 3. 20. There has been some scholarly confusion about this text. *Minor Poems of John Lydgate*, part 2, 433 ed. MacCracken, indicates that Shirley includes a running title in Trinity College Cambridge MS R. 3. 19 that identifies the poem as a mumming. I have examined the facsimile of this manuscript, and no such titles appear; see *Manuscript Trinity R. 3. 19: A Facsimile*, ed. Ruggiers, fos. 157v–159r. In fact, this running title appears in MS R. 3. 20, as Eleanor Hammond, in *English Verse Between Chaucer and Surrey*, 115, notes. The title reads: "þe fourome of desguysinges contreved by Daun Johan Lidegate / þe maner of straunge desgysinges. þe gyse of a mummynge." I am grateful to Joanna Ball of Trinity College Library, Cambridge, for assisting me with a photocopy of the relevant pages of MS R. 3. 20. I have not discussed "Bycorne and Chichevache" as a mumming here, because it is clear from Shirley's rubric that the text was designed to accompany a "peynted or desteyned clothe for an halle or parlour or a chaumbre" (*Minor Poems of John Lydgate*, part 2, 433). The running titles, with their repetition of phrases such as "þe maner of," "þe gyse of," and "þe fouorme of," simply indicate that Shirley noted the affinity between "Bycorne and Chichevache" and the other mummings, not that he considered it a mumming itself.

3 For an example of a speculative reading of the "Mumming at Windsor," filled with suggestions for possible performance, see Westfall, *Patrons and Performance*, 34–37.

A brief discussion that challenges the tendency to see the mummings strictly as precursors to Renaissance masques by focusing on them as instances of *Gesamtkuntswerk*, or panaesthesia, can be found in Rafael Vélez Núñez's "The Masque's Antecedents in John Lydgate's Mummings and Momeries: A Revisionist Approach," 185–89.

4 Strohm, "Rememorative Reconstruction," especially 8–11; see also Strohm, "Shakespeare's Oldcastle," in *Theory and the Premodern Text*, 132–48.

5 Kipling has recently argued that Lydgate's dramatic works are texts first and foremost, written as "devices" wholly separate from the performances that might have been based upon them; see "Lydgate: The Poet as Deviser," 98–99. In contrast, Sponsler, "Drama in the Archives: Recognizing Medieval Plays," suggests that if Lydgate's mummings seem especially "textual," it is because "that's what Shirley made them," through an "erasure of signs of performativity." Following Symes ("The Appearance of Early Vernacular Plays") Sponsler suggests that medievalists must rethink the generic division between dramatic and nondramatic texts, given that there is often little evidence in manuscripts to show that a particular text was or was not performed. As my argument will make clear, Lydgate's texts – while certainly designed for performance – are also, and deliberately, written to be read and analyzed.

6 See Wickham, *Early English Stages, 1300–1600*, vol. I, 207. Two thirteenth-century English precursors to the mummings are *Interludium de Clerico et Puella* and *Dame Sirith*, both of which contain dialogue and were clearly meant for performance. Both texts can be found in *Early Middle English Verse and Prose*, ed. Bennett and Smithers; for *Interludium*, see no. XV, pages 196–200, and for *Dame Sirith*, no. VI, pages 77–95. A French dialogue found in an English manuscript, Harley 2253, seems to have been intended for performance and describes an old woman lecturing a young woman about love; "Gilote et Johane" can be found in N. R. Ker, ed., *Facsimile of B. M. MS Harley 2253*, item 37, fos. 67v –68v. In lines 344–45 the text is dated September 15, 1293. For discussion of this text, see Revard, " 'Gilote and Johane': An Interlude in B.L. MS Harley 2253." Another important coupling of text and performance may be seen in Richard Maydistone's *Concordia*, a 548-line Latin poem describing a 1392 procession by Richard II and Queen Anne through London; see Smith, ed., "Concordia Facta inter Regem Riccardum II et Civitatem Londonie." The text is also printed by Thomas Wright in *Political Songs and Poems Relating to English History*, 282–301. The *Concordia* is discussed by Strohm in *Hochon's Arrow*, 107–11, and by Lerer in "Chaucerian Critique of Medieval Theatricality," 64–66. Gordon Kipling, *Enter the King*, 11–21, discusses the 1392 spectacle as a "civic triumph" that uses the liturgy of Advent in order to effect a reconciliation between Richard and London after a protracted dispute. Sylvia Federico reads the *Concordia* as imagining London as a "fantastic other, the feminine New Troy"; see "A Fourteenth-Century Erotics of Politics." John Bowers has recently discussed the *Concordia* in his *Politics of Pearl*, 31–34. For the details of Richard's dispute with the city, see Bird, *Turbulent London of Richard II*, 102–09.

7 Griffiths, *Reign of King Henry VI*, 178–94, 189.

8 Pearsall, *John Lydgate (1371–1449)*, 25.

9 Ibid., 25–26. See McKenna, "Henry VI of England and the Dual Monarchy" for a discussion of this poem in relation to other forms of Lancastrian propaganda during the minority (151–54, plates 27 and 28b). See also Rowe, "Henry VI's Claim to France in Picture and Poem." For the text of the poem, see *Minor Poems of John Lydgate*, part 2, ed. MacCracken, 613–22. It is probable that Lydgate was in France in 1426, and that he may have executed the commission there; in another poem translated from a French wall-painting, *Danse Macabre*, he indicates in an envoy that he has sent the text "fro Paris to

Inglond"; see Pearsall, *John Lydgate (1371–1449)*, 26–27. For discussion of Lydgate's poems written to illustrate pictorial images, including wall-paintings, banners, and *soteltes*, see Pearsall, *John Lydgate*, 179–83, as well as Hammond, "Two Tapestry Poems by Lydgate."

10 As Ralph Griffiths describes, the Duke of Bedford commissioned the poem, which emphasized Henry's descent from St. Louis. It aroused the ire of at least one Frenchman; the wall-painting at Notre-Dame was defaced by a canon of Rheims in 1425. Much later, the Earl of Shrewsbury would commission a presentation volume for Margaret of Anjou upon her wedding to Henry VI that included a copy of the genealogy; it survives in British Library Royal MS 15 E VI f. 3. See Griffiths, *Reign of Henry VI*, 218–19. Lydgate's "Title and Pedigree" is also discussed by Green in *Poets and Princepleasers*, 186–90; Green describes Lydgate as a Lancastrian "apologist" (189).

11 Patterson, "Making Identities in Fifteenth-Century England," 93. Patterson reproduces the genealogy and a schematic diagram on pages 90–91.

12 Ibid., 93.

13 Griffiths, *Reign of Henry VI*, 28–50, 68–93. Two examples of Gloucester's actions are his 1423 licensing of St. Mary's Abbey, York, to elect its abbot (which provoked a 1424 rule from the council that no councilor could make a grant alone), and, more seriously, his 1424 campaign in the Low Countries in support of his wife, Jacqueline of Hainault (Griffiths, *Reign of Henry VI*, 30). This campaign threatened the Anglo–Burgundian alliance on which much of England's rule over France depended, making the situation more unstable both at home and abroad (ibid., 179, 187).

14 Wolffe, *Henry VI*, 39–45. Beaufort was as guilty as Gloucester of attempting to usurp the collective authority of the council; when Gloucester was absent in Hainault, he acted as principal councilor and was widely blamed in London for repressive legislation enacted in the 1425 Parliament (ibid., 40).

15 Watts, *Henry VI and the Politics of Kingship*, 115.

16 Ibid.

17 Griffiths, *Reign of King Henry VI*, 189–90; Watts, *Henry VI and the Politics of Kingship*, 117–18.

18 *Minor Poems of John Lydgate*, part 2, ed. MacCracken, 622–30. Pearsall adds to these three "A Prayer for King, Queen and People," which anticipates the coronation; see his discussion of the coronation poems in *John Lydgate (1371–1449)*, 29–30.

19 See Bryant, "Configurations of the Community in Late Medieval Spectacles," for a complete description of the Paris entry; Bryant argues that the city of Paris put on a spectacle that "barely disguised [its] subversive politics" (17), making a less than subtle case for the authority of the French Parliament and the need for justice. Kipling reads the 1431 entry in relation to the liturgy and imagery of Advent, making a compelling case that the spectacle "conceived of Henry's civic triumph as a spiritual preparation for his coronation" (*Enter the King*, 93). For a French account of the entry, see *La Chronique d'Enguerran de Monstrelet*, ed. Douët-D'Arcq, book 2, chapter 109, 1–6.

20 Griffiths, *Reign of King Henry VI*, 193 notes that the coronation "was marred by an unseemly dispute between the canons of Notre-Dame and some of the English courtiers, an invasion of the banqueting hall by a number of Parisians, and the failure of King Henry II to distribute the customary largesse." For the text of Lydgate's poem, see *Minor Poems of John Lydgate*, part 2, ed. MacCracken, 624–48; for a full discussion of the 1432 entry, and Lydgate's part in it, see chapter 4 below.

21 I will not be discussing the three other texts MacCracken describes as "mummings" here. Two, the "Mumming at Hertford" and the "Mumming at London" are examined in the

following chapter; I will argue that they constitute substantially different modes of performance than the four Shirley "mummings" and thus should be considered separately. Shirley himself, as Wickham notes, refers to these poems as "disguisings" (*Early English Stages 1300–1600*, vol. 204); Pearsall points out that the Hertford and London poems are formally distinct from the other five works: they are far longer and in rhyming couplets, while the remaining five are brief and in rhyme-royal (*John Lydgate*, 184). Nor will I discuss the "Mumming at Bishopswood." Unlike the other mummings, this takes place on May Day and is the only mumming not to appear in Trinity College Cambridge MS R. 3. 20. It can be found in another Shirley manuscript, Bodleian Ashmole 59, and its date is unknown. It has been printed in *Minor Poems of John Lydgate*, part 2, ed. MacCracken, 668–71, and by Norton-Smith, *John Lydgate: Poems*, 7–10 and notes. Norton-Smith compares the ballad to the *soteltes* poem for Henry VI, a classification that in many ways is more logical than MacCracken's. The poem takes the form of a letter carried to the dinner by a "pursuivant," announcing that Flora, goddess of fresh flowers, has sent her daughter Ver with tidings of felicity and prosperity. The proper role for each of several estates – princes, Holy Church, judges, Mayor, provost, aldermen, sheriffs – is outlined. The most interesting moment in the poem comes in its envoy, when Lydgate includes a brief description of Parnassus and the muses, suggesting a desire to articulate for this audience the purpose and worth of the poetry to which they have been listening. Lancashire suggests that a likely date for Bishopswood would have been May Day 1430, which would be consistent with both Lydgate's other dramatic productions and with the general atmosphere of festivity attendant upon the king's coronations; see *London Civic Theatre*, 122.

22 Watts, *Henry VI and the Politics of Kingship*, 23.

23 See also Twycross and Carpenter's *Masks and Masking*, which covers much of the same ground but reaches quite different conclusions. Twycross and Carpenter see Lydgate's mummings as "ceremonial" (though "problematical"), part of a tradition of courtly entertainment appropriated from the "popular urban custom of mumming" (159–60); it is my argument that notions of "popular custom" should be approached with great caution. Some of their conclusions were anticipated by Twycross's "My Visor is Philemon's Roof," which adduces much of the same evidence I have derived from Ian Lancashire's *Dramatic Texts and Records of Britain* regarding records and prohibitions of mumming. See also Twycross's "Some Approaches to Dramatic Festivity," 7–8. It should be noted as well that E. K. Chambers paved the way for all subsequent work on mumming; he provided a basic map of the evidence to be found in later scholarship like that of Twycross and Carpenter, Ian Lancashire and Glynne Wickham, as well as the persistent thesis that Lydgate's mummings emerged from popular traditions. See Chambers, *Mediaeval Stage*, vol. I, 390–403. Two illustrative examples of the persistence of Chambers's narrative in discussion of Lydgate's mummings include William Tydeman's reading of the mummings, which asserts that mumming was "a sophisticated survival of a pagan folk-ritual, or of the Roman Saturnalia, and a prerogative of the *bourgeoisie* rather than the nobility" (*Theatre in the Middle Ages*, 73–74), and that of Marion Jones ("Early Moral Plays and the Earliest Secular Drama," 237–42). I have cited Chambers below where he supplies evidence not to be found in Ian Lancashire. The material in this section is also discussed by Anne Lancashire in her important book, *London Civic Theatre*, 41–43, which appeared after this chapter had been written; I have cited her work only where she introduces evidence not found elsewhere.

24 A description can be found in the *Anonimalle Chronicle*: "En celle tenps les comunes de Loundres firent une graunte desporte et solempnite al iune prince, qare le dymaigne

proschein avaunt la Purificacion de Nostre Dame a sayre et deinz noet furount vi^{xx} et x hommes degisement arrayes et bien mountez a chivalle pur moummere." *Anonimalle Chronicle*, ed. Galbraith, 102–3, cited in Lancashire, *Dramatic Texts and Records*, 160, no. 802. The passage is translated by John Stow in his *Survey of London*, ed. Charles Kingsford, vol. I, 96–97.

25 See Wickham, *Early English Stages 1300–1600*, vol. I, 191–207, for a discussion of Lydgate's mummings in relation to gift-giving and disguise as standard elements of the practice.

26 See, for example, Welsford, *Court Masque*; Twycross, "My Visor is Philemon's Roof"; Pettit, "Early English Traditional Drama," and "Tudor Interludes and the Winter Revels." Pettit's articles usefully summarize the scholarship on the "lost tradition" of mummings; though he is quite critical of attempts to derive that tradition from more recent folk customs such as the wooing plays or the sword dance, he ultimately concludes popular Christmas customs were gradually elaborated to produce the sophisticated interludes of the Tudor period. In his *Medieval Theatre*, Glynne Wickham wisely notes that if there were a lost tradition of mummings, "it is surely curious that no poet or diarist from Chaucer to Pepys should have even described such a play" (144), though he does ultimately assert that the mummer's play and other folk festivals have ancient origins.

27 Lancashire, *Dramatic Texts and Records*, 336, no. 1763.

28 One very curious record, dated by Lancashire as 1377–99 (*Dramatic Texts and Records*, 52, no. 224), appears in *Arnold's Chronicle*, a printed volume compiled in the late fifteenth/early sixteenth century by Richard Arnold, a London merchant who collected a variety of documents – lists of mayors, royal charters, municipal regulations, assizes of bread, receipts – for the use of the citizens of London. Article Eight of the "Charter of London, graunted bi Kynge Richard the ij" reads:

> Wetyth wel that we haue graunted our citezens of London that none of them pletee othor wythout the wallis of London of ony plee, but of plees of fre holde that ben with out the fraunchesis outake momers and our mynstrels.

A number of oddities crop up here. First, the article is directed at *citizens* of London, an elite group that appears to include "momers and our mynstrels." Second, those latter are excluded from the prohibition against bringing suit, or having suit brought against them – possibly because, as Robert Rodes of the Notre Dame Law School suggests, they are likely to travel outside the city walls. If so, however, it is strange to see these persons categorized as "citezens," though it does suggest that "mumming" was an occupation or practice associated with the London elite. Regardless, the date of the chronicle (*c*. 1500) means that the use of the word "momer" is later than the period under consideration here; Arnold is clearly translating from a Latin or French original. It is a tantalizing record, not least because it associates the king very directly with mumming and with a proprietary interest – "our mynstrels" – in performing practices. See *The Customs of London, otherwise called Arnold's Chronicle*, 17, as well as the introduction for discussion of the early printing history of the text. I am grateful to Professor Rodes for his generous assistance with this record.

29 Lancashire, *Dramatic Texts and Records*, 160, no. 802 (1377), 129, no. 633 (1393), and 177, no. 910 (1394). For the 1393 mumming, see also Barron, "Quarrel of Richard II with London 1392–7." To the three Ricardian mummings might be added a fourth; Anne Lancashire notes that the Mercers' accounts for 1395/96 record payment for a royal mumming (Mercers' MS Wardens' Accounts 1347–1464, fo. 19v). She does not indicate whether the term "mumming" itself is used. See *London Civic Theatre*, 42 and note 41.

30 *Calendar of the Letter-Books Preserved among the Archives of the Corporation of the City of London at the Guildhall*, ed. Sharpe, H:322, cited by Lancashire, *Dramatic Texts and Records*, 176, no. 904; the original French reads: "ne nul voise pur mummer ne nul autre ieu ieuer oue visure ne en nulle autre estrange gise par quelle il ne poet estre connue sur pein denprisonment a volunte des mair et aldermans." Quoted by Twycross, "My Visor is Philemon's Roof," 335.

31 The first record Lancashire cites that refers to masks or costume is no. 203 (1215–30) (*Dramatic Texts and Records*, 48); it is a condemnation of *histriones* by Thomas Chabham, subdean of Salisbury. There are of course references to *histriones*, theatres, and plays that predate Chabham's condemnation; the reference here is merely to show that disguise was a feature of English entertainment long before the mummings of Richard II. One analogous form of entertainment in which we find a gradually increasing use of costume and disguise is in the tournament. Wickham notes that during and after the reign of Edward III "some form of dressing up now becomes more usual in accounts of English Tournaments" (*Early English Stages 1300–1600*, vol. I, 20). Juliet Vale (*Edward III and Chivalry*) documents the development of mimetic behavior (costume and personification) in the tournaments and Christmas *ludi* of Edward III, arguing that the existence of mimetic episodes probably dated at least from Edward I's contact with late thirteenth-century French tournaments (73). One familiar example of a Christmas house visit that includes disguise and game-playing is, of course, *Sir Gawain and the Green Knight*; significantly, however, the term "mumming" is not used by the poet to describe the action. Arthur does refer to "enterludez" (line 472), interpreting the Green Knight's visit as part of the "craft" appropriate to Christmas, which includes laughing, singing, and dancing as well. Twycross and Carpenter interpret the visit as a mumming; see *Masks and Masking*, 154–55. Christine Chism reads the visit in relation to the 1377 entertainment before Richard II and provincial challenges to Ricardian courtliness; see *Alliterative Revivals*, 82–87. Susan Crane also discusses the Green Knight in relation to other forms of courtly entertainment and display; see *The Performance of Self*, 163–74. See *Sir Gawain and the Green Knight*, ed. Tolkien and Gordon, lines 467–73.

32 See Lancashire, *Dramatic Texts and Records*, nos. 888 (1334), 890 (1352), 894 (1372), 897 (1376), 900 (1380), 903 (January 1387), 904 (December 1387), 909 (1393), 913 (1404), 915 (1405), 921 (1417), 922 (1418).

33 The term "mumming" appears in French at roughly the same time as in English, though slightly earlier. The *Dictionnaire de l'ancienne langue française*, ed. Godefroy, 381–82, cites a number of fourteenth- and fifteenth-century appearances of the word or its variants, under the entries for "mome," "momeor," "momer," and "momon"; the earliest use of the term it cites is in 1293, though the majority of references are to late fourteenth-century and fifteenth-century sources, such as Monstrelet's chronicle. Charles d'Orléans mentions mumming twice in his verses; see *Poésies*, ed. Champion, vol. I, ballad LXXXVIII, 128–29, and vol. II, roundeau CXXI, 359–60. Crane discusses the first of these, noting that the ballad was written to be read aloud during an interlude; see *Performance of Self*, 141.

34 Portions of Maghfeld's account book are printed in Edith Rickert's "Extracts from a Fourteenth-Century Account Book"; the relevant entry reads: "Item appreste pour le mommyng al Roy a Eltham al feste de Noell xl s." Rickert dates the entry to December 1392, but as Caroline Barron's discussion of the occasion makes clear, it occurred in January, 1393; see Barron's "Quarrel of Richard II with London 1392–7," 195, n. 91.

35 From *Calendar of the Letter-Books*, fo. ccxxiii, cited in Riley, *Memorials of London and London Life*, 669; for the 1417 prohibition, see ibid., 658, cited in Lancashire, *Dramatic Texts and Records*, 179, nos. 921 and 922.

36 Lancashire records prohibitions from elsewhere in England from later in the fifteenth
century and the sixteenth century; see *Dramatic Texts and Records*, 89, no. 406 (Bristol,
c. 1479–1508); III, no. 534 (Chester, 1555); 232, no. 1198 (Newcastle upon Tyne, 1554). He
includes as well an Act of Parliament in 1511–12 forbidding the ownership of visors and
mumming. *Dramatic Texts and Records*, 60, no. 266; see also Luders, Tomlins, France,
and Taunton, eds., *Statutes of the Realm*, vol. III, 30, 3 Henry VIII. See also Twycross
and Carpenter, *Masks and Masking*, 83.

37 Wickham, *Early English Stages 1300–1600*, vol. I, 202–4.

38 Twycross and Carpenter, *Masks and Masking*, 82–83.

39 A well-known image of figures wearing animal masks in Oxford, MS Bodley 264 (fo.
181v) has been mistakenly interpreted in just this way; Michael Camille described it as
the "dance of peasant mummers," suggesting that the marginal mummers were designed
to contrast with the central image of lords and ladies dancing. See Camille, *Images on the
Edge*, 120–26. However, as Nancy Freeman Regalado has pointed out, the masked
figures are in fact "elegantly clad with belts, daggers, finely varied designs on the cloth of
their tunics, and heraldic devices on their capes." See her "Staging the *Roman de Renart*,"
140, n. 35. The manuscript also includes another image of figures with animal masks on
fo. 21v; digital images of the entire MS, as well as a description of its provenance and
date, can be seen at http://www.image.ox.ac.uk/show?collection=bodleian&manu-
script=msbodl264. MS Bodley 264 can be dated to approximately 1338–44 and was
illustrated by the Flemish illuminator Jehan de Grise; the illuminations I cite above
illustrate the *Romance of Alexander*. Other illustrations were added in England *circa*
1400. These illuminations do testify to the practice of masking at court, but the maskers
are not identified in the manuscript as "mummers."

40 Lancashire, *Dramatic Texts and Records*, 129, no. 634; see also *A Chronicle of London from
1089 to 1483*, ed. Tyrrell and Nicolas, 87. The 1400 event is described using the term
"mumming" ("men of London maden a gret mommyng to hym of xij aldermen and
there sones") though the chronicle probably dates from later in the century; see Antonia
Gransden's discussion of London chronicles in *Historical Writing in England ii: c. 1307
to the Early Sixteenth Century*, 228–30. An earlier record, in French, that uses the term
"momyng" can be found in the Merchant Taylors' accounts for 1400/01 (Guildhall
Library MS 34048/1, fo. 11r); payment is rendered "a le Guyhalle pur le Momyng a
Nowelle." I quote the passage from Lancashire, *London Civic Theatre*, 229, n. 43; it is
also referenced by Clode, *Memorials of the Guild of Merchant Taylors of the Fraternity of
John the Baptist*, 62. Ian Lancashire (*Dramatic Texts and Records*) cites this record as no.
912, 177. Clode suggests that the mumming took place at the Guildhall, but Anne
Lancashire argues more plausibly that the Merchant Taylors' payment was a contribution to the mumming at Eltham (*London Civic Theatre*, 42).

41 In her discussion of the 1393 performance, Caroline M. Barron states in a note that "the
mercers provided five men as mummers at a cost of £3, Mercers' Hall, Account Book
1347–1464, fo. 12." It is not clear if the account book uses the term "mumming," though
Barron also cites Maghfeld's account book, which does ("The Quarrel of Richard II with
London 1392–7," 195, n. 91).

42 *Westminster Chronicle*, ed. and trans. Hector and Harvey, 510–11 (1393) and 516–17
(1394). Lancashire, *Dramatic Texts and Records*, 129, no. 633 (1393) and 177, no. 910
(1393–94), cites the same text as the chronicle of John of Malvern, who continued
Higden's *Polychronicon*; see *Polychronicon*, book 9, 278 (1393) and 281 (1394). However,
Lumby mistakenly identified the *Westminster Chronicle* as part of John of Malvern's
continuation; see Hector and Harvey's introduction, xv and lxxv. See also Barron,

"Quarrel of Richard II with London," 190–96. For a fascinating reading of the gift of the bird to Queen Anne, which Malverne describes as "mirabilem habentem guttur latissimum" – having a wondrously wide throat – as well as a general account of the rift between Richard II and the Londoners, see Strohm, *Hochon's Arrow*, 106–07.

43 Capgrave, *Abbreuacioun of Cronicles*, ed. Lucas, 216. The date of the text is uncertain; Lucas concludes that it was written before 1461, and possibly begun before 1438 (xliii). It is clearly not contemporaneous with the events of 1400, however, and its use of the term "mumming" is consistent with a later date. Chambers, *Mediaeval Stage*, vol. I, 395, n. 1, noted the incident and cited several versions in various chronicle accounts; Lancashire, *Dramatic Texts and Records*, 285, no. 1510, similarly cites multiple accounts.

44 Gregory's *Chronicle of London*, in *Historical Collections of a Citizen of London in the Fifteenth Century*, ed. Gairdner, 108. Lancashire, *Dramatic Texts and Records*, 129, no. 635, notes the event but dates it incorrectly to 1415. Strohm discusses the incident briefly in *England's Empty Throne*, 65, but points out that Gregory's *Chronicle* is "a highly unreliable source" (229, n. 6). However, he also notes that in the Exchequer Issue Rolls for February 1414, "payment is authorized for manacles 'for certain traitors recently captured at Eltham and elsewhere, and imprisoned.' " See PRO, E403/614/mem.12. The chronicle itself dates from a slightly later period; Gransden, *Historical Writing in England*, vol. II, 230, asserts that it is "almost certainly by William Gregory, skinner, sheriff of London from 1436 to 1437 and mayor from 1451 to 1452." Gregory died in 1467, making it unlikely that he was composing the chronicle in 1414.

45 Sarah Beckwith has made this point in her analyses of the York cycle; see *Signifying God*, especially chapter 2, "Ritual, Theater and Social Space in the York Corpus Christi Cycle," 23–41. Sheila Lindenbaum argues cogently that forms that might seem to promote social cohesion also forcefully reiterate boundaries of class and status; see "The Smithfield Tournament of 1390."

46 The 1400/01 mumming is no. 634 in Lancashire, *Dramatic Texts and Records*; it was an entertainment by Londoners dressed as twelve aldermen and their sons in honor of the visit of Manuel II, emperor of Constantinople. See *A Chronicle of London, from 1089–1483*, 87. For a full account of Manuel's visit, see Nicol, "Byzantine Emperor in England," 215. Anne Lancashire notes that a collection of contributions for this mumming appears in the Mercers' accounts for 1400/01 (Mercers' MS Wardens' Accounts 1347–1464, fo. 32v); see *London Civic Theatre*, 42 and note 42.

47 Lancashire, *Dramatic Texts and Records*, 181, no. 935 (1437), and 182, no. 939 (1451).

48 The mummings also appear in British Library MS Additional 29729, a copy of Trinity College Cambridge MS R. 3. 20 made by Stow; see Boffey and Thompson, "Anthologies and Miscellanies," 284.

49 Richard Osberg notes the emergence in this mumming of classical figures, linking it to Maydistone's use of "Bacchus" in his description of the 1392 entry of Richard II, and to the appearance of Bacchus and Thetis in the 1432 entry of Henry VI; he also notes that Bacchus and Ceres appear, bearing wheat and grapes, in Pierre Gringore's pageants for the entrance of Mary Tudor into Paris on November 6, 1514; see "The Jesse Tree in the 1432 London Entry of Henry VI," 227, n. 29.

50 Queen Katherine is not named; Lydgate delicately addresses "yowe, Pryncesse, borne of Saint Lowys blood" (line 52), and Shirley provides a gloss: "ad Reginam Katerinam, mother to Henrie y° VI."

51 Scholars of the mummings have not agreed on a date for Eltham. In 1902, Rudolph Brotanek (*Die Englischen Maskenspiele*) dated the poem 1427–28, based on what he saw as its reference to Henry Beaufort's abortive attempt at a crusade against the Hussites in

those years. Brotanek's date was adopted by Robert Withington (*English Pageantry*, 106–07), and Chambers (*Mediaeval Stage*, 397h); again following Brotanek, Paul Reyher (*Les Masques anglais*, 109) gives the more general date 1427–30. Walter Schirmer (*John Lydgate*, 101) quotes Charles Kingsford in asserting that Lydgate had written mummings in 1424 and 1428, before arbitrarily assigning Eltham to 1424; no title for Kingsford's work is given and I have been unable to locate the reference. Pearsall, *John Lydgate (1371–1449)*, 29, notes that Henry was at Eltham for Christmas in 1425 and 1428, and suggests the latter date, given the cluster of mummings and occasional poems from 1428 to 1432. Wolffe asserts that Henry was at Eltham in 1426 and 1427 as well, citing the accounts kept by his chamber treasurer, John Merston, and printed in *Foedera*, ed. Rymer, x, 387–88, which record payments to "Jakke Travaill & ses Compaignons" and "Jeweis de Abyndon" for "diverses Jeuues & Entreludes" for Christmas (*Henry VI*, 37–38). I concur with Pearsall that the 1428 date is likely, but there is no conclusive evidence to date the mumming definitively.

For discussion of the hostilities with France, see Jacob, *Fifteenth Century*, 243–47. Jacob points out that "from the battle of Verneuil [August, 1424] to the siege of Orléans [1428] is a period of minor action," lending support to the 1428 date for the Eltham mumming.

52 Green, *Poets and Princepleasers*, 189 briefly mentions the "Mumming at Windsor" as one of Lydgate's "apologist" poems.

53 Pearsall, *John Lydgate (1371–1449)*, suggests the 1429 date as well.

54 The question of possible French influence on Lydgate's mummings must remain an open one. There are clearly parallels between French cultural practices and those of the English, and Lydgate might easily have seen French interludes or performances during his time in France in the train of the Duke of Bedford in 1426 (Pearsall, *John Lydgate(1371–1449)*, 27–28). Crane has described a number of French occasional performances in which aristocrats costumed themselves and performed for the court, but none of these includes a written script; see *Performance of Self*, 155–65. Regalado discusses a striking account of the Parisian Pentecost Feast of 1313, in which the life of Renart the fox was enacted in *tableaux vivant*, which may have included masked actors; see "Staging the *Roman de Renart.*" These shows did not include a script or dialogue, however. I am grateful to Carol Symes for this and the following reference. Roger Sherman Loomis describes a variety of French courtly performances at tournaments in his "Chivalric and Dramatic Imitations of Arthurian Romance"; again, though the performances include costumes and action, they do not include the kind of script that Lydgate provided. The example of thirteenth-century Arras, where vernacular plays were written and performed by such dramatists as Adam de la Halle, both at court and in the *puy* (an organized group of court poets) and the *confrérie* (a guild of *jongleurs*), suggests strongly that its rich performance tradition would have been transmitted to England, and thus would have been familiar to Lydgate. See Ardis Butterfield's recent discussion of Arras in her *Poetry and Music in Medieval France*, 133–50.

55 For discussion of this propaganda, see McKenna, "Henry VI of England and the Dual Monarchy"; he argues that "The very real though superficial interest which the Anglo-Gallic administrators showed in French royal history and traditions, and the use of those traditions in propagandist poetry and pageantry, testify to their determination that Henry VI's French antecedents should receive all possible publicity" (155).

56 Ibid. This image was particularly freighted with significance in 1429–30, not only because Charles VII had himself crowned at Rheims in July 1429, but also because Henry VI was not able to be anointed at Rheims and had to settle for being crowned at Paris. See Jacob, *Fifteenth Century*, 248–50.

57 David Benson has recently discussed these mummings, along with the "Mumming at London" and the "Mumming at Bishopswood," in relation to their status as London performances that affirm civic values and covertly suggest criticisms of the city's focus on wealth; see "Civic Lydgate: The Poet and London."

58 Shirley's introduction states that "þe goldesmythes of þe Cite of London mommed ... to þeyre Mayre Eestfeld, vpon Candelmasse day." According to Stow, Eastfield was mayor of London in 1429 and 1437 (*Survey of London*, ed. Kingsford, vol. II, 173); Brotanek, *Englischen Maskenspiele*, 306, and Schirmer, *John Lydgate*, 107, assert that since neither the Goldsmiths' nor the Mercers' mummings makes mention of the mayor being reelected, the texts were likely performed in 1429, though the absence of such a mention does not conclusively point to the earlier date. Pearsall concurs that the 1429 date should be accepted; after 1433 or 1434 Lydgate had retired to Bury and his "laureate" period had passed (*John Lydgate*, 223; see also *John Lydgate (1371–1449)*, 29). Anne Lancashire has shown, however, that the date would have been 1430, not 1429, if the reference is to Eastfield's first term as mayor; Eastfield was elected on October 13, 1429, and thus Twelfth Night and Candlemas performances would have taken place in 1430. See Lancashire, *London Civic Theatre*, 121 and notes 23–26.

59 For a discussion of the *Stirps Jesse* and one of its medieval commentators, Bishop Fulbert of Chartres, see Fassler, "Mary's Nativity, Fulbert of Chartres, and the *Stirps Jesse*," 410–11.

60 *The Mirour of Mans Saluacioune*, ed. Avril Henry, can be dated to approximately 1429 based on the paper and hand of the manuscript; see Henry's introduction, 20. It is a close translation of *Speculum Humanae Salvationis* (*SHS*), a compilation of sources including the *Historia Scholastica* of Petrus Comestor, Voragine's *Legenda Aurea* and Aquinas's *Summa Theologica*, that dates to 1310–14. *SHS* is a typological rendering of the life of the Virgin (which includes the life of Christ), giving three foreshadowing events for each incident narrated. Its popularity is attested to by the number of manuscripts – 394 – that have survived from the fourteenth and fifteenth centuries (Henry, ed., *Mirour of Mans Saluacioune*, 10).

61 Holsinger, *Music, Body and Desire in Medieval Culture*, describes the origins and transmission of this image over the course of the Middle Ages (27–60). He also discusses its appearance in *SHS*, examining in particular the woodcuts accompanying most of the manuscripts; see pages 203–08.

62 *The Letters of Bernard of Clairvaux*, trans. Bruno Scott James, 135, discussed by Clopper, *Drama, Play and Game*, 56–57; see also Bernard of Clairvaux, *Lettere*, ed. Ferruccio Gastaldelli, letter 87, vol. I, 434–36.

63 *Dives and Pauper*, ed. Priscilla Heath Barnum, 297, commandment 3, cap. 17, lines 31–35. Clopper discusses this text in *Drama, Play and Game*, 82–83, noting that the *Dives* author distinguishes between legitimate entertainments (legitimated by the Old Testament) and illicit recreation that leads to sin.

64 As Clopper notes, the story of David dancing before the ark also appears at the end of *A Treatise of Miraclis Pleyinge*, where it serves as an example of the proper kind of "pleyinge": "Than, frend, yif we I wilen algate pleyen, pleyne we as Davith pleyide bifore the harke of God" (*A Treatise of Miraclis Pleyinge*, ed. Clifford Davidson, 114, lines 724–25). Clopper's reading of the *Treatise* suggests that its indictment of "miraclis pleyinge" refers only to "clerical parodies and *irrisiones*" rather than to vernacular mystery cycles; thus its use of the David and Michol example would be consistent with its indictment of a specific kind of playing rather than of playing in general.

65 Duffy, *Stripping of the Altars*, 210.

66 Ibid., 213. Duffy further notes that Lydgate had a particular affinity for translating material from the Little Office: "Lydgate, for example, produced verse translations of the calendar, the 'Fifteen Oes,' the Marian antiphons from the Little Office such as the 'Salve Regina,' and a number of popular devotions from the primer, like the indulgenced hymn on the five joys of Mary, 'Gaude Virgo Mater Christi' (223).

67 The image of the city as a "New Jerusalem" had a long history in medieval culture, as Kipling points out in *Enter the King*, 15, citing Ernst Kantorowicz, "The 'King's Advent' and the Enigmatic Panels in the Doors of Santa Sabina." In England, both the 1392 reconciliation of Richard II with London, and Henry VI's 1432 entry exploited the image of London as "New Jerusalem"; see Kipling, *Enter the King*, 15–16, 143–44. Benson notes, however, that the latter occasion mixed earthly with spiritual imagery, celebrating the fecundity of trees and the abundance of wine; see "Civic Lydgate: The Poet and London." The "Mumming for the Goldsmiths" likewise mixes classical and Christian images of Troy and Jerusalem.

68 Clopper, *Drama, Play and Game*, 62, notes the correspondence of Lydgate's "konnyng, grace and might" to the Trinity. The three attributes of the Trinity were commonplaces in Middle English literature; Julian of Norwich expounds on the "myte, wisdam and love" of Father, Son, and Holy Spirit (*The Shewings of Julian of Norwich*, ed. Georgia R. Crampton, chapter 58, lines 2409–11). Further examples include *Piers Plowman*, B-text, passus XVI, lines 30, 36 and the *Prioress' Tale*, line 472 (where "Fadres Sapience" indicates Christ). I am grateful to Jill Mann for these references. Dante also refers to the "podestate, sapienza, amore" of the Trinity (*Inferno*, III. 5–6). J. P. H. Clark traces the attribution to Augustine in " 'Fiducia' in Julian of Norwich."

69 Sponsler, "Alien Nation," 236.

70 Shirley's glosses have been printed by Brusendorff, *Chaucer Tradition*, 466–67.

71 The question of the audience for Trinity College MS R. 3. 20 is a difficult one. As Margaret Connolly explains, though Shirley was affiliated with the household of Richard Beauchamp, earl of Warwick, for most of his career, his life records show that after moving to London in the late 1420s, in the early 1430s "he started to develop a wide range of civic connections across [London's] merchant class" (*John Shirley*, 55). Because Trinity College MS R. 3. 20 contains material dateable to the late 1420s ("Mumming at Windsor," 1429), Connolly dates its composition to the early 1430s (ibid., 77–80) – precisely the period of time in which Shirley was resident in London and making connections with the London mercantile elite. As such, it seems entirely possible that Shirley envisaged a mixed audience for his compilation, composed of both aristocrats – from the Beauchamp household – and London merchants.

72 See Sponsler, "Alien Nation," in which she argues that the Goldsmiths' and Mercers' mummings may be read as allegories for the troubled relation of Londoners to alien merchants that work by deploying symbolic others – Easterners and Jews. Although I find this reading insightful in many ways, it depends upon somewhat doubtful textual evidence. It is true that the main actors in the "Mumming for the Goldsmiths" are Israelites, specifically Levites. Although the fact that the historical Jews were expelled from England in the thirteenth century does suggest that Israelites would embody an "Other," this reading fails to account for the overwhelming *familiarity* of the Christian narrative of David and the Ark of the Covenant. As its appearance in the popular *Mirour of Mans Saluacioune* suggests, the story and the figure of David were well known, and would have signified not alterity but rather the incorporation of the secular into a dominant cultural and ideological narrative. Further, the easy fit between the exotic geography of the "Mumming for the Mercers" and the Orientalism thesis of

Said cannot be sustained in the face of a careful textual reading. Sponsler's argument depends on Wickham's speculation that the mercers are dressed as "Orientals," rather than on the evidence provided by the text itself; see Wickham, *Early English Stages 1300–1600*, vol. I, 201 and vol. I, 54. Unlike other medieval narratives – Middle English romances provide a good example – the encounter of Westerners with Eastern people is not staged by the "Mumming for the Mercers," insofar as the text (the only evidence available) records its dramatic action. In fact, though the ships are described as having "sayled ful fer towarde þe West" (line 80), they are identified as having *French* lettering on the sides – suggesting that the "East" is not very far away. Indeed, given the fraught nature of the relationship between England and France in 1429, the use of French phrases would surely have been a distinct gesture toward the French.

73 Green, *Poets and Princepleasers*, 10. In using the term *aristocracy*, Green is referring specifically to the literature and practices of the court, rather than to some more generalized notion of "gentlemen" or "gentility"; it is in this narrow sense that I use the term as well. It is an important distinction because, as Sylvia Thrupp demonstrated, the dividing line between "merchant" and "gentleman" was a thin one; see *Merchant Class of Medieval London*, 234–87. More recently, Rosemary Horrox has meticulously illustrated the fluidity of that boundary in the fifteenth century, suggesting that the "urban gentry" and the landowning gentry were participants in a shared elite culture; see "Urban Gentry in the Fifteenth Century," 22–44. A. I. Doyle has traced the production of manuscripts for courtly and noncourtly readers and shown that their tastes were very similar, and that the distinction became more blurred over the course of the fifteenth century; see "English Books in and out of Court from Edward III to Henry VI." For a similar understanding of fifteenth-century "middle-class" literacy, see Parkes, "Literacy of the Laity."

74 This abbreviated list is taken from the longer discussion in Carol Meale's "*Libelle of Englyshe Polycye* and Mercantile Literary Culture in Late Medieval London." In particular, Meale cites several books that were owned by mercers, including such texts as the *Awntyrs of Arthure, Piers Plowman,* and the *Confessio Amantis,* as well as several by Lydgate: *The Complaint of the Black Knight, The Temple of Glass, The Serpent of Division, The Life of Our Lady,* and *The Siege of Thebes.* Some of the texts she cites – *Confessio Amantis, Troilus and Criseyde, Siege of Thebes* – were owned by members of the mercantile class somewhat later than the period under consideration here, but I reference them to illustrate a general trend that began in the later fourteenth century and continued through the end of the Middle Ages. Parkes, "Literacy of the Laity," 290–94, gives a number of examples of mercantile ownership, including the ownership of Trinity College Cambridge MS R. 3. 21 by a mercer, Roger Thorney. This manuscript includes a number of works by Lydgate, and Connolly links it to the production of Shirley manuscripts such as Trinity College Cambridge MS R. 3. 20; see *John Shirley,* 180–81. See also Patterson, *Chaucer and the Subject of History,* 333, who argues that "English mercantile culture was largely confected out of the materials of other cultural formations – primarily aristocratic but also clerical – and lacked a center of its own." For further discussion of the development of "middle-class" culture, particularly in relation to literacy, see Coleman, *Medieval Readers and Writers: 1350–1400.* In describing a manuscript from the middle fifteenth century, Tanner 346, Lerer makes the point that "gentry readers sought to mime the structures of commission that granted authority to the patron" in aristocratic culture; see *Chaucer and his Readers,* 84.

75 In *The Merchant Class of Medieval London,* Sylvia Thrupp demonstrated the weakness of the dividing line between merchants and gentry, citing numerous instances of

intermarriage and friendship between the groups, as well as examples of gentlemen who engaged in trade and merchants who became knights (256–78). In particular, she noted the habit of powerful London guilds of admitting members of the nobility to their ranks; the Mercers admitted "over thirty members of gentle rank between the 1430s and the end of the century," and the Goldsmiths admitted another man because he was "'a man of substance and in great favor with lords'" (256–57). She further noted the similarities between mercantile and gentle cultures in their attitudes to education and their choice of reading materials (247–48). In order to draw this line as finely as possible, Carol Meale, citing Felicity Riddy, uses the term "subculture" to describe the different "textual communities" at play in the late medieval English mercantile and aristocratic worlds. Meale, "*Libelle of Englyshe Polycye*," 184; Riddy, "Reading for England."

76 Lindenbaum, "London Texts and Literate Practices," 285, 294–98. Lindenbaum's comprehensive discussion of mercantile culture focuses on its tendency toward uniformity and officialization during the fifteenth century; her emphasis is on the conservative qualities of cultural production during the period, rather than on the incoherences and inconsistencies that so fascinate Strohm in *England's Empty Throne*. The two share the notion, however, that the fifteenth century saw a retrenchment from the experimentation of Chaucer (or indeed, of John of Northampton) and toward more stable and uniform texts. For a brief reading of Lydgate's mummings that concludes that they are "politically conservative" and identifies them as political poems, see Ebin, *John Lydgate*, 86–91.

77 Christopher Baswell describes the way in which the mercantile culture of the late fourteenth century, in London and in Lynn, appropriated and deployed such aristocratic narratives as the founding of Rome by Aeneas; turning to manuscripts associated with the Rising of 1381, he demonstrates how "new and fractious urban agents might seek to imagine and consolidate communal identities under the aegis of ancient epic story." See his "Aeneas in 1381," 17. Similarly, in his discussion of the Shirley manuscripts, A. S. G. Edwards notes that they are typically down-market productions with up-market aspirations, showing how they "[offer] his audience glimpses into the life and more importantly the literary tastes of these great and good ... The most common element in a number of his rubrics is the stress on class." See "John Shirley and the Emulation of Courtly Culture," 316.

78 Mary Rose McLaren has shown that the adjective "rially" appears in the London chronicles as a kind of shorthand to emphasize the majesty of various processions in honor of kings; according to her, it is a London term with a very particular resonance in relation to the monarchy. See her *London Chronicles of the Fifteenth Century: A Revolution in English Writing*, 57–58.

79 See Isidore of Seville, *Etymologiae*, book 14, ch. 8, 11–12, for the basic description of Parnassus, including its location near Cirrea and Boeotia. In the *Troy Book*, Lydgate imitates the invocations to books 2 and 3 of *Troilus and Criseyde* by calling on both Clio and Calliope, whom he describes as having their homes on Parnassus; see the *Prologue*, lines 40–48, where Lydgate repeats a common medieval mistake, also made by Chaucer (*House of Fame*, line 522), in suggesting that Helicon is a well. As John Norton-Smith (*Lydgate: Poems*) points out, Helicon was in fact one of the ridges (*iuga*) of Parnassus (126). Robert Edwards, in his edition of the *Troy Book*, gives Persius's *Satires* as the source for the details of Parnassus, including the "welle Caballyn" (340, note to *Prologue*, line 44), but it is clear that the basic outlines of Parnassian geography derived primarily from Isidore, who in turn repeats them from Servius's commentary on Virgil (Norton-Smith, *Lydgate: poems*, 126).

80 My conclusion here has been anticipated to a certain extent by Pearsall, who suggests in *John Lydgate* that the tastes of the "upper bourgeoisie" were being "created as well as satisfied" by such texts as the "Mumming for the Mercers" (73); see his discussion of the literary appetites of this class, 71–76. Lerer discusses the *Mumming for the Mercers* briefly in *Chaucer and his Readers*, as an example of Lydgate's interest in laureation; see pages 36–37.

81 See for example the well-known passage in *Siege of Thebes*, ed. Axel Erdmann and Eilert Ekwall, lines 39–57, which calls Chaucer "Floure of Poetes thorghout al breteyne," and the *Prologue* to the *Fall of Princes*, ed. Henry Bergen, lines 246–357, where Lydgate catalogs Chaucer's works and links him explicitly to Tully, Petrarch, and Boccaccio, all the while complaining that the Muses of Parnassus are sure to reject his call for help. For a list of Lydgate's paeans to Chaucer see Pearsall, *John Lydgate*, 80, n. 28.

82 *Lydgate's Troy Book*, ed. Bergen.

83 Once again, Lydgate reveals his debt to Chaucer in his use of the term *poursuyant*; according to the *MED*, the first use of the word in English appears in the *House of Fame*, line 1321, "That pursevantes and heraudes, / That crien ryche folkes laudes" (*Riverside Chaucer*, 364).

3

Tragedy and comedy: Lydgate's disguisings and public poetry

In 1590 Edward Allde printed Lydgate's *Serpent of Division* together with Sackville and Norton's *Gorboduc* as illustrations of the dangers of civil war and strife. For Allde, the link between Lydgate's treatise and the revenge tragedy was one of content rather than form; both texts serve a didactic function by showing readers the terrible consequences of political division:

> Three things brought ruine vnto *Rome*,
> that ragnde in Princes to their ouerthrowe:
> *Auarice*, and *Pride*, with *Enuies* creull doome,
> that wrought their sorrow and their latest woe.
> *England* take heede, such chaunce to thee may come:
> *Foelix quem faciunt aliena pericula cautum.*[1]

But the sympathy between *Serpent of Division* and *Gorboduc* is not limited to their topicality. What Allde sensed about *Serpent* was that its fundamentally tragic structure resonated profoundly with the dramatic genre of tragedy as Sackville and Norton had defined it – and indeed, by identifying the tract as a precursor to *Gorboduc*, he constructed a literary history of tragedy that inserted the medieval into the humanist narrative of genre formation that moved from classical to Renaissance, Seneca to *Hamlet*.[2] In this alternate version of literary transmission, tragedy is quintessentially a political form, bound up with the production of sovereignty and the state, with a clearly defined function in relation to authority. That is to say, tragedy is a mode of address that inserts itself between the sovereign and the polity, a form of mediation that operates according to a distinctive didactic logic by which it interpellates both the monarch and his or her subjects. "Lordes and pryuces of renowne" may read *Serpent* as Caesar *and* as Romans, as ruler and ruled at once.

By using *Serpent of Division* to warn England of the hazards of internal dissension, Allde betrayed his own fundamentally medieval understanding of tragedy as a genre; just as Caesar and Pompey's sinfulness destroyed Rome, so too might the sins of rulers threaten the sixteenth-century realm. And like Lydgate, Allde found himself caught between two contradictory definitions of the tragic: one in which human agency – sin – precipitates a fall, and another in which Fortune – the "unwar strook" – overtakes the human capacity for willed action and plunges the unwitting ruler from the top of her wheel to the bottom. Avarice, pride, and envy may have "wrought their sorrow," but in the end, Allde insists, it is *chance* that must be guarded against ("England take heede, such chaunce to thee may come"). This particular contradiction was endemic to the genre of tragedy as it was articulated, defined, and practiced in the late fourteenth and fifteenth centuries. It was in part an effect of the introduction of classical texts and definitions of tragedy into late medieval vernacular discourse, and in part the result of the genre's status as a distinctly *public* form, one associated from the very beginning with matters of state. As Isidore of Seville stated in his *Etymologiae*, "sed comici privatorum hominum praedicant acta; tragici vero *res publicas* et regum historias."[3]

This chapter turns to certain vexed questions of medieval literary genre as a way of addressing the central problem raised by both *Serpent of Division* and Lydgate's mummings, both royal and mercantile. How was the idea of the literary itself translated by Lydgate into what I have called a "public culture"? That is, can the quality of "literariness" found in those texts be shown to be something more than classical and biblical allusion, an investment in a particularly poetic form of ambiguity? The answer to these questions is inextricably bound up with considerations of literary genre, specifically, tragedy and comedy – and their relationship both to broader historical narratives of the emergence of Renaissance literary forms and to the very local intertextuality of Lydgate and Chaucer as it was manifested in two dramatic, "public" texts: the "Mumming at London" and the "Mumming at Hertford."

These two poems are markedly different from the mummings I discuss in chapter 3, and indeed, Shirley himself appears to acknowledge that difference by referring to them as "disguisings" rather than "mummings": "Nowe foloweþe here þe maner of a bille by wey of supplicacion putte in to þe kyng ... as in a disguysing of rude vpplandisshe people" (Hertford), and "Lo here filoweþe þe deuyse of a desguysing to fore þe gret estates of þis lande" (London).[4] These poems are not only substantially longer than the mummings, but they are also written in rhyming couplets rather than rhyme royal – two formal differences that are matched by the poems' distinctive treatment of their subject matter, which is far more complex and elaborate than any found in the four mummings.[5] When Henry Noble MacCracken named these texts "mummings," he did so in order to signal their essential kinship as dramatic performances, and indeed, the Hertford and London poems are in many ways contiguous with Lydgate's other dramatic works. Like the mummings, these texts were written and performed during the 1420s, at Christmastime; like them, they provided entertainment for the royal and London elites, raising similar questions of sovereignty, succession, and authority in a festive and celebratory context.[6] And Anne Lancashire is surely right to insist that, in general, "[mummings and disguisings] are similar kinds of occasional entertainment, performed both at court and elsewhere."[7] However, given the clear formal differences between Lydgate's "mummings" and the Hertford and London poems, and given that they function very differently as *literary* texts, it will be useful here to refer to them with Shirley's term, "disguising." One of the clear lessons to be learned from all of Lydgate's dramatic works is that form – the ritualized form of the mumming, the stylized forms of the tragic and the comic – matters, that the semiotic weight it carries must be accounted for in any serious discussion of what such texts might mean. As such, it is with a formal label, however imprecise, that this discussion of the Hertford and London poems must begin.

The "Disguising at Hertford" has been the *locus classicus* of certain evolutionary arguments about the origins of Renaissance drama, beginning with Glynne Wickham's relatively mild assertion that "it is hard to distinguish in some respects from the regular comedy of the following century" and culminating with the publication of an edition of the text entitled *Lydgate's Disguising at Hertford Castle: The First Secular Comedy in the English Language.*[8] It will be my contention here that although these particular narratives are unsatisfactory, they do point to a characteristic shared by the Hertford and London performances: their affinity with two genres typically conceived as Renaissance phenomena, tragedy and comedy. By no means am I suggesting that these poems are proto-Shakespearean dramas; they are not lesser, fractured forms of sophisticated texts. But each of these disguisings poses a serious challenge to linear notions of literary history by simultaneously embodying both "medieval" and "Renaissance" ideas about genre and performance. The fact that they seem to be *traditional* renderings of medieval conventions (platitudes about good governance in the case of London, old saws about chiding wives in the Hertford text) turns out to be a chimera, an illusion produced in part by the texts' own need to clothe innovation in seemingly old-fashioned garb, and in part by a fundamental critical blindness to what constituted the "new" in the fifteenth century. Paul Strohm has used the phrase "unruly diachrony" to describe this phenomenon, the way in which the new and the old coexist uneasily (for modern critics) in certain texts, simultaneously gesturing toward the past and toward a future that "will have been."[9] It is a notion that pockets of futurity – moments that seem to belong to a later age or to be surprisingly "modern" – might lie interred within certain very traditional texts, unrecognized by later readers, or alternatively, *mis*recognized as embryonic versions of later forms. This latter phenomenon once characterized a whole strain of thought about fifteenth-century writing and performance, as is amply illustrated by the role that Lydgate's mummings have typically played in diachronic narratives of dramatic development and change. It is a dangerous misrecognition, not merely because it substitutes a very convincing diachronic narrative for the "unruly" temporality of the texts in question, but also because the rejection of such a narrative tends to foreclose considerations of precisely those moments of futurity that led to its construction in the first place. Thus, the suggestion that a Lydgate text might have a certain generic relationship to Renaissance texts and textual practices – might, in this case, be linked to "tragedy" and "comedy" as they came to be understood in the sixteenth century – seems to fly in the face of recent critical insistences on historical details, contexts, and moments. But the rejection of a particular historical narrative should not preclude a turn to the diachronic, or prevent the recognition that cultural and literary forms have a tendency to persist, even across major historical dividing lines and in the teeth of drastic cultural change. Nor should a resistance to seeing the "medieval" as the childlike predecessor of the "Renaissance" prevent us from seeking out those moments of intellectual ferment at which new forms and genres were emerging out of old.[10]

THE FORM OF TRAGEDY: CHAUCER AND LYDGATE

The suggestion that "tragedy" and "comedy" are terms relevant to Lydgate's dramatic works comes directly from the performance at London, where, having described Fortune and the falls of great men, he enjoins the audience to "Reede of poetes þe comedyes; / And in dyuers tragedyes / Yee shal by lamentacyouns / Fynden þeyre destruc-cyouns – / A thousande moo þan I can telle" (lines 123–27). Tragedy, as it is defined by Lydgate here, is a form of *de casibus* narrative – a definition familiar to readers of the *Monk's Tale*, the *Troy Book*, and the *Fall of Princes*, and one that plays a central role in our discussion. There has long been critical interest in medieval understandings of tragedy as a genre, and the nature and limits of Chaucer and Lydgate's knowledge of classical tragedy have been well mapped by scholars such as H. A. Kelly and Renate Haas.[11] Before describing the basic outlines of Lydgate's probable understanding of tragedy during the 1420s – a set of ideas he would build on and revise in his great collection of tragedies, the *Fall of Princes* – it will be useful to recall for a moment the fundamental historical contradiction at work in *Serpent of Division*, the tension between a world governed by providence and one afflicted by contingency. The London disguising unerringly points to this causal contradiction and enhances it by staging its resolution: the supersession of Fortune by virtue, specifically, the four cardinal virtues. It does so by allegorizing these five figures and displaying them to the audience, accompanied by a dramatic reading of the relevant portion of the poem. The didactic habit we observed in Lydgate's mummings is in full flower here; the performance is both a lesson and a consolation. What is crucial to recognize, however, is that though the problem of the "unwar strook" was certainly familiar to his audience – as were the virtues offered as remedy – Lydgate's citation of the "tragedies and comedies" of poets and his narration of the falls of great men, were for that audience surprising new ways of representing history and thinking about causality. As with *Serpent of Division* and the mummings, Lydgate introduces the modern in the garb of the traditional; what look like conventions and platitudes appear, from the proper angle, as very complex reworkings of older forms of culture into new modes of expression. The tragedy, in other words, despite its classical origins, constituted the cutting edge of English poetry.[12]

It should come as no surprise that the new form of the tragedy is rendered by Lydgate in terms that make it appear authoritatively ancient. Chaucer's use of the word "tragedy" in the *Monk's Tale* and *Troilus and Criseyde* had relied upon the *auctoritas* of figures like Homer, Virgil, Ovid, Lucan, Statius, Seneca, and Lucan, in order to legitimate the tragic enterprise.[13] In his exhaustive study of Chaucer's understanding of the classical form, Kelly has argued that these gestures toward the past in fact conceal the striking innovation at work in Chaucer's use of the concept; it was Chaucer, he suggests, who first conceived of tragedy as a living genre, one that could operate in the present rather than being consigned to a long-dead past.[14] The source for Chaucer's definition of tragedy was Boethius, in a passage we have already seen referenced by Lydgate in *Serpent of Division*:

> Quid tragoediarum clamor aliud deflet nisi indiscreto ictu fortunam felicia regna vertentem?[15]

> (What other thynge bywaylen the cryinges of tragedyes but oonly the dedes of Fortune, that with an unwar strook overturnth the realmes of greet nobleye?)[16]

Scholars have agreed that Chaucer used a copy of the Latin text that had been glossed by Nicholas Trivet, whose commentary on this passage in Boethius reads: "tragedia est carmen de magnis criminibus vel iniquitatibus a prosperitate incipiens et in aduersitate terminans" (tragedy is a song about great crimes or iniquities beginning in prosperity and ending in adversity).[17] It was this idea – that tragedy begins in "wele" and ends in "wo" – that Chaucer would repeat in the *Monk's Tale* and that Lydgate would take up in various texts over the course of the succeeding decades. There are two elements of the Boethian text and Trivet's gloss that are crucial to understanding how tragedy functioned in both Chaucer and Lydgate's work: first, the relationship between Fortune (the "unwar strook") and tragedy that the *Consolation of Philosophy* allows Chaucer to establish, and second, Chaucer's selective translation of Trivet's definition, the elision of "magn[arum] iniquitat[ium]."[18] These factors are particularly important because they are not characteristics of Chaucer's primary source, Boccaccio's *De Casibus Illustrium Virorum*, and indeed run counter to the prevailing ethos of that text, which, as David Wallace has described, "shapes the art of scholarly exemplification as a form of resistance to contemporary tyrannical rule."[19] For Boccaccio, it is the "magnae iniquitates" of despots that leads to their fall and the destruction of their rule, not the "unwar strook" of Fortune so compelling to Chaucer.[20] And it is precisely in Chaucer's revision of Boccaccio that we find the origins of that tension in *Serpent of Division* (and later in *Fall of Princes*) between providence and contingency, a tension expressed through and by the genre of tragedy itself as it evolved after Chaucer.[21]

It is in the *Monk's Tale* that Chaucer gives the definitions of tragedy that form the crucial vernacular subtext of Lydgate's work during the 1420s, definitions that Lydgate would complicate and modify and to which both *Serpent of Division* and the "Disguising at London" constitute considered responses. The Monk glosses tragedy explicitly three separate times:

> Tragedie is to seyn a certeyn storie,
> As olde bookes maken us memorie,
> Of hym that stood in greet prosperitee,
> And is yfallen out of heigh degree
> Into myserie, and endeth wrecchedly.
> And they ben versified communely
> Of six feet, which men clepen *exametron*.
> In prose eek been endited many oon,
> And eek in meetre in many a sondry wyse.
> (*Monk's Prologue*, 1973–81)

> I wol biwaille in manere of tragedie
> The harm of hem that stoode in heigh degree,
> And fillen so that ther nas no remedie
> To brynge hem out of hir adversitee.
> For certein, whan that Fortune list to flee,
> Ther may no man the cours of hire withholde.
> Lat no man truste on blynd prosperitee;

Be war by thise ensamples trewe and olde.
(*Monk's Tale*, 1991–98)

Tragediës noon other maner thyng
Ne kan in syngyng crie ne biwaille
But that Fortune alwey wol assaille
With *unwar strook* the regnes that been proude;
(*Monk's Tale*, 2761–65)

Tragedy is, for Chaucer's Monk, a *genre* with a distinctive narrative shape and a specific philosophical theme. As *Troilus and Criseyde* – "litel myn tragedie" – shows, Chaucer did not restrict his use of the term formally; it is not the length, medium, meter, or complexity of the narrative but rather the "wele to wo" trajectory, coupled with a meditation on Fortune, that produces a genuinely tragic story.[22] Renate Haas has argued that the Monk's incompetence, particularly his inability to produce a coherent philosophy of the tragic (some figures fall because they are evil, some because they are great; Fortune appears both as an independent figure and as God's agent), represents Chaucer's response to the early Italian humanist representations of tragedy following the reintroduction of Seneca's tragedies in the early fourteenth century.[23] In particular, she suggests that in introducing the genre to England, Chaucer understands himself to be disseminating a "potentially dangerous form."[24] The danger arises from precisely the point that proved so problematic in *Serpent of Division*: the question of contingency, or, put another way, the problem of the relative independence of Fortune from God. Because the Senecan texts imagined a pagan Fortune, to be resisted with "Stoic determinism and fortitude," they inevitably posed serious philosophical challenges to Christian providential understandings of causality and free will.[25] This reading of the *Monk's Tale* has much to recommend it, and clearly the philosophical tensions at work in the text become central to later iterations of the tragedy, as *Serpent of Division* and *Fall of Princes* show. What Lydgate recognized in this new Chaucerian genre was a discursive mode with a distinctive relationship to history, one in which particular historical narratives could both function as exemplars (and thus be relevant to the present) and seemingly be stripped of all historicity through the atemporality of form. This latter aspect of tragedy is of course an illusory one; history never retreats so easily. Nor, for that matter, did Lydgate shrink from testing the limits of the new genre. But as both *Troy Book* and the "Disguising at London" show, it is the transformation of Chaucer's new form into a mode of *public* discourse that ultimately lays bare both its inadequacies and its enormous potential.

In a famous passage from book 2 of the *Troy Book*, Lydgate defines tragedy and comedy at some length, focusing particularly on the performance of tragedy in the ancient world. Although Glynne Wickham's suggestion that this description accurately represents the performance of Lydgate's mummings and disguisings is certainly over-stated, it does point to a crucial link Lydgate forges between *genre* and *performance* here, one that has tended to recede in the face of interest in the textuality of Lydgate's account.[26] The description itself has pro-vided a fascinating subject for source study, and an index to the state of knowledge about classical theatre in the fifteenth century. What has been less generally acknowledged, however, is the clear resonance between the account in the *Troy Book* and the disguisings at Hertford and London – a link, I will argue, mediated through Chaucer's *Monk's Tale*, and critical to grasping the nature of Lydgate's role in producing a "public" literary culture during the 1420s. This passage represents Lydgate's clearest methodological statement about dramatic genre and public performance, not only because it provides an interpretive framework for his disguisings, but also because it places them within the broader context of his classicism.

After defining the content of tragedy and comedy, Lydgate turns to ancient spectacles of tragic performance:

> And whilom þus was halwed þe memorie
> Of tragedies, as bokis make mynde;
> Whan þei were rad or songyn, as I fynde,
> In þe theatre þer was a smal auter
> Amyddes set, þat was half circuler,
> Whiche in-to þe Est of custom was directe;
> Vp-on þe whiche a pulpet was erecte,
> And þer-in stod an awncien poete,
> For to reherse by rethorikes swete
> Þe noble dedis, þat wer historial
> Of kynges, princes for a memorial,

And of þes olde, worþi Emperours,
Þe grete emprises eke of conquerours,
  . . .
Al þis was tolde and rad of the poete.
And whil þat he in þe pulpit stood,
With dedly face al devoide of blood,
Singinge his dites, with muses al to-rent,
Amydde þe theatre schrowdid in a tent,
Þer cam out men gastful of her cheris,
Disfigurid her facis with viseris,
Pleying by signes in þe peoples siȝt,
Þat þe poete songon hath on hiȝt;
So þat þer was no maner discordaunce
Atwen his dites and her contenaunce:
For lik as he alofte dide expresse
Wordes of Ioye or of hevynes,
Meving & cher, byneþe of hem pleying,
From point to point was alwey answering–
Now trist, now glad, now hevy, & now liȝt,
And face chaunged with a sodeyn siȝt,
So craftily þei koude hem transfigure,
Conformyng hem to þe chaunteplure,
Now to synge & sodeinly to wepe,
So wel þei koude her observaunces kepe.
(*Troy Book*, 2: 860–72, 896–916)

The details of this passage have been thoroughly discussed, beginning as early as the eighteenth century with Thomas Warton's *History of English Poetry* and culminating with Kelly's treatment in his *Chaucerian Tragedy*.[27] Though it is not clear where Lydgate derived all of these elements of ancient performance practice, the general outline comes from Isidore's *Etymologiae*, possibly mediated through Vincent of Beauvais's *Speculum Doctrinale*, and enhanced with certain details from Boethius's *Consolation of Philosophy*.[28] Though the idea that ancient poets read "tragedies" while actors mimed the events and emotions of the narrative – "Pleying by signes in þe peoples siȝt, / Þat þe poete songon hath on hiȝt" – had become relatively common by the fifteenth century in Latin and Italian texts, largely due to the revival of interest in Seneca and Trivet's commentary on *Hercules Furens*, it was not a familiar notion in England.[29] Ranulph Higden had given the Isidorean account of "theatrum" in his *Polychronicon* – a text with which Lydgate was certainly well acquainted – but had not included Isidore's definitions of tragedies and comedies.[30] Significantly, on those occasions when Hidgen did use the word "tragedia," John Trevisa consistently translated it as "geste," betraying the extent to which the classical concept of tragedy remained alien and strange to an English audience before Chaucer.[31] If it was Chaucer who introduced the idea of tragedy into English, it was Lydgate who brought together tragic narrative and classical performance for English readers.[32]

Though English mummings were not generically understood in classical terms – as my discussion in the preceding chapter shows – Lydgate's two disguisings constitute specific responses to the Chaucerian "classicizing" notion of tragedy and comedy as genres, and explicitly mine the connection between ancient custom and contemporary practice.[33] This connection is not one that would necessarily have manifested itself in the details of the performance; I am not suggesting that the "Disguising at London" was read out from a "pulpet" on a "smal auter." But the connection between the ancient tragedies and comedies he had described in *Troy Book*, and the disguisings (both of which are specifically positioned in relation to the *Canterbury Tales*) he produced in the 1420s, could not have been lost on Lydgate. In all likelihood, Lydgate's mummings and disguisings were read out by a presenter, with a dumb show enacted before the audience illustrating the verses; thus, in the "Disguising at London," the figures of Fortune and the four cardinal virtues appear before the audience and are extensively described and glossed by the herald.[34] In the "Disguising at Hertford," a presenter reads a "bille by wey of supplicacion" as six husbands and their wives parade before the king; the grievances of the husbands are elaborated and explained as the twelve figures enact the domestic strife that has driven the husbands to seek monarchical remediation. In each disguising, the interaction between the verses and the actors is indicated by phrases such as "Loo *here* þis lady þat yee may see" (London, line 1, emphasis added) and "Lyke as þeos hynes, *here* stonding oon by oon" (Hertford, line 25, emphasis added). Shirley himself glosses the latter phrase, "demonstrando vj. rusticos," further suggesting that costumed figures silently enacted the words of the presenter, just as Lydgate imagined mimes performed in ancient Troy as poets "rad and songe" tragedies.[35]

It is not necessary simply to posit a logical connection between the disguisings and Lydgate's notions of ancient performance. The poems themselves specifically gesture to Chaucer's *Monk's Tale* and its *Prologue* and end link, the *Prologue* to the *Nun's Priest's Tale*, a set of texts in which the relationship between tragic and comic is explored through a series of dialogues among the Canterbury pilgrims. Lydgate's innovation in the *Troy Book* is to connect those Chaucerian ideas about tragedy and comedy to dramatic performance, an innovation he further elaborates by constructing specific performance texts that stage the "tragic" and the "comic" for elite audiences. As my discussion of the "Disguising at London" will show, Lydgate persistently linked dramatic practice (tragedies and comedies) to the problem of Fortune and causality. By 1422 that problem had become exquisitely pointed with the death of Henry V and the establishment of conciliar government. It is hardly surprising, then, to find that during the 1420s Lydgate chose Fortune as the subject of a public performance for the "gret estates" (those, as we know, most likely to be afflicted by tragedy) at London, and it is to that text that we now turn.

TRAGIC PERFORMANCE: THE "DISGUISING AT LONDON"

> Lo here filowebe þe deuyse of a desguysing to fore þe gret estates of þis lande, þane being at London, made by Lidegate Daun Iohan, þe Munk of Bury. of Dame Fortune, Dame Prudence, Dame Rightwysnesse and Dame Fortitudo. beholdeþe, for it is moral, plesaunt and notable. Loo, first komeþe in Dame Fortune.[36]

The "Disguising at London" invites the kind of misreading that has plagued Lydgate since the sixteenth century. It appears at first to be simply a tissue of late medieval conventions: a description of Fortune drawn from the *Romance of the Rose*, coupled with highly stylized portraits of the four cardinal virtues, and a series of exempla designed to illustrate a moral theme. Like other conventional texts of the fifteenth century, this performance teaches a lesson, showing its audience that the vagaries of Fortune may be resisted with the aid of virtue; that lesson is nicely packaged in the familiar genre of the mumming, with the four cardinal virtues functioning as a gift brought by the performers to the king's household. The text further solicits a reflexive historical reading;

if the death of Henry V constituted a damaging blow to the Lancastrian regime – to the "gret estates" – then this spectacle of Fortune's overthrow by virtue constitutes a form of consolation, a remedy for historical contingency and a public display of stability and order designed to enact Lancastrian power and affirm Lancastrian hegemony. The "Disguising at London" is indeed all of these things. But it is a far richer literary artifact than such readings suggest. Like the mummings for the Goldsmiths and the Mercers, the performance at London demands to be *read*; filled with allusions to Lydgate's vernacular precursors, it is a carefully crafted work of poetic art, embedded in a dramatic context which – once the possibility of its unconventionality has been allowed – illustrates both the "plesaunce" and the peril of "tragedye" after Chaucer.

The "Disguising at London" gives few clues as to the date of its production or performance; it is clearly written after the death of Henry V, since it refers to him in the past tense ("Empryses wheeche þat were bygonne / He lefft not til þey weere wonne" [lines 269–70]) but lacks other topical references; no extratextual evidence for such a performance has yet been found. Derek Pearsall has suggested a likely date of 1427, noting the clear contiguities between the text and Lydgate's mummings – all of which, as we have seen, can be reliably dated to the late 1420s – and the fact that Parliament (the "gret estates") opened at London on October 13, 1427.[37] More recently, Anne Lancashire has noted that Parliament also met at Westminster from September 22, 1429 to February 23, 1430, making it possible that the disguising was performed in 1429, though, as she points out, "the mumming need not have been associated in its performance with Parliament and/or its opening."[38] Because the disguising so explicitly addresses "gret estates," and does not directly reference the king, I find the earlier date – when Henry VI was younger and less involved in state occasions – more likely, though there is no way of knowing for certain when the text was written or performed.

Of all Lydgate's dramatic works, the "Disguising at London" is the one most marked by what Seth Lerer has called "political theatricality," a category in which he includes royal entries and other civic spectacles of the Ricardian period, arguing that the *Canterbury Tales* are animated by a continuing critique of the "relations between literary form and political action."[39] In particular, he suggests that Chaucer understood contemporary forms of public drama – royal entries, guild plays, the Rising of 1381 – as threats to his own authorial autonomy, and thus sought throughout the *Canterbury Tales* to explore the limits and dangers of the theatrical as a mode of representation.[40] In contrast, the "Disguising at London," with its address to the "gret estates," its use of the mumming form of gift-giving (itself, as we have seen, a medium for the negotiation of relations between king and subject), and its moral subject matter (the four cardinal virtues) would appear to be an ideal illustration of "political theatricality" at work:

> It is not so much that theater is the medium for royal power crassly or intimidatingly displayed. Rather, it is that theater becomes the rhetorical device, the official venue, for consolidating potentially divisive and dividing social groups ... What matters, in the end, is the ethos of political theatricality: the sense ... of the bodily relations among ruler and ruled.[41]

In Lydgate's four "mummings," as I argued in chapter 2, the Ricardian form is exploited not only to *negotiate* such relations, but also – in an almost ontological sense – to call them into being by the simple iteration of a form that demands a ruler in order to be legible at all. As the mummings for the Goldsmiths and the Mercers and the mummings at Eltham and Windsor show, the status and definition of that ruler were far more uncertain in the late 1420s than during the tumultuous years of Richard's reign; then, the problem to be resolved was the onerous omnipresence of the king, not the dangerous absence produced by a child on the throne. In one sense, Lydgate responds to this uncertainty by turning to a familiar form; thus mumming functions as a mode of citationality that reflexively names the king simply by virtue of being a traditional discourse of authority and subjection, an "ethos of political theatricality" with well-defined (not to say rigid) locative positions of address and response. In this reading, the hermeneutics of London civic drama – including mummings, royal entries, and spectacles such as the Midsummer Watch – derive meaning from a single referent: monarchical power. And what Lydgate seeks to evoke by turning to that mode of theatricality is the authority of the throne at a moment when it seems most vulnerable.

The vision of Lydgate as conservative avatar, always already buttressing the most traditional social and political values and forms, has become a familiar one. But this image of Lydgate's uncritical apology for tradition ultimately cannot retain explanatory force in the face of the complexity of a poem like the "Disguising at London," in which an intricate network of allusions to Chaucer – and to Chaucerian ideas about theatricality – produce a text that simultaneously embraces and challenges its precursors as it seeks to carve out a space for literary art in public performance. The poem begins with an elaborate description of Fortune drawn from the *Romance of the Rose*, which so closely parallels that text that it functions as a loose translation.[42] Unlike many of Lydgate's vernacular sources, this one is explicitly acknowledged:

> Loo here þis lady þat yee may see,
> Lady of mutabilytee,
> Which þat called is Fortune,
> For seelde in oon she dooþe contune.
> For as shee haþe a double face,
> Right so euery houre and space
> She chaungeþe hir condycyouns,
> Ay ful of transmutacyouns.
> Lyche as þe Romans of þe Roose
> Descryveþe hir, with-outen glose,
> And telleþe pleyne, how þat she
> Haþe hir dwelling in þe see.
> (lines 1–12)

Lydgate takes pains to emphasize to readers and viewers the "pleyneness" of Jean de Meun's description, the fact that the text needs no gloss. But the passage from the *Romance of the Rose* is in fact highly symbolic; it demands interpretation from its readers, just as its visual counterpart would have required viewers to make connections between the images associated with Fortune and her intangible qualities of doubleness and instability. Fortune lives on a "bareyne roche" (line 13) whose weather alternates between summer and winter, and she has a hall, "departed and wonder desguysee" (line 39), with one side made of precious metals and stones and the other of clay, "in ougly wyse" (line 45). All of these visual details are then glossed by Lydgate in a simple demonstration of allegorical hermeneutics: "And as hir hous is ay vnstable, / Right so hir self is deceyuable: / In oo poynt she is neuer elyche" (lines 57–59). The opening passage on Fortune thus serves a double purpose, both thematic and formal; it introduces Fortune (and the *Romance of the Rose*) and teaches the audience how to interpret properly – how to forge links between the spectacle they see and the meaning it is supposed to impart. This latter lesson is important, because it establishes a community of readers and spectators whose task is to make meaning out of the text or performance with which it is presented. And far from producing a simple allegory, Lydgate creates for that community a deeply ambiguous engagement with past and present history in the guise of providing exemplary advice.

Given that the explicit function of the disguising is to demonstrate the remedies for Fortune's instability – to mitigate her potential to create catastrophe by articulating the capacity of the human will to embrace virtue – one might expect to find various exempla invoked as negative and positive models for the audience, and indeed Lydgate obliges with a series of historical victims of Fortune: Alexander, Julius Caesar, Gyges, and Croesus, all great men who came to bad ends. And it might further be predicted that, since Lydgate seems to be articulating a philosophical understanding of Fortune that is consistent with a Gowerian notion of individual responsibility, those victims would have fallen as a result of their own weaknesses or sins. This is indeed the case for two of the exemplars, Gyges and Croesus – the former "came to al his worthynesse ... by fals mourdre" (lines 99–100), and the latter was "surquydous in his pryde" (line 103) – but neither Alexander nor Caesar is described in any but triumphant terms. These two would seem to be merely hapless victims of Fortune's indiscriminate violence, exemplars not of the danger of rejecting the four cardinal virtues (the ostensible subjects of the disguising), but of the sheer contingency of Fortune's operation in the world. Matters are made more difficult by the very complicated intertextuality of Lydgate's exemplary figures; he draws on at least three sources here, each of which carries with it a particular relation to the problem of historical causality. Taken together, then, these figures introduce to the relatively simple form of the disguising an almost terminal ambiguity, which not only undermines its message but also challenges the limits of the discursive field out of which it emerges.

The first and most obvious source for Lydgate is the one he explicitly cites, the *Romance of the Rose*; Jean de Meun describes several exemplary figures in Reason's discourse on Fortune as illustrations of her changeability and power, including Socrates, Seneca, Nero, and Croesus. Though each is adduced in order to bolster Reason's claim that the lover should reject Fortune and seek virtue, the overall effect of the examples is to suggest that Fortune afflicts both good and evil men. While the falls of Nero and Croesus might imply that tragic ends are produced by evil actions, Seneca and Socrates are destroyed *despite* their explicit embrace of honor; they perfectly illustrate the principle of Fortune's radical changeability by demonstrating that no human action, good or bad, can prevent her wheel from turning.[43] As Lydgate well knew, Jean was adapting and responding to book 2 of the *Consolation of Philosophy*, precisely the book in which Boethius defines both Fortune and tragedy – and in which Chaucer uses the phrase "unwar strook" for the first time. Nero, Seneca, and Croesus all appear as exemplars in the *Consolation*, the latter as an illustration of good fortune, and the two former as demonstrations of the dangers of power, of the way in which the great power of kings leaves them vulnerable to even greater falls.[44] For Boethius, and for Jean, the relative virtue or tyranny of a king makes little difference in determining the effects of Fortune; though both may inveigh against the wickedness of a figure like Nero, it is the extent of his power, not his sinfulness, that instigates his fall. So too, as we recall, in Boethius's definition of tragedy, the genre is merely one of lamentation for the falls of great men, "What other thynge bywaylen the cryinges of tragedyes but oonly the dedes of Fortune, that with an unwar strook overturneth the realmes of greet nobleye?"[45] This Boethian understanding of the place of Fortune in both the world and in art is perfectly illustrated by the example that follows, one that both Jean and Lydgate employ (and one that the Wife of Bath references in her *Prologue*):

> Lernedest nat thow in Greek whan thow were yong, that in the entre or in the seler of Juppiter ther ben cowched two tonnes, the toon is ful of good, and the tother is ful of harm? What ryght hastow to pleyne, yif thou has taken more plentevously of the gode side? [46]

The critical question asked here by Fortune herself (as ventriloquized by Lady Philosophy) is, "What ryght hastow to pleyne?" In other words, tragedy itself emerges as an aesthetic mode without philosophical justification, a purposeless "pleyning" or "cryinge" whose exercise reveals the human failure to adequately comprehend the place of Fortune – contingency – in the world. In this, Fortune's question is consistent with the providential vision of the *Consolation*, in which lament is repeatedly set aside in favor of a philosophy of world rejection, a turning away from earthly matters and toward the divine, toward a universe bound up by love.

When Lydgate sets out to translate Jean's version of Boethius's book 2, then, he is responding doubly to the visions of Fortune that appear in both texts – and, as we shall see, he explicitly raises the question of tragedy as a means of linking the philosophical problem articulated by Boethius with a set of questions emerging from both Chaucer's and his own understanding of theatricality. His gloss on Fortune's dwelling, which invites the audience to *read* the spectacle before them, also opens the door for a more complex interrogation of the text itself, one in which the multifarious traditions out of which Lydgate has crafted the poem can be acknowledged and understood. Lydgate takes from Jean (who copied Boethius) the idea of using exemplars to illustrate the depredations of Fortune; like Jean, his illustrative figures are a mix of innocent and guilty men. But they are not the same men. While he keeps the story of Croesus, Lydgate replaces Socrates, Seneca, and Nero with Alexander, Caesar, and Gyges, a shift that marks his turn to a new – and very familiar – source, Chaucer's *Monk's Tale*. With the exception of Gyges, a very brief example rendered in six lines, the remaining figures all appear in the *Canterbury Tales* in precisely the order in which Lydgate gives them: Alexander, Caesar, Croesus. In each case, Lydgate's version resembles Chaucer's in that he maintains the relative guilt or innocence of each figure; Chaucer's Alexander and Caesar are examples of heroic men destroyed by Fortune, as are Lydgate's, and Croesus remains a villainous fool, brought down by his own pride. By invoking the *Monk's Tale*, of course, Lydgate inevitably calls to mind not only the "tragedyes" of that text, but also the fundamental problem of guilt and innocence – the problem of causality – that Chaucer had raised. The symptomatic refusal by Chaucer to link "magnes iniquitates" to tragedy by describing only the falls of evil men is repeated here, but while Chaucer's Monk simply veers away from the contradiction between contingency and providence, Lydgate forces it into the open for both readers and spectators. Not only does he pair Caesar and Croesus as positive and negative exemplars – their descriptions are far longer than those of Gyges and Alexander – but he also, as we will see, explicitly contrasts "tragedyes and comedyes" with his own poetic enterprise in the disguising: the evocation of virtue. It will be my contention here that despite its insistence on the possibility of finding remedies for Fortune, the genre of tragedy haunts this text from the very beginning – and that the specter itself has a particular identity: Henry V.

The spectrality at work in Lydgate's disguising is familiar to us from *Serpent of Division*, where the absence of the king, the loss and recovery of sovereignty, saturated the narrative of Caesar's life and heightened the effect of his death. And indeed, the "Disguising at London" specifically recalls the earlier text by adducing Caesar as an illustration of Fortune's instability.

> So did sheo Sesar Julius:
> She made him first victorious,
> Þaughe to do weel sheo beo ful looþe
> Of a bakers son*n*e, in sooþe,
> She made him a mighty emperrour,
> And hool of Roome was gouuernour,
> Maugrey þe Senaat and al þeyre might;
> But whanne þe sonne shoone mooste bright
> Of his tryumphe, fer and neer,
> And he was corouned with laurier,
> Vnwarly thorughe hir mortal lawe
> With bodekyns he was eslawe
> At þe Capitoyle in Consistorye,
> Loo, affter al his gret victorye.
> (lines 67–80)

Lydgate makes two changes to Chaucer's account; he adds the detail that Caesar was a baker's son – thereby showing how he had been raised up by Fortune – and inserts the line, "Maugrey þe Senaat and al þeyre might."[47] It is in this latter line that a window onto *Serpent of Division*, and the deeply ambiguous status of Caesar in medieval texts more generally, is opened. Chaucer had described the emperor in steadfastly positive terms and his murder in resolutely tragic tones, as the downfall of a "grete conqueror," so virtuous that even as he lay dying he covered his "privetee" with a mantel. Lydgate complicates this picture by suggesting that Caesar ruled, "maugrey þe Senat" – that, in fact, he was the tyrant we occasionally see in *Serpent of Division*. On the one hand, this alteration seems to push the disguising in precisely the direction we would expect; by implying that Caesar's fall came about because of his tyranny, and not despite his "honestee," Lydgate moves toward an ideology of individual responsibility and virtue. But on the other, it is at just this moment that he inserts the image of Jupiter's "two tonnys," drawn from Boethius and Jean, and altered slightly to enhance its effect. In Lydgate's version, the two "tonnys" belong to Fortune herself: "Whoo tasteþe oon, þer is noon ooþer, / He moste taaste eek of þat toþer" (lines 89–90). The explicit lesson to be drawn from Caesar's exemplum, then, remains that of Fortune's perpetual changeability; Lydgate never moves beyond innuendo and implication to suggest – as he does in *Serpent* – that Caesar's fall is his own fault. And indeed, by contrast with the story of Croesus, whose fall is blamed on pride, Caesar appears as the embodiment of martial virtue. The suggestion otherwise, however, remains. It is a small point, to be sure, but it is sufficient to expose the inherently contradictory nature of exempla such as these, illustrations of the remorseless workings of Fortune in a world governed by ideals of virtue and restrained by the notion of sin.

In light of the seemingly propagandistic function of "political theatricality," Lydgate's resistance to providing a simple narration of the falls of evil men seems inexplicable. Were the purpose of the disguising merely to stage an optimistic account of human initiative in a world of instability and sudden change, it would be easy enough – as the example of Croesus shows – to display for the "gret estates" a series of notorious tyrants, figures who explicitly eschewed virtue and were punished as a result.[48] But the complicated series of negotiations that Lydgate makes around and through his three main sources here – Boethius, Jean, Chaucer – displays an impulse at odds with the seemingly didactic function of the disguising overall. That impulse may be characterized as excessive, in that Lydgate embraces those moments of contradiction found in and between the texts of his precursors; it is fundamentally a drive to produce semiotic complexity through stylistic as well as discursive means. In other words, Lydgate relies upon formal cues – the length and order of his exemplars, for example – to signal to audiences that an act of interpretation is required. We have seen already that he "teaches" viewers and readers a simple form of exegesis in his description of Fortune; this mode of interpretation (in which particular descriptive and narrative details are construed to provide a generalization, making the doubleness of Fortune's dwelling a symbol of her abstract quality of doubleness) necessarily fails when confronted with contradictions philosophically impossible to resolve. The inadequacy of this hermeneutic is signaled by Lydgate in explicitly generic terms:

> Reede of poetes þe comedyes;
> And in dyuers tragedyes
> Yee shal by lamentacyouns
> Fynden þeyre destruccyouns –
> A thousande moo þan I can telle – ,
> In-to mescheef howe þey felle
> Dovne frome hir wheel, on see and lande.
> (lines 123–29)

To claim, as I am doing here, that Lydgate's gesture to "tragedyes and comedyes" constitutes an invocation of literary form at odds with both the simple hermeneutics of Fortune's description and the overall moralization of the disguising itself, is to insist on both the capacity of genre to contain specific cultural, ideological, or epistemological impossibilities, and on the legibility of these particular genres within the discursive field defined by the text. That field is not identical with either Lydgate's "intention" or the audience's recognition of the viability of such genres within its reading and viewing experience. In the first case, though an examination of Lydgate's alterations to his source texts may yield information that suggests a certain self-consciousness lurking behind such lines as "maugrey þe Senaat" (and should rescue Lydgate from charges of incompetence), it is nevertheless important to see the philosophical problem of causality and the formal problem of genre – both usefully denominated by the term "tragedy" – as more general phenomena produced by the intersection of texts and histories at given moments in time. Thus, in Chaucer's response to Boethius and Boccaccio, in Lydgate's response to Jean and Chaucer, we may find articulations of certain broader cultural impasses – and it will be my argument here that it is precisely at the juncture of history and form that the outer limits of such impasses are reached.

This formulation bears directly on the question of audience, both its response and its capacity to comprehend the subtleties of "tragedye" or the ambiguities of Caesar's portrait. The "Disguising at London" addresses both a reading and a viewing audience, the "gret estates." In some ways, of course, this duality merely concretizes the fiction of the *Canterbury Tales*, substituting for the imaginary audience of pilgrims an actual group of spectators. At the same time, however, it must be acknowledged that for present-day readers, the pilgrims are far more tangible than the mysterious, absent audience for the disguising (or indeed, for any of Lydgate's dramatic works). The question of whether or not a viewing audience could have recognized the semiotic complexity of this text – could have called to mind, for example, other representations of Caesar that were more negative – seems at one level to be very important. A great deal of effort, and not a little speculation, might be expended on answering that and other questions of audience, through such expedients as historical reconstruction, manuscript analysis, examination of wills and library lists, and so forth; many scholars have in fact performed precisely this kind of study for other Middle English texts and performances.[49] Indeed, as I showed in chapter 2, the audience for Lydgate's mummings – mercantile or royal – is a crucial factor in determining what those texts might mean. Certainly, in the case of the "Mumming for the Mercers," we have a concrete illustration of the expectations of one reader, John Shirley, regarding the audience's capacity to appreciate and understand the literary references in the text; his manuscript glosses clearly indicate that he considered Lydgate's allusions obscure and in need of explanation. But the "Disguising at London" (as well as the "Disguising at Hertford," to a lesser extent) present very different textual scenarios, and demand a different kind of critical practice. Lydgate presents his audiences – readers and viewers – with texts whose meaning is produced in layers, with a surface that is easily legible to the casual consumer (with a seemingly digestible moral meaning), but one that consistently and explicitly points toward other, more ambivalent texts and contexts: the *Romance of the Rose*, the *Canterbury Tales*, the *Consolation of Philosophy*. And it is precisely this intertextual complexity that marks Lydgate's most profound innovation: he has brought to "political theatricality" a working notion of vernacular poetics that insists upon its adequacy to the most serious philosophical and historical questions.

To return for a moment to the question of intention, it should be clear by now that in my view Lydgate can be understood to have a "limited intentionality," by which I mean that while the marks of poetic self-consciousness are everywhere in a text like the "Disguising at London" – deliberate adaptations, additions, and elisions of source texts abound, for example – that self-consciousness can only reach so far. The text reaches the limits of cultural legibility at those moments at which unspeakable or incomprehensible historical truths flash up, highlighting what are irreconcilable contradictions buried in the very forms through which history itself is rendered. When Lydgate exhorts his audience to "reede … comedyes [and] tragedyes," he has reached a moment of impasse; when he contrasts Fortune's "two tonnys" with the four cardinal virtues, he has exposed a contradiction. This contradiction is, of course, intimately related to that impasse, and Lydgate attempts to sidestep them both by gesturing outward to other poets, as if to quarantine the problem of tragedy outside the purview of the disguising proper. His gesture marks a signal moment of "limited intentionality," in that he clearly identifies the problematic at work in his exempla (the question of guilt or innocence), and just as clearly knows its origin (the new notion of "tragedye"), and is wise enough to wish to expel it from his text – but finds himself caught between imperatives he cannot reconcile. On the one hand, Lydgate has a mandate to produce a performance "moral, plesaunt and notable," which means constructing a remedial text, in every sense of that term, one that will console, soothe, and edify an audience situated at a moment of historical instability, concerned to affirm the solidity and strength of the minority regime. On the other, Lydgate evidently understood himself to be a poet's poet, not a hack writing propaganda (though he was certainly capable of doing so), and was almost irresistibly drawn to the complexities and ambiguities he found in the texts of his precursors. It is when this latter impulse is coupled with the intractability of history itself – the refusal of certain unspeakable problems to recede behind a veil of moralization – that intentionality reaches its final limit. As we will see, nothing can lay to rest the ghost of Henry V.

Between Lydgate's invocation of tragedy and the inevitable appearance of the dead king himself we find a long interpolation on virtue. An interpolation, that is, only within the formal logic of the text overall (a logic, as *Serpent of Division* shows, propelled by the risks and pleasures of contingency), for by any other estimation the passages that follow the description of Fortune constitute the moral, political, and dramatic heart of the enterprise. It is worth examining Lydgate's presentation of the four cardinal virtues, as well as the sources and analogues he uses, by way of contrast with the disguising's somewhat fraught beginning and in anticipation of its troubled end, for the four ladies seem at first to promise precisely the kind of resolution that the performance demands:

> Four ladyes shall come heer anoon,
> Which shal hir power ouergoone,
> And þe malys eeke oppresse
> Of þis blynde, fals goddesse,
> Yif sheo beo hardy in þis place
> Oonys for to shewe hir double face.
> (lines 133–38)

The appearance of the four cardinal virtues marks the "Disguising at London" as an attempt to develop a notion of virtue fit for the public realm of politics, a secularized (though hardly secular) code of behavior particularly suited to the governing classes. The cardinal virtues tradition derives ultimately from Cicero's *De Inventione* and Macrobius's *Somnium Scipionis*, and it was disseminated widely throughout the Middle Ages, appearing in such authors as Aquinas, Alain de Lille, Dante, and John of Wales, to name but a few.[50] The only source Lydgate cites is Seneca, in his description of Prudence, which points toward a twelfth-century treatise often attributed to Seneca (but by Martin of Braga) entitled *De Quatuor Virtutibus Cardinalis*, which was translated into French in 1403 by Jehan de Courtecuisse and which would certainly have been familiar to Lydgate.[51] The four cardinal virtues developed a special association with kings and rulership in textual, visual, and dramatic traditions over the course of the Middle Ages.[52] In addition to the popular pseudo-Senecan text, they appear in Hoccleve's *Regiment of Princes* and in Trevisa's translation of its source, *De Regimine Principum* of Aegidus Romanus, as well as in Lydgate's

Fall of Princes and in a 1422 translation of the *Secreta Secretorum* by James Yonge, dedicated to Henry V.[53] A representation of the virtues triumphant over the vices appeared in the famous Painted Chamber at Westminster.[54] The four cardinal virtues also became popular subjects for pageantry; they appeared in the 1501 pageant for the wedding of Katherine of Aragon and Prince Arthur and in the 1503 wedding pageant honoring Margaret of England and King James IV of Scotland.[55] The appeal of the virtues to the merchant classes in the fifteenth century can be seen in the rebuilding of the London Guildhall between 1411 and 1430; the porch doorway was flanked by statues of Discipline, Justice, Fortitude, and Temperance.[56] Most importantly, in all of these instances the four cardinal virtues were firmly linked to the secular realm of politics. Ernst Kantorowicz has described a process beginning with Aquinas's assertion that the moral, intellectual virtues could independently produce good actions (without the infusion of the three theological virtues, faith, hope, and charity), and reaching fruition in Dante's *Monarchia*, where the two sets of virtues are firmly separated and a space carved out for the specifically secular realm of monarchical politics.[57] The four cardinal virtues thus come to signify, in both the rarefied sphere of Dante's political commentary and in the common world of public art, an ideology of secular governance focused on the moral well-being of the monarch as the embodiment of the realm.

Lydgate clearly understands the four cardinal virtues as belonging to the art of governance; each of his descriptions of Prudence, Rightwysnesse, Fortitudo, and Attemperance focuses on right rulership in the face of Fortune's instability. Each is rendered according to an iconographic tradition that is carefully explicated and illustrated; the speaker gestures toward the figure – "Loo, heer þis lady in youre presence" (line 139) – and glosses her appearance and costume. Lydgate's use of the virtues provides a signal instance of his penchant for linking words and pictures, text and illustration. Each figure has some distinguishing characteristic that metonymically reveals its significance to the spectators and that provides the occasion for the speaker's gloss. The visual functions here as an incitement to the textual rather than as a supplement to it; theatricality, Lydgate implies, is brought into being by the need for explication, driven by a fundamentally didactic impulse. But unsurprisingly perhaps, his use of images has a distinctly literary resonance. Prudence, the first of the ladies to appear, is described as having three eyes:

> For Senec seyþe, who þat can see,
> Þat Prudence haþe eyeghen three,
> Specyally in hir lookynges
> To considre three maner thinges,
> Alweyes by goode avysement:
> Thinges passed and eeke present,
> And thinges affter þat shal falle.
> (lines 147–53)

As a visual representation, this image is unusual.[58] Nor does the figure of Prudence with three eyes appear in the pseudo-Senecan *De Quatuor Virtutibus Cardinalis*. But the image has a venerable vernacular literary genealogy. In Dante's famous representation of the chariot of the ideal Church in *Purgatorio* 29, which includes all seven (three theological and four cardinal) virtues, three-eyed Prudence leads the group:[59]

> Da la sinistra quattro facean festa,
> in porpore vestite, diestro al modo
> h'una di lor ch'avea tre occhi in testa.

(By the left wheel four other ladies made festival, clothed in purple, following the measure of one of them that had three eyes in her head.)[60]

Chaucer adopts the image in *Troilus and Criseyde*, when Criseyde laments her loss of Troilus, she complains that she lacks one of Prudence's three eyes:[61]

> To late is now to speke of that matere.
> Prudence, allas, oon of thyne eyen thre
> Me lakked alwey, er that I come here!
> On tyme ypassed wel remembred me,
> And present tyme ek koud ich wel ise,
> But future tyme, er I was in the snare,
> Koude I nat sen; that causeth now my care.
> (book 5, lines 743–49)

Much as he did in *Serpent of Division*, Lydgate substitutes a classical source – Seneca – for his "maistere Chaucer," eliding his vernacular debts and invoking Latin authority. This turn away from the vernacularity of the first segment of the disguising, from the explicit citation of the *Romance of the Rose* and the clear reference to the *Monk's Tale*, emblematically marks the difference between the discourse of Fortune (associated explicitly with the vernacular) and the discourse of virtue (here linked to classical *auctoritas*). This contrast between the mutability of the former and the reliability of the latter that Lydgate sets in place is of course doomed from the start; the disguising is itself a vernacular text, and subject to precisely the same instabilities and contradictions that infect the poetry of Jean and Chaucer, even (or perhaps especially) at those moments when it attempts to set in place an ideology of immutability using the language of virtue.

This point becomes even more pressing as the disguising progresses. Lydgate uses the discourse of virtue to develop an English lexicon of terms and phrases that constitute prescriptive utopian gestures toward an ideal polity, a lexicon to which he seeks to lend the authority of both classical precedent and Christian morality. Prudence resists Fortune with foresight, making her followers "fraunchysed and [at] liberte, / From hir power to goo free" (lines 169–70). Rightwysnesse operates with the "balaunces of equytee" (line 214); existing "euer in oon" (line 218), she refuses gifts, bribes, and favoritism, making " ... but of raysoun" (lines 191–92). This concern for the welfare of the state is extended and expanded in the description of Fortitudo; she carries a sword, working only for "comune profit" (line 231):

> And most she dooþe hir power preove
> A communaltee for to releeve,
> Namely vpon a grounde of trouthe.
> (lines 236–38)

She has "stidfastnesse" (line 241), a quality akin to the "stabulnesse" (line 287) associated with Attemperance, who "restreynes" the other virtues "from vyces" and "þer-inne gyf hem libertee" (lines 289–91). This vocabulary – of stability, equity, liberty, restraint, unity, "commune profit," "trouthe" – performs for the spectators a public iteration of the values of the English polity, carefully crafted to appeal to rulers and the ruled alike. It is a familiar set of terms to readers of fourteenth- and fifteenth-century texts; as both Anne Middleton and Richard Firth Green have shown, a language of "commune profit" and "trouthe" developed during the

Ricardian period in both poetic and documentary texts, as a means of articulating social and political ideals in the vernacular.[62] It is this language that Lydgate takes up in the "Disguising at London," much as he deploys the language of succession and sovereignty in his four mummings, and it is through his use of this English political vocabulary that the basic didactic purpose of the text can be discerned – a purpose, moreover, distinctly at odds with the aesthetic and philosophical impulses driving the early portion of the text.

The central concern of the "Disguising at London" is governance. This word is repeated obsessively throughout the text, frequently as part of an injunction to govern the self, often as a way of describing the function of virtue in the world. Those who are "gouuerned" (line 172) by Prudence "goo free" (line 170) of Fortune's power; Rightwysnesse uses her scales to set all the virtues "in gouuernaunces" (line 176); Attemperaunce sets "al thing in gouuernaunce" (line 284). We are urged to "gouverne" ourselves in "soburnesse" (line 300); and finally, all "who by þeos foure is þus gouuerned" (line 314) will escape the depredations of Fortune. Virtue and "gouuernaunce" imply self-regulation, the control of the impulses of the flesh, a refusal of the temptations of the world and excessive behavior; Attemperaunce in particular enables the self to resist "gloutonye," "dees and þe taverne," and "deshoneste compaignye" (lines 297–299). This focus on the restraint of the self recalls Gower's image in the *Prologue* to the *Confessio Amantis* of man as a microcosm of the world – "The man, as telleth the clergie,/Is as a world in his partie,/And whan this litel world mistorneth,/The grete world al overtorneth" (lines 955–58) – an image and an idea familiar to fifteenth-century readers of advice to princes, which conceived of the personal rule of the king (including self-rule) as extending outward to encompass the realm.[63] As Larry Scanlon has described, the tradition of thinking of the king as the moral center of the realm emerged out of the *Fürstenspiegel,* or "mirror for princes" genre, in which:

> In order to propose the ideal of the Christian prince, the text has to overcome the moral anarchy of temporal existence and find within it a source of order; once that source has been defined in the prince, the prince must overcome his own sinful nature to make the ideal actual.[64]

147

It is this logic, by which the moral standing of the prince provides an index to the state of the realm, that underpins the concern of the "Disguising at London" with self-governance through the embrace of virtue. At the same time, though, it is precisely this logic that the text overall cannot sustain. Scanlon's analysis makes it clear that the *Fürstenspiegel* tradition was part of a much broader development within the medieval understanding of the role of the king in relation to the polity; following Kantorowicz, he points to the continuing articulation and rearticulation of the monarch as the head of the social body, whose actions and decisions constituted, in their ideal form, the only possible embodiment of lay political authority.[65] In the case of the "Disguising at London," of course, that authority has been diffused; because the king himself cannot yet rule, because this *Fürstenspiegel* addresses the "gret estates" rather than Henry VI himself, the "governaunce" with which it is so concerned lacks a crucial focal point. This becomes especially evident at the end of the performance, when the narrator explains that the virtues will remain in the household for one year:

> And yee foure susters, gladde of cheer,
> Shoule abyde here al þis yeer
> In þis housholde at libertee;
> And ioye and al prosparytee
> With yowe to housholde yee shoule bring.
> (lines 333–37)

The gift-giving that seems at first to be absent from this performance – an absence that marks the difference between the "Disguising at London" and the more traditional Ricardian mumming – makes its appearance here, transformed from the literal presentation of objects (gold cups and rings) to the more abstract bestowal of virtue itself. The physical presence of the king, too, has been replaced by the more generalized notion of the household, a household whose residents are curiously undefined and unremarked. The decentered quality of the "Disguising at London," the way in which its object of address is continually obscured by gestures toward "yee" and "you," suggests that it functions according to a supplemental logic produced by an absence at the very heart of the realm. The traditional form of mumming, which fundamentally serves as a mode through which power (the king, even the mayor) may be safely addressed – must be translated here out of its governing structure of simple exchange and into the more distant realm of ideas. The disguising's lack of focus is of course produced by the attenuated operation of power in the early years of the minority; to address such an entertainment to any individual would be to fix the locus of authority in a manner inimical to the function of government by council. By invoking the *Fürstenspiegel* tradition, then, Lydgate has animated a discourse about monarchical power that inexorably points to the foundational inadequacy of minority rule, when rule is understood as part of an ideology of the self-governance and self-restraint of a single figure.

Given the generic demand for a prince in the "mirror for princes" genre, one might expect to find some gesture toward the king in the "Disguising at London," and indeed, Lydgate includes several rulers in his description of Fortitude, the virtue most closely associated with kings and rulership.[66] It is in his turn to examples of good kings that the two generic strands I have identified here – the *de casibus* tradition and the *Fürstenspiegel* – collide, producing out of this seemingly conventional text a startling moment of anticipation, a genuine instance of tragic drama. As Lydgate's description makes clear, the task of Fortitude is to battle injustice, to take on "enpryses" (line 234) and to do "thinges gret" (line 233); it is the chivalric virtue *par excellence*. Both "philosophres oolde" (line 245) and martial leaders were inspired by Fortitude; Diogenes, Plato, Socrates, Cypion, and Hector, as well as the Nine Worthies, are all presented as examples of Fortitude at work. Lydgate here returns to the precedent established at the very beginning of the text, citing exemplars to illustrate his descriptions, and it is in this formal gesture that a link emerges between the "fall of princes" model of the first portion of the disguising and the "mirror for princes" structure of the presentation of the virtues. If the figures of Alexander, Caesar, Gyges, and Croesus had provided illustrations of the changeability of Fortune by coming to notoriously bad ends, the three exemplars given here – Cypion, Hector, and, crucially, Henry V – demonstrate the rewards of embracing Fortitude through the great "empryses" they undertook. Cypion was inspired by Fortitude "to vnderfongen in his aage / For comune proufyte thinges gret" (lines 250–51); Fortitude made Hector, "as a mighty chaumpyoun, / In þe defence of Troyes toun / To dye with-outen feer or dreed" (lines 257–59).[67] The invocation of Hector begins to suggest the fundamental problem that these examples pose within the logic of virtue, for if Fortitude enables the "chaumpyoun" to resist Fortune, she cannot, it would seem, help him to escape death. And in Lydgate's final example we see this suggestion come to fruition:

> Herry þe Fyfft, I dare sey soo,
> He might beo tolde for oon of þoo
> Empryses wheeche þat were bygonne
> He lefft not til þey weere wonne.
> And I suppose, and yowe list see,
> Þat þees ladyes alle three
> Were of his counseyle doutelesse,
> Force, Prudence and Rightswysnesse.
> Of þeos three he tooke his roote,
> To putte Fortune vnder foote.
> (lines 267–76)

Lydgate's invocation of the recent history of the realm reanimates the tension between innocence and guilt, chance and necessity, that so marked the opening four exemplars. It is a tension that sets in opposition the abstracting impulse of the turn to virtue, which allows an escape from history, and the grounded particularity of present history embodied in Henry V. It is made manifest in the slight sense of danger evoked – "I dar sey soo" – with the name of the dead king; the articulation of the immediate past is, like the work of "champyouns," a daring "empryse" in and of itself. In part, the inclusion of Henry V in the list of exemplars marks precisely an attempt to insert him into a generalized and platitudinous set of narratives about great men. But at the same time, any citation of the king necessarily recalls his loss; when Lydgate asserts that he "putte Fortune vnder foote," the fact of his untimely demise automatically reminds spectators that the ultimate weapon of Fortune – death – proved greater than any "empryses" Henry "wonne." In calling to mind the figure of the dead king, Lydgate gestures toward what James Simpson sees as the "oppositional" character of fifteenth-century clerical writing, the way in which the tragic mode – in texts such as *Troy Book* and *Siege of Thebes* – becomes a means of critiquing the martial violence of aristocratic culture, of the very idea of "empryses" so critical to aristocratic self-understanding.[68] But the questions Lydgate raises are not specific to Henry V and the problem of violence, though they certainly touch on those points. They are primarily questions of genre – never an historically innocent category, and least of all here. In the exemplar of Henry V, that is, the lesson of the *Fürstenspiegel* (that "gouuernaunce" depends on an individual ruler), becomes fundamentally, and dangerously, subject to the logic of the *de casibus* narrative.[69] When the realm depends upon a single man, his generic vulnerability to Fortune's wheel – in both a literary sense and a real way – undermines the very foundations of the state.

In functional terms, the "Disguising at London" must be understood not only as didactic, but as an imaginary, public negotiation of a series of irreconcilable conflicts and strains both explicit and unspeakable. As *Serpent of Division* makes clear, the difficulty of reconciling a Christian notion of causality based on sin with the historical experience of contingency (of radical, unprovoked change) pervaded attempts to articulate a basic philosophical program of aristocratic self-understanding. Were the examples in the "Disguising at London" limited to ancient heroes – if Lydgate started with Caesar and ended with Hector – it might be argued that the negotiation of this contradiction between the contingent and providential visions of Fortune occurs in a very limited sense, for a sophisticated readership well able to recognize the complex intertextuality of the disguising and its sources. But once Henry V has been conjured as an illustration of "putting Fortune under foot," his spectral presence catapults what had been a hermeneutically difficult, highly self-referential poetic problem into the public sphere of the "gret estates." The irony of claiming that a victim of Fortune's "unwar strook" exemplifies freedom from Fortune could not have been lost on an audience made up of precisely those persons most drastically affected by the king's loss. Nor is there any sign in the disguising that Lydgate imagines Henry V as a type of Troilus, a victim of Fortune who achieves freedom through death, who laughs at those left behind enmeshed in a world of pointless struggle. On the contrary, the efficacy of human action in the world is explicitly affirmed; "Force, Prudence and Rightwysnesse" not only enabled Henry V, but will enable the spectators, to resist Fortune *in the world* – which is a far different lesson than the *contemptus mundi* of that other tragic hero, Troilus. This message of faith in virtue – this moral lesson – might be said to constitute the functional intention of the text, that element of the disguising in which a public purpose may be discerned: consolation. As a text with a mandate, a task to accomplish, the "Disguising at London" apparently functions very well, or at least according to a discernible and rational logic. The lost king is called up, memorialized, and abstracted, his life rendered as an illustration, his death as an affirmation, of the transformative power of virtue – the "gift" of the performance to its audience.

All gifts come with a price, however, or at least with a string attached. In this case, the price of virtue is history. Once Henry V has entered the dramatic world of the disguising, the fragile hold it had retained on its exemplars (the hold of moralization upon such disruptive figures as Caesar) is shattered. Contradictions multiply; paradoxes become obvious to even the densest viewers. With history comes tragedy. Once again, when Lydgate introduces Henry V, we find that he is following Chaucer's lead in positing a relation between the genre of tragedy and the seemingly indigestible events of the recent past, imbued as they are with a concreteness unmatched by any happening of long ago. In the *Monk's Tale*, Chaucer notoriously includes four "modern instances," examples drawn from the immediate past, and, as David Wallace has argued, from his own experience.[70] In Wallace's view, the "modern instances" prove to be the undoing of *de casibus* narrative, "entail[ing] endless textual destabilization"; their very modernity confers on them a semiotic complexity that the narrative drive of the genre cannot quite contain.[71] Indeed, as Wallace points out, the *Monk's Tale* strangely prefigures the Lancastrian need to assimilate Richard II to a narrative that could declare him safely dead. The *public* function of *de casibus*, that is, emerges at moments of loss and rupture – the death of kings, the overthrow of tyrants:

> As it nudges ever closer toward the present, then, *de casibus* narration maintains an increasingly complex, dialectical relation with historical events. It determines to a considerable extent just how the fall of a "myghty man" will be experienced, but it requires other forms of discursive practice in the public realm (public execution, funeral, *tidynges*) to activate the simple and brutal mechanics of its genre.[72]

These "other forms" – public forms – of the *de casibus* narrative lurk uneasily behind the "Disguising at London" 's treatment of Henry V; Lydgate does not quite wish to submit the hero-king to its "simple and brutal mechanics." At the same time, however, he cannot resist including Henry V in his list of exemplars, even though to do so opens the door to the problem of contingency, allowing chance to haunt the disguising and trouble its viewers. What Wallace's formulation permits us to see is that the public realm becomes the *sine qua non* of *de casibus* narratives at precisely those moments at which history seems to exceed the limitations of genre. In fact, those instances of historical contingency (the death of kings) that provoke terrible, destabilizing uncertainty prove far safer than certain moments whose causes can be clearly articulated (the usurpation of the throne, for example). It is better to suffer unpredictability than to allow the unspeakable to become public – to openly iterate a historical causation based on the raw assertion of power in the face of monarchical ideology. To see Henry V as a victim of the "unwar strook" of Fortune may indeed pose a radical challenge to the logic of virtue. But it introduces a necessary principle of uncertainty into a dangerously linear chain of causes and effects; if virtue enables resistance to Fortune, than surely Fortune's victims share in the blame for their downfalls – an unpalatable conclusion when the victim, according to the logic of *Fürstenspiegel*, embodies the realm.

"Logic" itself – the rational accounting of causes and effects – proves useless in articulating the genuinely tragic, because tragedy itself, as Lydgate was beginning to understand, is a form to which the most terrifying historical contradictions and aporias are necessary and intrinsic. As a genre, the tragic marks the limits of cultural logics and tests the validity of rationalization itself. We have seen that Chaucerian tragedy – in the *Monk's Tale* and in *Serpent of Division* – is fundamentally riven by the competition between Christian moralization and pagan contingency. We have seen as well that the former mode is an ahistorical, world-rejecting solution to the problem posed by the latter, by the obduracy of history and its refusal to be assimilated to the logic of linear causality (even when that logic calls upon the metalogic of philosophy or theology, as in the Boethian notion of providence). It is facticity that makes tragedy out of exemplarity; it is the spectral *reality* of Henry V that transforms Lydgate's spectacle of virtue into tragic drama *avant la lettre*:

> In relation to every other form, including *Trauerspiel,* genuine tragedy has a special and extraordinary quality, a kind of surplus value that no play, however perfect, can attain because a play, unless it misunderstands itself, does not even want to attain it. This surplus value lies in the objective reality of tragic action itself, in the enigmatic involvement and entanglement of indisputably real people in the unpredictable course of indisputably real events. This is the basis of the seriousness of tragic action, which, being impossible to fictionalize or relativize, is also impossible to play. All participants are conscious of an ineluctable reality which no human mind has conceived – a reality externally given, imposed and unavoidable. This reality is the mute rock upon which the play founders and the foam of genuine tragedy rises to the surface.[73]

The "indisputable reality" (Carl Schmitt's formulation) of Henry V goes beyond even Chaucer's "modern instances" in producing a *public* expression of the tragic, for an audience who shares in that reality and for whom it constitutes the "mute rock" upon which *de casibus,* in its moral form, ultimately founders. It is a reality that, as *Serpent of Division* shows, bears an uneasy relationship to pleasure, to the "plesaunce" of exemplarity; it undermines consolation by exposing the exquisite shudder at the heart of the tragic process of recognition. Inevitably, of course, the "Disguising at London" retreats from this unruly moment and retrenches; the appearance of Henry V is followed by a description of "Attemperaunce," perhaps the best antidote to the aesthetic of excess that makes the tragic what it is. But the ghost has been conjured; tragedy and drama have collided for an instant, making an evanescent but nevertheless real appearance and transforming – momentarily to be sure – an old genre into a new form.

ANSWERING TRAGEDY: COMEDY AND THE "DISGUISING AT HERTFORD"

After narrating what will be his final tragic example, that of Croesus, the Monk rearticulates his definition of tragedy:

> Tragediës noon oother maner thyng
> Ne kan in syngyng crie ne biwaille

> But that Fortune alwey wole assaille
> With unwar strook the regnes that been proude;
> For whan men trusteth hire, thanne wol she faille,
> And covere hire brighte face with a clowde.
> (lines 2761–66)

It is this repetition that seems to arouse the Knight, who interrupts with his own definition of a "gladsom" story:

> And the contrarie is joye and greet solas,
> As whan a man hath been in povre estaat,
> And clymbeth up and wexeth fortunat,
> And there abideth in prosperitee.
> (lines 2774–77)

The Knight's description would seem to fit the medieval definition of comedy, a tale that moves from "wo to wele," reversing the trajectory of tragedy and standing in opposition to it.[74] This perception of the Knight's words stems in part from the specific distinction that Chaucer makes between the two genres in *Troilus and Criseyde*:

> Go, litel bok, go, litel myn tragedye,
> Ther God thi makere yet, er that he dye,
> So sende myght to make in som comedye!
> (book 5, lines 1786–88)

"Som comedye," it has traditionally been assumed, became the *Canterbury Tales*. This pairing of comedy and tragedy, in both the Knight's response and in *Troilus and Criseyde*, has its roots in various classical and early medieval definitions of the genres, and Lydgate clearly understood them to be complementary modes.[75] His injunction in the "Disguising at London" to "Reede of poetes þe comedyes; / And in dyuers tragedyes / Yee shal by lamentacyouns / Fynden þeyre destruccyouns" emerges out of his more general understanding of the opposition between the two forms.[76] More importantly, he conceives of the two modes of tragedy and comedy in dialectical terms, each responding to the other and to the vision of the world it promotes and imagines. The notion that the answer to the bleakness of tragedy lies in comedy – and the corresponding idea that the only answer to comic excess is tragic lamentation – comes directly out of Lydgate's reading of the *Canterbury Tales*, particularly the *Prologue* to the *Monk's Tale* and the *Prologue* to the *Nun's Priest's Tale*, both moments at which the comic and tragic sensibilities animated by Chaucer mix and mingle in dialogic fashion. We have already seen that Lydgate positioned the "Disguising at London" in direct relation to the *Monk's Tale*, and to Chaucer's notion of tragedy; in the remainder of this chapter I will show that he wrote its companion piece, the "Disguising at Hertford" as a specific rejoinder to Chaucer's use of comedy and the comic in the *Canterbury Tales*. In so doing, I will be arguing that for Lydgate, comedy is an unworkable genre, the comic an impotent mode – indeed, that it is the antithesis of the extreme form of the tragedy, in which past and present collide to expose the insoluble contradictions of ideology and radical unknowability of the contingent. From these heights, Lydgate descends in the "Disguising at Hertford," only to find that the Chaucerian answer to tragic extremity – "solaas," or "game" – does not function in his changed and changing world.

In making this argument, I will be countering the critical tendency to see the "Disguising at Hertford" as the single most "modern" work that Lydgate wrote, the one text in which he might be said to have produced a genuine literary innovation. The sense that the "Disguising at Hertford" represents a departure, not only for Lydgate but in Middle English literature more generally, has been articulated by Derek Pearsall, who argues that, "there is no denying that [Lydgate] had stumbled, with Chaucer's encouragement, into something new."[77] And Alan Renoir's characterization of the text as a "landmark in the history of the English drama" embeds it firmly in the evolutionary narrative of dramatic history through which all of Lydgate's theatrical works have been understood. But of course, for Lydgate and his audience, the "Disguising at Hertford" represented not the embryonic form of a fully-fledged comedy, nor a landmark on the way to Shakespeare and the masque, but a synthesis of various familiar tropes and figures whose entertainment value lay precisely in their capacity to evoke recognition and identification.[78]

The "Disguising at Hertford" is somewhat easier to date than the "Disguising at London"; Shirley's headnote gives four crucial pieces of information that, taken together, suggest a date of Christmas 1426 or 1427.[79] He tells us that the disguising was held before the king at

Christmas, at Hertford Castle, "at þe request of þe Countre Roullour Brys slayne at Loviers." As Alan Renoir has shown, the *terminus ad quem* for the work must be the 1431 siege of Louviers; Richard Firth Green proposes 1425 as the *terminus a quo*, based on the assumption that the mumming would not be performed before a child younger than four.[80] Following Mabel Christie's itinerary for Henry VI, Green suggests that since the Christmases of 1425 and 1428 were spent at Eltham, of 1430 at Rouen, and of 1431 in Paris – and in all likelihood 1429–30 was spent at Windsor enjoying Lydgate's "Mumming at Windsor" – 1426 or 1427 must be the date for the "Mumming at Hertford," giving slight preference to 1427 as the king spent Easter 1428 at Hertford.[81] However, Bertram Wolffe has argued that Christie's itinerary is flawed, because it relies upon dating under the great seal, which reveals the location of the chancellor rather than the king; citing a contemporary account book, he suggests that Henry VI was at Eltham in both 1426 and 1427.[82] But the entries to which Wolffe refers were recorded in 1428, for the 1427 Christmas season, including one which records an expense for bringing the king and the "femmes du Roi" from Eltham to Hertford, making it possible that Christmas was spent in Hertford.[83] Like the "Disguising at London," the "Disguising at Hertford" cannot be dated precisely, but I think it likely that both were performed *circa* 1426–1427, based on the evidence for the location of the king, the dates of Lydgate's other mummings, and on their striking similarity in style.

The disguising stages before the king a debate over sovereignty between husbands and wives; it is, in Shirley's terms, "a bille by wey of supplicacion" presented by "rude vpplandissche peple compleynyng on hir wyves." It is enmeshed in a variety of Middle English sources, conventions, and analogues. As a debate, it recalls a poem like *Wynnere and Wastoure*, which similarly stages a conflict to be judged by the king; as a performance of marital conflict, it reminds readers of the Noah plays or the *Second Shepherds' Play*, as a form of satire, it specifically recalls *Piers Plowman*, and as an interrogation of wifely sovereignty, its language and concepts are explicitly Chaucerian.[84] Wickham, Renoir, and Pearsall are all correct to note that in its synthesis of these elements, the mumming breaks new ground – but at the same time it must be recognized that in every aspect the text is entirely traditional. In particular, Lydgate hews very closely to the definition of comedy he provides in the *Troy Book*, one, as we shall see, drawn from standard medieval sources and enriched by his Chaucerian intertext:

> A comedie hath in his gynnyng,
> At prime face, and maner compleynyng,
> And afterward endeth in gladnes;
> And it þe dedis only doth expres
> Of swiche as ben in pouert plounged lowe
> (2: 847–51)

The two criteria Lydgate sets forth here – that comedy moves from "wo to wele" and that it involves people of low estate – can be found in Vincent of Beauvais (*Speculum Historiale* and *Speculum Doctrinale*) and in Isidore's *Etymologiae*, both sources with which Lydgate was familiar, as well as a variety of other authoritative texts.[85] Isidore defines comedy in books 8 and 18 of the *Etymologiae* as the acts of "privatorum hominum," a definition that Vincent repeats in the *Speculum Doctrinale*.[86] "Private men" become rustics in the *Speculum Historiale*, where Vincent describes the origins of comedy as "villanus cantus," rustic song, before explaining that Latin comedy fell into two categories, the *togata*, regarding "personis ignobilium" and the *pretextata*, concerning the doings of noble persons.[87] Lydgate would appear to have linked Isidore's "private men" with Vincent's "rustics" in determining that comedy concerned "swiche as ben in povert plounged lowe." The idea that comedy moves from "compleynyng" to "gladnesse" is clearly articulated by Vincent in the *Speculum Doctrinale*, who states that "est autem comoedia poesis, exordium triste laeto fine commutans" ("comedy is, moreover, poetry beginning in sadness and changing to a joyful end").[88] And as we have seen, this definition closely resembles the Knight's response to the *Monk's Tale* in identifying a particular narrative arc for the genre, and in opposing comedy to tragedy, which Vincent defines in the same passage as "poesis a leto principio in tristem finem desinens" ("poetry from a joyful beginning concluding in a sad end").[89] Lydgate combines the two elements – low degree and "wo to wele" – to produce the definition of comedy he puts forth in the *Troy Book* and to which he opposes tragedy, both of which he imagines to be genres of performance, "song and rad."

Read in this context, the blueprint for the "Disguising at Hertford" is distinctly comic: "rude, vpplandissche people" come to court in order to "compleyne" (line 8) of the "bonde of sorowe, a knott vnremuwable" (line 14) that is marriage; they are seeking to turn the "wo that is in mariage" into "wele" by asking the king for relief. The disguising begins with an address to the king and his mother – "Moost noble Prynce, with support of Youre Grace" – and the introduction of the cast of characters, six unhappy rustics who have been tormented by their wives. The narrator describes the miserable domestic lives of the husband and wife pairs; the wives are drunkards, they feed their husbands "leene growell and ... colde potage" (line 46), they beat the hapless men with distaffs, fists and ladles, and they never stop scolding. This portion of the disguising is filled with the kind of realistic detail to be found in such texts as the *Miller's Tale* or *General Prologue*, details that give Chaucer's renderings of various figures their seeming authenticity as well as their comic and dramatic potential. And indeed, Lydgate makes it clear throughout the disguising that his model and interlocutor is Chaucer; it is pervaded by Chaucerian vocabulary and snippets from various *Canterbury Tales*. Cecely Soure-Chere "*qwytts*" her husband Colyn Cobeller (line 65); Beautryce Bittersweete "hathe for þe collyk *pouped* in þe bolle" (line 40), a word cited by the *MED* as occurring only in this text, and in the *Nun's Priest's Tale* (line 3399) and the *Manciple's Prologue* (line 90); Pernelle the butcher's wife, "cast hir not to dyen in his *dette*. / She made no *taylle*, but *qwytt* him by and by" (lines 110–11), recalling Chaucer's pun on *taille* in the *Shipman's Tale* (line 416) as well as the Wife of Bath's discussion of the marriage debt (lines 129–32); the wives claim in their defense that "þe bakoun was neuer of hem fette, / Awaye at Dounmowe in þe Pryorye" (lines 186–87), a custom described by the Wife of Bath in her *Prologue*, lines 218–19. Finally, in two passages I discuss below, the familiar Chaucerian opposition between "earnest and game" appears; responding to Colyn Cobeller's predicament, the narrator comments that "Hit is no game but an hernest play, / For lack of wit a man his wyf to greeve" (lines 72–73), and in his summary of the husbands' plight, he remarks that "It is no game with wyves for to pleye" (line 161).[90] The latter recalls again Justinius's advice to January in the *Merchant's Tale*, "it is no childes pley / To take a wyf withouten avysement" (lines 1530–31).

These echoes, however, are small in comparison to the disguising's references to its two major intertexts, the *Wife of Bath's Tale* and the *Clerk's Tale*. That these two tales form the subtext for the disguising becomes clear midway through the first segment; after describing the particularly egregious violence of "Mabyle" – a wife seemingly unattached to a particular husband – the narrator turns heavenward:

> Blessed þoo men þat cane in suche offence
> Meekly souffre, take al in pacyence,
> Tendure suche wyfly purgatorye.
> Heven for þeyre meede, to regne þer in glorye,
> God graunt al housbandes þat beon in þis place,
> To wynne so heven for His hooly grace.
> (lines 85–90)

The coupling of "pacyence" – Griselda's virtue – with "wifely purgatorye" – the Wife of Bath's punishment for her husbands – firmly establishes the "Disguising at Hertford" as a *poetic* response to Chaucer as well as a dramatic adaptation of Chaucerian characters and stories.[91] And indeed, when the wives respond to the accusations of their husbands, they make explicit the narrator's implicit comparisons:

> And for oure partye þe worthy Wyff of Bathe
> Cane shewe statutes moo þan six or seven,
> Howe wyves make hir housbandes wynne heven,
> Maugre þe feonde and al his vyolence;
> For þeyre vertu of parfyte pacyence
> Parteneþe not to wyves nowe-adayes,
> Sauf on þeyre housbandes for to make assayes.
> Þer pacyence was buryed long agoo,
> Gresyldes story recordeþe pleinly soo.
> (lines 168–76)

The wives' reading of Chaucer derives from the envoy to the *Clerk's Tale*;[92] it asserts the irrelevance of Griselda as a model by consigning wifely patience to a long ago past and embracing the modernity of the Wife of Bath. Indeed, as a brief quotation from the envoy will show, Lydgate's wives are constructed specifically as readers of the Clerk's injunction:

> Grisilde is deed, and eek hire pacience,
> And bothe atones buryed in Ytaille;

. . .

O noble wyves, ful of heigh prudence,
Lat noon humylitee youre tonge naille,
Ne lat no clerk have cause or diligence
To write of yow a storie of swich mervaille
As of Grisildis pacient and kynde,
Lest Chichevache yow swelwe in hire entraille!

. . .

Ye archewives, stondeth at defense,
Syn ye be strong as is a greet camaille;
Ne suffreth nat that men yow doon offense.
And sklendre wyves, fieble as in bataille,
Beth egre as is a tygre yond in Ynde;
Ay clappeth as a mille, I yow consaille.
(lines 1177–78, 1183–88, 1195–1200)

Not only does Lydgate directly reference this passage by having the wives insist that "it longeþe to vs to clappen as a mylle / No counseyle keepe, but þe trouth oute telle" (lines 177–78), and that "pacyence was buryed long agoo / Gresyldes story recordeþe pleinly soo" (line 175), but he also creates a powerful fictional reader's response to the Clerk.[93] The Lydgatean wives' behavior, that is, demonstrates the efficacy of Chaucerian poetry in the world; the "Disguising at Hertford" is, at one level, a nightmarish imaginary in which the comic world of the *Canterbury Tales* has become a real world of gendered strife, a world turned upside down by the "archewyves" exhorted by the Clerk. The delicately balanced resolutions of the *Wife of Bath's Prologue* and *Tale* and the *Clerk's Tale*, in which the question of "maistrye" is settled through various forms of compromise, are elided in favor of a rhetorically aggressive feminism, for which power – far from being a negotiable and variable commodity – can only be allocated *in toto* to one party in the debate. This extreme binarism might appear to be simply a particularly uncomprehending reading of Chaucer's texts by Lydgate (or, more charitably, by the wives), with the mumming constituting merely a logical extension of the Clerk's envoy and providing further evidence that fifteenth-century readers were incapable of grasping the true complexity and depth of the Chaucerian engagement with questions of gender and power. But despite the suggestive parallel that might be drawn between Lydgate the poet/cleric and the Clerk as figures who fail to understand the implications of their own texts, Lydgate's transformation of Chaucerian narrative into monarchical drama bears all the marks of a self-conscious authorial making entirely congruent with his "maistere Chaucer." Of course, even granting a certain form of intentionality to the text cannot free it from the weight of its own history or abstract it out of the cultural and semantic fields in which it is embedded. Lydgate uses Chaucerian terms in the "Disguising at Hertford" in order to establish a vocabulary that can evoke, even as it dismisses, serious political questions. Indeed, he uses a whole series of Chaucerian techniques for evading historicity even as he produces a debate that fundamentally revolves around the problem of legitimacy and the right to rule.

Lydgate's choice of Chaucerian narratives and vocabulary is revealing; both the Wife of Bath and Griselda are in different ways figures that appear to negate the political by turning away from the social. The Wife of Bath both mounts challenges to authority and consistently asserts traditional social values; Griselda's capacity to attain near allegorical status as a figure for patience stands as an interpretive bulwark against the exploration of tyranny undertaken by the tale itself.[94] Lydgate recognizes this potential for negation when he couples "pacyence" with "purgatorie" in his description of the husbands' plight (lines 86–97); not only does the rustic domesticity of the characters militate against an overtly political reading of the text, but Lydgate has set in place a Christian model for interpretation that allows the subjugation of the husbands to be seen in transcendent rather than earthly terms. In the *Canterbury Tales*, such turns to the abstract are always countered by the heteroglossia of the pilgrimage itself or they are enclosed within a particular narrative that inevitably must make way for a new story. Custance's "joye after wo" must yield to the Wife of Bath's "joly tale." When Lydgate appropriates this material, however, he strips away both the multiplicity of voices and the multivalence of narrative, setting in their place a series of oppositions – husbands and wives, Griselda and the Wife of Bath – that demand not narrative but legal resolution.

The echoes of and references to the *Canterbury Tales* in the "Disguising at Hertford" mine two different comic veins in Chaucer's poetry, one that involves rustics (familiar from the *Miller's Tale* and the *Reeve's Tale*, among others) and one that takes up marriage (the *Clerk's*

Tale, the *Merchant's Tale*, and the *Wife of Bath's Prologue* and *Tale*, to name only those to which Lydgate directly gestures), joining them to produce a text we would expect to be doubly comic, with a joyful resolution leading to marital harmony. Lydgate clearly understands the mode of domestic comedy as one in which serious political questions may be posed and their implications explored, a lesson he certainly learned from Chaucer, but one that will prove oddly ineffective as the disguising progresses. If comedy exaggerates the real in order to defang it, to make it, paradoxically, manageable through rendering it excessive and thus *un*real and insubstantial – if comedy, that is, makes the unpalatable stuff of history easier to swallow – then, as we shall see, the "Disguising at Hertford" fails to maintain the unreality necessary to this task.[95] If on the other hand, comedy is, as Lee Patterson has argued, a "socially antithetical form" – a mode of critique in which the unreality of the form conceals a pointedly oppositional perspective on the real – then the "Disguising" fails as well; for all of its embrace of a "world turned upside down" with "conquest of wyves," it is ultimately unable to sustain (or contain) the social critique such a vision invokes.[96]

The failure of the comic mode becomes evident when Lydgate begins to articulate the logic of the husbands' requests. As the narrator defines the specific terms of the husbands' request to the king, he invokes a series of categories familiar from the political discourse of the "Disguising at London." Unlike Griselda, "þeos holy martirs" plead for relief from their torment:

> Lowly beseching in al hir best entent,
> Vn-to Your Noble Ryal Magestee
> To graunte hem fraunchyse and also liberte,
> Sith þey beoþe fetird and bounden in maryage,
> A sauf-conduyt to sauf him frome damage.
> Eeke vnder support of youre hyeghe renoun,
> Graunt hem also a proteccyoun.
> (lines 135–42)

"Fraunchyse and liberte," "sauf-conduyt," and "proteccyoun" are all words that describe the proper relationship of kings to subjects (and part of a vocabulary familiar from the "Disguising at London"), making it clear that though the riotous depictions of wives run amok were amusing, the serious business of the disguising is now at hand. Lydgate's narrator here recasts the problem of wifely dominance, moving it out of the realm of "pacyence" and "purgatorie" and into a world in which rights and privileges may be granted by the king. A new opposition is introduced; though the wives claim "of right to haue þe hyegher hande" (line 144) the narrator suggests that right must be tempered with mercy:

> Conquest of wyves is ronne thoroughe þis lande,
> Cleyming of right to haue þe hyegher hande.
> But if you list, of youre regallye,
> Þe Olde Testament for to modefye,
> And þat yee list asselen þeyre request,
> Þat þeos poure husbandes might lyf in rest,
> And þat þeyre wyves in þeyre felle might.
> Wol medle among mercy with þeyre right.
> (lines 143–50)

Like Christ, the king can "modefye" the wives' claim to authority by right – and like Christ, too, he cannot erase or invalidate that claim, despite the fact that nature itself impeaches it:

> For it came neuer of nature ne raysoun,
> A lyonesse toppresse þe lyoun.
> (lines 151–52)

But despite the fact that "conquest of wyves" is unnatural, the king is merely urged to grant "sauf-conduyt" and "proteccyoun," not to overturn the wives' claim to rule; it is relief from tyranny that is sought here, not the overthrow of the tyrant. The contradiction that emerges between nature and custom will be repeated and multiplied in the wives' response, which answers the charge of tyranny by proposing a series of justifications for their claim to "right." It is a scattershot defense that operates according to a logic of accretion rather than progression; its foundational assumptions coexist uneasily under the rubric of "right," and indeed, would threaten to impeach each other were it not for the speed with which they are asserted. The details may be tenuous, but the overall effect is formidably authoritative.

One of the most remarked features of the wives' response is its use of the first person.[97] The husbands' complaint is firmly anchored in the third person, with a presenter ventriloquizing the "bill" as spokesman to the king, suggesting that, as in Lydgate's other mummings, the actors simply mime the action described by the herald or pursuivant. But the wives answer the charges directly:

> Touching þe substance of þis hyeghe discorde,
> We six wyves beon ful of oon acorde,
> Yif worde and chyding may vs not avaylle,
> We wol darrein it in chaumpcloos by batayle.
> (lines 163–66)

The apparent shift in speakers from presenter to the wives themselves is necessitated by the extreme binarism of Lydgate's representation of gender; no man may speak for these women because it is precisely their right to speak – to chide – that they are defending. It is further unimaginable that the distance implied by the use of the third person – the illusion of objectivity conferred by the male presenter – be granted to the utterly subjective and excessive wives. Dramatic innovation emerges, in this case, from the highly traditional understanding of gender that subtends the disguising as a whole; Lydgate permits women to speak in order to show that, like the Wife of Bath, they are by nature *compelled* to speak. And what they say, in fact, is as jumbled and contradictory as the Wife's attack on patristic authority.

The discourse of the wives strings together a familiar set of legal justifications for rule: they offer to defend themselves in battle; they gesture toward the authority of written texts (the *Wife of Bath's Prologue*); they cite statutes; and they invoke genealogical and customary precedent ("successyoun" and "prescripcyoun" [lines 203–04]). As a legal defense of their "right," and as a mode of legitimation of rule, this series of claims proves effective; the king, having considered the evidence, confirms the wives' franchise for one year while legal remedy is found for the husbands. When the presenter restates the wives' claim, it seems obvious that the king is bound to rule in their favor:

> Custume, nature, and eek prescripcyoun,
> Statute vsed by confirmacyoun,
> Processe and daate of tyme oute of mynde,
> Recorde of cronycles, witnesse of hir kuynde.
> (lines 235–38)

Leaving aside for the moment the question of the king's clear subjection
to the law – he cannot overturn the wives' franchise even though it is
unreasonable and unnatural – it must be noted that this summary
statement obscures the logical impossibilities and contradictions that
permeate the wives' response. Specifically, the presenter abstracts the
legitimating categories – "custume, nature, prescripcyoun," and so
forth – out of the particular context of the wives' speech, and by so
doing stabilizes and codifies what are in fact quite fragile assertions. The
wives' very first claim, that they will "darrein" their right "in chaump-
clos by bataylle," immediately confirms the suggestion made by the
presenter that they are unnatural, not only by conjuring the specter of
women doing chivalric battle, but also by effecting an equally unnatural
appropriation of aristocratic prerogative. Having confirmed, in essence,
the accusation leveled against them – that they are unfeminine and
hence unnatural – the wives proceed to cite the Wife of Bath's *Prologue*
and the Clerk's *Envoy* as both legal authorities and historical records.
The Wife of Bath "cane shewe *statutes* moo þan six or seven"; Griselda's
story "recordeþe pleinly" that "pacyence was buryed long agoo." This
turn to Chaucer specifically aligns his poetry with the "clapping" of the
wives – with feminine chiding – and sets in place an opposition between
the Chaucerian model of comic poetry to be found in the *Canterbury
Tales* and the serious complaints of the battered husbands. When the
presenter states "hit is no game with wives for to pleye," we see the
counter-assertion by Lydgate of the value of poetic seriousness,
"ernest," in the face of historically real questions of "fraunchise" and
"libertee." Indeed, the opposition in the "Disguising at Hertford"
between "ernest and game" must be read against the use of the opposition
in the *Clerk's Tale*, where it appears twice. In the first instance, Chaucer
describes Griselda's *silence* using the phrase – "ne nevere hir doghter
name / Ne nempned she, in ernest nor in game" (lines 608–09) – and
in the second, he describes Walter's cruel behavior in the same terms:
"But nathelees, for ernest ne for game, / He of his crueel purpos nolde
stente; / To tempte his wyf was set al his entente" (lines 733–35). For
Chaucer, the opposition between "ernest" and "game" marks the
implacability of both the main characters in the tale; both are so fixed
in their positions that they cannot enter into the dialogic relationship
defined by the two terms, each of which is modified by the other. But

when Lydgate takes up the opposition, he redefines that relationship by coining the phrase "hernest play" (line 72), a juxtaposition that puts forth a claim for a new form of seriousness, "ernest" to be sure, but in the form of "play."

"Play" means most simply "strife" or "debate."[98] But the word inevitably both suggests Chaucerian "solaas" and recalls Lydgate's own description of theatrical performance, the "pleies in Troye . . . þe ryyt [of] tragedies olde" (*Troy Book*, 2: 922, 924).[99] Lydgate's "hernest play" is set over and against the Chaucerian model of rustic domestic comedy (which might be defined as "ernest *in* game") exemplified here by the Wife of Bath – a figure whom Lydgate represents as having superseded and replaced the static Griselda ("buried long agoo"), who transcended the "ernest and game" opposition through a certain intransigence characteristic of the Clerk's very discourse. The Wife of Bath, of course, is superseded in her turn, as Chaucerian comedy is marked as a form of feminine "clapping" – which itself is constituted over and against the allegorical mode of representation defined by the *Clerk's Tale*. What emerges is an opposition between comedy and complaint, "hernest play," which is staged by Lydgate as a gendered debate. But the disguising's real subject is neither gender nor women. Nor is it contemporary politics, though the battle of the sexes overlays a serious consideration of pressing political questions about the extent of sovereignty (the kind of consideration with which readers of the *Clerk's Tale* are familiar). In the end, the real subject of the "Disguising at Hertford" is genre, conceived in the broadest sense as a mode of organizing the historical – a form of mediation – and manifested here and in the "Disguising at London" as the comic ("clapping") and the tragic ("hernest play").

When the king responds to the pleas of the husbands, he does so by acknowledging his own subjection to the law, allowing the wives to maintain their franchise for one year in the hope that "man may fynde some processe oute by lawe, / Þat þey shoulde by nature in þeyre lyves / Haue souerayntee on þeyre prudent wyves" (lines 242–44). The clear political message sent by this conclusion – that "souerayntee" rests upon the law – makes perfect historical sense in the context of the minority; as we have seen, it was precisely questions of legal precedent that underwrote both challenges to and affirmations of conciliar government. But

Lydgate does not allow matters to rest with this indeterminate conclusion. Instead, he turns to what seems like blatantly misogynistic discourse:

> A thing vnkouþe, which was neuer founde.
> Let men be-ware þer-fore or þey beo bounde.
> Þe bonde is harde, who-soo þat lookeþe weel;
> Some man were leuer fetterd beon in steel,
> Raunsoun might help his peyne to aswaage,
> But whoo is wedded lyeuþe euer in seruage.
> And I knowe neuer nowher fer ner neer
> Man þat was gladde to bynde him prysonier,
> Þough þat his prysoun, his castell, or his holde
> Wer depeynted with asure or with golde.
> (lines 245–54)

The "thing vnkouþe" refers to that "souerayntee" over women – which according to Lydgate "was neuer founde."[100] These lines are, of course, illustrations of an antifeminist position typical of "clerkes," as the Wife of Bath's Jankyn and his "book of wykked wives" demonstrate. What is more important, however, is that they introduce a temporal marker – "soueryantee" "*was* founde" – that divides the past of the disguising from the present of its audience and its readers, distancing them from what has been a performance distinguished by its modernity, with its up-to-date references to the Wife of Bath and its cast of characters familiar from contemporary vernacular poetry. This is not the first such moment in the disguising; as we have seen, the wives aggressively insist on inhabiting the Chaucerian "now" and displacing the patient Griselda into "then." But its effect is crucial to understanding the poem as a whole. First, it dramatically asserts the *reality* of Chaucerian comic fictions, taking the humor of the Clerk's *Envoy* and the Wife of Bath's *Prologue* seriously as a description of the historical present. Secondly, and more importantly, it transforms that humor into a bleak and unsatisfying conclusion to what should have been a comic performance. The beautifully balanced endings we find in the *Canterbury Tales* to narratives of domestic strife – in the Franklin's, Merchant's, Wife's, Clerk's, and even Shipman's *Tales* – are rejected in favor of the most pedestrian antifeminism. Though some persons might find the conclusion of the "Disguising at Hertford" funny, it is not *comic* in the sense in which Lydgate understood comedy as a mode or form. The disguising travels from "wo to wo," from complaint to complaint; its end is as unsatisfying and unsettled as its beginning.

The key to understanding what causes this failure – what makes the disguising unable to either sustain the illusion of unreality produced by comic excess, or to mount any kind of social critique (even a conservative one) – lies in the figure of the king. Like the comic form itself, the king is impotent in the face of history, powerless to reverse the "conquest of wyves," unable to produce "wele" for his lieges. This impotence is not explicable by means of topical allegory, in which the child-king Henry VI's immaturity is staged for an audience eager to see their political dilemmas made comic and thus easier to bear – though such a reading is certainly made available by the text. Rather, the king's impotence functions as a sign of a much deeper historical unease, one arising from a generalized sense that politics are an effect, rather than a cause, of epistemological doubt. The trouble does not lie with the particular king now, but with the fact of kings and their mortality, with the vulnerability of realms to Fortune, to radical contingency. The true content of this "uneasiness" is manifested most clearly when the genres and forms through which it finds expression are acknowledged, when the particular content of cultural expressions is muted and its form given precedence. In the case of Lydgate's disguisings, the form in question is that of tragedy.

To fully understand how tragedy functions in relation to the "Disguising at Hertford" – as well as its companion, the "Disguising at London" – we must return to its point of origin in Chaucer. In the *Prologue* to the *Monk's Tale*, when Chaucer's Host responds to another story of a patient wife – the *Melibee* – he does so in terms that strikingly (and unsurprisingly) anticipate the "Disguising at Hertford":

> Oure Hooste seyde, "As I am feithful man,
> And by that precious corpus Madrian,
> I hadde levere than a barel ale
> That Goodelief, my wyf, hadde herd this tale!
> For she nys no thyng of swich pacience
> As was this Melibeus wyf Prudence.
>   . . .
> And if that any neighebor of myne

Wol nat in chirche to my wyf enclyne,
Or be so hardy to hire to trespace,
Whan she comth hoom she rampeth in my face,
And crieth, "False coward, wrek thy wyf!
By corpus bones, I wol have thy knyf,
And thou shalt have my distaf and go spynne!"
Fro day to nyght right thus she wol bigynne.
"Allas," she seith, "that evere I was shape
To wedden a milksop, or a coward ape,
That wol been overlad with every wight!
Thou darst nat stonden by the wyves right!"

. . .

Al be it that I dar nat hire withstonde,
For she is byg in armes, by my feith:
That shal he fynde that hire mysdooth or seith –
But lat us passe awey fro this mateere.
(lines 1891–96, 1901–12, 1920–23)

The figure of "Goodelief," it should be clear, is the kernel from which the "Disguising at Hertford" grew; her violence, her chiding, her insistence upon "wyves right" all appear, in exaggerated form, in Lydgate's domineering wives. Goodelief is originally conjured in response to the seriousness of Chaucer's own tale, which deploys a gendered dialogue in order to articulate the values of good counsel, patient "suffraunce" and resistance to Fortune (all values, critically, to be found in the "Disguising at London").[101] Herry Bailley misreads the *Melibee* by interpreting it literally, by concretizing the genders of Melibee and Prudence and applying their examples to his own experience. The generic clash staged here by Chaucer, between the somber mode of the *Fürstenspiegel* and the comic mode of gendered debate, is promptly resolved by the introduction of a third genre: the tragedy.[102] The Host explicitly turns away from the excessiveness of his own self-presentation and toward the Monk's imagined sexual excesses ("Thou woldest han been a tredefowel aright" [line 1945]), demanding a story that can "quite" his own tale of marital woe and masculine submission. What the Host wants, in effect, is an equal and opposite account of male dominance over women, told by a "myghty man"; what he gets, as we know, is tragedy.[103]

Lydgate could not have missed the strategic positioning of the Host's comic turn between the *Fürstenspiegel* of the Melibee and the tragedies of the Monk, nor was he blind to the implication – produced by the Nun's Priest's comic answer to them both – that neither mode (of somber advice or tragic lament) could adequately represent the fullness of human experience.[104] Lydgate, however, is far less interested in quotidian experience than Chaucer, and far more invested in an over-wrought vision of history on the edge of catastrophe – in "hevynesse" as a discursive mode. In the "Disguising at Hertford" we see the comic made tragic, the narrative arc of the former subverted and Harry Bailley's mockery brought to life, unpleasantly so. The failure of the disguising enacts the failure of one mode of Chaucerian discourse, the comic, to remain adequate to the representation of the present in the face of dramatic historical change. Its failure to resolve questions of "right" and "souerayntee," even in the most attenuated and domesti-cated form, marks the intrusion of a kind of "tragic reality" into the comic unreality of the *Canterbury Tales.* Lydgate is simply unable to make the story move from "wo to wele"; the best he can do is to settle for an endlessly bleak world turned upside-down in which women have "souerayntee" and the king himself is paralyzed and impotent. But the comic does not become inadequate because Henry V dies unexpectedly. The particular sequence of historical events that created the minority was distinctly vulnerable to tragic representation, creating a dialectical relationship between form and event in which each crafted and shaped the other. Chaucer may have introduced tragedy to English poetry, but when Lydgate recognized Henry V as a tragic figure – or perhaps more accurately, when such a recognition became possible – tragedy moved out of the comic fiction of the *Canterbury Tales* and into the public world of events and their representation.

The emergence of tragedy into public discourse, marked by the "Disguising at London," and the supersession of Chaucerian comedy illustrated by the "Disguising at Hertford" both represent a critical moment of "unruly diachrony," a moment at which genre steps outside of literary historical time and enforces its own modernity. The tempor-ality of tragedy has everything to do with the problem of contingency that called it into being, with the "unwar strook" that shatters historical causality and violently creates the space for new forms with which to organize catastrophic experience. But it is equally important to remember that even as the operations of contingency produce a need for the tragic, so too the tragic demands the catastrophic event – and even in its absence, will seek out the "unwar strook" as a means of making "hernest" what cannot be said in "game." As my final chapter will show, Lydgate's instinctive sense that "hernest pley" – a new kind of public discourse – was a critical means of mediating a profound cultural tension between an ideology of virtue and the horrifying fact of contingency, emerges out of a much broader metahistorical tendency, a new mode of historical thinking, with its origins in the Latin exemplary tradition of the fourteenth century. At the beginning of this chapter I suggested that the emergence of tragedy and comedy in Lydgate's disguisings would enable a broader diachronic picture of the "public culture" this book has described to emerge. The supersession of the comic by the tragic in these texts, the irruption of a new "tragic reality" into the discursive and performative world of public representation, marks an instance of what might be called "uneasy temporality," a moment at which the future rends our understanding of the past. It is critical to understand this "uneasy temporality" as a matter of form, as the collision of form with history – and if it is chance that disrupts historical causality, it is the future that, like the ghost of Henry V, is called into being by contingency and thus made ineluctably, terrifyingly real.

NOTES

1 The Serpent of Deuision Wherein is conteined the true History or Mappe of Romes ouerthrow . . . Whereunto is annexed the Tragedye of Gorboduc, sometime King of this Land, and of his two Sonnes, Ferrex and Porrex. Printed by Edward Allde for Iohn Perrin, 1590. STC (2nd edn) 17029.
2 Franco Moretti argues that *Gorboduc* represents a distinct departure from medieval understandings of tragedy, exemplified by the *Monk's Tale*, in that it substitutes for the "story of a king opposed by fate" the "story of a tyrant" ("'A Huge Eclipse,'" 17). For Moretti, *Gorboduc* instantiates tragedy as a form whose "task" is "the destruction of the fundamental paradigm of the dominant culture" (ibid., 7) – absolutist monarchy. As an examination of fourteenth- and fifteenth-century tragedy will show, however, Chaucer's emphasis on fate instead of individual sin as the cause of tragic falls was in fact unusual; far more typical was Lydgate's frequent depiction in the *Fall of Princes* of the king brought low by his own crimes.
3 Isidore, *Etymologiae*, book 8, ch. 7, 6.
4 MacCracken, ed., *Minor Poems of John Lydgate*, part 2, 675, 683.
5 This has also been noted by Pearsall, *John Lydgate*, 184 and Wickham, *Early English Stages*, vol. 1, 204–05.
6 For a full discussion of the dates of these texts, see below.

7 Lancashire, *London Civic Theatre*, 275, n. 17. For a different use of the terms, in which "mumming" refers to a dumb-show, and "disguising" to a more elaborate performance, see Westfall, *Patrons and Performance*, 33, n. 21.

8 Wickham, *Early English Stages*, vol. I, 205. The text has recently been edited by Derek Forbes (with a foreword by Wickham); see *Lydgate's Disguising at Hertford Castle: The First Secular Comedy in the English Language*. Though Forbes does not mount a sustained argument for the continuity of comedy from the 1420s to the sixteenth century, the implications of his subtitle are clear.

9 Strohm, *Theory and the Premodern Text*, 93. Strohm is describing a specific text – *Troilus and Criseyde* – and the way in which Chaucer's translation of Petrarch's sonnet 132 stands out as a "Renaissance" moment in a medieval text, bespeaking multiple and contradictory temporalities and challenging conventional understandings of periodicity.

10 For two critical accounts of the emergence of tragedy in the fifteenth century that invoke this diachronic view, see Scanlon, *Narrative, Authority and Power*, 343–50 (his discussion of Lydgate's *Fall of Princes* and tragedy), and Simpson, *Reform and Cultural Revolution*, 558–61.

11 H. A Kelly's work is essential to any discussion of medieval tragedy, from its classical origins to its late medieval manifestations. See *Ideas and Forms of Tragedy* and *Chaucerian Tragedy*; I cite him below where relevant. For a discussion of Chaucer's understanding of tragedy (corrected by Kelly, but still useful), see Norton-Smith, *Geoffrey Chaucer*. An important analysis of "tragedy" and its relationship to continental humanism in the *Monk's Tale* can be found in Haas, "Chaucer's *Monk's Tale*." W. A Davenport discusses fifteenth-century cycle plays and morality plays in relation to tragedy (meaning a great man brought low); see *Fifteenth-Century English Drama*, 20–35. For a discussion of "romance tragedy" – that is, tragedy involving a love story – see Clough, "Medieval Tragedy and the Genre of *Troilus and Criseyde*." D. Vance Smith's recent discussion of tragedy focuses on its relationship to the household and to death, particularly the plague; he usefully defines tragedy as that mode which "follows the transformation of a place that may be topographical, political, mnemonic, or psychological into a space that is threatened by and involved in the flux or oblivion of time" – a transformation that I will be mapping, albeit in a different vocabulary – in my discussion of the "Disguising at London." See Smith, "Plague, Panic Space, and the Tragic Medieval Household," 367.

12 See Haas, "Chaucer's *Monk's Tale*," 56–57, who argues that the tale is "an ingenious response to the most advanced contemporary literary and philosophical discussion."

13 These are all figures that Chaucer cites in the two poems; Seneca and Lucan appear in the *Monk's Tale*, line 2503 (the story of Nero), and line 2719 (the story of Julius Caesar; he also cites "Swetoun" and Valerius). Homer, Ovid, Virgil, Lucan, and Statius are famously listed at the end of *Troilus and Criseyde*, book 5, line 1792, in the same stanza in which Chaucer identifies the poem as a "tragedye." For discussion of *Troilus and Criseyde* as a tragedy, see the essays collected in *The European Tragedy of Troilus*, ed. Piero Boitani, especially Derek Brewer's "Comedy and Tragedy in *Troilus and Criseyde*" (95–109, especially 100), Barry Windeatt's "Classical and Medieval Elements in Chaucer's *Troilus*" (111–31, especially 120–23), and Anna Torti's "From 'History' to 'Tragedy': The Story of Troilus and Criseyde in Lydgate's *Troy Book* and Henryson's *Testament of Cresseid*" (171–97).

14 Kelly, *Chaucerian Tragedy*, 140.

15 Boethius, *Consolation of Philosophy*, trans. Tester, 182–83, book 2, pr. 2.

16 Chaucer, *Boece*, book 2, pr. 2. 409.

17 See the notes to the *Riverside Chaucer's Boece*, 1004–08, and Kelly, *Ideas and Forms of Tragedy*, 128, for the complete passage from Trivet, which cites Isidore's description of theatre and tragedy in book 18 of the *Etymologiae*. Trivet's commentary on Boethius has not been published, but an unfinished edition of the work by Edmund Silk is available at the Sterling Memorial Library, Yale University, titled *Exposicio Fratris Nicolai Trevethi Anglici Ordinis Predicatorum Super Boecio de Consolacione*. The quotation cited here is on page 200 of the typescript; it can be found in book 2, prose 2 of Trivet's commentary.

18 Both of these points are noted by Kelly (*Chaucerian Tragedy*, 50–52), and Haas ("Chaucer's *Monk's Tale*," 59–62). Kelly explores the question of whether the copy of the glossed Boethius text that Chaucer used was incomplete, leading him to eliminate "magn[as] iniquitates" as a result, and cites the abbreviated gloss in Cambridge University Library MS Ii. 3. 21; he is unable to come to a definitive conclusion (52–55).

19 Wallace, *Chaucerian Polity*, 305.

20 Boccaccio elaborates his reasons for describing the falls of great men in his preface to *De Casibus*, asserting that, having seen the immorality of great men, he sought to turn them away from vice and toward virtue through his exempla, hoping they might "learn to place a limit upon their joys" ("letis modum ponere discant"). See Kelly's discussion and translation of this passage (*Chaucerian Tragedy*, 26–28) as well as his broader analysis of the text as a whole (11–39). For the text of the preface, see *Tutte Le Opere Di Giovanni Boccaccio*, ed. Branca, vol. IX, 8–10. In his classic analysis of the concept of tragedy in medieval vernacular writing, Willard Farnham explores the contradiction between the *contemptus mundi* tradition and Boccaccio's clear interest in the potential of humans to will action in the world, noting that this contradiction would become a central problem within later representations of tragedy. See *Medieval Heritage of Elizabethan Tragedy*, 69–128.

21 In an essay he was kind enough to share with me in draft, Paul Strohm describes this tension as a "latent and unrecognized implication" in Boccaccio's text, in which the providential idea of Fortune as God's executress clashes with the partial autonomy she is granted in the world. See "Lydgate and the Emergence of *Pollecie* in the *Mirror* Tradition."

22 For an important reading of the *Monk's Tale* that understands it in relation to the problem of human destructivity, see, among others, Fradenburg, *Sacrifice your Love*, 113–54. For Fradenburg, the Monk's tragedies "show us that we are susceptible to making universalizing forms and codes as much to shelter ourselves from our own sentience as to enhance it . . . The *Monk's Tale* strips the group down to the bare bones of the law that structures it, and shows us that the law is arbitrary and inanimate" (151). In these terms, the function of *de casibus* narrative is anything but consolation, a point I would agree with in relation to the "Disguising at London"; see my discussion below.

23 Nero is "vicius / As any feend" (line 2463), while Julius Caesar is "so manly . . . of herte" (line 2711); Fortune raises up Anthiochus in pride, but God gives him an incurable wound (lines 2583–600), while it is Fortune who punishes Nero and laughs at his suicide (line 2550). See Haas, "Chaucer's *Monk's Tale*," 60.

24 Ibid., 57.

25 Ibid., 54. The text that Haas sees as best representing the early humanist use of Seneca is Petrarch's *De Remediis Utriusque Fortunae*, which Chaucer clearly knew and in which Fortune appears in her pagan guise. For a different view of the Petrarchan influence on the *Monk's Tale*, see Wallace, *Chaucerian Polity*, 308 *et passim*; Wallace rightly argues that the Petrarchan notion of "remedie" is precisely that which Chaucer rejects, and

suggests that Petrarch's *De Viris Illustribus* forms a countertext to Chaucer's tale, which ultimately interrogates the authority of "great men."

26 Wickham, *Early English Stages*, vol. I, 193–95. Wickham states that "misconceived as it may be as a reconstruction of Roman, Greek or Trojan practice, [it] may still portray quite accurately the London indoor 'theatre,' *circa* 1430, for which Lydgate wrote. What he is describing is a Mumming or Disguising" (195). An opposing view is held by Lawrence Clopper; though he does not discuss the *Troy Book* passage, he does argue that "tragedy" and "comedy" were understood to refer only to classical literature, not to contemporary drama. See *Drama, Play and Game*, 9–12. I take his point, but argue below that Lydgate makes the connection between genre and drama in his two disguisings at Hertford and London.

27 See Warton, *History of English Poetry*, 301–02, noted by Wickham, *Early English Stages*, vol. I, 379, n. 6. See also Welsford, *Court Masque*, 60–61, and Chambers, *Mediaeval Stage*, vol. II, 161, n. 1; both are cited by Wickham, *Early English Stages*, vol. I, 379, n. 6. All of these early discussions of the text point out that it is an incorrect rendering of classical performance practice. Norton-Smith discusses the passage briefly in *Geoffrey Chaucer*, 185–86, as does Tydeman, *Theatre in the Middle Ages*, 49. Kelly's discussion of Lydgate's view of classical tragedy and comedy occupies an entire chapter in *Chaucerian Tragedy*; see 149–75, especially 152–60, for discussion of the *Troy Book* passage.

28 For the relevant passage, see Isidore, *Etymologiae*, book 18, 41, "De Theatro" and "De Scena." Isidore's account is repeated very closely by Vincent of Beauvais in his *Speculum Doctrinale*, 1044. The details Lydgate takes from the Isidorean account are the pulpit from which the poet speaks, the semicircular nature of the altar (the altar itself is not a detail from Isidore), and the miming of the actors as the poet reads or sings; see Kelly, *Chaucerian Tragedy*, 156–58. It is also possible that Lydgate derived his version of ancient theatre from Higden; the *Polychronicon* includes an account drawn from Isidore with many of the same details. See Higden, *Polychronicon*, book 3, 24, 98–102. From Boethius, probably mediated through Chaucer's translation, Lydgate gets the "Muses al torent"; the opening of the *Consolation of Philosophy* describes "lacera[s] camena[s]," which Chaucer translates as "rendynge Muses" (*Consolation of Philosophy*, trans. Tester, book I, m. I, 130; *Boece*, book I, m. I, 397). The idea that the actors emerge from a tent ultimately derives from Hugutio of Pisa's *Derivationes*, in which the word "umbraculum" is used to describe the *scena*; as I show in chapter 4, it is entirely possible that Lydgate knew this text. See Nencioni, ed., *Uguccione da Pisa: Derivationes*, fo. 78v. Hugutio also includes actors wearing masks, the "visers" of Lydgate's account. The best treatment of medieval notions of "theatrum" remains that of Mary H. Marshall; see "Theatre in the Middle Ages: Evidence from Dictionaries and Glosses." There are two odd details in Lydgate's account that cannot be accounted for in any of his sources: the use of the "altar" and its Eastern orientation. Kelly cites a Dominican chronicler of the fourteenth century, Galvano Flamma, whose account (or a similar one) might have suggested these details to Lydgate, but can reach no conclusion about Lydgate's source (*Chaucerian Tragedy*, 157–58).

29 See Kelly, *Ideas and Forms of Tragedy*, 132–34, as well as chapter 5 more generally.

30 See Hidgen, *Polychronicon*, book 3, 34, 98–102.

31 See ibid., book 7, 16, 460–61, for example, where Trevisa translates Hidgen's "tragediam" as "geest"; see the definition of *geste* in the *MED* for this and other uses of the word. See also Kelly, *Chaucerian Tragedy*, 41.

32 The *Alliterative Morte Arthure* has been discussed as a type of tragedy of Fortune, though Robert Lumiansky has argued strongly that its representation of the cardinal virtue Fortitude makes it incompatible with the notion of tragedy as a fall from high to low

produced by the sinfulness of the protagonist. See "The Alliterative *Morte Arthure*, the Concept of Medieval Tragedy, and the Cardinal Virtue Fortitude."

33 It is certainly clear that Lydgate did not view the classical past in anachronistic, "medievalizing" terms; as Benson, "Ancient World in Lydgate's *Troy Book*" points out, he takes pains to emphasize the "awncien" character of tragic performance in *Troy Book*, assembling a series of details that highlight the strangeness of classical custom: the Eastern orientation of the altar, the "gastful" and "disfigurid" faces of the mimes, and so forth. Benson's argument is thus consistent with Kelly's view that the *Troy Book* description did not constitute a representation of contemporary English dramatic practice, but rather an erroneous understanding of classical drama: "No doubt any similarities between Lydgate's understanding of ancient drama and the practices of his own day in England are largely coincidental" (*Chaucerian Tragedy*, 160). My argument is slightly different, in that it emphasizes the extent to which Lydgate would have recognized those "coincidental" similarities.

34 See Wickham, *Early English Stages*, vol. 1, 193–95. The two disguisings appear in MacCracken, ed., *Minor Poems of John Lydgate*, part 2, the "Mumming at London" on pages 682–91, and the "Mumming at Hertford" on pages 675–82.

35 Contemporary visual evidence from various manuscript representations of poetic performance is suggestive. Several scholars cite, as evidence of the spread of Isidorean ideas about the theatre, a manuscript of Terence's comedies, Bibliothèque Nationale Latin MS 7907A, fo. 27v, which includes a frontispiece in which the presenter sits in a curtained booth (the *scena*) while masked players dance in front. The manuscript was presented to Jean, duke of Berry, on January 1, 1408. See Jones, "Isidore and the Theatre," 41; Jones also notes two other fifteenth-century representations of the Isidorean theatre, one in a French manuscript of Virgil dated 1410 and one in a French manuscript of the *City of God*, circa 1425 (42). See also Kelly, *Chaucerian Tragedy*, 159. Laura Kendrick notes another very similar Terence manuscript, Paris, Arsenal Lat. 664, fo. iv; see "*Troilus* Frontispiece and the Dramatization of Chaucer's *Troilus*," 85, n. 10. Both frontispieces are reproduced in Meiss, *French Painting in the Time of Jean de Berry*, vol. II, figs. 209, 210. Kelly also notes an illustrated fourteenth-century manuscript of Seneca's *Hercules Furens*, Vatican Library MS Urb. Lat. 355, fo. lv, in which the poet appears in a booth, with a lectern, and shares the stage with a chorus and actors; see *Chaucerian Tragedy*, 18, n. 41, and the frontispiece of *Ideas and Forms of Tragedy* for a reproduction of the image. By far the best-known and most debated illustration for readers of Chaucer and Lydgate is the *Troilus* frontispiece to Corpus Christi College Cambridge MS 61. S. Kendrick links this representation of Chaucer in a pulpit, declaiming before a courtly audience, specifically to Lydgate's description of Trojan tragedy in *Troy Book*, arguing that the illustrator recognized *Troilus and Criseyde* as a tragedy performed according to Lydgate's Isidorean model (82–85). But Elizabeth Salter and Derek Pearsall have argued strongly that the frontispiece is an illustration of preaching; see "Pictorial Illustration of Late Medieval Poetic Texts," 118. See also Pearsall, "*Troilus* Frontispiece and Chaucer's Audience." Lerer sees the frontispiece as a "drama of commission and response," part of a Lydgatean model of patronage; see *Chaucer and his Readers*, 55–56.

36 MacCracken, ed., *Minor Poems of John Lydgate*, part 2, 682.

37 See Pearsall, *John Lydgate (1371–1449)*, 28 and note 65.

38 Lancashire, *London Civic Theatre*, 122–23, n. 33.

39 Lerer, "Chaucerian Critique of Medieval Theatricality," 74. A suggestive comparison of the "Disguising at London" to Skelton's *Bowge of Courte* has been made by Kozikowski, "Lydgate, Machiavelli, and More and Skelton's *Bowge of Courte*."

40 Lerer, "Chaucerian Critique of Medieval Theatricality," sees Chaucer's relationship to the cycle dramas of northern cities as distant and attenuated; the *Miller's Tale*, he argues, not only comically inverts the civic theatricality of the *Knight's Tale*, but does so while suggesting that the provincial theatricality it exploits is suffused with "intractable otherness" (70). The Corpus Christi plays, he argues "may well have seemed as distant or as different to Chaucer as they do to us" (70). By the time Lydgate writes his own dramatic works, however, that distance between the theatrics of the London court and the northern play cycles had certainly diminished – and perhaps was never so great as Lerer suggests. Lydgate himself has been proposed as the author of the N-town plays, by Gail Gibson ("Bury St. Edmunds, Lydgate, and the N-Town Cycle"); whether or not such authorship can be proved, it is definitely the case that Lydgate would have been thoroughly acquainted with East Anglian drama as a result of his tenure at Bury St. Edmunds.

41 Lerer, "Chaucerian Critique of Medieval Theatricality," 66.

42 An interesting analogue to Lydgate's theatrical use of Fortune here can be found in Adam de la Halle's *Le Jeu de la feuillée*, in which Fortune mimes various actions while other characters speak. See *Le Jeu de la feuillée*, ed. Dufournet.

43 See *Le Roman de la Rose*, ed. Langlois, vols. II and III; for Socrates, see lines 5842–69 (vol. II, 273–74); for Seneca, lines 6175–250 (vol. II, 286–89); for Nero, lines 6175–250, and 6411–88 (vol. III, 4–6); and for Croesus, lines 6489–6630 (vol. III, 7–12).

44 For Croesus, see *Boece*, book 2, pr. 2, 409; for Nero and Seneca, see book 3, m. 4 and pr. 5, 425–26.

45 Ibid., book 2, pr. 2, 409.

46 Ibid., book 2, pr. 2, 410. See also the Wife of Bath's *Prologue*, line 170, and *Le Roman de la Rose*, lines 6813–54.

47 The detail of Caesar as a baker's son can be found in Hoccleve's *Regiment of Princes*, ed. Blyth, lines 3513–21. His source is the *Chessbook* of Jacob de Cessolis. For a Latin version of the text, see *Libellus de Moribus Hominum et Officiis Nobilium ac Popularium super Ludo Scachorum*, ed. Burt, 67; for a French version, see *A Critical Edition of Le Jeu des Eschés, Moralisé translated by Jehan de Vignay*, ed. Fuller, 206. See also the notes to Charles Blyth's edition of the *Regiment of Princes*, 234.

48 Lydgate's version of the Croesus story is consistent with both Jean's (*Le Roman de la Rose*, lines 6489–630) and Chaucer's (*Monk's Tale*, lines 2727–60), with the exception of a single detail. In the earlier accounts, Croesus is visited by a dream that his daughter, "Phania" or "Phanye," interprets as portending his death; Lydgate retains the dream, but names the daughter "Leryopee," a name that comes from Ovid's *Metamorphoses*, book 3, lines 339–50, where "Liriope" is the name of Narcissus's mother. See Ovid, *Metamorphoses*, trans. Miller, 148–49. "Liriope" asks Tiresias if her son will have a long life; he responds affirmatively, as long as Narcissus does not get to know himself. Lydgate may have found the figure of Liriope appropriate because of her association with prophecy; as the story of Narcissus shows, Tiresias was correct. Dreams and portents, of course, pose particular philosophical problems within a Christian understanding of free will; though Lydgate does not take up the question here, his alteration to the Croesus narrative suggests a particular concern with prediction and prophecy.

49 For discussion of recent work on manuscripts, see Hanna, "Middle English Manuscripts and the Study of Literature." Kathryn Kerby-Fulton has discussed Langland's "coterie" of readers, as well as the *Piers Plowman* manuscripts and their transmission, in "Langland and the Bibliographic Ego." See also Coleman, *Medieval Readers and Writers*. Scholars of medieval drama have gone to some lengths to recover

the fact of performance; Twycross summarizes much of this work in her "Theatricality of Medieval English Plays." Sarah Beckwith turns to more recent stagings and film representations of medieval drama in her important reading of the parameters of sacred performance in the York plays, *Signifying God.*

50 See Tuve, *Allegorical Imagery*, 57–88. See also Harris, *Skelton's Magnyfycence*, 73–84. For the passage in Cicero, see *De Inventione*, trans. Hubbell, vol. II, 53–4, 326–33; for the passage in Macrobius, see *Commentary on the Dream of Scipio*, book 1, ch. 8 (*Macrobius*, vol. II, ed. J. Willis, 36–39).

51 The pseudo-Senecan text was in fact written by Martin of Braga and entitled *Formula Vita Honestae*; see *Opera Omnia of Martin of Braga*, ed. Barlow. See also Tuve, *Allegorical Imagery*, 73–76. An interesting version was printed in Paris in 1491 by Antoine Vérard and ascribed to Laurent de Premierfait, one of Lydgate's favorite authors, and titled *Les Euvres de Senecque*, with the subtitle, *De quattuor virtutibus cardinalibus* or *Des mots dorez des quatre vertus*. I examined the microfilm of the book held by the Huntington Library, San Marino, California.

52 Watts has demonstrated the prevalence of the four cardinal virtues in discussions of late medieval kingship; see *Henry VI and the Politics of Kingship*, 23–26, 58–59.

53 Hoccleve identifies the virtues in his discussion of Prudence; see *The Regiment of Princes*, ed. Blyth, line 4747 *et passim*. For Trevisa's text see *The Governance of Kings and Princes*, ed. Fowler, Briggs, and Remley, 47–54. Yonge's translation appears in *Three Prose Versions of the Secreta Secretorum*, ed. Steele; the cardinal virtues appear in chapters 18–27, pages 145–63. The four cardinal virtues are mentioned in the *Fall of Princes*, ed. Bergen, book 7, lines 1132–36.

54 For the paintings in the king's bedchamber, see Binski, *Painted Chamber at Westminster*, especially 41–43. Adolf Katzenellenbogen has described the tradition of representations of both the virtues and the vices, in *Allegories of the Virtues and Vices in Medieval Art from Early Christian Times to the Thirteenth Century*; see especially 30–56. For other representations of the virtues, see Mâle, *Art religieux de la fin du moyen âge*, 295–346.

55 Withington, *English Pageantry*, 168–69.

56 Barron, *Medieval Guildhall of London*, 27 and plates 9a, 9b, 10.

57 Kantorowicz, *King's Two Bodies*, 468–83.

58 See Mâle's discussion of Prudence in *Art religieux de la fin du moyen âge*, 321; he does note that Prudence is occasionally represented with three heads, but suggests that in the fourteenth century at least, she usually has merely two faces. For a broader discussion of the Aristotelian virtue of prudence, and its relationship to both political and ethical thought in the fourteenth century, see Coleman, "Science of Politics and Late Medieval Academic Debate," 196–200.

59 For images of three-eyed Prudence in Dante manuscripts, see Matthews, "Troilus and Criseyde, V. 743–49," and Matthews, "Chaucer's Personification of Prudence in *Troilus* (V.743–49)."

60 Dante Alighieri, *Purgatorio*, ed. Singleton, canto 29, lines 130–32, pages 322–23.

61 For discussion of Chaucer's use of Dante here, see Schless, *Chaucer and Dante*, 141, nn. 75 and 76.

62 Middleton, "Idea of Public Poetry," 100, and Green, *Crisis of Truth*, 1–40. Middleton and Green differ in their views of the extent to which these ideals were seen as workable social concepts in the late fourteenth century; Middleton emphasizes the way in which Ricardian poets worked to articulate a public poetic voice grounded in the experiential world of everyday political life, while Green shows that ideals like "trouthe" were severely tested and strained by both broad social shifts and the particular crises of

Richard II's reign. Both, however, note the emergence of an English vernacular vocabulary for social ideals, and it is this vocabulary that Lydgate inherits. For further discussion of Middleton's notion of "public poetry," see my introduction.

63 For a discussion of the image of the "ethical microcosm" in Gower, and particularly its source in the *Secretum Secretorum* and *De Regimine Principum*, see Porter, "Gower's Ethical Microcosm and Political Macrocosm."

64 Scanlon, *Narrative, Authority and Power*, 83.

65 Ibid., 98–105.

66 This is particularly the case in the "Disguising at London" because Lydgate gives Fortitude the alternative name "magnyfysence," a quality thought to be especially important for rulers. As Tuve describes, "magnyfysence" was identified as a subset of Fortitude in both the Ciceronian and Macrobian traditions; see *Allegorical Imagery*, 57–60. Harris discusses magnificence at length, particularly its role in Aquinas; see *Skelton's Magnyfycence*, 46–70. See also Lumiansky, "Alliterative *Morte Arthure*," 102–03, for discussions of Fortitude within the four cardinal virtues tradition. Richard Osberg has suggested that the 1432 pageants for Henry VI's return from France make reference to the cardinal virtues, especially Fortitude, in their representation of the seven liberal arts, which were associated with the four cardinal virtues and the three gifts of the Holy Spirit. The pageants do not explicitly identify the cardinal virtues, however. See "The Jesse Tree in the 1432 London Entry of Henry VI: Messianic Kingship and the Rule of Justice," 224–25.

67 Oddly, Lydgate seems to think that Scipio was a Carthaginian; the full passage reads: "She made Cypion of Cartage / To vnderfongen in his aage / For comune proufyte thinges gret; / And for no dreed list not leet, / Ageynst Roome, þat mighty tovne, / For to defende his regyoun" (lines 249–54). In the version he gives in the *Fall of Princes*, which he derives from Laurence de Premierfait's translation of Boccaccio, he does identify Scipio Africanus as a Roman, and describes his defeat of Carthage, as well as his later exile from Rome. See *Fall of Princes*, ed. Bergen, book 5, lines 1030–141, 1622–712. "Sypion" also appears in "King Henry VI's Triumphal Entry into London, 21 Feb. 1432," line 520, and is clearly identified as the conqueror of Carthage. See chapter 5 for discussion of this poem.

68 Simpson, *Reform and Cultural Revolution*, chapter 3, "The Tragic," 68–120, especially 103 for a definition of the "oppositional" quality of the tragic and its appropriation by clerics in the fifteenth century.

69 Strohm sees the reverse movement at work in the *Fall of Princes*, from *de casibus* to "advice to princes," noting that Lydgate affirmatively states both that Fortune may be resisted with virtue, and that bad Fortune is a sign of the sinfulness of the fallen ruler; see *Fall of Princes*, book 2, lines 1–126, which includes lines such as "It is nat [Fortune] that pryncis gaff the fall, / But vicious lyuyng" (lines 45–46) and "Vertu conserueth pryncis in ther glorie / And confermeth ther dominaciouns" (lines 64–65). See Strohm, "Lydgate and the Emergence of *Pollecie*." Wallace makes the important observation that the *Fall of Princes* includes no "modern instances" to challenge Lydgate's assertion that rulers rise and fall according to their sinfulness and virtue; see *Chaucerian Polity*, 334. Lydgate does collect seven "modern instances" in "Of the Sodein Fal of Princes in Oure Dayes," a poem that appears in Trinity College Cambridge MS R. 3. 20, along with the mummings. As Pearsall points out, it weds words and images like many of Lydgate's works during the "laureate" period, and is likely to have been written during the minority. Unlike the *Fall of Princes*, however, not all of Lydgate's "modern instances" fall because of their own sinfulness or weakness; two – Thomas, duke of

Gloucester, and John, duke of Burgundy – fall despite their "trouthe" (line 32). This split between the idea that falls come about because of sin, and that fortune strikes unexpectedly, would appear to be more characteristic of the minority period than slightly later. One measure of reader response to both Chaucer's *Monk's Tale* and Lydgate's *Fall of Princes*, and the notions of tragedy contained therein, can be found in Cambridge, Trinity College MS R. 3. 21, where Chaucer's poem is framed by selected passages from the *Fall of Princes*; Edwards suggests that the Trinity redactor was dissatisfied with Chaucer's insistence on the irrationality of Fortune, and compensated by adding a Lydgatean notion of moral causality and human agency. See "The Influence of Lydgate's *Fall of Princes c.* 1440–1559: A Survey," 436.

70 See Wallace, *Chaucerian Polity*, 313–29, for discussions of what Chaucer might have known about each of the "modern instances" he adduces.

71 Ibid., 314.

72 Ibid., 330.

73 Schmitt, "Source of the Tragic," 142–43.

74 See Kelly, *Chaucerian Tragedy*, 79.

75 Kelly discusses the question of Chaucer's understanding of comedy as the opposite of tragedy in *Chaucerian Tragedy*, 79–90, concluding that it is likely that Chaucer had encountered definitions of comedy in such sources as William of Conches's glosses on Boethius, Isidore's *Etymologiae*, or Vincent of Beauvais's *Speculum Historiale* (see 80–81). He disagrees with Patterson's definition of Chaucerian comedy as a "socially antithetical form," arguing that the state of Chaucer's knowledge of comedy was more fragmentary than such a definition would suggest (83); see Patterson, *Chaucer and the Subject of History*, 242–43, and my discussion of Patterson's thesis in relation to Lydgate below.

76 In his descriptions of tragedy and comedy in the *Troy Book*, Lydgate sets out to describe the "final difference" between them; see *Troy Book*, ed. Bergen, book 2, lines 842–59, line 846.

77 Pearsall, *John Lydgate*, 188.

78 An interesting French analogue to the "Disguising at Hertford" can be found in the *Farce nouvelle très bonne des drois de la Porte Bodès et de Fermer l'huis*, printed in Gustave Cohen, ed., *Recueil de Farces Françaises Inédites du XVe Siècle*, 159–64. In it, a cobbler and his wife have a quarrel about who should shut the door, which naturally becomes a dispute about sovereignty in the household. After several stanzas of debate, including a game of "who speaks first," they seek a judge. The cobbler, much like the husbands in the Disguising at Hertford, complains that he is henpecked and that his wife wants to be mistress of the house. The wife, like the wives in Hertford, responds with legal language, insisting that a certain provost of her town has issued a doctrine that gives wives dominion over husbands in the house. The judge reads the doctrine and agrees, and renders the judgment that men must submit to women. The farce probably dates to the later fifteenth century (see Cohen, ed., *Recueil de Farces*, xxi). Of course, stories of such domestic disputes were popular throughout the Middle Ages, and, as Jody Enders has shown, the use of a legal setting for drama was endemic from a very early period. See her *Rhetoric and the Origins of Medieval Drama*, especially chapter 4. Her discussion of the farce described above appears on pages 210–16.

79 The text has been printed several times, beginning with Hammond's edition in 1899; see "Lydgate's Mumming at Hertford." MacCracken printed it with Lydgate's other mummings in *Minor Poems of John Lydgate*, part 2, 675–82; most recently, Forbes has printed both the text and a translation in *Lydgate's Disguising at Hertford Castle*, 2–11 (translation) and 29–36 (original).

80 Renoir, "On the Date of John Lydgate's 'Mumming at Hertford'"; Green, "Three Fifteenth-Century Notes." Green makes the important point that Brice was not in fact the Controller, but the Cofferer, his deputy.

81 Green, "Three Fifteenth-Century Notes," 15; see Christie, *Henry VI*, 375–76.

82 Wolffe, *Henry VI*, 361 and 37. See also John Merston's account book, in *Foedera*, ed. Rymer, vol. X, 387–88.

83 The full entry reads, "Item, *Donne a Deux Hommes* de l'Abbe de Waltham, esteantz ovec nostre *Sire le Roi* ovec une Couple des Chivalx, pur carier les Femmes du Roi en une Chare de Eltham jusques Hertford"; see *Foedera*, ed. Rymer, vol. X, 387.

84 In a paper he was kind enough to share with me in draft, Robert Epstein notes the resemblance between certain passages of the disguising, the *Second Shepherds' Play*, and the Wakefield *Noah*; see "Lydgate's Mummings and the Aristocratic Resistance to Drama." These resemblances are part of a broader discursive similarity between the disguising and that strain of English poetry that focuses on rural satire; Epstein also notes the similarities between the text and such poems as "The Song of the Husbandmen" and "God Spede the Plough." Further, though Epstein does not draw this comparison, three characters in the "Disguising at Hertford" also appear in *Piers Plowman*: Thome Tynker (from passus 5, line 310), Pernelle, Berthilmewe the Butcher's wife and Phelyce, the waferer wife of Colle Tyler (characters named Pernele and Felice appear in passus 5, lines 26–29).

85 These sources have been traced by Wilhelm Cloetta, *Komödie und Tragödie im Mittelalter*, and include Isidore, Donatus, Vincent, Dante's *Epistle to Can Grande*, Dante's commentators. See also Patterson, *Chaucer and the Subject of History*, 242–43, and Kelly, *Chaucerian Tragedy*, 80–83. Kelly also describes various other twelfth-century versions of comedy, including Geoffrey of Vinsauf's in his *Documentum de Arte Versificandi*, who defines comedy as "cantus villanus de humilibus personis contextus, incipiens a tristicia et terminans in gaudio" ("a rustic song put together of humble persons, beginning in sadness and ending in joy"), much as Lydgate does. See Kelly, *Ideas and Forms*, 94–102, 99, and Lawlor, *Parisiana Poetria of John of Garland*, appendix 2, "The Two Versions of Geoffrey of Vinsauf's *Documentum*," 327–32, excerpt 4 (332). For discussions of medieval comedy, largely in terms of classical and more recent models, see the essays collected in Ruggiers, ed., *Versions of Medieval Comedy*. Ruggiers also analyzes Chaucer's use of comedy in Aristotelian terms in "A Vocabulary for Chaucerian Comedy: A Preliminary Sketch," 193–225. For a discussion of comedy in the Croxton *Play of the Sacrament* and the N-town Nativity play in relation to Jews and women, see Lampert, *Gender and Jewish Difference from Paul to Shakespeare*.

86 Isidore, *Etymologiae*, book 18, 46. See also Vincent of Beauvais, *Speculum Doctrinale*, book 11, chapter 95, 1046, for the repetition of Isidore's definition.

87 Vincent of Beauvais, *Speculum Historiale*, book 5, chapter 72, 158–59.

88 Vincent of Beauvais, *Speculum Doctrinale*, book 3, chapter 109, 287.

89 The translation is Kelly's (*Ideas and Forms of Tragedy*, 126).

90 For the relevant passages in Chaucer, see the *Miller's Tale*, line 3186; the *Legend of Good Women*, line 2703; the *House of Fame*, line 822; the *Manciple's Tale*, line 101; the *Merchant's Tale*, line 1594; the *Clerk's Tale*, lines 609, 733; and *Troilus and Criseyde*, book 3, line 254.

91 The notion of "wifely purgatorie" is also taken up by the Merchant, who has the wise counselor Justinius warn January that May may be his "purgatorie" (line 1670).

92 For a general discussion of the *Envoy*'s place in the *Canterbury Tales*, and a survey of scholarship on the text, see Chickering, "Form and Interpretation in the *Envoy* to the

Clerk's Tale." In *Chaucer and his Readers,* Lerer has argued that the Clerk's *Prologue* and *Envoy* held special significance for Lydgate, forming "the model of Lydgate's own practice in the *Fall of Princes* . . . as if Lydgate had read the *Clerk's Tale* for its drama rather than its moral" (39). Though he does not discuss the "Disguising at Hertford," its relevance to his argument is clear.

93 This passage from the *Clerk's Tale* clearly exerted a strong influence on Lydgate's imagination; the reference to "chichevache" (lean cow) is taken up by him in a poem, "Bycorne and Chichevache," that is often associated with the mummings. See the note to this line in the *Riverside Chaucer,* 883–84, for discussion of the word "chichevache." "Bycorne" is a fat beast who feeds on patient husbands; "chichevache" is a skinny animal who feeds on patient wives. Hammond, *English Verse from Chaucer to Surrey,* 113–15, explores the various forms of the name "Chichevache" and its textual history in the French tradition.

94 For example, Patterson argues that "What Chaucer's Wife wants is not political or social change; on the contrary, the traditional order is quite capable of providing the marital happiness she desires"; see *Chaucer and the Subject of History,* 282. In contrast, Scanlon argues that the Wife "disables" the antifeminist tradition; see his "What's the Pope got to do with it?," 165. Wallace has shown that, read in conjunction with Petrarch and Boccaccio's versions of the Griselda story, the *Clerk's Tale* mounts a powerful critique of tyranny (especially as it was represented by Petrarch), and thus is itself a political tale; my point here is merely that the allegorical reading of Griselda as "patience" is available to readers wishing to eschew the implications of that critique. See Wallace, *Chaucerian Polity,* 260–93.

95 Scott-Morgan Straker makes an analogous point about the relationship between Chaucer's depoliticized domestic narratives and Lydgate's tendency to "[make] the political implications of his narratives overt" ("Deference and Difference: Lydgate, Chaucer, and the siege of Thebes," 16), suggesting that "In Lydgate's work the move-ment is in the opposite direction: domestic crises require political resolutions" (15). This argument is clearly relevant to the "Disguising at Hertford," in which domestic strife is referred to the king for resolution.

96 Patterson, *Chaucer and the Subject of History,* 243.

97 Lydgate's use of the first person was first noted by Chambers in *Mediaeval Stage,* vol. I, 398; Wickham, *Medieval Theatre,* also remarks on it, commenting that the "Disguising at Hertford" "trembles on the brink of dialogue" (162); Pearsall, *John Lydgate,* 188, identifies it as a "striking innovation." Clopper, *Drama, Play and Game,* 163, remains unconvinced that the wives actually speak, arguing that the disguising "probably reflects a Hocktide game like that at Coventry."

98 see *MED,* s.v. "ple"; the word is defined as both "strife, contention, complaint" and "a legal conflict, case at law, lawsuit." These are clearly the literal senses in which Lydgate is using the term here.

99 See the *MED* definition for "pleie," which includes a wide range of meanings, includ-ing merriment, children's play, sexual play, theatrical plays, martial play, and joke play. Clopper points out that the term *play* did not mean "drama" in the contemporary sense of an acted, emplotted narrative on a stage, but rather that it referred more generally to modes of entertainment thought to give delight; see *Drama, Play and Game,* 12–17. See also Coldewey, "Plays and 'Play' in Early English Drama."

100 Green, "Three Fifteenth-Century Notes," 16, suggests that the "asure and golde" to which Lydgate refers is in fact a reference to Queen Katherine's alliance with Owen Tudor ("asure and golde" being the colors of the French royal arms), making the

"Disguising at Hertford" a "rather clumsy piece of contemporary satire." Pearsall, *John Lydgate (1371–1449)*, strongly disagrees, pointing out that Queen Katherine was a member of the king's household – and a very powerful one – until 1430, and arguing that it is "inconceivable that anyone, least of all Lydgate, would be making sly digs at her" (28). I am inclined to agree with Pearsall here, though the choice of "asure and golde" is suggestive.

101 Jill Mann reads the *Melibee* as a potential "core of the *Canterbury Tales*," arguing that the values of submission and "suffraunce," first elucidated through Melibee's submission to Prudence, and then to his enemies, are presented by Chaucer as a human ideal, a way of living in the world for both men and women; in this light, the Host's immediate turn to gendered, antifeminist comedy and interest in the Monk's sexual prowess illustrates the reaction of one man to the potentially world-altering lesson of the *Melibee*. See *Feminizing Chaucer*, 95–98.

102 In identifying the *Melibee* as a *Fürstenspiegel*, I am following Scanlon, who has described both it and the *Monk's Tale* in relation to the form, as part of a broader argument about Chaucer's development of a lay political discourse; see *Narrative, Authority and Power*, 206–29.

103 Wallace discusses the phrase "myghty man" in *Chaucerian Polity*, arguing that the Monk represents the Host's "fantasy of a virile man" and reflects the frequent desire of "male-dominated associational polity" for "strong and masterful men" (309–10). It is striking that the "Disguising at Hertford" does not articulate such a desire, though the "Disguising at London" 's evocation of Henry V falls into precisely the category defined by Wallace here.

104 James Simpson has argued that the comedy in the *Canterbury Tales* in fact falls into two types, the prudential comedy of the *fabliaux*, and the providential comedy of romance, a point illustrated by the contrast between the Wife of Bath's *Prologue* (bourgeois prudential comedy) and her *Tale* (providential comedy). His reading of the *Melibee*, like mine, sets it in opposition to the comic, in this case, the providential comedy of the *Tale of Sir Thopas*. Simpson is concerned to rehabilitate Chaucer's relationship to the romance, demonstrating that far from dismissing the form, Chaucer in fact explored the potential and limitations of providential comedy; in this reading, the *Clerk's Tale* becomes a comic tale, one that demonstrates that "Christian narrative is itself a romance" (321). The two forms of comedy are both rejected by the "Disguising at Hertford," as Lydgate's invocation of the Wife of Bath's *Prologue* and the *Clerk's Tale* shows. See Simpson, *Reform and Cultural Revolution*, 302–21.

4

Spectacular culture: the Roman triumph

In 1432, having been crowned in both England and France, Henry VI returned to his native soil to take up his reign as an adult. The minority, for which Lydgate had written so much and such varied verse, was officially over, though Henry VI would continue to be carefully supervised as he exercised his royal will. The citizens of London greeted their king with a lavish display as he processed through the streets, and unsurprisingly, one of the most vivid records we have of that occasion is a poem written by Lydgate, titled by MacCracken "Henry VI's Triumphal Entry into London."[1] The entry itself was one of the most splendid to have been mounted in England, in part as compensation for English losses in France, and in part to reassert the authority of the young king after a protracted absence.[2] Lydgate's poem is a mediated account of the events of the day; most likely written after the fact, it describes in detail the various pageants and tableaux that Henry VI encountered in his procession through London. The poem has attracted a certain amount of critical attention, as scholars have come to recognize that the royal entry was a crucial means by which medieval kings represented themselves to their subjects, a highly ordered and sophisticated cultural practice through which monarchical power was elaborated and constructed.[3] Like the practice of mumming, the royal entry also provided the occasion for the negotiation of the relationship between king and city, displaying each to the other in spectacular and public fashion. Indeed, the 1432 verses stand as an important cultural and historical document, revealing much about the poetic theatricality at the heart of late medieval urban culture.[4]

But the most significant lines in Lydgate's account are not, in fact, part of the poem's record of the entry's visual pyrotechnics. At the very end of the text Lydgate added a series of lines praising the king in his own voice, including a striking comparison between the king's entry and one of Caesar's triumphs: "Such ioye was neuere in the Consistorie, / Made ffor the tryvmphe with alle the surplusage, / Whanne Sesar Iulius kam home with his victorie" (lines 517–19). At first glance, Lydgate's comparison of Henry VI's entry to Caesar's triumph would appear to be simply one of many flattering tropes and images used on the 1432 occasion, which included allegorical figures (Nature, Grace, and Fortune, for example), illustrious ancestors (Saints Edward and Louis), symbolic animals (two antelopes), and biblical imagery (a Jesse tree), to name just a few.[5] Indeed, Lydgate's verses describe the typical medieval practices associated with royal entries, including the association of London with a "New Jerusalem" and the identification of the king as a type of Christ.[6] But his gesture to Caesar at the end constitutes a serious divergence from the relatively simple praise that makes up the majority of the poem. As my discussion of *Serpent of Division* in chapter 1 showed, no fifteenth-century evocation of Caesar could be simple or purely flattering.[7] By recalling Caesar's triumphs, Lydgate not only brings to mind a complex narrative of Roman history; he also references a long textual tradition of commentary and exegesis on Roman triumphs, one that existed side by side with royal entries over the course of the fourteenth century, but did not intersect with them in any explicit way. This written tradition would have been familiar to a wide audience of medieval listeners and readers; it was transmitted in a variety of exempla and sermon collections, and described the triumph in specific detail. Lydgate himself used this tradition in *Serpent of Division* to describe Caesar's triumph, drawing not on his primary source, Jean de Thuin, but instead on the iterations and reiterations of the exemplum to be found in Latin dictionaries, chronicles, and sermon handbooks. Thus, when he compares the 1432 entry to one of Caesar's triumphs – "whanne Sesar Iulius kam home with his victorie" – Lydgate fuses two distinct formal traditions, one written (the triumph as exemplum) and one spectacular (the royal entry), as a means of inserting the particular event into a legible historical narrative, one that can transform the youthful king into an exemplary figure much like his father: a latter-day Caesar, conqueror of France. Coupled with his description in *Serpent*, this comparison suggests an entirely new intersection between the textual and the real, between the Roman triumph as it appeared in sermon handbooks – as a popular exemplum – and the historical triumphs of both Caesar and the English kings. The notion that a king's entry resembles a Roman triumph seems obvious, not least because by the sixteenth century a whole variety of London spectacles – including royal entries, coronations, marriages, and Lord Mayor's shows – were intentionally modeled after the Roman practice.[8] But it was not so, and as I will show, in England it was not until Lydgate's account of Henry VI's 1432 entry that the connection was explicitly forged.[9]

As with so many of Lydgate's "propagandistic" works, his verses on Henry VI's entry, when examined closely, open a window on to a complex cultural history – this time, the history of the Roman triumph as exemplum and as cultural practice. In exploring that history, I have taken a different path than in the other chapters of this book; rather than exploring the meanings and implications of a set of texts in stasis (like the mummings or *Serpent of Division*), I have adopted a broadly diachronic view. Indeed, I return to *Serpent* and place it within this newly defined diachronic trajectory, shifting the kaleidoscope a bit to look at Lydgate, and a series of other poets and writers such as Holcot, Bromyard, Higden, and Gower, in a new way. With this shift, we can see the triumph exemplum signify over time in multifarious and complex ways, far in excess of the simple comparison between the entries of English king and Roman emperor. As such, it provides a signal instance of the capacity of form to acquire layers of meaning, the excavation of which can – and does – enable the construction of an alternative literary history, one that sees in Lydgate's minor writings merely the surface manifestations of deeply rooted social and aesthetic movements. Tracing a trope over time is a venerable practice. But despite that venerability, it remains no less capable of rendering old texts new again, of exposing countercurrents in the prevailing seas of literary-historical narrative. In this case, a look at the iteration of a single exemplum across two centuries captures the history of textual transmission and translation from Latin to vernacular from a slightly different angle – a shift in perspective that allows us to see texts like *Serpent of Division*, or Lydgate's verses commemorating the 1432 entry, as palimpsests overlying (and perhaps superseding) a variegated and multifaceted field of discourses and modes of representation.

In exploring that field, this chapter makes two related arguments. The first proposes that the triumph exemplum illustrates the emergence of a new interest in the classical past *as past* in the work of both Latin and vernacular writers of the fourteenth century, a past whose difference from the present provoked not the desire for assimilation (as in moralizing readings of pagan history), but an urge to analyze and classify. The second reads Lydgate's uses of the triumph exemplum – in *Serpent of Division* and especially in the 1432 verses – not only as vernacular illustrations of this historical impulse but also as crucial moments in the making of public culture, moments at which form, historicity, and spectacularity collide to produce a new place for the classical past in literary and dramatic history. All of the examples discussed here are small parts of much larger works and projects – entries in dictionaries, exempla in sermon handbooks, illustrations in biblical commentaries, narrative digressions – and as such have been largely overlooked in scholarly discourse. But the patterns they form, taken together, are significant – indeed, it is because of, and not in spite of, the seeming triviality of these shards of discourse that the argument that takes shape around them acquires a certain solidity. These bits of text – variations on a single theme – have a history worth writing. They are the workaday materials out of which English vernacular literature was forged, the mold that falls away to reveal the crafted object inside. And it is from the gradual accretion of such dross that something resembling a literary tradition becomes naturalized and familiar, becomes pedestrian, and is finally forgotten.

Although the first use of the word "triumph" in English appears as early as the ninth century, in the Ælfredian *Orosius*, it is not used again until the late fourteenth century, when it surfaces in a cluster of texts referencing the Roman practice.[10] The term may be found in Chaucer – in *Anelida and Arcite*, the *Man of Law's Tale*, and the *Monk's Tale* – and descriptions of the Roman triumph appear in book 7 of Gower's *Confessio Amantis*.[11] But by far the most elaborate treatment of a Roman triumph appears in *Serpent of Division*. Lydgate's interest in the exemplum is produced by the significance of the triumph within the narrative as a whole; it is the denial of a triumph to Caesar by Pompey that sparks the civil war and ultimately leads to the subjugation of Rome. Lydgate's description of the triumph, like *Serpent of Division* itself, reflects his interest in the classical past as both exemplar and other to the present, an interest that he derives in part from Chaucer and that is clearly evident in such works as *Troy Book* and *Siege of Thebes*.[12] It is this interest that would seem to undergird Lydgate's approach to the triumph, as an unfamiliar custom in need of an elaborate gloss. His impulse to define and explicate the words and practices of the Romans firmly assigns Caesar and his triumph to the realm of the unfamiliar, producing a distance between past and present, Roman and English, that belies the exemplary function of the text as a whole.

The triumph, Lydgate tells us, is a "treble gladnesse," "ordeyned for victors" (53, lines 14–15) that celebrates conquest in three ways. First, when the conqueror enters the city, he is greeted by "all the peplis of hiȝe estate and lowe" (53, line 19); second, he is surrounded in his procession by "fetrid and manaclid" (53, line 21) prisoners; and third, he is clothed in purple, with a crown of laurel, a necklace in the likeness of a palm, and a scepter topped with an eagle, and carried to the Capitol in a chariot drawn by four white steeds.[13] Lydgate's rendering contains what had become the standard elements of the triumph exemplum:

> Firste ȝe schall vndirstonde þat Triumphus bi descripcion is as mochell to seyne in pleyne englisch, as a treble gladnesse, or ellis a singulere excellens of Ioye in þre maner of wise, ordeyned for victors, which þorowȝe here hiȝe renovne and manly prowes hadde browȝte regions and Citeis be wey of knyȝtly conqueste to be soget and tributarie to þe Empire of Rome. And þe firste of þese iij worschippis done to a conquerrowre was þis: firste in his repeire to þe Citie, all the peplis of hiȝe estate and lowe schulde with grete Ioye & reuerence, in þer beste and richeste aray, mete him on þe waye; and þis was þe furste. The seconde was þis: þat all þe prisonneres, and þey þat weren in captiuite, schulde fetrid and manaclid gone rownde abowte environ his chare, some toforne and somme behynde. And þe þirde worschip done vnto him was þis, þat he schulde be clad in a purpurat mantell of Iubiter liche a god, and sitte with a crowne of lawrer vpon his hed in a riche chare of golde, and abowte his nekke in maner of a Cercle schulde environe abye made of golde in similitude and likenes of a palme. And [if so were þat his conqveste was accomplisshed and perfourmed withoute swerde or sheding of blood thanne shulde the coroune of þe palme] be forged withowte prikkes or spynis and ȝif so were þat his victori was fynisschid bi þe cruell fate of were þan of

custome his cercle or his pectorall was forgid full of scharpe prikyng
þornes to declare and specifie þat þer is none conqueste acomplischid
[fully] to þe fyne bi [mediacioun] of werre withoute þat þer be [felt
and found] therinne þe scharpe prikkynge thornes of aduersite and
þat oþer [bi deth] oþer bi pouerte. And þis riall and þis victorius chare
toforeseide was drawe with fowre white stedis þorowe the moste riall
stretis of þe Cite to þe chapitoile hauynge a septre in his honde full
richely devisid and þervppon in Signe of victori an Egle of golde.
(53, lines 13–34, 54, lines 1–3)

Lydgate's sources for the triumph episode are Isidore's *Etymologiae* and
Higden's *Polychronicon*, in the latter he found the basic outline of the
custom – the triple honor, the wretch, and the Greek admonition to
"Know thyself" – and from Isidore he took the further details of the
eagle-topped scepter, the use of palm, and the difference between
"triumph" and "trophe."[14] Similar accounts of Roman triumphs appear
in the *Gesta Romanorum, Fasciculus Morum*, in John Bromyard's *Summa
Praedicantium*, and Holcot's *Super Libros Sapientiae*, all thirteenth- and
fourteenth-century texts that were widely distributed, in written and oral
form. Each of these versions of the exemplum has something to reveal
about both Lydgate's version of the triumph and fourteenth-century
understandings of the classical past; each constitutes a small piece of
the larger puzzle being assembled here. Lydgate's turn to the triumph in
Serpent of Division and in "Henry VI's Triumphal Entry" is neither
arbitrary nor simple; both uses reflect new ways of thinking about the
classical past in relation to the present, and both form part of a complex
meditation on the relation between sovereign power and spectacular
display. But neither is comprehensible without a careful examination of
the triumph tradition from which Lydgate's representation emerged.
This chapter starts with the base texts of that tradition – Isidore's
Etymologiae and Hugutio of Pisa's *Derivationes* – and traces the development of the triumph exemplum in such texts as *Fasciculus Morum* and the
Gesta Romanorum, before turning to the more complex renderings of
Holcot, Bromyard, and Higden. These discussions form the basis for my
consideration of the vernacular tradition, which begins with Chaucer and
Gower and ends in 1432, at the moment at which the triumph at last
became "real," when Lydgate merged the royal entry with the exemplum
of the preachers, commentators, and historians.

DICTIONARIES AND ETYMOLOGIES: HISTORY IN WORDS

The two foundational sources for the triumph exemplum in the later Middle Ages are Isidore of Seville's *Etymologiae* and Hugutio of Pisa's *Derivationes*.[15] The version found in the *Derivationes* appears in slightly different forms in the *Gesta Romanorum* as well as in Higden's *Polychronicon*, the sermon tradition, Gower, and Lydgate.[16] Although Hugutio was clearly influenced by Isidore, he diverged significantly from the account of the triumph found in the *Etymologiae*, including some elements of Isidore's version but adding several new details from other classical and medieval sources. Both Isidore and Hugutio were drawing on an ancient tradition when they anatomized the triumph; classical writers had frequently mentioned triumphs, and each individual element of the Isidorean and Hugutian descriptions can ultimately be traced to a classical source, though there is no single classical text that synthesizes them all.[17] Most of the elements of Lydgate's version of the triumph are present in Hugutio; the line of transmission from the *Derivationes* to *Serpent of Division* is revealed by the precise repetition of phrases from the Latin dictionary, phrases that recur throughout the triumph tradition and that had clearly become conventional by the fifteenth century. The triumph, Hugutio explains, has "triplex leticia" (triple joy).[18] First, the triumphator enters the city and is greeted by the people "magno exultatione et magno gaudio"; second, the triumphator's chariot is followed by his captives, with their hands tied ("ligatis manibus"); and third, he wears the tunic of Jove ("tunica Iovis"), and four white horses ("quattuor equi albi") draw him to the Capitol. But the triumphator also confronts annoyances – "molestia[e]" – that temper the great joy ("magno gaudio") of the occasion; a slave is placed with him in the chariot, who hits him repeatedly, saying "nolisolitos," or "know yourself" ("nesce te ipsum") in Greek. This "molestia" occurs for two reasons, both to keep the triumphator from becoming proud ("ne ipse nimis superbiret"), and to give hope to men of "vilis condicionis" that they might achieve honor if they too are upright and honest. Finally, on the day of the triumph the people are permitted to say what they please to the triumphator, without punishment ("illa die licebat cuique dicere in personam triumphantis quicquid vellet"). This basic scenario is repeated over and over in the triumph tradition with minor variations and shifts of emphasis. Crucially, Hugutio never makes explicit the link between the behaviors of the Romans and contemporary Christian practices, nor does he turn to allegorical exegesis in order to assimilate and familiarize the alien elements of the pagan past. The only moment at which a potentially Christian reading surfaces – Hugutio's only commentary on the way the triumph makes meaning – occurs when he explains the function of the slave. In asserting that the presence of the slave gives hope to other men that they too may achieve merit, Hugutio diverges significantly from Isidore, whose account of the triumph is embedded in a meditation on the vagaries of fortune – in war and in spectacle – that runs throughout the chapter "De Bello et Ludis." Isidore describes the chastizing figure as a hangman – a misreading of Pliny's "carnifex" – and in his version the hangman simply serves as a reminder of the ultimate baseness of human existence; it is part of an overall notion of fortune that emphasizes the instability and contingency of the world.[19] In contrast, Hugutio's editorial remarks about the significance of the slave's speech and actions introduce a thesis about human agency and the capacity for self-knowledge ("nolisolitos") that provided moralists with the groundwork for a thoroughly allegorical reading.

In order to fully grasp the extent of the innovation wrought by Higden, Gower, and especially Lydgate in their versions of the triumph, it is important to examine what I am calling the "moral" tradition – the development of the triumph as an exemplum in sermon collections, devotional works, biblical commentaries, and the like. In focusing on the triumph, I will be pulling a single thread in a loosely woven but extremely intricate network of manuscripts and texts, sources, and contexts that might broadly be labeled "exemplary" but which includes a wide variety of materials and evinces a bewildering series of textual affiliations and connections. Though examining the triumph exemplum does shed some light on the nature of such connections, it cannot break through what have become scholarly impasses; for example, while a look at the triumph can help to show with some precision *how* texts like the *Fasciculus Morum* and the *Gesta Romanorum* are related, it does not address the problems of chronology and sequence – which redaction came first, and when each version originated – that scholars have struggled to resolve. What the triumph exemplum does reveal, however, is the wealth of material a poet like Lydgate would have drawn upon in fifteenth-century England, material that has received little scholarly attention and that is usually neglected in discussions of the emergence of vernacularity.

THE MORAL TRIUMPH: *FASCICULUS MORUM* AND
THE *GESTA ROMANORUM*

The versions of the triumph in such texts as *Fasciculus Morum* and the *Gesta Romanorum* appear "traditional" to modern readers because they are accompanied by moral or allegorical commentaries that render the specificities of the exemplum in highly abstract and theological terms. And in this sense, they do indeed represent a traditional form of hermeneutics with its roots in Augustine's *On Christian Doctrine* and in the letters of Paul. However, it is important to recognize the extent to which the use and collection of exempla was an emergent phenomenon in the late thirteenth and early fourteenth centuries. The content of the *Gesta Romanorum*, for example, may not have been particularly innovative, but neither was its form entirely traditional. While collections of exempla appeared in the late twelfth century – and while the use of exempla dates from the patristic period – it was in the thirteenth and fourteenth centuries that the wholesale production of exempla collections and sermon handbooks began; as Larry Scanlon and others have described, the growth of the exemplum form can be directly tied to the reforms of the Fourth Lateran Council and the emergence of mendicant preaching.[20] Indeed, it is because exemplary material proliferated so rapidly at this time that determinations of lines of influence and chronological sequence are so difficult to make. What is clear, however, is that compilations like *Fasciculus Morum* and *Gesta Romanorum* were part of a dynamic and energetic intellectual movement that sought to bridge the gap between clerical learning and lay spirituality by providing illustrative exempla for preachers and readers.

To begin, then, I will focus on two early texts in which the triumph is described that provide a baseline from which to evaluate the multiple versions of the exemplum scattered throughout fourteenth-century Latin and vernacular writing. These texts – *Fasciculus Morum* and the

192

Gesta Romanorum – do not function as sources in a simple sense for figures like Holcot, Bromyard, and Higden; though those authors clearly knew one or both of the compilations, there is strong evidence that they used other source texts – Hugutio and other classical and patristic texts – and rejected the specific moralizations (though not the practice of moralizing) to be found in the earlier redactions. But the two collections stand as the earliest versions of the triumph as an exemplum, and thus demonstrate the process by which Hugutio's and Isidore's historical descriptions were transformed into morally meaningful vignettes. In its own moment, the kind of exemplarity found in *Fasciculus* and the *Gesta* had not yet become hegemonic – and in England it is in these texts that the moralizing power of such exemplarity was first brought to bear on an alien and inscrutable past.

Judson Allen has argued that the early fourteenth century saw a shift in exemplarity, away from an emphasis on historical truth as manifested in biblical and patristic texts and toward secular and marvelous material drawn from a wide variety of sources.[21] While such a thesis must be approached with caution – after all, figures like Hugutio and Vincent of Beauvais testify to the abiding interest in the classical past found throughout the Middle Ages – a shift does seem to have occurred in the quantity and quality of engagements with antiquity, produced in part by the emergence of mendicant scholarship, which emphasized the practical applications of clerical learning. Beryl Smalley's fourteenth-century "classicizing friars" are perhaps the best examples of this tendency in England, but it was developing even earlier, as *Fasciculus Morum* and the *Gesta Romanorum* show. As writers of exemplary texts sought new material, they inevitably drew in stories and episodes from the pagan past, which were then subjected to moralization and rendered in familiar Christian terms. Such uses of classical material would have unintended consequences; the pagan past brought with it a whole series of ideological and philosophical questions that poets such as Chaucer, Gower, and Lydgate found attractive and troubling. But in collections like *Fasciculus* and the *Gesta*, such questions remain latent; the links between Christian moralization and antiquity are newly forged and thus appear deceptively simple. One reason that the triumph exemplum provides such a compelling case study is precisely because it resists that simplicity by virtue of its atypical status. Unlike most exempla, it is not a narrative. As a description of a cultural custom rather than a story about a character or exemplary figure (usually, in the *Gesta*, an "imperator") the triumph both accentuates the difference between past and present and highlights the hermeneutic at work in the exemplary tradition; in the absence of narrative's capacity to familiarize and domesticate the strangeness of the past by subjecting it to the conventions of storytelling, the authors of *Fasciculus Morum* and the *Gesta Romanorum* had to rely upon the sheer power of allegoresis in order to render the triumph meaningful within a Christian context.

While the origin, history, and date of both *Fasciculus* and the *Gesta* are difficult to pin down, what has become clear in the work of scholars such as Brigitte Weiske and Siegfried Wenzel is that both emerged in the late thirteenth century in England, and both became enormously influential over the course of the fourteenth century.[22] Wenzel argues, and Weiske concurs, that *Fasciculus Morum* precedes the *Gesta Romanorum* in its earliest form; according to this argument, the triumph exemplum that appears in the former text would constitute the earliest rendition of the triumph in England, and thus a potential source for all of its later iterations. But accurate dating is less important than establishing the intertextual network that can be glimpsed through the lens of the triumph exemplum, a network that forms the largely unspoken and uncited – perhaps even unconscious – substratum of later vernacular textual productions

It is obvious from the outset that *Fasciculus* is indebted to Hugutio, or to a Hugutian text. Though the *Fasciculus* version is shorter, it uses words and phrases directly taken from the *Derivationes*:

> Si ergo vestigia Christi sequi optamus, eodem modo oportet quod in seipso contumelias recipiat sicud honores. Et ecce hystoria ad hoc. Legitur in *Gestis Romanorum* quod si aliquis strenuus foret in civitate qui trina vice pro civitate pungnasset et vicisset, quod triplex honor sibi debebatur: primo quod sederet in curru deaurato et quatuor equi albi ipsum traherent per civitatem; secundo quod inimici eius ad dictum currum afflicti ligarentur; tercio quod duceretur ad templum Iovis et ibi tunica dei sui indueretur. Set ne de hiis superbirent, tria opprobria eadem die et tempore sustinerent: primum, quod servus

quidam rurissime condicionis iuxta eum sederet equalis honoris cum
eo; secundum, quod hic servus eum colaphizaret dicens, "Nothos
olitos," idest cognosce teipsum; <tercium>, quod illo die inimici
eius contra ipsum dicerent <impune> quicquid vellent.

(If we then wish to follow in Christ's footsteps, we must in the same
way as he did accept for ourselves reproaches as well as honors.
A story relevant to this appears in the *Deeds of the Romans*, where it is
reported that if there was a hardy champion in the City who had
fought for it and won a victory three times, he deserved a threefold
honor: first, he was to sit in a golden chariot and four white horses
were to draw him through the City; second, his enemies were in
their defeat to be bound to his chariot; and third, he was to be led
to the temple of Jupiter and there clothed in the cloak of his god.
But that he should not be too proud in these honors, he was to suffer
threefold shame on the same day: first, a slave of the lowest class was
to sit next to him in equal honor; second, this slave was to strike him
and say, "Gnothi seauton," that is, "Know thyself"; and third, on
that day his enemies could with impunity say anything they wanted
against him.)[23]

Like Hugutio, the *Fasciculus* author describes three honors and three
"opprobria," though they are neither precisely the same nor in the same
order.[24] In particular, the words of the slave to the triumphator,
"Nothos olitos" recall Hugutio's description: "Et ideo ut daretur spes
unicuique quantumcumque vilis condicionis esset perveniendi ad similem honorem si probitas sua promereretur, dicebat semper 'nolisolitos'
id est 'nosce teipsum,' quasi noli superbire de tanto honore."[25] But the
Fasciculus version compresses the Hugutian text, eliminating the reasons Hugutio gives (that others may hope for honor and so that the
triumphator not become arrogant) for the slave's presence in the
chariot, thus stripping the exemplum to its bare bones in order to
open the conceptual space for allegory to work. It does so in a relatively
straightforward fashion, identifying the triumphator as the self, strug-
gling against the flesh, the world, and the devil and glossing such details
as the four wheels of the chariot as the four cardinal virtues – an
allegorical practice that will continue, in a different way, in the *Gesta
Romanorum*.

If, as Wenzel's dating suggests, *Fasciculus* was a source for the *Gesta*,
we might expect to find that the triumph exemplum in the latter

strongly resembles the former, and indeed it does.[26] But there is one crucial difference. Where the *Fasciculus* account truncates the Hugutian model, eliminating the reasons he gives for the appearance of the slave, the *Gesta* quotes Hugutio with some precision:

> Ne cum hiis honoribus oblivisceretur sui, triplicem molestiam oportebat illum sustinere. Prima est, quod cum eo ponebatur in curru quidam servilis condicionis, ut daretur spes cuilibet quantumcumque vilis condicionis pervenire ad talem honorem si probitas mereretur. Secunda molestia erat, quod iste servus eum colaphizabat, ne nimis superbiret, et dicebat: Nosce te ipsum et noli superbire de tanto honore! Respice post te et hominem te esse memento! Tercia molestia erat, quod illa die licebat cuilibet dicere in personam triumphantis quicquid vellet, scilicet omnia obprobria victori.

> (Lest, with these honors, he might forget himself, it was necessary for him to endure a triple annoyance. The first is, that a certain person of vile condition was placed with him in the chariot, so that hope might be given to anyone of vile condition that he might attain such an honor if his honesty merited it. The second annoyance was that this slave hit him, so that he would not become too arrogant, and said, "Remember yourself, and do not become proud of such honor. Look behind you and remember that you are a man." The third annoyance was that on that day it was permitted that anyone should say whatever he wished against the person of the triumphator, that is, all sorts of insults.)[27]

The *Gesta* version is far closer to the Hugutian text than that found in *Fasciculus,* except in one detail: the use of the Greek phrase "nolisolitos." In the *Derivationes,* the slave says "nolisolitos" and Hugutio explains ("id est") what the word means. In the *Gesta* the phrase has been removed and replaced with a quotation from Tertullian's *Apologeticus,* "Respice post te et hominem te esse memento" ("Look behind you and remember that you are a man"). Despite the fact that the latter phrase has traditionally been associated with triumphs in later renderings of the practice (including in recent scholarship), "respice post te" in fact appears very late in the tradition; not until Tertullian's *Apologeticus* in the second century – which does not describe an actual triumph in historical terms, but uses the image of the triumph in order to mount an argument against the divinity of emperors – does the slave in the chariot speak.[28]

The *Gesta* author thus turns to Tertullian in order to produce a version of the triumph susceptible to Christian exegesis, a process that begins in the *Apologeticus*, where the Roman practice is used in an exemplary rather than an historical fashion. In contrast, both Isidore and Hugutio emphasize, to different degrees, the historicity of their accounts; both present themselves as translators, mediators between past and present, who provide readers with a means of understanding the Roman past on its own terms. Hugutio's use of the pseudo-Greek "nolisolitos" – deliberately excised in the *Gesta* – functions synecdoch-ally as an emblem of the alien nature of Roman customs; triumphs, that is, require translation in order to be legible to medieval readers. The *Gesta* author too is engaged in a process of translation, in the continuing project of reimagining the classical past as always already Christian, Christian in spite of itself. But the two projects are funda-mentally at odds. The *Gesta*'s quotation from Tertullian lays the groundwork for the moralization to follow, in which Hugutio's expla-nations for the function of the slave – to prevent the triumphator from becoming proud and to give hope to other men – are superseded, replaced by an allegorical reading that erases the secular meaning of the Hugutian text: "Secunda molestia erat quod servi eum colaphiza-bant. Sic Judei Christo fecerunt dicentes: Prophetisa nobis, quis est, qui te percussit?" ("The second annoyance was the slave that was hitting him. So the Jews hit Christ, saying, 'prophesy to us, who is it that struck you?'"). By substituting the figures of Christ and the Jews for trium-phator and slave, the *Gesta* author radically transforms the meaning of the text, putting in place a hermeneutic by which the transcendence of Christian narrative over the historical world of facts and events is asserted and authorized. Rome serves simply as the locus for a set of symbols that signify a more profound and universal meaning; the letter – the triumph – falls away, replaced by the endlessly iterable story of Christ's passion.

In the end, the compilers of the *Gesta Romanorum* and *Fasciculus Morum* perform the same operation upon the text of the exemplum; the description of the triumph retains a certain integrity throughout, but its meaning is subject to change depending on the rhetorical purpose to which it is put. The interpretive freedom such changes signal illumin-ates an aspect of exemplarity infrequently emphasized. Once the initial act of moralization has occurred – once the original text has been subjected to the exemplary impulse – it becomes a flexible and plastic signifier, available to a wide variety of rhetorical intentions and constructions. Most importantly, perhaps, the turn to exemplarity in the *Gesta* tradition marks a turn away from the historicity of the triumph that was preserved in both Isidore and Hugutio's accounts – a historicity that depended upon the notion of linguistic stability subtending the very enterprise of the *Etymologiae* and *Derivationes*. In both cases the description of the triumph is produced by a definitional impulse that begins from the word "triumphus" itself; it is to define this term that Isidore and Hugutio engage in narrativizing the Roman practice. To be sure, the process of definition is merely one strategy among many possible tactics for organizing a large mass of data. But as a mode of representation it calls upon history in a very specific way: the past is rhetorically understood to be intact as past, to be translatable but not transformable. Even though Hugutio's account differs significantly from Isidore's, he presents the triumph as if it were a set of facts recounted from history that are of necessity tied to the word itself. In contrast, the moralized versions of the exemplum – which do not use the term "triumph" – function as a means to an end, a kind of double exemplarity. On the one hand, the exemplum provides a starting point for a creative and imaginative use of allegory, which subjects the texts to various forms of exegesis in an attempt to derive a Christian meaning. That meaning, however, resists the historicity of the exemplum and asserts its own univocality, insisting upon the transcendence of the spirit over the letter and betraying its lack of interest in the past as past.[29]

Dominant though this type of exemplarity was in the early fourteenth century, however, there were intertwined with it (and at moments, indistinguishable from it) competing modes of exemplary representation that challenged the moral tradition in specifically historical terms. What I will describe in the next section is only a tiny portion of a very understudied body of work, one that has critical ramifications for the writing of English vernacular literary history. Beryl Smalley first coined the phrase "classicizing friars" to describe what she saw as a minor intellectual movement in the early to mid-fourteenth century, characterized by a new interest in the classical past, in its texts and histories.[30] Figures such as John Ridewall, Robert Holcot, Thomas Waleys, and Nicholas Trivet, as well as others, form a coherent (if somewhat diffuse) group of thinkers undertaking the project of engaging with antiquity in a new way, through chronicle histories, biblical and classical commentaries, exempla collections, and treatises of various kinds. To Smalley's group should be added the Dominican John Bromyard and the Benedictine monk Ranulph Higden, each of whom, to different extents, was also reshaping the genre in which he worked – the sermon handbook for Bromyard and the universal history for Higden. Much work remains to be done on these figures, and I can only gesture here toward the enormous significance they had for later vernacular writers by examining the work of three of them. Before looking at Higden's *Polychronicon*, I will turn to Holcot and Bromyard, each of whom used the triumph exemplum in radically different ways from *Fasciculus Morum* and the *Gesta* (and from each other as well), signaling a slight shift in the representation and iteration of the classical past – a shift that both gestured forward, to later poets, and backward, to the authority of antiquity.

CLASSICAL PAST, ENGLISH PRESENT: *SUPER LIBROS SAPIENTIAE* AND THE *SUMMA PRAEDICANTIUM*

One of the most elaborate iterations of the triumph exemplum appears in Robert Holcot's commentary on the Book of Wisdom, *Super Libros Sapientiae*. Holcot represents a particularly important – if rarely discussed – figure for understanding the line of influence I will argue extends from Higden through Gower to Lydgate, a line in which the classical past is both articulated *as past* and mined for its relevance, in a secular sense, to the present. Although Holcot's scholarly practices were not atypical of his historical moment, a close examination of his use of the triumph exemplum will confirm Smalley's fundamental assertion that his mode of "classicizing" differed from the exemplary tradition as it appeared in sermons and compilations, and as it has usually been understood in contemporary scholarship.[31]

As a commentary on the Book of Wisdom, Holcot's *Super Libros Sapientiae* specifically addresses political questions of right rulership and kingship; as Smalley notes, it was preceded in some manuscripts by a note making the "public" form of the text explicit:

> Although wisdom is found in each part of Holy Scripture, it is contained especially and in a particular form in this book [the Book of Wisdom], where kings and princes are instructed on the worship of God and on right conduct.[32]

At the same time, the commentary was written as part of a series of lectures given at Oxford or Cambridge and designed to train students as preachers; it is divided into lectiones and refers specifically to certain dates, as if the text was to be read on specific occasions.[33] The Wisdom commentaries were enormously popular, "a standard part of the equipment of every good theological library in the later middle ages," and would have been read by preachers, scholars, and poets alike, as Chaucer's use of the text (in the *Nun's Priest's Tale*) shows.[34] As such, Holcot's representation of the triumph exemplum is particularly significant. If the exemplum form does indeed, in Larry Scanlon's terms, transform "fallen historical reality" into "moral value," we would certainly expect to find such a transformation at work in Holcot's text, a doubly exemplary work aimed at both a clerical audience and a lay audience.[35] What his use of the triumph shows, however, is another impulse – a desire, like Isidore and Hugutio, to allow for and preserve the integrity of the past.

The triumph exemplum appears in lectio 164, as part of a commentary on Wisdom 14.17, which concerns idols. Holcot's commentary on this text is typically wide-ranging, filled with a variety of exempla and multiple gestures to authorities both classical and biblical – Aristotle, Helinand, Seneca, the Old Testament and the New Testament. Smalley attributes this capaciousness to Holcot's lighthearted understanding of his role as scholar, arguing that he "chose the role of romancer and *raconteur*" rather than striving for "exact scholarship" – a too simple assessment that nonetheless helpfully pinpoints his fundamentally *poetic* grasp of the relation between classical past and biblical precedent. Lectio 164 appears at first glance to be a mélange of somewhat carelessly assembled illustrations for the Wisdom text, one whose ordering principle resembles an associative train of thought rather than an orderly exposition of doctrine. But it is precisely those links and associations forged by Holcot that produce the text's poetic logic. It is a logic, I will argue, that bears a particular relationship to an emergent understanding of the ways in which the past might signify in the present, a very different understanding than that we find, for example, in the *Gesta Romanorum*. Smalley's articulation of the "classicizing" movement among friars in the first half of the fourteenth century provides a starting point as well as a helpful field of reference; Holcot is hardly alone in his interest in antiquity, as the examples of Thomas Waleys, John Ridewall, Nicholas Trivet, and others show. My use of Holcot's Wisdom commentaries here is a metonymic one, in that I will look in a limited fashion at a single lectio, and within that lectio, at a single exemplum. But what this slice of Holcot's text reveals is instructive; it demonstrates the intersection of Latin and vernacular within the broad aesthetic developments of the fourteenth and fifteenth centuries, revealing how intimately related the ideas of vernacular poets such as Chaucer and Gower were to those of Latin commentators and scholars.

The passage from Wisdom that forms the basis for lectio 164 links the making of images to kingship and forms part of a larger condemnation of idolatry. Holcot dilates upon the inherent ambivalence of this link between reverence for the king and the sinful worship of images – after all, the practice of image-making pervaded medieval culture, both secular and clerical alike – by turning to the related, but perhaps less fraught, topic of honor. If the first cause of image-making was the excessive love of men for friends and parents, the second (and far more problematic) cause was the pride and ambition of kings for gifts and honors ("superbia et vana ambitio regum et principum ad donationes et honores"). In the remainder of the lectio, Holcot explores the meaning of honor as both a positive and a negative social force, drawing a distinction between righteous forms of honor (for king, parents, and neighbors) and false honors such as clothing, sacrifices to pagan gods, and earthly wealth. Each step in the argument is illustrated by exempla that demonstrate for readers how the definitions of honor being proffered might apply to various historical scenarios, particularly involving kings and bishops. Nebuchadnezzar's demand in Judith 3.13 that Holofernes destroy all the gods of the earth so that he might be worshipped as the only god is adduced as evidence that kingly desire for honor leads to idolatry; in contrast, a prior of Clairvaux who refuses a bishopric illustrates the wisdom of resisting earthly rewards. The triumph exempla are embedded within this broad frame of honor and idolatry; in the simplest sense, their relevance to the Wisdom passage is derived from the fact that they describe honors granted to victors and thus historicize the biblical text. But Holcot's use of the triumph is in fact a particularly good illustration of the complexity of his relation to the classical past, as well as a signal instance of the distinctive method of exposition that characterizes his commentary. He repeats *both* the Isidorean and the Hugutian versions of the exemplum, a repetition that not only suggests that he found it an especially relevant text, but also points to a certain ambivalence about Roman customs and practices, an ambivalence amply illustrated elsewhere in the lectio.

A close examination of the way in which Holcot presents the triumph suggests that the twofold exemplum is part of a broader methodological binarism, in which positive and negative illustrations and dicta are paired as a way of both exhausting the topic at hand and of resisting the immediate historical implications of the texts being subjected to exegesis. The traditional triumph exemplum – the Hugutian text – appears first, following Holcot's meditation on a passage from the *City of God*, which describes how the Romans built two temples, one to honor and one to virtue; by tradition, no one was permitted to enter the temple of honor unless he first visited the temple of virtue. Though the two temples might easily stand as examples of pagan idolatry, particularly given the passage from Wisdom being glossed here, Holcot (and Augustine) choose to interpret the Roman passage metaphorically, as a positive exemplum rather than as an alien historical practice. Similarly, Holcot's use of the triumph exempla oscillates between the allegorical, assimilative mode found in texts like the *Gesta*, and a more historical – and more negative – iteration of Roman culture as subject to Christian judgment. But even at those moments in which Holcot appears to be embracing the allegorical mode – in which the triumph stands in for some other, more profound meaning – he does not elucidate specific connections between details of the Roman custom and various allegorical significances (Christ as triumphator, for example). Instead, the Hugutian version is briefly introduced and minimally glossed:

> Unde Ro. II. Honor et pax omni operanti bonum. Et quisquis honor debeatur virtuti sicut premium quiddam insufficiens: tum nihilominus honor plerusque derogat virtuti dum mentes honor in superbiam nititur eleuare. Et ideo ad istam pestem rationabiliter euitandam legimus quod victoribus triumphantibus et rhomam redeuntibus triplex honor impendabatur et triplex iniuria inferebatur.

> (Romans II [says]: Honor and peace to every man who does good. And whatever honor is owed to virtue as a [kind of] reward is insufficient: then nevertheless honor detracts from virtue for the most part, so long as honor strives to raise the minds to pride. And therefore, in order to avoid this disease rationally, we read that a triple honor was paid and triple annoyance was suffered by triumphant victors returning to Rome.)[36]

If honor does indeed detract from virtue ("derogat virtuti"), then the three "inuriae" of the triumph constitute a rational response to the disease of pride – a response, moreover, that "we read" ("legimus"). Holcot's direct first-person citation of the audience for his commentary, "legimus," suggests strongly that the metaphorical mode subtending Augustine's description of the temples of honor and virtue has collapsed, replaced by a metonymic historicism in which the *similarity* between past and present – signaled by the gesture toward an all-encompassing "we" – overrides the alienating divide between the pagan practices of the Romans and contemporary Christian morality. It is this refusal to acknowledge the otherness of the past that seems to "medievalize" Holcot's text and to confirm Smalley's assertion that the classicizing friars of the fourteenth century "did not periodise history, making some ages 'bad,' but enjoyed all equally."[37]

But "legimus" is one word among many, and Holcot's description of the triumph is far more thorough than any found in similarly "medievalized" exempla collections. If he betrays a desire to familiarize the past, he also reveals an equal and opposite impulse, similar to that found in Isidore and Hugutio, to render it in its full and unfamiliar complexity. At the end of his description of the three honors and three injuries given to the victor, for example, Holcot refers to Julius Caesar: "Unde Iulio cesari reuertenti post multas victorias fuereunt gravissime contumelie dicte, nulla penitus ultione sequente" ("Wherefore the most grave insults were said to Julius Caesar, as he returned after so many victories, and no punishment at all followed"). This detail of the insults shouted at Caesar during his triumph does not appear in any of the exempla collections or sermons discussed above; it is taken from Ranulph Higden's *Polychronicon*, which in turn derives the incident directly from Hugutio's *Derivationes*.[38] Neither Holcot nor Hidgen reproduces Hugutio's text in full, perhaps because it seemed confusing (or unspeakable); the story refers to the rumor that Caesar committed sodomy with King Nicomedes in Bithynia; during his subsequent triumph, the crowd supposedly shouted "regina."[39] Higden leaves out the references to Bithynia (though he includes them in his account of Caesar's life later in the *Polychronicon*) and merely records (with a touch of humor) the crowd's sarcastic "Salve, calve!" and "Ave, Rex et Regina!"; Holcot in turn simply asserts that "gravissime contumeliae" were shouted.[40] Leaving aside for the moment the more general significance of Higden's account, to which I return below, it must be noted that the puzzling nature of Holcot's inclusion of this detail confounds the expectations that the beginning of the commentary have set in place. If the exemplum from the *City of God* implied that the triumph exemplum was to function allegorically, as in the *Gesta*, the citation of Caesar introduces a new principle of reading. The thematic point, that honor must be tempered with injury in order to prevent excessive pride, is proven historically rather than allegorically; the point of reference becomes an actual Roman rather than a Christian abstraction (the soul, the flesh) or a figure from salvation history (Christ, the devil). History, Holcot suggests, is adequate *in itself* as a demonstration of the truth of his assertions about honor. In part, Holcot's use of Caesar seems to confirm the apparent slide into metonymy that began with "legimus," evoking an unbroken link between the rulers of the past – with the genealogy of Caesar stretching forward to contemporary England – and the need to temper honors in the present. But it also suggests a different kind of historical thinking, one in which the concrete example from the past not only illustrates a maxim, but also is meaningful in and of itself, as history and not as allegory, and thus functions as a crucial nodal point in Holcot's text – and by extension, in the trajectory I am defining here.

To be sure, this alternate mode of thinking history is no more than a suggestion; the idea that instances from the classical past may be used to illustrate moral points forms the very basis of the exemplarity that flourished in texts like *Fasciculus* and the *Gesta*. In and of itself, it merely demonstrates the assimilative power of the allegorical operation. But Holcot's use of his sources reveals a fundamentally different impulse at work in the text. Immediately after citing Caesar, he turns to Isidore:

> Aliter aliquantulum de isto honore scribit Isidorus viii ethymo. ca. ii et allegat tranquillum dicentem quod triumphus dicitur ab eo quia triumphans cum urbem ingrederetur: tripertito iudicio honorabatur.[41]

> (Isidore writes a little about this honor in a different way in *Etymologiae* 7, chapter 2, and cites Suetonius, saying that a triumph is so called from the fact that when the triumphator enters the city he was honored by a threefold judgment.)

Holcot has read Higden's text, which opens by citing both Isidore and Hugutio – "Isidorus, libro octavo decimo, capitulo de triumphis, et Hugutio, capitulo Tris."[42] But the *Polychronicon*'s account of the triumph in fact relies solely on Hugutio; like Lydgate after him, Holcot turns directly to Isidore for further details of the Roman practice. Rather than integrating the separate versions, however, Holcot is content to let the Hugutian and Isidorean accounts stand side by side, exposing their differences and resisting the impulse to assimilate the historical contradictions that emerge from the pairing. He does so in order to exploit the didactic potential of the two versions; by coupling the triumph exempla, Holcot sets in place a method of doubling that fundamentally shapes his mode of argument in the lectio overall. Positive exempla are paired with negative exempla, producing a curiously ambivalent effect even while imposing a relatively sturdy structure on the mass of material comprising the commentary. This doubling, of course, is a form of argument by opposition, a familiar scholastic technique and one used extremely effectively by Holcot here. As a result, the passage from Isidore ultimately functions as the negative counter to the Hugutian version. If the first triumph account illustrated the rational response of the Romans to giving honors, with the three "inuriae" constituting an appropriate curb to the pride of the triumphator, the second represents a dangerously unbalanced combination of glory and restraint, so much so that Holcot ultimately glosses the text with a biblical verse. Isidore's account includes a long list of the accoutrements worn and carried by the triumphator; Holcot's version emphasizes these adornments by iterating and reiterating their use:

> Erat autem mos rhomanorum ut triumphans quadrigis veheretur colore rufo perlinieretur purpura et palmata toga indueretur. Palma aurea vel lauro coronaretur scipione seu sceptro super quod sedebat aquila ornaretur. Et istis omnibus preparatis ei carnifex pro socio preponeretur. Ideo vero in quadriga vehebatur. Quia illo genere vehiculi primi proeliantes vtebantur. Ideo colore rubeo perliniebatur quasi divini ignis invictam effigiem imitaretur. Ideo super scipionem siue sceptrum aquilam habebat eo quod per victoriam ad summam magnificentiam ascendebat. Coronabatur corona palmea, si in bello vel in conflictu triumphasset. Palma autem aculeos habet et significat conflictum. Coronabatur corona laurea si sine conflictu contingeret triumphare videlicet hostes sine pugna fugando. Quia laurus aculeos vel spinas non habet. A carnifice contingebatur ut ad tantum fastigium euectus mediocritatis humane conmoneretur.

> (It was, however, the custom of the Romans that the triumphator was carried by a team of four, was smeared with red color, and was dressed in a purple and palm-embroidered toga. He was crowned with golden palm or laurel and was adorned with a staff or scepter upon which an eagle was sitting. When all these things had been prepared, a scoundrel was placed before him as a companion. So, he was carried in the chariot because the first centurions were carried in that type of vehicle. He was smeared with red color as if he were imitating an indelible image of divine fire. He had an eagle on top of his staff or scepter because he was ascending through victory to the height of magnificence. He was crowned with a crown of laurel if he happened to triumph without battle – that is, by routing the enemies without fighting – because laurel does not have pricks or spines. He was touched by the scoundrel so that, having been elevated to such dignity, he would be reminded of the meanness of human life.)

Just as in the *Gesta* version, each detail of the Isidorean triumph carries a specific meaning relevant to the triumph as a whole – as a signifying unit with an entire series of subordinate elements that contribute variously to the overall import of the event.[43]

But these meanings are not transhistorical: they are embedded in a distinctively Roman past, a past that does not work according to a Christian moral logic. In the same way that he resists the allegorizing drive familiar to him from texts like the *Gesta* in recounting the Hugutian triumph, Holcot is content – for the most part – to let the Isidorean text stand without invoking salvation history or Christian abstraction. However, the Isidorean triumph fundamentally differs from the Hugutian text; in it Holcot confronted an account in which symbolic meanings had already been assigned to the performative details of the Roman practice – symbols whose referents were not Christian but pagan, not moral but ideological. What is surprising about Holcot's response to this version, then, is that he does not attempt to assign Christian significance to the various elements of the triumph. Indeed, he *enhances* the import of Isidore's allocation of symbolic meaning by repeating several details twice, the first time declaratively and the second time with an explanatory phrase beginning "ideo" ("for that reason"). The red color of the triumphator, the staff, the crowns of palm and laurel, and the hangman are all introduced and meticulously explained. Nothing is added to Isidore's text, but the overall effect of Holcot's revision – the reiteration of each detail – is to emphasize the alien quality of the Roman customs. Just as in Isidore, the red color signifies divine fire, the crowns of palm and laurel reveal what kind of victory the triumphator has achieved, the staff indicates the height of magnificence to which he will ascend. These are *historical* meanings conferred by the Romans for the Romans and described by Holcot in an anthropological rather than a moral sense. Indeed, he passes over an ideal opportunity to condemn idolatry (the ostensible subject of the commentary) when he explains the meaning of the "color[is] ruf[i]."

There is in Holcot's rewriting of Isidore's account a consciousness of the past as alien, other, and complete unto itself; it is a consciousness wholly absent from texts like the *Gesta Romanorum*. It is, however, produced less by a genuine interest in the *facta* of the Roman past (the one detail Holcot leaves out of Isidore's text, for example, is a brief digression explaining the staff) and more by a notion of fidelity to his source texts. Holcot's historicism is a *literary* phenomenon; having seen in Higden the citation to Isidore, he is compelled to look it up, and equally driven to record it with some accuracy. This is not to say, however, that Holcot has any notion of objectivity in relation to the past; he still regards his Roman exempla as subject to positive and negative moral judgments. It is merely to suggest that his literary practice – his method of exposition – is subtended by an understanding of the classical past very different from that found in the exemplary tradition with which he is associated.

Lest the case be overstated, however, it should be remarked that although Holcot reproduces the historical symbolism of Isidore's text, he embeds it within a formal structure that produces a moral reading – the doubling or pairing of positive and negative exempla I noted above. At the very end of the Isidorean exemplum, Holcot appends a gloss from Ecclesiasticus to the description of the hangman: "Ac si sibi diceretur illud Eccl. xj. In vestitu ne glorieris unque: nec in die honoris tui extollaris" ("as if it was said to him from Eccl. 11, 'Glory not in apparel at any time, and be not exalted in the day of thy honor' " [Douay-Rheims translation]). This passage marks a departure from the strict reportage of the remainder of the exemplum; not only is Holcot suggesting what the hangman might have said ("ac si"), he is also retrospectively commenting on the triumph as a whole. Unlike the Hugutian version, in which the triumph itself contains its own discursive critique (the words of the slave), the Isidorean triumph is entirely visual. It relies on surfaces and appearances, clothing, adornments, and trappings to communicate its meaning. It is this one-dimensionality – a certain interest in exterior form – that compels Holcot both to supply a content (what the hangman might have said) and to condemn the triumph itself. The verse from Ecclesiasticus provides the ideal gloss, allowing the exemplum to stand as the negative counterweight to the three honors and three injuries of its double. In the end Holcot subordinates what might be called his "literary historicism" to the moralizing energies of his exegesis. But the Isidorean exemplum remains, along with the claim it makes upon the past *as* past – a claim that Holcot may ultimately resist but one that exerts a profound pull on his vernacular inheritors. Holcot's doubles, that is, do not advance an argument in any philosophical or theological sense. They simply demand from the reader a response to the words on the page, one that notes the oppositions and engages curiously with the unfamiliar and the alien, the past and its strangeness.

If Holcot marks a turn away from the exemplarity of the *Gesta* tradition, an equally distinct – though very different – departure can be found in John Bromyard's *Summa Praedicantium*, one of the most influential preaching handbooks of the fourteenth century and an important, though hardly noted, precursor for Gower and Lydgate's iterations of the triumph. A full consideration of Bromyard's influence on vernacular English writing has never been written, in part because of the unavailability of the text, and I can only gesture here toward some of the ways in which his rendition of a single exemplum anticipates the dominant philosophical concerns of the late fourteenth and early fifteenth centuries. Like Holcot's *Super Libros Sapientiae* and the *Gesta Romanorum*, Bromyard's text is a product of the first half of the fourteenth century, and like them, it is replete with exempla both classical and Christian.[44] On first look, the *Summa* resembles Hugutio's *Derivationes*; it is organized alphabetically by topic, ranging from "avaritia" to "iudicium" to "tribulatio." But the two texts are epistemologically very different. If Hugutio was interested in defining an authoritative and historical meaning for words and concepts, Bromyard is primarily concerned with exegesis and exemplarity. He assembles under various rubrics – such as "tribulatio" – a whole series of *distinctiones*, or divisions, that illustrate the theme from various angles with different exempla and authorities.[45] This alphabetical method for ordering compilations for preachers emerged in the late thirteenth century and flourished in the fourteenth century; Bromyard's was one of the most influential of these texts.[46] In this model, the exemplum itself is entirely subordinated to the major theme and its subdivisions, which are designed to provide the preacher with both the structure and the component parts of his sermon; the exempla may be selected or rejected based on their usefulness to the task at hand. Bromyard specifically denies any interest in the truth or falsity of the exempla he deploys: "Istud non adduco pro veritate hystoriali – quam [fabulam] non credo veram; sed pro tanto valet ad propositum" ("I do not adduce it for its historical truth, as I do not believe the story true, but insofar as it fits the purpose").[47] Ultimately, the formal similarity between Bromyard's text and Hugutio's dictionary can only be viewed as a structural analogue; the purpose and method of the *Summa* are far removed from the historical impulse at work in the *Derivationes*. At the same time, though it shares some ideological and methodological similarities with collections like the *Gesta*,[48] Bromyard's text finds its closest analogue in Holcot's commentary, in that it assembles exempla and citations from the Bible and other authorities in a thematic rather than an allegorical way, stitching together an argument from a wide variety of texts. But as a look at his version of the triumph will show, unlike Holcot, Bromyard ruthlessly subordinates his exempla to the task at hand.

Given its status as an encyclopedic resource for preachers, it is unsurprising that the *Summa*'s version of the triumph is far more learned than those found in the *Gesta* and in *Fasciculus Morum*. Bromyard has embedded the exemplum in a long analysis of "tribulatio," drawing on a set of biblical texts and on St. Gregory's *Moralia* in order to articulate the spiritual meaning of worldly tribulation; what captures his interest about the triumph has little to do with the Roman past or with the fourteenth-century present. It is, rather, the fact that the triumphator endures various *tribulations* that makes the exemplum relevant to Bromyard's overriding purpose. He quotes Gregory's *Moralia* in order to establish his theme:

> Sicut, inquit, vnguenta latius redolere nesciunt, nisi commota. Et sicut aromata fragrantiam suam non nisi incendantur, expandunt: ita veri sancti omne, quod virtutibus redolent, in tribulationibus innotescunt.
>
> ([Gregory says,] Just as unguents cannot give off a scent unless they are stirred, and incense does not spread out its fragrance unless it is burned, so true saints make known in their tribulations everything which they are redolent of in respect of virtues.)[49]

Once the relationship between tribulation and virtue has been established, Bromyard can turn to the triumph exemplum:

> In hoc enim operatur Deus circa electos suos, quod facere solebant Romani circa victores, & triumphatores suos. Triumphus enim secundùm Isidorum dicitur a tribus: quia triumphator Romanus cum victoria versus ciuitatem veniens tres honores habere debuit: captiuos vinctos post currum suum ducebat: tota ciuitas ei occurebat, & quatuor palefredi albi currum suum ducebant. Sed ne de his superbiret, tria vituperabilia eum sustinere oportuit. Vnum quod

minimus de populo ei illo die impune maledicere potuit. Secundum quod deiecta, & vilis persona secum in curru sederet. Tertium quod infortunatus eum leuiter tangere debuit, & dicere. Talis fuissem, si fortuna mihi ministraret, nec tua fortitudo: sed fortuna te victorem fecit. Sicut ergo ille si causam nescisset, admirari potuisset: ita electi in praesenti nescientes omnium tribulationum causas, & vtilitates admirantes dicunt: Domine quid multiplicati sunt, qui tribulant me in Psal. 3. Cui respondetur, sicut patet responderet in tali casu filio, quaerenti quare permitteret eum frequenter à magistro verberari? & quare plus eum verberari iuberet, quàm illum, vel illum? Pater responderet quaerenti talia: quia tu es filius meus, te de (sic) curam habeo, & non de alieno. Sic etiam seruo proprio responderet, quando eum castigat, &c. In hoc enim boni se patrem ostendit tribulati potius quam prospere viuentis, quia flagellat omnem filium, quem recipit. Prouer. 3. Et Heb. 12. Quem vero non flagellat, ostendit non esse suum filium: quia secundùm beatum Gregorium. Qui exempti sunt a numero filiorum. In hoc etiam ostendit differantiam inter amicos, & inimicos: sicut patet supra eod. Cap. 11. Sicut patet. G. 3. 13.[50]

(In this indeed God works in respect to his chosen ones as the Romans were accustomed to do in respect to their victors and triumphators. Triumph, indeed is, according to Isidore, so called from three things: because the Roman triumphator coming toward the city with victory ought to have three honors: he led the conquered captives after his chariot; all the people met him and four white horses drew his chariot. But so that he might not become arrogant about these things, it was proper for him to endure three censures. First, that the lowliest of the people was able to malign him on that day with impunity. Second, that a low-down, vile person should sit with him in the chariot. Third, that the unfortunate ought to touch him irreverently and say, "I would have been such a one, if fortune had served me; not your bravery, but fortune made you a victor." Just as, therefore, if he had been ignorant of the cause, he might have wondered, so the chosen ones in the present, not knowing the causes and benefits of all tribulations, say in wonder: God, why are they multiplied, who trouble me? (Psalm 3). To which it is responded, just as a father would respond in such a case to his son, who was asking why he permitted him to be beaten frequently by his teacher, and why he commanded that he be beaten more than this other one or that other one. The father would respond to his son who was asking such things "because you are my son. I care about you, and not about anyone else." So he would respond to his own servant, when he castigated him, etc. In this, indeed, he shows himself to be the father of the good man who suffers tribulation rather than of the one who lives prosperously, because he scourges his sons, whom he receives. Truly, whom he does not scourge, he reveals not to be his son, because, according to the blessed Gregory, "Those who are cut off from the number of his sons ..." . In this he reveals the difference between friends and enemies; just as it appears above in the same place (cap. 11). As it appears. (G. 3. 13))

It is worth quoting the passage at length to illustrate the extent to which Bromyard has fixed the meaning of the exemplum by embedding it within a tissue of biblical and patristic authorities. His is a general, rather than a particularized, use of the exemplum; while the *Gesta* and *Fasciculus Morum* anatomized each element of the triumph, Bromyard is primarily concerned to illustrate an abstract theme. Just as Holcot fixed on honor as that element of the exemplum that could serve as a hermeneutic key to its meaning, so too Bromyard invokes "tribulatio" as the genuine significance of the Roman practice. And if Holcot alternated between metaphor and metonymy – between a vision of the past as different from the present and an understanding of the past as essentially contiguous with fourteenth-century England – Bromyard's figure is the simile: the Roman world must be aligned with biblical and patristic authorities – "sicut ergo" – in order to draw out an essential moral meaning, which ultimately supersedes the letter of the text. For this reason, the exemplum itself is only superficially rendered. Bromyard perfunctorily describes the three honors – the captives following the chariot, the greeting of the people, and the four white horses – in a different order from any of the texts that might have functioned as his sources (*Fasciculus, Gesta*, Hugutio's *Derivationes,* even Holcot's commentary), leaving out familiar details such as the purple toga, the binding of the captives, and the procession to the Capitol. The intensity of Holcot's anthropological gaze is entirely absent here. It is not merely the fact that Bromyard understands history differently than Holcot – that for him, the pagan past provides grist for a moralizing mill – but also that he envisages textual authority in a very different way. Bromyard's citation of Isidore, for example, is reflexive, clearly copied from a source; there is no evidence that he read the text.

The authorities that matter to him, on the other hand (Gregory and the Bible) are carefully and exactly quoted. This selective emphasis on the accuracy of his exempla and authoritative citations contrasts sharply with Holcot's consistent striving for a certain fidelity to what he understands to be original sources – a fidelity, as we have seen, at odds with the impulse to moralize that also pervades his commentary. In *Super Libros Sapientiae* the result is a curious doubling, the reproduction in full of both the Isidorean and the Hugutian versions of the triumph; it is a method utterly alien to Bromyard. As a result, he might seem in comparison to Holcot a more traditional figure – and indeed he is, if the trajectory being outlined is one of progress toward Renaissance humanism. But if such linear narratives are discarded, it becomes possible to see that the paradoxical freedom that exemplarity allows – the way in which a text may be shaped and reshaped in order to produce meaning – in fact creates the opportunity for serious innovation within what appears to be a predictable and very "medieval" text.

Bromyard's version of the triumph is striking in part because it is so compressed; he sums up in a minimum of words the honors and injuries familiar from the texts of the Hugutian tradition. But he does make one drastic and unprecedented change to the exemplum. Rather than having the slave say "noli solitos" or even "respice te hominem," Bromyard introduces the notion of Fortune into the text; *his* slave says, "Talis fuissem, si fortuna mihi ministraret, nec tua fortitudo; sed fortuna te victorem fecit" ("Such a one I might have been, if fortune had served me; not your fortitude, but fortune made you a victor"). The connection between fortitude and fortune is a common one, but it is typically described in nearly opposite terms; in Alan of Lille, for example, fortitude is the virtue through which fortune may be vanquished: "Qui fortis est liber est, non servit fortunae, non varietati mundanae. Vide, quanta fuerit in martyribus fortitudo, qui tormenta vicerunt, qui sua magnanimitate ipsi illusere tyrannis, qui projecti corpore, non sunt projecti mente; qui adversitati terga non verterunt, sed magnanimiter restiterunt" ("He who is brave is free; he does not serve fortune, or worldly mutability. See what great bravery was in the martyrs, who conquered over their torments, who mocked the tyrants with their greatness of soul, who were laid low in body, but not in mind. They did not turn their backs on adversity, but bravely stood firm").[51]

For Bromyard, however, Fortune holds sway over the victor; virtue alone is not enough to confer worldly glory, or indeed to prevent tribulation. In this he is consistent with the Boethian model that clearly underlies his innovation here; both human success and human failure may be ascribed to Fortune and must ultimately be understood providentially, as experiences of the world that will fall away, discarded when the soul achieves salvation. Though Bromyard does not cite Boethius in this instance, he uses exempla from the *Consolation of Philosophy* elsewhere in the *Summa*, and it is evident that he has read and absorbed the text.[52] His seeming rejection of the principle that virtue provides protection from the depredations of Fortune must be understood in this Boethian light; the "fortitudo" described by the slave is the military bravery of the soldier, rather than the Christian virtue described by Alan. Bromyard's interpolation thus constitutes, at one level, a judgment rendered upon the pagan world in which earthly victories are glorified. In this sense he is drawing a line between pagan and Christian, Roman past and English present, suggesting that the distant classical world is simultaneously other to and subject to the evaluation of, contemporary preachers and their audiences. At the same time, however, Bromyard insistently makes his account historical. What seems like a Christian judgment embedded in the text is, after all, placed in the mouth of a *Roman* slave – a figure deployed by the Romans themselves to curb the pride of their victor. Further, when he replaces the Greek "noli solitos" with the idea of Fortune, Bromyard re-Romanizes the exemplary text. As a reader of Boethius and a huge variety of other Latin authorities, Bromyard would have associated the very notion of Fortune with the Roman past, and would certainly have understood his own invocation of Fortune in part as a gesture to the classical tradition.

Bromyard's Boethian alteration to the triumph exemplum is extremely important, not only because it appears in Gower and Lydgate, but also because it indicates his interest – parallel to, but not intersecting with that of Holcot – in classical modes of understanding the past. A hasty dismissal of Bromyard's *Summa* as a medievalizing source for more innovative vernacular thinkers ignores what is, at the moment of the text's composition, a certain modernity, similar to Holcot's, though perhaps not as marked. His willingness to manipulate the triumph exemplum, to eliminate the discursive gloss that it traditionally contains – "noli solitos" – in favor of a Boethian maxim (but not one drawn directly from the *Consolation*), indicates that his impulse to moralize is coupled with a distinctly philosophical interest in causes and effects, an interest, moreover, that leads him back to Roman models. Even as he subjects the exemplum to moralization, that is, Bromyard gestures toward a framework for understanding events in the world – in history – that ultimately provides the vocabulary for serious vernacular considerations of contingency and historical change: Boethian philosophy.

SECULAR HISTORY AND VERNACULAR MORALIZATION: THE *POLYCHRONICON* AND THE *CONFESSIO AMANTIS*

The phrase "historical thinking" provides a relatively vague way to categorize a particular kind of relation to the past I am arguing obtains – to greater and lesser degrees – in texts like Isidore's *Etymologiae*, Hugutio's *Derivationes*, Holcot's Wisdom commentaries, and Bromyard's sermons. It is not a scientific or taxonomic phrase, and the phenomenon I am describing is not easily categorized or defined. It is, indeed – as the example of Holcot shows – an ephemeral mode of thought, one that asserts itself at moments and just as quickly recedes behind moralizations or allegories. But for all of its fragility, the "historical thinking" I locate in these texts has several distinctive characteristics. First, it proposes a relation between past and present that is one of unfamiliarity; the past is unlike, strange to, the present. It further refuses to ameliorate this strangeness with recourse to the abstract – that is, to allegorical reading or genealogical narratives – and in so doing makes an uneasy commitment to a factual, rather than a truthful, rendering of history. The facticity that emerges in tandem with this historical thinking has nothing to do with modern facts; it is instead a notion of textual fidelity, an urge to return to, and reiterate, the most authoritative originary texts and documents. Finally, it is distinguished by its secularism – by which I mean simply that it tends to imagine the past in particulars that are divorced from (though perhaps ultimately subordinated by) eschatological or salvific versions of history. It is in some sense *anthropological*, in that it is interested in the study of human beings, their practices and behaviors, their customs and traditions, their vocabularies and languages, rather than theological, except in some very generalized sense. I am using this phrase "historical thinking" to cut across several generic and diachronic categories and narratives – the exemplary tradition, historiography, the emergence of vernacularity, the growth of humanism – into which most, if not all, of the examples I have adduced here might be profitably slotted. It is worth resisting such modes of classification now and again, however, in order to follow the meandering trail of an idea as it wends its way across time and space, emerging here and there in different guises, being shaped and reshaped by different hands. The Roman triumph is one such idea, and its historical peregrinations are more than instructive. Its iteration is frequently also a moment at which some version of the historical thinking I have been describing emerges, in variously inflected ways. This is not a coincidence, nor is it a case of wishful reading. The fact that a Roman custom that constituted both a spectacle of power and of its restraint, that literally performed military sovereignty and its limits, proved so compelling to medieval thinkers testifies to the extent to which the problem of state power and its representation lay behind the most innovative works of history writing. As a deeply sedimented cultural form – one that could legitimately be traced from antiquity to the fourteenth-century present, the Roman triumph both carried an aura of strangeness and provoked the shock of recognition – a double response that made it an inevitable catalyst for the historical thought of thinkers such as Holcot, Higden, Gower, and finally Lydgate.

It should be clear by now that I am not suggesting that there was a "movement," a "new historiography," or "new exemplarity" (though those are all perfectly possible) but rather that a mode of thought – one among many far more visible and codified systems of thought – came into being at a certain moment and made itself available to poets, commentators, and moralists alike. No one consistently embraced this new mode – but all of the most important writers of the fourteenth and early fifteenth centuries deployed it in one way or another. In this section, I turn at last to the vernacular texts in the trajectory I am defining, to Gower and Lydgate, each of whom mined the triumph tradition, and each of whom found himself thinking *with* it, about questions of sovereignty, causation, and ultimately, literary form.

The primary source for both Lydgate and Gower's renditions of the triumph is Ranulph Higden's *Polychronicon*, written between the late 1320s and the early 1360s.[53] Though its iteration of the triumph clearly falls within the Hugutian tradition, as a universal history (rather than a biblical commentary or exempla collection) the *Polychronicon* differs radically from all of the works I have discussed so far. The generic demands of the universal history necessarily produce their own distinct set of epistemological and philosophical problems; Higden is attempting both to write an account of history from Creation to the present day, and to construct an exhaustive encyclopedia of geography and peoples. Despite the fact I will argue here that Higden's version of the triumph is distinguished by its secularism, the *Polychronicon* overall is a Christian enterprise, dependent on a narrative model drawn from salvation history; it can easily be read as a large-scale moralization of history, a systematic subsumption of all that was known under the sign of Christian eschatology. But as Gower and Lydgate's responses to the text show, the *Polychronicon* is not that simple.

Higden's account of the triumph appears in book 1, the encyclopedic portion of the project, as part of an extensive description of peoples and their customs. Though most of book 1 is drawn from Vincent of Beauvais, Higden cites Isidore and Hugutio as his sources for the description.[54] He has clearly consulted Hugutio – he includes the details of Caesar's triumph and "contumelia[rum]," which appear nowhere else – and just as clearly has not read Isidore; he leaves out the lines in Hugutio that are quoted from the *Etymologiae*. His version differs slightly – he uses "honor" instead of "leticia," for example – but is generally very close to Hugutio's text. In addition to Caesar's triumph, one other detail from the *Derivationes* appears in Higden that is not found in *Fasciculus*, the *Gesta*, Holcot, or Bromyard: he cites Ovid.[55] Higden would certainly have been familiar with the version of the triumph found in exempla collections, as well as with the practice of allegorical moralization; he himself wrote two aids to preaching, the *Ars Componendi Sermones* and the *Speculum Curatorum*.[56] But his interest in the triumph is not a moral one. Because his aim is (in part) to reproduce knowledge rather than to read, or interpret, signs, he eliminates the moral and focuses solely on the custom itself. In doing so, he harkens back to an older tradition embodied by Hugutio, in which history, while it may be broadly contextualized as part of a Christian scheme, stands on its own *as* history, as an account of another time or another place that maintains a distance from the present. The Romans appear in Higden not as prefigurations of Christians, nor yet as the letter from which the spirit must be extracted, but rather as members of a different culture whose mores and practices can be described and articulated but never assimilated. This is not to suggest that Higden is any less theocentric than the moralizing writers of the exemplary tradition; indeed, he explicitly states that the reason for using pagan exempla was to "serve the Christian religion" ("Christianae tamen religioni famulantur"), just as Virgil sought wisdom in the "dross of the poet Ennius" ("Licuit enim Virgilio aurum sapientiae in luto Ennii poetae spoliare").[57] But he tempers this assertion:

> In quibus paene cunctis aliunde membratim excerptis, sed hic lineamentaliter concorporatis, ita seriosis ludicra, ita religiosis ethnica vicissim sunt admixta, ut succinctis tritis laxatisque exoticis processus series observetur, et integra pro posse veritas non vacillet; aequalis tamen utrobique per omnia teneri non poterit certitudo.

> (Þat is in oþer bookes i-write welwyde and parcel mele i-plaunted, here it is i-putte togidre in rule and in ordre; so merþe to sadnesse and heþen to Cristen, eurich among oþere, þat straunge stories beeþ so abregged, schorted and i-lengþed þat þe storie is hool, in sooþnesse nou3t i-chaunged. Neuerþeles more certeyn som is i-holde þan oþir.)[58]

What is most significant about this description is Higden's clear interest in the process of history writing, in the *method* – "membratim excerptis, sed lineamentaliter concorporatis" – through which the past should be articulated and made meaningful. He links historical practice firmly to questions of truth and falsity, as well as to a broad notion of reader investment in knowing the past. Higden is distinctly aware of the differing uses of history (edification and enjoyment, "seriosis ludicra") and he invokes a notion of historical certainty ("certitudo") divorced from spiritual meaning. In this, he differs drastically from Bromyard, who, as we have seen, disavowed any concern for the truth or falsity of his exempla, as long as the moral truth that they signified was communicated adequately. Higden's historical imagination is a double one; he both envisages the past as a morally useful object of analysis, and considers historical knowledge valuable in and of itself, on its own terms. While moralization may be his ostensible purpose for writing history, he is also compelled by a desire to *preserve* the past as past.[59] As his version of the triumph shows, this desire produces a text in which the past stands alone, without reference to allegorical or moral interpretive schema.

Like Holcot, Higden is concerned to articulate the particulars of the triumph with reference only to their significance in Roman, not Christian, terms; thus, he allows Hugutio's reasons for the slave's presence – that the triumphator should not become proud, and that all men should have hope of achieving such worship – to stand alone, as sufficient in and of themselves to explain the meaning of the Roman custom: "Colaphizans vero saepius dicebat triumphanti, 'Nothissolitos,' id est, *nosce teipsum*, quasi diceret, 'Noli superbire de tanto honore.'" It is this insistence on Romanness that offered to Gower and Lydgate an account detached from the moralization found in the exemplary tradition, an account that both asserts its textual authority (by citing Isidore and Hugutio) and insists on its historicity by embedding the triumph in an entire sequence of descriptions of Roman customs. This sense of the historical can be found in varying degrees in the two poets – Gower understands the triumph as an exemplum in a way that Lydgate does not – but both of them have clearly absorbed the *Polychronicon* and its perspective on the past.

There are a number of vernacular English versions of the triumph exemplum – in the Middle English *Gesta Romanorum*, Mirk's *Festial*, and the Middle English *Secreta Secretorum* – but Gower's and Lydgate's are both the earliest and the only ones that make significant alterations to the standard text.[60] As I argued in chapter 1, Gower is an important, though unacknowledged, source for *Serpent of Division*; a closer look at his use of the triumph exemplum will demonstrate the extent to which Lydgate, once again, depended on the *Confessio Amantis* for the conceptual underpinnings of his representation of the Roman past.[61] Gower's triumph, embedded in book 7 of the *Confessio Amantis* – the book in which he most powerfully articulates a vision of political (that is, monarchical) order, and the book in which he breaks away from the penitential structure of the text as a whole – illustrates precisely how limiting Chaucer's tag "moral Gower" proves to be. The old critical assumption – that Chaucer was a sort of protosecular humanist while Gower was "moral" and thus more "medieval" – has been thoroughly laid to rest, as critics have argued that Chaucer, like Gower, was interested in the preservation of social hierarchies and the communication of moral truth.[62] The reverse is also true: Gower, like Chaucer, was interested in moments at which the moralizing tradition broke down or proved insufficient to the task of negotiating the relation of particulars (individual lives or historical contingencies) to authoritative generalities (religious and social orthodoxies).

Modeled on the *Secreta Secretorum*, Brunetto Latini's *Trésor*, and the *De Regimine Principum* of Giles of Rome, book 7 attempts a comprehensive taxonomy of medieval political life and sciences of knowledge, based on the central organizing metaphor of man as a microcosm of the world.[63] In this model, the ethical self-governance of the king becomes the key to the well-being of the realm; the king himself becomes a kind of exemplum for those he governs – making the theme of exemplarity, both moral and political, central to the work of the book as a whole.[64] Given the overriding concern of book 7 with ethics and kingship, then, the suitability of the triumph exemplum, as an illustration of martial authority chastened and exalted at once, becomes obvious. But Gower's particular rendering of the triumph, especially when considered in light of the tradition I have been outlining here, does not function simply as an exemplary instance of the proper relation between king and people. Instead, it raises questions about the philosophical underpinnings of the microcosm model, particularly when juxtaposed to an equally powerful narrative of monarchical life: the tragedy, or fall of princes.

Gower's triumph forms part of a discussion of flattery, which is itself a subset of "Largesse," the second of five points of "Policie" – which is in turn a subdivision of the branch of knowledge called "Practique" (the others are "Theorique" and "Rhetorique"). Though he includes a warning of the dangers of ill-used and false words in the section on "Rhetorique" ("Word hath beguiled many a man" [7: 1564]), Gower reserves his most scathing critique of language for his warning against flatterers: "Ther myhte be no worse thing / Aboute a kinges regalie, / Thanne is the vice of flaterie" (7: 2203–05). As a solution to the problem of flattery, Gower holds up the example of the Roman emperors, who insisted on "wordes pleine and bare" (7: 2350) from their soothsayers. The triumph, in this context, is described as an illustration of the Romans' penchant for plain speaking – particularly embodied in the words of the slave, and the license to the people to say what they pleased to the triumphator. The familiar elements of the triumph are all here, though in slightly different order than in Higden:

> Whil that the worthi princes were
> At Rome, I thenke forto tellen.
> For when the chances so befellen
> That eny Emperour as tho
> Victoire hadde upon his fo,
> And so forth cam to Rome ayein,
> Of treble honor he was certein,
> Wherof that he was magnefied.
> The ferste, as it is specefied,
> Was, whan he cam at thilke tyde,
> The Charr in which he scholde ryde
> Foure whyte Stiedes scholden drawe;
> Of Jupiter be thilke lawe
> The Cote he scholde were also;
> Hise prisoners ek scholden go
> Endlong the Charr on eyther hond,
> And alle the nobles of the lond
> Tofore and after with him come
> Ridende and broghten him to Rome,
> In thonk of his chivalerie
> And for non other flaterie.
> And that was schewed forth withal
> (7: 2360–81)

Gower's familiarity with the triumph exemplum as it was rendered in the moral tradition is made even more evident in the Latin gloss that accompanies the text:

> Hic narrat super eodem, qualiter nuper Romanorum Imperator, cum ipse triumphator in hostes a bello Rome rediret, tres sibi laudes in signum sui triumphi precipue debebantur: primo quatuor equi albissimi currum in quo sedebat veherent, secundo tunica Iovis pro tunc indueretur, tercio sui captiui prope currum ad vtrumque latus cathenati deambularent. Set ne tanti honoris adulacio eius animum in

superbiam extolleret, quidam scurra linguosus iuxta ipsum in curru sedebat, qui quasi continuatis vocibus improperando ei dixit, "Notheos," hoc est nosce teipsum, "quia si hodie fortuna tibi prospera fuerit, cras forte versa rota mutabilis aduersabitur."

(Here he relates, on the same subject, how not long ago the Roman emperor, when having triumphed over his enemies, he returned to Rome from the war, three praises in particular were owed to him as a sign of his triumph. The first was that four white horses drew a chariot in which he sat. The second was that for the occasion he was dressed in the tunic of Jove. The third was that his captives walked in chains near the chariot on both sides. But so that his spirit should not be exalted in pride by such honor, a talkative ribald sat next to him in the chariot, who as if taunting him with a stream of words, said to him, "Notheos," that is, "Know yourself, because if today fortune favors you, perhaps tomorrow her changing wheel will have turned and be against you.")
(7: marginal gloss)

These Latin phrases are (with one exception) certainly recognizable by now; the question is not whether Gower knew the moral tradition, but rather, which of the many texts in that tradition he used.[65] Despite the fact that Gower uses the *Secreta Secretorum* in book 7, and despite the fact that a version of the triumph does appear in some versions of that text, the source from which he draws the exemplum is Higden's *Polychronicon*. In his discussion of the relationship between the exempla in book 7 and the version of the *Secreta* used by Gower – thought to be a French translation from the latter half of the thirteenth century by Jofroi de Waterford – George L. Hamilton noted that despite close correspondences, Gower has not taken the word "Notheos" (a corruption of a corruption, "nolisolitos") from Jofroi's text.[66] "Nolisolitos" does, however, appear in the *Polychronicon*. Further, Gower immediately follows the triumph exemplum with a tale of a Roman custom in which the emperor, on the first day of his reign, receives at his throne his masons, who ask him what kind of stone they should use in making his sepulcher, and what should be engraved upon it (lines 2412–31). A similar story appears immediately following the triumph description in the *Polychronicon*, which is attributed to John the Almoner; though it differs in some details (the gravemakers ask what kind of metal, rather than stone, to use), the juxtaposition of the two episodes argues strongly for Higden as Gower's source.[67] Finally, and most conclusively, Gower twice states that he is following a "Cronique" (lines 2352 and 2415) – an attribution that has puzzled critics, but that makes perfect sense if his source is identified as the *Polychronicon*, the only one of the potential candidates that could legitimately be called a chronicle.

Gower's use of the *Polychronicon* here is important, because it demonstrates his interest in the accuracy and historical truth of his exempla, as well as the influence of Higden's descriptive method; like Higden, Gower links the two exempla – the triumph and the masons – because they concern Romans and together suggest a particular quality of Romanness (a willingness to be confronted by unpleasant truths) he wishes to hold up as an example to present-day kings. Indeed, Gower includes a third exemplum, a story of Caesar's wisdom in resisting flattery, to round out his Roman illustrations. The principle of selection at work here is thematic, much like that found in any sermon or treatise, but it is *also* historical. There are many examples Gower might have chosen to illustrate his point about flattery; the fact that he links three *Roman* exempla suggests that, like Higden, part of his purpose is to describe Rome as a culturally distinct and historically distant entity – which then functions in exemplary terms as a model for princes by virtue of its very difference from the present. In more general terms, Gower's representation of the past embodies a fundamental contradiction in the mode of historical thought I have been describing; it is at once an attempt to acknowledge the alienness of the past *and* an insistence upon its exemplarity. Romans are both strange objects and reflective mirrors, both other and same. Indeed, the very notion of historical temporality undergirding this mode of thought is deeply riven, combining a powerful sense of genealogical continuity – seamless time – with an equally compelling articulation of rupture and fragmentation. This double temporality, which might just as well be described in generic terms as the uneasy union of historicity and exemplarity, can be seen in the work of Higden and Holcot, though the sheer power of Christian moralization generally overwhelms the urge to acknowledge historical difference. But in the move to the vernacular, the balance between the two modes or temporalities shifts, lurching fitfully toward a recalibrated understanding of the ways in which the past might make meaning for the present.

It is Bromyard who first provides the key to understanding the transition, the metamorphosis in progress, with his Boethian "sed fortuna te victorem fecit" – and it is Gower who expands the citational gesture into a fully-fledged meditation on the role of Fortune in the world. Fortune, as we shall see, is precisely the agency by which historicity may be severed from moralism, and reattached to exemplarity. Gower's triumph exemplum – both in the Latin gloss and the vernacular text – invokes Fortune to explain the presence of the slave:

> Wher he sat in his Charr real,
> Beside him was a Ribald set,
> Which hadde hise wordes so beset,
> To themperour in al his gloire
> He seide, "Tak into memoire,
> For al this pompe and al this pride
> Let no justice gon aside,
> Bot know thiself, what so befalle.
> For men sen ofte time falle
> Thing which men wende siker stonde:
> Thogh thou victoire have nou on honde,
> Fortune mai noght stonde alway;
> The whiel per chance an other day
> Mai torne, and thou myht overthrowe;
> Ther lasteth nothing bot a throwe."

The Latin gloss reads, "quia si hodie fortuna tibi prospera fuerit, cras forte versa rota mutabilis aduersabitur" (because if today Fortune is favorable to you, tomorrow her wheel will be turned changeably). Whether or not Gower knew Bromyard's exemplum, it is clear that he made a similar connection between "know yourself" and the notion of Fortune's changeability – an odd connection, since in effect the two maxims imply entirely different structures of causation. To "know yourself" suggests the possibility of human agency – much as Lydgate's address to "wyse governours" in *Serpent of Division* counseled action in the face of contingency – while the image of Fortune's turning wheel insists on human helplessness in a world of chance and change, the "unwar strook."

This paradox is particular to rulers. To rule is to assert the efficacy of human action in the world; the will of the ruler is an embodiment of agency itself. The idea of Fortune – and, as we saw in chapter 3, the genre of tragedy – constitutes one way of limiting this agency by subordinating it to a principle of uncertainty that is itself, in the Boethian model, then made subject to providence and ultimately to the divine will. And it is indeed possible to suggest a Boethian reading of Gower's version of the triumph exemplum, one in which Fortune constitutes the axis for a Christian moralization ultimately contiguous with the forms of allegoresis found in the sermon tradition. But the central incongruity between "knowing oneself" and acknowledging contingency remains an epistemological problem in at least two ways. Not only does the evocation of agency belie the image of the turning wheel (a problem to which Boethius provides a solution) but the introduction of a principle of causation that can itself be historicized as part of an alien system of belief – the workings of Fortune in the pagan world of the Romans – disrupts the structure of moralization and suggests a new function for exemplary history. In this new model, a provisional one to be sure, the metonymic structure of allegorical moralization, in which past events are not only signifiers of present truths but concretely, genealogically *prefigure* those truths, begins to be replaced by a fundamentally metaphorical understanding of historicity. The past is *unlike* the present, alien to it; profitable comparisons may be drawn between then and now but they remain separated by a necessary distance. It is this distance that enables Gower, and Lydgate after him, to construct a secular mode of exemplarity addressed to rulers – precisely those embodiments of human agency whose will seems most in need of Christian tempering. Such a secular exemplarity becomes necessary because the metonymic mode, the process of moralization and allegoresis, carries with it certain perils that make it inadequate to the task of providing advice to princes. *Imitatio Christi* does not function as a useful model for princes charged with administering a highly complex governmental and social structure, even one imagined in familial and personal terms. To be sure, the moralized type of the exemplum was deployed by preachers as a means of commenting on the state of the realm. But because Gower and Lydgate are particularly interested in articulating a place for a vernacular, quasisecular form of advising that can also perform the work of writing history *as history*, the moralizing mode ultimately proves insufficient in both literary and philosophical terms – even at those moments when both poets appear to be fully invested in traditional understandings of the social and political world.

Neither Gower nor Lydgate is a radical thinker or innovator. But what their writings reveal are the structural tensions at work at the intersection of what might loosely be called written culture (which includes histories, moralities, commentaries, and fictions) and the experientially real world of particular kings and specific events. Reconciling the pagan past with the Christian present produces one set of problems; advising the king creates another. Negotiating the generic boundaries and limits set by a tradition of authoritative writing, and doing so in the vernacular, raises further questions. These are all tasks attendant on writing texts like *Confessio Amantis* or *Serpent of Division* – that is, on the enterprise of writing a certain kind of history for a particular audience at a specific moment in time. What had remained relatively latent in Holcot and Bromyard becomes pressing in Gower and Lydgate precisely because of the intersection of past *auctoritas* with present-day rulership – and indeed, recall that Holcot's *Wisdom* commentaries, where some of the same attitudes to history appear, were themselves conceived as a form of advice to princes.[68]

Neither Gower nor Lydgate explicitly articulates a new vision of secular history, or could be said to have any intention of doing so. But each is clearly striving to negotiate the tensions inherent in the vernacular historical enterprise, tensions created by the instability of the poet's role in relation to structures of power. Gower's interest in defining that role is manifest in the triumph exemplum, which attains a particular importance in book 7 and in the *Confessio* as a whole as a highly self-referential episode. After describing the elements of the triumph, and introducing the idea of Fortune, Gower continues by explaining the significance of the "Ribald"'s role:

> With these wordes and with mo
> This Ribald, which sat with him tho,
> To Themperour his tale tolde:
> And overmor what evere he wolde,
> Or were it evel or were it good,
> So pleinly as the trouthe stod,

He spareth noght, bot spekth it oute;
And so myhte every man aboute
The day of that solempnete
His tale telle als wel as he
To Themperour al openly.
And al was this the cause why;
That whil he stod in that noblesse,
He scholde his vanite represse
With suche wordes as he herde.
(7: 2360–374)

Two things become evident in this passage. First, that quality of plain-speaking that Gower associates with the Romans forms part of a self-conscious meditation on the role of the poet as advisor to princes. Like the Ribald, poets such as Gower should not spare the truth when they address the king, an injunction that – paradoxically enough – the metaphorical structure of the exemplum itself belies. The lesson articulated in this passage, one that does not appear in any source or in the Latin gloss, is simply that kings should listen to the truth. But by embedding the triumph exemplum in a section on flattery and flatterers, and by adding this concluding moral, Gower conceals the more dangerous message it contains, allowing the content of the Ribald's speech – that kings are subject to Fortune – to remain safely part of the Roman past. The double structure of exemplarity articulated here, in which an explicit conclusion overlays an implicit, more troubling lesson, exploits the historicity of the exemplum itself, its dissimilarity from the English present, in order to safely contain the implications of the Ribald's speech within the confines of an alien cultural practice. Thus, though Gower holds up the Roman ideal of truth-telling, he himself evades speaking "al openly" in his own poetry. Second, the demand that advisors to princes tell the truth introduces another audience – of king's counselors – further undermining the potential of the exemplum to produce a one-to-one correspondence between king and Roman emperor. That audience is further alienated by its figuration as the "Ribald," an embodiment of the otherness of the past who allows readers to refuse identification with the exemplum, even if they accept the legitimacy of the lesson it propounds. In the end the most powerful correlation in the exemplum overall is that between

Gower himself and the Ribald, suggesting a fundamental ambivalence in Gower's representation of counsel; it may be important to speak the truth, but truth-tellers are likely to look like fools.

The complex workings of identification in Gower's triumph exemplum are produced by the exigencies of writing advice to princes in a relationship of extreme inequality.[69] The original dedication of the *Confessio* to Richard II, and the subsequent substitution of a dedication to Henry of Lancaster, testify to the concreteness of Gower's understanding of the role of his writing in public life, as do his explicit commentaries on contemporary politics, on the realm in *Vox Clamantis*, and in poems such as "In Praise of Peace."[70] As his practice in the triumph exemplum shows, Gower is acutely aware of the hazards of occupying the role of counselor, and it is that awareness – rather than an intentional literary or philosophical program – that ultimately compels him to render the Roman past in a distinctly historical way. The triumph, of course, is merely one exemplum in a long work, which includes multiple genres and modes of thought and which is itself organized by a narrative structure – the seven deadly sins and the confession – that insistently proposes a meaning for the poem as a whole. As the *Prologue* to the *Confessio* shows, Gower is fully capable of articulating a notion of causality that proceeds from individual morality to good or bad fortune; as I argued in chapter 1, it is the inadequacy of this understanding of history in the face of contingency that Lydgate exposes in *Serpent of Division*. When Gower directly addresses the question of counsel in book 7, he too must confront the insufficiency – and danger – of moral exemplarity in a political world.[71] Imagining a pagan past that bears a metaphorical rather than an allegorical relation to that world is only one response to those dangers, and it is by no means the dominant mode of representation in the *Confessio* overall. But, as Lydgate's depiction of the triumph shows, it has important future implications for the representation of history at the juncture of the written and the real.[72]

LYDGATE'S TRIUMPHS

Like Holcot, Lydgate describes both the Isidorean and the Hugutian versions of the triumph. In contrast, however, he compiles details from both into a single elaborate account, beginning with the Hugutian tripartite structure of honors, and interpolating such Isidorean particulars as the distinction between the necklace with spines and without:

> And [if so were þat his conqveste was accomplisshed and perfourmed withoute swerde or sheding of blood thanne shulde the coroune of þe palme] be forged withowte prikkes or spynis and ʒif so were þat his victori was fynisschid bi þe cruell fate of were þan of custome his cercle or his pectorall was forgid full of scharpe prikyng þornes to declare and specifie þat þer is none conqueste acomplischid [fully] to þe fyne bi [mediacioun] of werre withoute þat þer be [felt and found] therinne þe scharpe prikkynge thornes of aduersite and þat oþer [bi deth] oþer bi pouerte.

In explaining the difference between the two necklaces, Lydgate betrays the same willingness to let the Roman custom signify on its own terms that we find in Holcot's lectio 164, amplifying Isidore's explanation and emphasizing the symbolic pagan meaning of the detail. But while Holcot eventually resorted to Ecclesiasticus to gloss the Isidorean passage in moral terms, Lydgate follows Bromyard and Gower in elaborating the role of Fortune:

> But to schewe clerely þat all worldely glorie is transitori and not abidynge and evidently to declare þat in hiʒe estate is none assuraunce þere was set at þe back of þis conquerour behyndyn in þe chare the most vnlikly persone and þe moste wrecche þat in eny Cowntrey myʒt be fownde disfigured and Iclad in the moste vgly wise that eny man cowde devise and amyd all þe clamour and noyse of þe peple to exclude þe false surqvedie veyneglory and Idill laude this forseide wrecche schulde of custome & of consuetude smyte þe conqverroure euer in þe necke and uppon þe hed and stowndemele seyne vnto hym in greke þis worde Nothis politos, which is as mochill to seyne in owre englische tonge as knowe þiselfe, which declarith and vnclosith vnto him þat he nor none oþer schulde for no suche worldely glorie be surquedous nor wex prowde. And þilke day hit was lefull without punyschynge to euery man of hiʒe estate and of lowe to seine to him þat was victour whate some euer he wolde, were it of honoure or of worschip, of reprefe or of schame, as this was admittid withowte vengeaunce for þis cause, þat he schulde truly consideren and aduerte þat þer is none erþely glorie þat fully may ben assured withowte the dawngere of Fortune. (54, lines 4–19)

Lydgate's debt to Gower in this passage is obvious; though he has clearly read both Isidore and Higden's accounts (and possibly Bromyard's as well), he takes from the *Confessio Amantis* the notion that the vagaries of Fortune constitute the lesson of the exemplum, a lesson he later directly applies to present-day rulers, "wise gouernours of euery londe and region" (65, lines 25–26).[73] As in the *Confessio Amantis*, the classical past appears in *Serpent of Division* as a mirror for the present; Lydgate articulates the same metaphorical link between past and present that characterizes the historical thought of Holcot and Gower. And like Gower, Lydgate omits a crucial detail from Higden's text. One of the reasons given in the *Polychronicon* – and in Hugutio – for the presence of the wretch is that he gives hope to all men that they too might achieve glory through their own actions: "ut daretur spes cuique probo perveniendi ad consimilem honorem, si probitas sua hoc promereretur" ("for euerich man schulde hope to come to þat worschippe, ȝif he made hym self worþy by his dedes").[74] The omission of this reason skews the original logic of the Hugutian version, diminishing the importance of human agency and erasing its idealized vision of a world in which great deeds are rewarded. In its place we find Fortune, that principle of causation both providential and radically contingent, both Christian and pagan – and the appearance of Fortune signals, in both Gower and Lydgate's texts, a moment of constitutive, structural incoherence at the heart of the vernacular exemplary enterprise. Either the great deeds of victors produce triumphs, or Fortune does; either those deeds are to be imitated, or they are to be rejected as chimerical and worldly. These conundra raise critical questions about the status of the pagan past: is its relation to the present one of difference or similarity? Or, to be more precise, is the relation to be defined in concrete, material terms (in which specific past events may be compared to present happenings while retaining a fundamental distance from them), or in abstract, moral ones (whereby both past and present signify the same thing, and teach the same lesson)? In the *Confessio Amantis*, as we have seen, these ambiguities are centrally related to the problematics of the advice-to-princes genre; Gower's refusal to fix the meaning of the triumph exemplum in moral terms is produced by a need to allow his reader – the prince himself – sufficient interpretive room for the exercise of will. *Serpent of Division* is similarly aimed at a powerful patron, Humphrey of Gloucester, and reveals precisely the same contradictory drives toward moralization, on the one hand, and a distancing notion of history on the other.

But a great deal changes between the reigns of Richard II and Henry VI, and after 1422 Gower's particular mode of political intervention – the long, discursive poetic treatise dedicated to the king himself – no longer suits the needs of the minority regime or the desires of its primary commentator, Lydgate himself. Further, and more importantly, the very conditions of possibility for poetic production have been altered profoundly, and with them the genres, tropes, modes, and discourses through which poetry is created in fifteenth-century English culture. As the preceding chapters have shown, there emerged during the minority new forms of public discourse, forms that combined traditional kinds of spectacle with the layered and complex poeisis of figures like Chaucer and Gower. Thus, when Lydgate writes an exemplary treatise, when he engages with the problem of the pagan past as possible exemplar, he does so in distinctly *dramatic* fashion, expanding and amplifying Gower's version of the triumph to emphasize its status as performance, as cultural spectacle. His turn to Isidore appears in this light as a quest for visual detail – the eagle-topped scepter, the necklace with or without spines – that can complete the picture of triumphs he is drawing for readers. Similarly, Lydgate's depiction of the wretch – simply described by Higden as "servus" and by Gower as "Ribald" – accentuates the figure's spectacularity: "þere was set at þe back of þis conquerour behyndyn in þe chare *the most vnlikly persone* and *þe moste wrecche* þat in eny Cowntrey my3t be fownde *disfigured* and *Iclad in the moste vgly wise* that eny man cowde devise." These are not merely instances of the Lydgatean penchant for amplification. Rather, they illustrate the profoundly theatrical way in which Lydgate conceives of and represents history itself.

If the mummings and the disguisings of the latter part of the minority reveal anything, it is the tremendous rhetorical potential of the alliance between dramatic form and literary form, a potential that Lydgate's version of the triumph exemplum in *Serpent of Division* anticipates and explores. But the particular narrative in which the triumph is embedded – the story of Caesar's rise to power and ultimate fall – also suggests the dangerous potential of public spectacle. It is, after all, the denial of the triumph to Caesar that sparks civil war and incites Caesar to conquer Rome. For Lydgate, the links among dramatic expressivity, didactic efficacy, and state power are both tangible and complex. That a theatrical event – a procession or entry, for example – could have material as well as ideological effects in the world would have been obvious to any medieval person. That Lydgate should assign to the denial of the triumph the cause of civil war is in this sense a measure of precisely how efficacious he understood social dramas to be. The notion of drama that subtends this structure of causality is crucially bound up with Lydgate's understanding of the didactic function of the literary, as well as the fundamentally theatrical nature of his concept of fifteenth-century political life. But it would be a mistake to see the triumph episode in simple historical terms, as either an expression of Lydgate's predictable interest in dramatic ritual or as a reflection of a social practice both common and mechanistic. It is, of course, both of these things. At the same time, however, the dangerous aura the triumph achieves when its denial is adduced as the cause – "root and begynnyng" – of political and social catastrophe suggests that, for Lydgate, dramatic expressivity is fundamentally double-edged. As a means of reflecting authority and constructing relations of subjection, it is a mode of surpassing power – but one that perpetually threatens to turn back upon its masters and create not social harmony but "contageous deuysion."

Lydgate's insertion of a reference to Caesar in his account of Henry VI's 1432 London entry, then, inevitably calls to mind this ambivalence, the double sense in which spectacle might function as a unifying mechanism or divisive engine. Indeed, Lydate's final representation of Caesar, in the *Fall of Princes*, makes the point even more explicitly:

> Among the Senat was the conspiracye
> Alle of assent & of oon accordaunce, –
> Whos tryumphe thei proudli gan denye;
> But maugre them was kept thobseruaunce,
> His chaar of gold with steedis of plesaunce
> Conveied thoruh Roome, this prince [most] pompous,
> The moordre folwyng bi Brutus Cassius.[75]

Despite the clear condemnation of the Senate in these verses, the narrative effect is that of a movement from "assent and accordaunce" to division and death – a movement produced by Caesar's willful insistence on celebrating his triumph, "maugre them." It is the triumph, here, that is the proximate cause of Caesar's murder; he is "conveied thoruh Roome . . . the moordre folwyng." Not only should it be clear from *Serpent of Division* and *Fall of Princes* that Lydgate's citation of Caesar's triumphs in his "Verses on the Triumphal Entry" directly connects that occasion to those ill-fated victory processions denied to, and celebrated by, the emperor – but the nature of Lydgate's ambivalence about Lancastrian propaganda should be becoming evident. It is an historical ambivalence. If Roman history has any lesson to teach, it is (as Gower also knew) that the mightiest prince *will* fall, that Fortune's wheel will turn. The moment at which Lydgate invokes Caesar, then, is both a moment at which the Roman past is understood in metaphorical terms, as parallel to but not intersecting with the present, and an effort at a secular exemplarity, a way of issuing a warning to "lordes and prynces" of the dangers of embracing Caesarian spectacularity.

THE FORM OF PUBLIC CULTURE: THE END
OF THE MINORITY

By 1432, Lydgate had largely retired from his job as Lancastrian apologist, and in 1433 or 1434 was to retreat to Bury to work on his massive commission from Humphrey of Gloucester, the *Fall of Princes*.[76] His verses on Henry VI's entry represent some of his last work in the "propagandistic" vein; the public poetry I have described in this book became a thing of the past, as Lydgate turned his attention to the longer and more philosophical work of his later years. Though Henry VI's reign continued to be a troubled one – Humphrey of Gloucester remained in perpetual conflict with the other lords of the realm, while matters in France deteriorated still further – the unique historical nexus that had called forth Lydgate's public poetry ceased to exist.[77] The protectorate and, in essence, the dual monarchy had both come to an end, though Henry VI would continue to be guided by his councilors and the claim to the French throne would be maintained.[78] With hindsight, it becomes clear that the 1432 verses constitute a kind of valedictory address to the public that Lydgate had helped to shape and form during the years of the minority. The uneasy union between theatrical forms – the mumming, the triumph, the royal entry – and poetic discourse that characterizes Lydgate's writing during this period came, in one sense, to an end with his retirement and Henry VI's assumption of personal rule. In another, more important way that union (about which Lydgate himself was ambivalent) would prove durable. The idea that not merely verse but fully formed and complex poetic discourse constitutes a central means of shaping a public comprised of various and multiple groups – even if that public is a small one – would become, with the advent of print, a compelling and useful one.

The 1432 verses are not, as was once thought, a script for the entry itself. As MacCracken showed long ago, they are largely translated from a Latin letter of John Carpenter, town clerk of London, and follow his descriptions of the occasion very closely. Whether or not Lydgate witnessed the pageants is an open question; there are a number of important additions and changes to Carpenter's letter that imply that he did, though of course he could have been working from a lost version of the letter or from another account.[79] These include the allegorical figures of Mercy, Grace, and Pity, and flattering compliments to the mayor, John Wells, who Lydgate tells us commissioned the poem, as well as a description of the happenings in St. Paul's Cathedral and Westminster Abbey that differs substantially from that of Carpenter. At the very least, it is clear Lydgate was substantially involved in disseminating an account of the entry that was used by some chroniclers as an historical account and that presents itself as a firsthand narration of a quintessentially public event. The entry itself has been thoroughly analyzed for its liturgical symbolism, as well as its political import and nuances; Gordon Kipling has convincingly shown that the entry exploits the liturgies of Advent and Epiphany, staging minor epiphanies throughout that are linked to both liturgical and biblical passages and identifying Henry as a type of messiah.[80] In his comparison of the 1432 entry to Henry's 1431 entry into Paris upon his coronation, Lawrence Bryant argues that Londoners (unlike the Parisians) "treated the king intimately and personally," as part of the Lancastrian habit of creating spectacles "as precise images of the urban place in the existing political order."[81] These readings, the liturgical and the political, complement each other in creating a complex picture of the entry as staged for the king and the city, with each pageant forming part of an overriding theme that exalts Henry while gently suggesting he make use of various elements of good governance; such scenes as the giving of the seven gifts of the Holy Ghost – intelligence, "sapience," strength, good counsel, "konnyng, drede, pite and lownesse" – demonstrate the way in which the sacred and the secular are inextricably linked in the production.[82]

What makes Lydgate's verses so significant is not their rendering of the 1432 event *per se* or of its details; these are available in Carpenter's account, and it is obvious from Lydgate's use of that text that his verses can in no way be described as a "script." But they are all the more important for that. The 1432 verses are a mediated representation of a public event that works to point and shape the *historical* interpretation of Henry VI's entry, so much so that they prompt a rethinking of the very term "public." When Lydgate was commissioned by Mayor Wells to write a poetic account of the entry – of which the mayor, as the ruler of the very city that staged the event, must have been justifiably proud – he was asked not only to record the occasion for posterity (Carpenter's letter, or one like it, would have sufficed for that), but to transform it into poetry. It has been a large part of the argument of this book that complex modes of representation that might loosely be described as "poetic" became, in Lydgate's hands during the minority, privileged discourses for making of the public as an imaginary (but no less real) new construct. The 1432 verses constitute an arbitrary end point in this process, to be sure, but they remain particularly instructive both because they allow us to see what Lydgate imagined a public spectacle *should* be, and because they show us that at least one figure – the mayor – understood and valued the kind of public discourse that Lydgate helped to create.

To gain some insight into what made the 1432 verses necessary – to what made Carpenter's letter insufficient – it is necessary to look at those moments at which Lydgate deviates from the text. Some are clearly driven by the patronage of Wells, and might seem for that reason to be insignificant. In stanzas 49–50, for example, Lydgate elaborately compliments the mayor by punning on his name:

> The wyn of **Mercy** staunchith by nature
> The gredy thristis off cruell hastynesse,

Grace with hire likour cristallyne and pure
Defferrith vengaunce off ffurious woodnesse,
And **Pitee** blymsith the swerde of Rithwysnesse;
Convenable welles, moste holsom of savour,
Forto be tasted off euery governour.

O! how these welles, who-so take goode hede,
With here likours moste holsome to atame,
Affore devysed notably in dede
Forto accorden with the Meirys name;
Which by report off his worthy ffame
That day was busy in alle his gouernaunce,
Vnto the Kyng fforto done plesaunce.
(lines 335–48)

This is a simple and indeed typically Lydgatean compliment in many
ways. But the final line of the stanza tells us that the mayor's task was to
do "plesaunce" to the king, and this is a task with which Lydgate – who
describes himself in *Serpent of Division* giving "plesaunce" to "wyse
governours" – is intimately familiar. Wells is Lydgate's patron, but he is
also a double for the poet, engaged, like Lydgate, in the task of creating
an aestheticized fictional world for the pleasure of others. Indeed,
Lydgate follows his compliment to the mayor with a virtuoso display
of poetic skill, translating Carpenter's succinct "stellatum floribus et
arboribus fructiforis" as[83]

There were eke treen, with leves ffressh off hewe,
Alle tyme off yeer, ffulle of ffruytes lade,
Off colour hevynly, and euery-liche newe,
Orenges, almondis, and the pome-gernade,
Lymons, dates, theire colours ffressh and glade,
Pypyns, quynces, blaunderell to disport,
And the pome-cedre corageous to recomforte;

Eke the ffruytes which more comvne be –
Quenynges, peches, costardes and wardouns,
And other meny fful ffayre and ffressh to se;
The pome-water and the gentyll ricardouns;
And ageyns hertes ffor mutygaciouns
Damysyns, which with here taste delyte,
Full grete plente both off blak and white.
(lines 349–62)

The insertion of a poetic set piece like this one into a text otherwise presented as a firsthand account has two crucial effects. First, it denaturalizes the verses even as it seems to intensify the gaze of the narrator at the pageants. The reader is taken out of the world of pageantry – the mayor's preserve – and into the world of poetic composition, a world in which ekphrasis gives "plesaunce," not to viewers but to sophisticated readers. Second, it insists that such ekphrasis can substitute for, and literally become, historical reality – as indeed it did, when Lydgate's verses were copied into chronicles, edited, and printed. In some senses, of course, Carpenter's letter is equally fictitious for later readers; no one can know "what happened" when Henry VI processed through London. But there is a crucial difference between the two texts: Carpenter's text is presented simply and directly, without rhetorical flourish, in a style that suggests that he is merely stating what he has seen, while Lydgate's poem – though it gives the surface impression of being a firsthand account (Carpenter's letter is never mentioned) – contains too many poetic devices and embellishments to be mistaken for a straightforward report of events. Mayor Wells, perhaps motivated by pure self-aggrandizement, perhaps by a recognition that the highly aestheticized entry demanded an equally ornamented account, solicited from Lydgate a text that transformed the real into the fictional as a way of writing – or rewriting – history.

This "imaginary history" constructs its public in two ways. One of the critical changes that Lydgate makes to Carpenter's account is that he describes actors in the pageants speaking to the crowds, rather than merely holding or gesturing toward "scriptures" on which biblical and liturgical texts were written. Lydgate's actors speak in English; their counterparts in Carpenter's letter display placards or scrolls written in Latin. Lydgate did find precedent for English speech in Carpenter's letter; the clerk records both the speech of the mayor as he greeted the king and the song of the seven virgins offering gifts to Henry.[84] But elsewhere in the letter Carpenter repeatedly specifies that various phrases were *written*, using words like "rescribere" and "subscribere" to make his point.[85] In contrast, Lydgate translates Carpenter's Latin into English and puts it into the mouths of the various figures in the pageants.[86] This vernacularization of the pageants' Latin "scriptures" works in two ways; it makes the meaning of the written word in the pageants legible to English readers of the verses, and it imagines a royal entry in which a wide public was orally addressed in its native tongue. Carpenter's version of the king's entry is one in which only a tiny portion of the viewers could understand the deeper meanings of the pageants as presented; Lydgate envisions a spectacle in which all viewers are addressed in a poetic idiom – a new form of public discourse. His interest in this new public is particularly evident in his account of the words of Sapience, who occupies a "tabernacle" along the procession route and is surrounded by the seven liberal arts:

> The chieff pryncesse called Sapience
> Hadde to-forn hire writen this scripture:
> "Kynges," quod she, "moste of excellence,
> By me they regne and moste in ioye endure,
> For thurh my helpe, and my besy cure,
> To encrece theyre glorie and hyh renoun,
> They shull off wysdome haue ffull possessioun."
> And in the ffront of this tabernacle,
> Sapience a scripture ganne devyse
> Able to be redde with-oute a spectakle,
> "Vnderstondith and lernyth off the wyse,
> On riht remembryng the hyh lorde to queme,
> Syth ye be iuges other ffolke to deme."
> (lines 258–70)

What is striking about this passage is the way in which writtenness and orality are mixed together; Sapience has a scripture before her, which she proceeds to read aloud – signaled by the use of "quod," a word used in direct quotation, as the *MED*'s examples show.[87] Having spoken, she presents another scripture, this time one that can be read "with-oute a spectakle" in English. In both cases, we can see Lydgate's concern for the transmission and dissemination of these "scriptures" – whether read aloud or written in large letters so that viewers could read them from a distance, these Latin texts are transformed in Lydgate's versions into direct addresses to the London citizenry.

On the first level, then, the verses as written describe an event in which a public is addressed that does not exist in Carpenter's version. It is an imaginary public. Secondarily, Lydgate draws this new public

out of the fictional world of his verses and into the "real" world of the
mayor and the city by addressing it directly in the poem's envoy:

> O noble Meir! be yt vnto youre plesaunce,
> And to alle that duelle in this citee,
> On my rudenesse and on myn ignoraunce,
> Off grace and mercy fforto haue pitee,
> My symple makyng fforto take at gree;
> Considre this, that in moste lowly wyse
> My wille were good fforto do yow servyse.
> (lines 531–37)

I began this book with a reading of *Serpent of Division*, a tract directed
to "wyse governours," and have argued that over the course of the
minority Lydgate developed new forms of address to the "public" and
invested old forms with new meanings at the same time. In the envoy to
his 1432 verses we see that the audience has changed from "wyse
governours" to mayor and "alle that duelle in this citee," an audience
that, both real and imaginary, has dramatically expanded since 1422.
This expansion is, of course, illusory in one sense; there is no docu-
mented sudden increase in numbers of readers of Lydgate's poems, nor
is there any evidence that the London citizens were given the pedagogical instruction that Lydgate describes in his verses. It is far more likely
that they were left to content themselves with the purely visual experience of the pageants. What is important, however, is that Lydgate has
begun to imagine a *form* – a way of doing "plesaunce" – in which such a
public might be addressed. That form is a poetic one. It is complex,
multilayered, and ornamented. Such a form of address does not imagine an audience of everyone – it is not populist in any way – but it does
imagine a wider, and smarter, audience than ever before.

But there is always a sticking point in imaginary worlds, and one is
provided here by Lydgate's gesture to Caesar at the end of his poem, the
reminder of public spectacles gone wrong. It is in this gesture that the
alternate mode of historical thinking found in Holcot, Bromyard,
Gower, and Lydgate intersects with the new forms of public culture
I have been describing. Caesar the secular exemplar walks out of the
world of literature and into the rough and tumble of the real world of
politics, kingship, and Lancastrian rule – and when he does, he brings

with him all the historical ambiguity he has accreted over the long years since his rule in Rome. What is critical is the evident unease with which Lydgate regards this phenomenon, manifested in his concern for contingency – the "unwar strook" – and his compelling suggestion that spectacles of power (triumphs, royal entries) might just as easily become invitations to strife. One reason for this caution may be an emerging recognition of the historical import of such new modes of thought and new forms of culture. That recognition is never made explicit, of course. But at some level Lydgate surely knew that in imagining a larger public – one to which he addresses this new discourse of secular exemplarity – he was opening a Pandora's box of profound historical change.

I began my exploration of medieval triumphs by describing it as an investigation of form and of the ways that literary, social, and cultural forms structure and shape experience and discourse. It has been my contention over the course of this book that the texts I have examined – *Serpent of Division*, Lydgate's mummings and disguisings, the various versions of the triumph exemplum – are all distinguished by a special relationship to form. In each of these cases Lydgate has animated and deployed a cultural or literary form for a distinct, often propagandistic purpose. And in every instance that form has carried with it a set of sedimented meanings and implications that have exceeded the brief of the text in question. To note the excessiveness of literary signification is hardly to make a new point. But when the notion of using literary ambiguity to articulate the subterranean tensions and conflicts within a particular *socius* has only recently developed, and at an historical moment demanding unique cultural compensations for the fragmentation of power at its very center, then form assumes a new and critical role. This role is a public one. At the same time, that public is an imaginary construct. As the triumph exemplum shows, the shift from collections like the *Gesta Romanorum* and sermon handbooks to vernacular poetry and prose is in fact a diminution of the audience, a narrowing of the group of readers or hearers likely to encounter the text. But when Lydgate deploys that familiar exemplum in both *Serpent of Division* and in his 1432 verses, he addresses an entity that constitutes *a* public imagined as a representative body. In other words, for Lydgate, the aristocratic and London elites to whom *Serpent*, the mummings, and the verses are directed constitute the public because they metonymically stand for everyone in the realm. This representative capacity is created by form: by social forms like Parliament, by cultural practices like royal entries, and by aesthetic forms – exempla, tragedies, and histories. These are all ideological categories, and indeed at moments they appear to express pure ideology and little else. But the need for form in the expression of ideology does not, and cannot, evacuate from those forms the excesses they inevitably contain. To compare Henry VI to Caesar is an ideological act; it is also a deeply ambiguous gesture. In the end, it would seem, the persistence of form achieves a kind of victory over the insistence of ideology precisely because forms contain histories. And history, as Chaucer taught Lydgate, always conceals an "unwar strook."

NOTES

1 MacCracken, ed., *Minor Poems of John Lydgate*, part 2, 648.
2 It is likely that Lydgate reconstructed the pageants from a Latin letter written by John Carpenter, town clerk of London (preserved in Guildhall Letter Book K, fos. 103b–104b, and MS Lambeth 12). The letter has been printed in the *Liber Albus*, ed. Henry Thomas Riley, 457–64, as well as in *Collection générale des documents français qui se trouvent en Angleterre recueillis et publiés*, ed. J. Delpit, 245–48. I have cited the copy found in *Liber Albus*. An important early article by MacCracken compared the letter to Lydgate's poem and concluded that the similarities were so precise that Lydgate must have used Carpenter's letter as a source; see "King Henry's Triumphal Entry into London, Lydgate's Poem, and Carpenter's Letter." Other scholars have since agreed; see Osberg, "Jesse Tree in the 1432 London Entry of Henry VI," n. 12, and Kipling's important discussion in *Enter the King*, 142–69, especially n. 59. But Kipling also notes that the allegorical figures of Mercy, Grace, and Pity, which Lydgate describes, do not appear in the two extant versions of Carpenter's letter; he nevertheless takes them as genuine elements of the spectacle. Thus, while Lydgate may have used a version of the letter no longer extant, he might also have seen the pageants himself. Lydgate's verses were recorded in a number of chronicles; see MacCracken, ed., *Minor Poems of John Lydgate*, part 2, 101–02, and Kipling, *Enter the King*, 143, n. 59. They have been printed in MacCracken, ed., *Minor Poems of John Lydgate*, part 2, 624–48, in Kingsford, ed., *Chronicles of London*, 97–115 (from MS Julius B II), and in Nicolas, ed., *Chronicle of London, from 1089 to 1483*, 235–50. Schirmer, *John Lydgate*, 139–43 argues that Lydgate must have been the "devisor" of the pageants, in collaboration with Carpenter, pointing out that the wording of the letter and the verses only coincides exactly when describing the inscriptions on each pageant. Pearsall, *John Lydgate (1371–1449)*, 33–34, takes the safest position when he suggests that Lydgate followed Carpenter, but may have been present. Benson reads the entry in relation to Lydgate's status as a London poet, noting that the imagery and structure of the spectacle highlighted the important role of London as the "King's Chamber," and emphasized the independence of the city from the monarch. See "Civic Lydgate." David N. DeVries discusses the entry in relation to the problem of clean

water in London, and makes the important point that the procession is modeled after the literary paradigm of the visionary journey, such as that in Alan of Lille's *Anticlaudianus*; see "And Away go Troubles Down the Drain," 409–10. For a brief discussion of prose accounts of the 1432 entry as they appear in London chronicles, see McLaren, *London Chronicles of the Fifteenth Century*, 52–58.

3 Two recent collections of work on urban theatricality contain a wide variety of approaches to the subject; see *City and Spectacle in Medieval Europe*, ed. Barbara Hanawalt and Kathryn Reyerson, and *Moving Subjects: Processional Performance in the Middle Ages and the Renaissance*, ed. Kathleen Ashley and Wim Hüsken. Studies of medieval English processions and entries were preceded by important work on Tudor spectacularity; see David Bergeron, *English Civic Pageantry, 1558–1642*, Sidney Anglo, *Spectacle, Pageantry, and Early Tudor Policy*, and Gordon Kipling, *The Triumph of Honour: The Burgundian Origins of the English Renaissance*. The first major work on English pageantry was done by Robert Withington; though it has been superseded, it still provides useful summaries; see *English Pageantry: An Historical Outline*, vol. I. Wickham's discussion of medieval English pageantry in *Early English Stages*, vol. I is comprehensive and helpful; see "Pageant Theatres of the Streets," 51–111. Two discussions of theatricality that explicitly take up the difficulties entailed in using theoretical models of wholeness and integration are Lerer's "Chaucerian Critique of Medieval Theatricality," and Clopper's "Engaged Spectator." Sheila Lindenbaum has also challenged the "social wholeness" thesis; see "Ceremony and Oligarchy: The London Midsummer Watch," and "The Smithfield Tournament of 1390," as well as "London Texts and Literate Practices."

4 In a series of important articles, and in his book *Enter the King*, Kipling has argued that the "civic triumph" first emerged during the reign of Richard II as a dramatic form; by the sixteenth century it had reached its zenith as one of the most "popular and influential" means of civic and theatrical expression in London. It is my argument here that "triumph" was not a label that was applied to royal entries in the fourteenth century. See Kipling's "Triumphal Drama: Form in English Civic Pageantry," 38, as well as "Richard II's 'Sumptuous Pageants' and the Idea of the Civic Triumph," 83–103. Kipling has modified his views on the influence of Roman triumphs on medieval civic triumphs; see *Enter the King*, 10 and note 11. The first "triumph" he describes occurred in 1377, at Richard's coronation, with a second – a welcome for his wife, Anne of Bohemia – following closely in 1382; these were relatively simple affairs, with a single pageant; see "Richard II's 'Sumptuous Pageants,' " 84; *Enter the King*, 6. The royal entry of 1392 was markedly more elaborate and spectacular; like the 1432 coronation entry of Henry VI, it used multiple pageants, stages and actors. See *Enter the King*, 12–21.

5 Lydgate's reference to Caesar is made more significant by the fact that it constitutes an addition to his source text, John Carpenter's Latin letter describing the 1432 pageants. For a discussion of Caesar's role in French pageantry of the fifteenth and sixteenth centuries, see Josèphe Jacquiot, "De l'entrée de César à Rome à l'entrée des Rois de France dans leurs bonnes villes."

6 For example, Lydgate compares London to Jerusalem, "And lyke ffor Dauyd affter his victorie, / Reioyssed was alle Ierusalem, / So this Citee with lavde, pris, and glorie, / For ioye moustred lyke the sonne beem" ("King Henry VI's Triumphal Entry," lines 22–25; MacCracken, ed., *Minor Poems of John Lydgate*, part 2, 631), and describes Henry's lineage as descending, like Christ, from Jesse; as Kipling notes, "just as his own genealogical trees are here revealed to be a type of the Jesse Tree, so Henry stands revealed as the type of royal Saviour come to the world as those trees have foretold" (*Enter the King*, 145).

7 Indeed, the closest analogue to Lydgate's reference to Caesar's triumph in the 1432 verses can be found in Chaucer's *Man of Law's Tale*, lines 400–03, a passage in which Custance's arrival in Syria is compared to Caesar's triumph: "Nought trowe I the triumphe of Julius, / Of which that Lucan maketh swich a boost, / Was roialler ne moore curius / Than was th'assemblee of this blisful hoost." Given Custance's fate while in Syria – and the line immediately following Chaucer's reference to the triumph, "But this scorpioun, this wikked goost, / The Sowdanesse" – Lydgate's echo of this passage suggests the deep ambivalence of his reference to Caesar in the verses for Henry's entry.

8 *OED*, s.v. "triumph," definition 4. In his important article "Triumphal Drama," Kipling cites a number of instances in which sixteenth- and seventeenth-century triumphs make reference to the Roman model, including a Lord Mayor's Show written by Thomas Dekker that imagines the Mayor as *triumphator*, the sheriffs as consuls, and the aldermen as senators, as well as the "Arches of Triumph" deployed in King James's 1603 coronation procession (40–41). By far the most complete treatment of the Roman triumph, from its classical origins to its Renaissance revival, is Anthony Miller's *Roman Triumphs and Early Modern English Culture*. A wave of interest in triumphs appeared in England at the end of the sixteenth century; see Miller's "Elizabethans and the Armada," 62–82, and "Marlowe and Spenser," 82–106. Robert Payne discusses the Renaissance triumph in his *Roman Triumph*, 225–46, adducing a large number of examples from the Continent and England. For a discussion of "triumphal forms" in the English Renaissance, including some treatment of Dante, Petrarch, and the Roman triumph, and with numerous examples of the uses of the triumph during the period, see Alastair Fowler, *Triumphal Forms: Structural Patterns in Elizabethan Poetry*, especially 23–61. For illustrations of the sixteenth-century interest in imitating Roman cultural practices and forms, whether mediated through Petrarchanism or directly copied, see Miller, *Roman Triumphs* (70), and D. D. Carnicelli's introduction to *Lord Morley's* Tryumphs of Fraunces Petrarcke, 55. The very fact of Henry Parker, Lord Morley's translation (printed between 1553 and 1556), illustrates the interest of sixteenth-century aristocrats in the idea of the triumph; as Carnicelli points out, Queen Elizabeth herself translated part of the "Triumph of Eternity" and Shakespeare, Spenser, and Sidney all included processions resembling those in the *Trionfi* in their works (36, 56–66).

9 While it seems likely that kings did enter cities in state from the very earliest times – as Ernst Kantorowicz demonstrated, the Roman "adventus" exerted a deep influence on the imagery and liturgy that accompanied Christian kings of the early Middle Ages – it is by no means clear that medieval kings imagined themselves as Roman triumphators; see "The 'King's Advent' and the Enigmatic Panels in the Doors of Santa Sabina." Using evidence from coins, liturgical orders, poems, and various visual images, Kantorowicz argues that there was "an unbroken tradition from antiquity insofar as the Christian ceremonial of royal receptions appears, with few *mutatis* and even fewer *mutandis*, as the continuation of the ceremonial observed at the epiphanies of Hellenistic Kings and Roman Emperors" (211). It is this essay that most deeply informs Kipling's *Enter the King*, and his vision of the thematic continuity of the "adventus" from the classical period to late medieval period. One body of evidence that Kantorowicz does not adduce, however, is records of actual royal entries, which begin much later in the medieval period; one of the earliest mentions of such an entry in England occurs in 1189, at the coronation of Richard I; see Withington, "Early Royal Entry." "Adventus" and "triumphus" did merge, to a certain extent, in papal entries; see Payne, *Roman Triumph*, 211–24, for examples of papal processions and their similarities to Roman triumphs. Susan Twyman, *Papal Ceremonial at Rome in the Twelfth Century*, 7–8, 47, has shown how the "adventus"

and "triumphus" tended to merge in papal ceremonial, through the appropriation of the *imperium* by the popes, but as her exhaustive accounts of "adventes" show, the ceremonies had very little in common with the classical model of the triumph.

10 Cited in the *OED*, s.v. "triumph," 1a. The word or a variant of it appears seventy-nine times in the *Dictionary of Old English Corpus*; most of those uses are Latin. It occurs eighteen times in Old English, all in the *Orosius*; see Bately, ed., *Old English Orosius*. I am grateful to Katherine O'Brien O'Keeffe for this reference.

11 See *Anelida and Arcite*, line 43; *Man of Law's Tale*, B, line 400; *Monk's Tale*, B, lines 3553 and 3886. See also *Confessio Amantis*, book 7, lines 2355–411 and gloss, and *Serpent of Division*, 53–54.

12 Benson has argued that both Chaucer and Lydgate represented the classical past as different from the present, emphasizing at various points in *Troilus and Criseyde* and the *Troy Book* that Troy was an alien culture, far removed in place and time from late medieval England; see "Ancient World in Lydgate's *Troy Book*," 299.

13 In Jean de Thuin's version, the victor is greeted by Roman citizens, including the dignitaries of the city, placed in an elaborately decorated chariot, clothed in a garment of gold and precious stones, and brought inside Rome. As in Lydgate's version, he shares the chariot with a "sierf"; but rather than beating him and telling him to "Know yourself," the "sierf" holds a golden palm as a token of humility. There is also a tablet covered with gold and precious stones that records the deeds of the conqueror, and the victor recounts his deeds for the people as he processes. He reaches the palace and is placed on a throne and crowned with laurel; he then divides his spoils among the barons and departs, scattering largesse to the people along the way. See *Li Hystore de Julius Cesar*, 8–10. The source of Jean's account is unclear. The editor of *Li Hystore*, Franz Settegast, cites Isidore and Tertullian (xxxiii, n. 1), but neither of those accounts corresponds particularly closely to Jean's. An exemplum appearing in some versions of the *Gesta Romanorum*, "Triumph, Beschreibung," has many similarities to Jean's account – the greeting by the people, the decorated chariot, and the distribution of the spoils – and may very well have served as his primary source; it is directly taken from a passage in Honorius of Autun's *Speculum Ecclesiae*.

14 Lydgate's use of Isidore is flexible. Lydgate adds this distinction to his account of a triumph, and also includes a number of other Isidorean details, some of which he modifies. Lydgate acknowledges the difference between palm and laurel, but locates it in the necklace of palm, which, he tells us, can have thorns or not, depending on the nature of the victory; he also adopts the eagle-crowned scepter. It is entirely possible that Lydgate found Isidore's version in Vincent of Beauvais's *Speculum Doctrinale*, 1043, where it is rendered verbatim.

15 Isidore's *Etymologiae* was the standard source for medieval thinkers who wished to know the meaning of a Latin word; as Mary Marshall in "Theatre in the Middle Ages: Evidence from Dictionaries and Glosses," 8, points out, there survive over one thousand manuscripts of the text, which may be dated to the early seventh century. Hugutio of Pisa (Uguccione da Pisa), bishop of Ferrara, 1190–1210, compiled the *Derivationes* during the later part of the twelfth century; it was a hugely influential work, known to modern scholars largely through its influence on Dante (see Toynbee, "Dante's Latin Dictionary," and the entry on Uguccione in *Enciclopedia Dantesca*, vol. v, 800–02, by Giancarlo Schizzerotto). A modern edition, *Derivationes*, ed. Cecchini et al., was published too late for me to use here. For a list of manuscripts (over two hundred), see Aristide Marigo, *I Codici manoscritti delle 'Derivationes' di Uguccione Pisano*. The text exists in both microfilm and facsimile. See Uguccione da Pisa, *Magnae Derivationes*, Bodl. MS Laud 626, MLA-Library

of Congress Collection of Photographic Facsimiles, no. 30, 1925. A facsimile of MS Laurenziano Plut. XXVII sin. 5 from the library at Crusca has recently been published; see Giovanni Nencioni, ed., *Uguccione da Pisa: Derivationes*. For a general discussion of Hugutio's life and works, see Wolfgang Müller, *Huguccio: The Life, Works, and Thought of a Twelfth-Century Jurist*, especially pages 35–48.

16 It is not clear where Hugutio derived the triumph account. The dictionary upon which he modeled his text in part was Osbern of Gloucester's *Derivationes*, but the triumph appears only as an entry with various Latin forms of the word; see Ferruccio Bertini and Vincenzo Ussani, eds., *Osberno: Derivazioni*, vol. II, 707. For a discussion of Osbern's sources, and of the meaning of such categories as "etymology" and "derivation," as well as a printed version of Osbern's preface, see Hunt, " 'Lost' Preface to the *Liber Derivationum* of Osbern of Gloucester." Another source for various entries is Papias's *Elementarium Doctrinae Erudimentum*, printed as *Papias Vocabulista* in Venice in 1496; the entry "triumph" repeats Isidore's version precisely (page 359). As I note below, there are various classical sources for the elements of Hugutio's description, but no one source accounts for them all. For a discussion of Hugutio's text and sources, see Riessner, "*Magnae Derivationes*", particularly 21–37. For a consideration of Papias, Osbern, and Hugutio and their relationships to each other and to the evolution of the dictionary form, see Weijers, "Lexicography in the Middle Ages."

17 The standard work on Roman triumphs is H. S. Versnel's *Triumphus: An Inquiry into the Origin, Development and Meaning of the Roman Triumph*; Versnel identifies the sources of most, but not all, of the elements of the triumph as described in medieval accounts. See also the review of Versnel's book by Larissa Bonfante Warren. T. Corey Brennan discusses the historical triumph, and the alternative of a triumph in Monte Albano, in "Triumphus in Monte Albano." Robert O. Payne's *Roman Triumph* is a more popular, but still useful account. The article by William Ramsay, "Triumphus," in *A Dictionary of Greek and Roman Antiquities*, ed. William Smith, contains many helpful references to classical sources for various elements of the practice. Künzl describes the Roman triumph in detail, including an appendix with German translations of several classical accounts and a brief final chapter describing the use of the triumph in Germany through the Middle Ages to the present; see *Der Römische Triumph: Siegesfeiern im Antiken Rom*. For extensive descriptions of specific triumphs, see Barini, *Triumphalia*; a brief account can be found in Scullard, *Festivals and Ceremonies of the Roman Republic*, 213–15. The most recent account of Roman triumphs is Holliday, *Origins of Roman Historical Commemoration in the Visual Arts*, especially chapter 1, "Images of Triumph," 22–62, which includes a large amount of material on visual representations of triumph not found elsewhere. These scholars are more interested in the cultural and historical contexts of the Roman practice than in the literary transmission of an idealized account of the triumph; for such an account of the Renaissance understanding of the triumph, see Anthony Miller, *Roman Triumphs and Early Modern English Culture*. Miller does not, however, discuss the medieval understanding of the triumph.

18 The full passage from Hugutio reads:

> Nam reverenti solebat totus populus exire obviam victori cum magno exulta-tione et magno gaudio. Et hic erat una leticia. Alia leticia erat quia omnes capti sequebantur currum suum ligatis manibus post terga. Tercia enim leticia erat quia ipse indutus tunica Jovis sedebat in curru quem trahebat quattuor equi albi. Ovidius: quattuor in niveis aureus ibis equis. Et cum tanto honore ducebatur ad capitolium, hanc tamen habebat molestiam quia ponebatur quidam servus una

cum eo in curru et semper colaphizabat triumphantem ne ipse nimis superbiret. Et ideo ut daretur spes unicuique quantumcumque vilis condicionis esset perveniendi ad similem honorem si probitas sua promereretur, dicebat semper "noli-solitos" id est "nosce teipsum," quasi noli superbire de tanto honore. Et illa die licebat cuique dicere in personam triumphantis quicquid vellet. Unde Cesari triumphanti fertur quidam dixisse cum debetur induci in civitati "Aperite portas regi calvo et regine Bitinie," volens significare quod calvus esset et quod regi britanie [sic] succubus extiterat. Et alius de eodem "ave, rex et regina."

(Returning to Rome, all the people were accustomed to go forth toward the victor with great exaltation and joy. This was the first joy. The second joy was that all of his captives followed his chariot with their hands tied in back. The third joy was that the triumphator himself was dressed in the tunic of Jove, sitting in a chariot drawn by four white horses. Ovid says, "quatuor in niveis aureus ibis." And as he was led to this Capitol with such honor, he nevertheless had this annoyance, which was that a slave was placed with him in the chariot, who was constantly striking the triumphator so that he would not become too arrogant. And therefore, in order that hope might be given to anyone, of however base a condition, that he might come to such honor if his virtue merited it, the slave was constantly saying, "noli solitos," that is, "Know yourself." And so that the triumphator did not become proud of such honor, on that day it was permitted that anyone might say against the person of the triumphator whatever he wished. Whence it is said that when Caesar was to be led in triumph into the city, someone said, "Open the gates to the bald king and the queen of Bithinia," wishing to signify that he was bald and that he had been a succuba of the king of Bithinia. And others said about him, "Hail, King and Queen!")

See Nencioni, ed., *Uguccione da Pisa: Derivationes*, 85v.

19 Isidore reads Pliny's remark that in Roman triumphs, "iubetque eosdem respicere similis medicina linguae, ut sit exorata a tergo Fortuna, gloriae carnifex" ("and the similar physic of the tongue bids them [the triumphators] look back, so that behind them, Fortune, the slayer of glory, may be appeased"), and interprets the word "carnifex" as "hangman"; see Pliny, *Natural History*, vol. VIII, ed. and trans. W. H. S. Jones, book 28, vii, 30–31. I have modified Jones's translation slightly. See the notes to the version of the *Etymologiae* printed in the *Patrologia Latina*, vol. LXXXII, col. 642D; see also Ramsay, "Triumphus."

20 See Welter, *Exemplum dans la littérature religieuse et didactique du moyen âge*, particularly part 2, chapter 1 for a survey of exempla collections and manuals for preaching in the thirteenth and fourteenth centuries. Welter's definition of an "exemplum" was very broad: "Il devait renfermer trois éléments essentiels, à savoir: un récit ou une description, un enseignement moral ou religieux, une application de ce dernier à l'homme" (3). For further discussion of the origins of exempla collections see Scanlon, *Narrative Authority and Power*, 65 and 70; Fleming, *Introduction to the Franciscan Literature*, 110–14, 142–4; and Allen, *The Friar as Critic*, 45–47. Scanlon's account is inestimably valuable in assessing the place of the exemplum in English literary history; he argues that vernacular writers such as Chaucer, Gower, Hoccleve, and Lydgate were deeply and formatively influenced by exemplarity, particularly its "transformation of fallen historical reality into moral value" (98). Each of these poets had to define himself in relation to the exemplum tradition, Chaucer in the *Melibee* and *Monk's Tale*, Gower in the *Confessio Amantis*, Hoccleve in the *Regiment of Princes*, and Lydgate in the *Fall of Princes*.

21 Allen, *Friar as Critic*, 46–47.

22 Wenzel discusses the question of the date for *Fasciculus Morum* in *Verses in Sermons*, 26–41; he elaborates the manuscript tradition in his edition and translation of the text, *Fasciculus Morum: A Fourteenth Century Preacher's Handbook*, 1–28. The question of the date of the *Gesta Romanorum* has been an extremely vexed one. The most recent treatment of the question is Weiske, *Gesta Romanorum*, which expands on and revises the work of Hermann Öesterley, the nineteenth-century editor of the *Gesta*, and until Weiske, the standard reference work on the text; see *Gesta Romanorum*, ed. Öesterley. Like Öesterley, Weiske distinguishes between the Anglo-Latin *Gesta* (represented by British Library MS Harley 2270) and the Germano-Latin tradition (two groups, w and z, with z preceding w and best represented by Innsbruck Universitätsbibliothek, Cod. Lat. 310), and notes the distinct differences between the English version and the later, continental texts. The Innsbruck MS is dateable to 1342 and represents the earliest manuscript of the *Gesta*; it has been printed by Wilhelm Dick as *Die Gesta Romanorum nach der Innsbrucker Handschrift*. In an article published in 1991, Weiske argued that the *Gesta* existed in a relatively developed form prior to 1284, showing that Hugo von Trimberg used exempla from the *Gesta* in his *Solsequium*; see "Die 'Gesta Romanorum' und das 'Solsequium' Hugos von Trimberg." In her book, she expands upon this thesis (see her discussion of Hugo, 77–81), showing that group z was ultimately of English origin, as evidenced by the use of English words in the Germano-Latin texts (vol. I, 30–41) – though both groups w and z remain distinct from the "insular" tradition. For descriptions of several manuscripts containing the *Gesta*, see Herbert, *Catalogue of Romances*.

23 Wenzel, *Fasciculus Morum*, 76–78, lines 218–29.

24 *Fasciculus* also includes a detail not found in Hugutio, but found in Lydgate: the fact that the chariot is gold.

25 Nencioni, ed., *Uguccione da Pisa: Derivationes*, 85v.

26 The first step in any discussion of the *Gesta Romanorum* must be to determine exactly what version(s) of the text will be analyzed, by no means an easy or obvious decision and one with important implications for questions involving dating or sources. In the case of the triumph, the situation is made more complex by the fact that some later redactions of the *Gesta* contain *two* versions of the exemplum, one that resembles the Hugutian description, and one that is drawn from Honorius (of Autun), called "Triumph, Beschreibung" by the principal editor of the text, Hermann Öesterley. Further, it is only the latter version that uses the term "triumph"; like *Fasciculus Morum*, the *Gesta*'s account of the three honors and the three discomforts given to the victor elides the Roman label found in Hugutio. Because "Triumph, Beschreibung" appears in far fewer manuscripts than the standard Hugutian account, and does not appear to have had the same influence on later commentators and sermonists, I will not be discussing it here. For the exemplum, see Öesterley, *Gesta Romanorum*, 657–58, no. 252; for the passage in Honorius, see the *Speculum Ecclesiae*, in *Patrologia Latina*, vol. CLXXII, cols. 955C–957A. The exemplum is indexed by Frederic Tubach, *Index Exemplorum*, as no. 4126 (317). The Hugutian triumph is indexed as no. 5084 (384).

27 Öesterley, *Gesta Romanorum*, 328–29, no. 30.

28 Tertullian, *Apologeticus and De Spectaculis*, trans. Glover, book 33, 156–57. The full passage reads: "Hominem se esse etiam triumphans in illo sublimissimo curru admonetur. Suggeritur enim ei a tergo: Respice post te! Hominem te memento!" ("Even in the triumph, as he rides in that most exalted chariot, he is reminded that he is a man. It is whispered to him from behind: 'Look behind thee; remember thou art a man!' ").

29 One other "moral" use of the triumph exemplum should be mentioned here, though I do not have space for a full discussion of the text: the sermons of Bishop Brinton. In three sermons – 7, 36, and 106 – Brinton uses the triumph exemplum as part of a more thematic excursus on the nature of honor; he is particularly concerned with ill-gotten honor and riches, using the three "molestiae" to illustrate the danger of embracing worldly recognition and gain. See *The Sermons of Thomas Brinton, Bishop of Rochester* (1373–89), ed. Devlin, vol. I, 14–22 (sermon 7), vol. I, 152–53 (sermon 36), and vol. II, 487–91 (sermon 106).

30 Smalley, *English Friars and Antiquity.*

31 In his discussion of Holcot's "mythographic learning," Allen argues that "Holkot's medieval sources are much more important to him, apparently, than classical ones" (*Friar as Critic,* 725).

32 In London, British Museum MS Additional 31216, fo. 175va and Cambridge, Pembroke College Cambridge MS 181, fo. 138vb; see Smalley, *English Friars and Antiquity,* 148 and note 2. The Latin reads: "Quamvis ista sapientia in qualibet parte scripture sacre valeat inveniri, specialiter tamen et quadam peculiari forma in libro sapentie continetur, in quo reges et principes de cultu Dei et bonis moribus informantur."

33 As Smalley points out, "in *lectio* liv, he refers to the feast of the Conversion of St. Paul (January 25) as to be celebrated tomorrow"; in lectio lxxxiii, a marginal note indicates "i post Pascha" and at the end of lectio c, he refers to the Whitsuntide break (*English Friars and Antiquity,* 140).

34 Ibid., 141–42. The manuscript was repeatedly copied, and was printed several times; see Smalley, "Robert Holcot, O. P.," 11–14, for a brief discussion of the manuscripts and printed editions. For a more exhaustive list, see Stegmüller, *Repertorium Biblicum Medii Aevi,* vol. V, no. 7416, 143–46. For Chaucer's use of the text, see Pratt, "Some Latin Sources of the Nonnes Preest on Dreams."

35 Scanlon, *Narrative, Authority and Power,* 98.

36 *Super Libros Sapientiae,* lectio 164.

37 Smalley, *English Friars and Antiquity,* 306.

38 Higden's text reads: "Unde et Julio triumphanti multae dicebantur contumeliae, nulla tamen ultione subsequente. Nam a quodam dicebatur, 'Salve, calve;' et ab alio, 'Ave, Rex et Regina' " (*Polychronicon,* lib. I, 240).

39 The story conflates two incidents in Suetonius's *De Vita Caesarum,* vol.I, xlix, in which Caesar is separately called "regina" and accused of sodomy; see Rolfe, ed., *Suetonius,* 96–97. Dante understood the meaning of the story plainly; as Toynbee, "Dante's Latin Dictionary," showed, he used Hugutio's "triumphus" in *Purgatorio* XXVI in his account of Caesar's sodomy. See also Charles Singleton's commentary on *Purgatorio,* 633–36, for the passage from Suetonius.

40 The full story appears in volume III of the *Polychronicon,* where it forms part of Higden's narrative of Caesar's rise and fall; Suetonius is cited as the source, though the same conflation occurs as in Hugutio. See *Polychronicon,* vol. III, 214.

41 I have emended the 1494 edition, which reads "tranquillum ducem," to "tranquillum dicentem," which is the reading found in the 1489 Reutlingen edition printed by Johanne Otmar.

42 *Polychronicon,* vol. I, 238.

43 Isidore's rendering is a relatively straightforward description of the custom; Isidore asserts that the triumphator was honored with a triple judgment ("tripertito iudicio") by the army, the senate, and the people. The conqueror entered Rome in a chariot drawn by a team of four, crowned either with the golden palm (in the case of a battle, because it

had spines) or with spineless laurel (for bloodless victories). He wore a purple toga embroidered with palms and carried a scepter topped with an eagle; his face was daubed with red coloring as an imitation of divinity ("quasi imitarentur divini ignis effigiem"). A hangman touched him in order to remind him of the insignificance and ordinariness of the human condition ("mediocritatis humanae"). See Isidore, *Etymologiae*, ed. Lindsay, lib. XVIII, ii, iii. These details can be found in a number of classical accounts; for a full discussion, see Versnel, *Triumphus*, 56–93. In his *History of Rome*, Livy gives a relatively full description of the classical triumph; see the *History of Rome*, book 10, vii, in *Livy: History of Rome Books VII–X*, trans. Foster, 382–85. We see the tunic embroidered with palms, the chariot, the ride to the Capitol, and the laurel wreath, along with the general idea that the triumphator is imitating Jove. The detail in Isidore that the conqueror's face was daubed with red coloring appears in Pliny; see *Natural History*, vol. IX, ed. and trans. Rackham, book 33, xxxvi, 84–85, among other places. See also Versnel, *Triumphus*, 59–60.

44 Leonard Boyle ("The Date of the *Summa Praedicantium* of John of Bromyard") dates the text to the years *circon.* 1330–52, based on internal evidence and references to current historical conditions. In particular, he dates Bromyard's work on "Tribulatio" to the summer of 1348; the text refers to recent heavy rains, a phenomenon remarked upon by several chroniclers, including Higden, and identified as occurring in the summer of that year.

45 For a useful discussion of the place of "division" in the art of sermon-making, see Wenzel, *Preachers, Poets and the Early English Lyric*, especially chapter 3, "The Sermon as an Art Form" (61–100).

46 Nolcken, "Some Alphabetical Compendia and how Preachers used them in Fourteenth-Century England," has shown how Bromyard's *Summa* fits into a well-established tradition of *artes predicandi* that had emerged in the thirteenth century with such texts as the *Speculum Laicorum*. In the fourteenth century a new kind of compendium emerged that "systematically amalgamated in an encyclopedic manner material drawn from various sources" (271); Bromyard's *Summa* was among the earliest and most important of these.

47 John Bromyard, *Summa Praedicantium*, "Dedicatio," 183, cited by Owst, *Literature and Pulpit in Medieval England*, 155, n. 2. It is largely through Owst's work that the *Summa Praedicantium* is known to scholars; it has not been printed in a modern edition. I have consulted the copy owned by the University of Pennsylvania's Van Pelt Library.

48 The difficult questions of dating the *Gesta Romanorum* and the *Summa Praedicantium* make it impossible to determine if one text preceded the other. Owst assumed that the *Summa* dated from the later part of the century (see Boyle, "Date of the *Summa Praedicantium*," 534) and that Bromyard used the *Gesta* as his source; it is equally possible that the reverse is true. The *Gesta* was not listed by Welter in his comprehensive list of the sources specifically cited by Bromyard in the *Summa*; see *Exemplum dans la littérature religieuse et didactique du moyen âge*, 333–34. The triumph episode indicates that Bromyard and the *Gesta* author read a similar source, but the accounts are sufficiently different to suggest that each independently rendered the exemplum.

49 Bromyard, *Summa Praedicantium*, 411. The analogy was a popular one in patristic texts. Bromyard quotes Gregory's *Moralia*; see part 6 of the preface to *Moralia in Job, Libri I–X*, ed. Adriaen, 12.

50 Bromyard, *Summa Praedicantium*, 411. There are several errors in the text: "Te de" should be "de te," "in hoc enim boni" should be "in hoc enim bonum," and "sicut patet responderet" should be "sicut pater responderet." A point of interest concerns the

marginal notation, "exemplum," part of the original printing of the copy held by the Van Pelt Library, which appears frequently throughout the text, but not next to the triumph exemplum. One provisional reason for this absence might be the nonnarrative character of the illustrative example; the triumph tends to recede in Bromyard's rendition, buried in the list of authorities and citations with which he surrounds it.

51 Alan of Lille, *De Arte Praedicatoria* (*Patrologia Latina*, vol. CCX, cols 109–98, caput xxiv, "De Fortitudine"); see also Patch, *Goddess Fortuna in Mediaeval Literature*, 83, for an extensive list of classical and medieval iterations of the maxim, "fortune favors the bold" – which is not necessarily the same thing as "Qui fortis est liber est," though Patch tends to imply that it is. The maxim appears, for example, in Gower's *Confessio Amantis*, book 7, lines 4902–03, in the story of the rape of Lucrece: "Fortune unto the bolde / Is favorable forto helpe." Since the words are spoken by Lucrece's rapist, they signal a similar resistance on Gower's part to the idea that Fortune responds to human incentive – though perhaps not to the notion that virtue enables man to resist Fortune.

52 Owst, *Literature and Pulpit in Medieval England*, 48; Welter, *Exemplum dans la littérature religieuse et didactique du moyen âge*, 333.

53 Gransden, *Historical Writing in England*, vol. II, 44. Higden was summoned before the king's council in 1352, "with all your chronicles," suggesting that he was well known as an historian by that date; see Edwards, "Ranulf, Monk of Chester," 94.

54 Higden's version reads:

> Venienti duci, regi, consuli, sive imperatori post insignem victoriam ad urbem Romam triumphus parabatur, id est, honor triplex triumphanti exhibebatur. Nam totus populus cum exultatione varia exibat obviam victori. Captivi quoque sequebantur currum ejus ligatis post terga manibus, et ipse victor induebatur tunica Jovis in curru sedens, quem trahebant quatuor equi albi usque ad Capitolium: unde Ovidius:
>
> Quatuor in niveis, Caesar, abibis equis.
>
> Hanc tamen ferebat molestiam sic honoratus, ne sui ipsius oblivesceretur, quia cum eo ponebatur servus in eodem curru, qui jugiter colaphizaret triumphantem; et hoc duplici de causa, ne scilicet triumphans nimis ex tali gloria superbiret, et etiam ut daretur spes cuique probo perveniendi ad consimilem honorem, si probitas sua hoc promereretur. Colaphizans vero saepius dicebat triumphanti, "Nothissolitos," id est, nosce teipsum, quasi diceret, "Noli superbire de tanto honore." Et eo die licuit unicuique de populo dicere victori impune quicquid vellet. Unde et Julio triumphanti multae dicebantur contumeliae, nulla tamen ultione subsequente. Nam a quodam dicebatur, "Salve, calve"; et ab alio, "Ave, Rex et Regina."
>
> (Whan duke, kyng, consul, oþer emperour hadde i-doo greet viage and victorie, and come into Rome, at his comynge he schulde wiþ þre manere worschippe be vnderfonge. Al þe peple schulde come aȝenst hym wiþ all þe solempne merþe, comforte, and ioye þat þey kouþe make; all þe prisoneres schulde folwe þe chaar wiþ hire hondes i-bounde byhynde her bakkes; þis victor hym self schulde were on Iupiter his cote and sitte in a chaar þat fyue white hors schulde drawe anon to þe Capitol. Þerof spekeþ Ouidius:
>
> Wiþ foure hors all snowe white Þou schalt, sire Emperour, wende.

ʒit among all þis worschippe, for he schulde not forʒete hym self, þis onnuy he
hadde: a cherle was wiþ hym in his chare, and smote hym all wey in þe nekke; and
þat for tweye skilles; þat oon was, for he schulde nouʒt be proude of þat greet
worschippe; þat oþer skile was, for euerich man schulde hope to come to þat
worschippe, ʒif he made hym self worþy by his dedes. While þe cherle smoot þe
victor, he schulde ofte seie to hym in þis manere: Nothisselitos, þat is to
menynge, *Know þyself*, as who seiþ, Be nouʒt to proude of þis worschippe. And
also þat day euerich man hadde leue to seie to þe victor what euere he wolde, and
no blame schulde take. And so were meny dispitous worde i-seide to Iulius Cesar
[and he took þerof no maner wreche. On seide to Iulius Cesar] at such a tyme:
"Salve, calve"; þat is, "*Hail, ballard*"; and anoþer seide: "Heile, kyng and quene."
(*Polychronicon*, vol. I, 238–41, and Trevisa's translation)

55 The line from Ovid comes from *Ars Amatoria*, vol. I, 214; see *Art of Love and Other
Poems*, trans. Mozley, 26–27. Ovid's description of a triumph can be found in *Amores*, I,
ii, 19–52; see *Ovid: Heroides, Amores*, trans. Showerman, 322–25. The reference to Ovid
does appear in one odd text, the *Tractatus de Diversis Historiis Romanorum*, which is an
early fourteenth-century collection of exempla found in a single manuscript. This text
does not include the "contumelia" shouted at Caesar, and therefore cannot be considered Higden's source. See Herzstein, ed., *Tractatus de Diversis Historiis Romanorum
et Quibusdam Aliis*. The triumph exemplum also appears in the *Dialogus Creaturarum*;
see *Die Beiden Ältesten Lateinischen Fabelbücher des Mittelalters*, ed. Grässe, dialogue 60,
titled "De gallina et columba," 202.

56 These texts are discussed briefly in Taylor, *Universal Chronicle of Ranulf Higden*, 4–5,
and by Jennings, "Monks and the 'Artes Praedicandi' in the Time of Ranulph Higden."

57 *Polychronicon*, vol. I, 16.

58 Ibid.

59 For example, Taylor, *Universal Chronicle of Ranulf Higden*, 77, cites Higden's refutation
of Virgil – that "Aeneas could not have seen Dido, because Aeneas died more than 300
years before the foundation of Carthage" – in order to show Higden's "classicizing"
impulse, aligning him with the figures treated by Smalley. The desire to "classicize" is
also a desire to historicize. Higden's source was John Ridewall's commentary on *City of
God*; see Smalley, *English Friars and Antiquity*, 320. His refutation of Virgil appears
twice in the *Polychronicon*; see vol. I, 66 and vol. II, 432.

60 The Middle English version of the *Gesta Romanorum* is based on the Anglo-Latin
tradition; the triumph appears in the "cockcrows exemplum," with four honors and
four discomforts. Sidney Herrtage, who edited the three manuscripts containing the
Middle English *Gesta*, dates them to the reign of Henry VI, around 1440; see *Early
English Versions of the Gesta Romanorum*, xix. The exemplum itself appears on pages
174–79. A fourth manuscript, Gloucester Cathedral MS 22, is a fragmentary version of
the text and does not include either the triumph or the cockcrows exemplum; see
Middle English Version of the Gesta Romanorum, ed. Sandred. Mirk's *Festial* is a
fifteenth-century collection of vernacular sermons compiled by John Mirk, from the
Augustinian house at Lilleshall; see *Mirk's Festial: A Collection of Homilies, by Johannes
Mirkus*, ed. Erbe, 114–16. See also Cannon, "Monastic Productions," 347. The exemplum claims to be from the "Gestys of þe Romayns," and indeed is very similar to the
Gesta account, although it does include the phrase "Another selitos." It is part of a
sermon for Palm Sunday, and makes the link between Christ's entry into Jerusalem and
the triumph explicit. The Middle English version of the *Secreta Secretorum* that includes

the triumph is that translated by James Yonge in 1422 from the French version of Jofroi de Waterford (extant in only one manuscript, Paris, Bibliothèque Nationale, fonds français, 1822); for discussion of the text, and Gower's use of it, see Hamilton, "Some Sources of the Seventh Book of Gower's 'Confessio Amantis,' " 326. Yonge's text is printed in *Three Prose Versions of the Secreta Secretorum*, ed. Steele, 119–248; the triumph exemplum appears on pages 154–55. This version is ultimately indebted to Hugutio; it includes the Greek phrase and the distinctive suggestion that the slave is present in order to give hope to the people that they too might achieve worship. See also my discussion of Gower below.

61 Chaucer was clearly aware of the triumph exemplum; he refers to triumphs three times, in *Anelida and Arcite*, the *Man of Law's Tale*, and the *Monk's Tale*, mentioning the details of the crown of laurel (*Anelida and Arcite*) and the procession of captives before the chariot (*Monk's Tale*) and citing one of Caesar's triumphs (*Man of Law's Tale*). The relevant lines and line numbers are: *Anelida and Arcite*, line 43, "With his tryumphe and laurer-corouned thus" (referring to Theseus's return to Athens); *Man of Law's Tale*, lines 400–03, quoted above; *Monk's Tale*, lines 2363–64, "Biforen his triumphe walketh shee, / With gilte cheynes on hire nekke hangynge" (referring to Aurelian's capture of Zenobia).

62 Scanlon demonstrates the fundamental similarities between the two poets in his *Narrative, Authority and Power*; as he notes, both poets were dependent on clerical traditions, both questioned authority (albeit in different ways), and both fundamentally affirmed modes of social order (Gower, the political, and Chaucer the religious). See particularly page 296, but generally chapters 7–9. Aers argues that the two poets' positions in relation to the Peasants' Revolt were fundamentally similar, and betray a similar investment in the maintenance of hierarchy; see " *Vox Populi* and the Literature of 1381," 450.

63 Copeland has argued that book 7 is "a guide to the structure of the *Confessio Amantis* as a whole"; see *Rhetoric, Hermeneutics and Translation in the Middle Ages*, 211. See also Porter, "Gower's Ethical Microcosm and Political Macrocosm."

64 For a discussion of the relationship between the *Confessio Amantis* and exemplarity, see Scanlon, *Narrative, Authority and Power*, 282–97.

65 The relationship between Gower's Latin glosses and the vernacular text is a critical one, though in the particular instance of the triumph exemplum I do not find it to be especially vexed. As Winthrop Wetherbee has described, however, the glosses frequently express a tension between *exemplum* and *moralitas*, providing as they do a "dogged, schoolmasterly moralism" and the vernacular text often articulating a Boethian naturalism through the figure of Genius. See "Latin Structure and Vernacular Space: Gower, Chaucer and the Boethian Tradition," 9. See also Minnis's essay, "De Vulgari Auctoritate: Chaucer, Gower and the Men of Great Authority," which explores the relationship between the moralizing glosses and the Latin commentary tradition.

66 The question of Gower's use of the *Secreta Secretorum*, particularly for the triumph exemplum, is made very vexed by the complex textual history of that work. Briefly, Jofroi's translation followed one of the Latin versions of the *Secreta*, though the triumph exemplum was clearly added; in examining Roger Bacon's edition of the Latin text, as printed by Robert Steele, as well as the eleven English versions of the *Secreta*, all translated from the Latin, I have found no instance of the exemplum. See *Opera Hactenus Inedita Rogeri Baconi, Fasc. V: Secretum Secretorum*, ed. Steele, and *Secretum Secretorum: Nine English Versions*, ed. Manzalaoui, as well as *Three Prose Versions of the Secreta Secretorum*, ed. Steele, and the helpful introductions to each of those editions.

The one exception, which I noted above, is the translation of James Yonge, in which the exemplum appears, complete with "Notisclotos." Yonge may have derived his use of the Greek term from any number of sources, including Gower. Jofroi himself derived the exemplum from the *Breviloquium* of John of Wales – another of Smalley's "class-icizing friars" – and cited it as an example of memory, a subset of prudence, in a discussion of the four cardinal virtues. See Norbert D'Ordal, *Breviloqui*, 73–74 and note 71 above; for a brief description of Jofroi's use of the triumph exemplum, see Monfrin, "Sur les sources du *Secret des Secrets* de Jofroi de Waterford et Servais Copale." Various critics and editors have discussed Gower's use of the triumph exemplum and its probable source. Porter, "Ethical Microcosm and Political Macrocosm," 156, notes the relationship of Yonge's text to Gower's, and speculates that Gower may have read a glossed version of the *Secreta*. Hamilton, "Some Sources," 7–8, suggests that Gower read one of the many possible Latin accounts of the triumph that include "Nolisolitos," but does not mention Higden. Macaulay, *Complete Works of John Gower*, vol. III, 530, note to lines 2355ff., cites Bromyard and the *Gesta*, but notes that neither of those sources would provide "Notheos."

67 The story of the emperor and his masons has also proved troubling to scholars. Neither George Hamilton nor Elizabeth Porter cites a source for the episode. In his edition of the *Confessio*, Peck notes – as does Macaulay – that the same story appears in Hoccleve's *Regiment of Princes*, itself modeled on the *Secreta*, and is accompanied by a marginal gloss, "in vita Johannis Elemosnia." The original *Vita S. Johannis Eleemosynarii*, in the *Patrologia Latina*, vol. LXXIII, col. 354, has the grave-makers asking what metal to use; it is clearly Higden's source. Gower seems to have substituted stone for metal, and removed the explanation (that the grave-makers did so in order to remind the emperor that he was mortal) in order to make the story fit his theme of flattery and Roman plain-speaking. Hoccleve's version corresponds closely to Johannes's – though he does appear to incorporate Gower's version by having the grave-makers ask "of what metal or what stoon" the grave should be made. See Blyth, ed., *Regiment of Princes*, 123, lines 2857–70 and note. Peck attributes this story to Jofroi's *Secreta* in his note on the passage; I do not believe this to be correct, as Hamilton does not cite it, nor does it appear in Yonge's translation of Jofroi's text. See *Confessio Amantis*, ed. Peck, 517, n. 16.

68 Minnis has also noted the similarities between Holcot's *Wisdom* commentaries and Gower's book 7, suggesting that the Sapiential books provided a model for the integra-tion of pagan and Christian sources undertaken by Gower. See "John Gower, *Sapiens* in Ethics and Politics," 169–74.

69 For discussion of Gower's writing during this period and its relationship to contem-porary politics, see Ferster, *Fictions of Advice*, 108–36.

70 The dedication to Richard appears in the first and second recensions of the manuscript, written between 1386 and 1392; it includes a story about Gower meeting Richard on the Thames and being commissioned to write the work. In the third recension, written in 1392, Gower substitutes a dedication to Henry of Lancaster and omits the narrative about the commissioning of the text. See Peck, *John Gower: Confessio Amantis*, vol. I, 44. In the third recension, Gower's mention of Chaucer is also omitted. John Fisher notes that Gower received two grants from Henry, the first in 1393, when he was Earl of Derby, of a collar, and the second in 1399, after the accession, of two pipes of Gascony wine annually; see *John Gower: Moral Philosopher and Friend of Chaucer*, 68. Judith Ferster discusses Gower's satire in *Vox Clamantis*, pointing out that he is far more direct in his Latin writing than in English; see *Fictions of Advice*, 111. Frank Grady describes Gower's Lancastrianism in "In Praise of Peace," arguing that it is a "poem of

exasperation and a valediction to the mirror-for-princes genre . . . a text that is always on the verge of revealing the intractable paradoxes of that form and the incoherence (or tendentiousness) of that philosophy" ("Lancastrian Gower and the Limits of Exemplarity," 570). See Macaulay, *Complete Works of John Gower*, vol. IV, *Latin Works*, 1–314, for *Vox Clamantis*, and vol. III, *The English Works*, 481–92, for "In Praise of Peace."

71 William Robins makes a similar point about Gower's use of the genres of romance and exemplarity, arguing that they propose two different notions of temporality: romance, a temporality of contingency, and exemplarity, one of moral necessity. See "Romance, Exemplum, and the Subject of the *Confessio Amantis*," 181. For a discussion of Gower's use of exemplarity that describes its relation to rhetoric, and argues that the purpose of the *Confessio* as an exemplum is "not to restrict, but to liberate Gower and [his] audience morally," see Olsson, "Rhetoric, John Gower and the Late Medieval *Exemplum*," 196.

72 In his discussion of Lydgate's representation of the classical past in the *Troy Book*, Benson, following Smalley, argues that Lydgate, in imitation of Chaucer and as part of a "general antiquarian movement in England" ("Ancient World," 300, n. 5), deliberately sharpened the distinctions between past and present by representing Trojan cultural practices as substantially different from Christian customs. Benson locates this "classicizing" trend as part of a burgeoning interest in writing accurate history, and sees Lydgate trying "to preserve the true record of an ancient civilization" (312). For an important discussion of the difference between Lydgate and Chaucer's relationships to a Renaissance notion of history and the classical past (one that, in my view, somewhat overstates the extent of Lydgate's "medievalism"), see Spearing, "Renaissance Chaucer and Father Chaucer."

73 Lydgate makes a similar point in "The Debate of the Horse, Goose, and Sheep," dated 1436–37 by Pearsall (*John Lydgate (1371–1449)*, 51), telling his readers that "thees emperours . . . with ther victories & triumphes" (lines 638–39) are subject to Fortune and fall. The political message is explicit: "Beth war, ye pryncis, your suggettis to despise" (line 643). See MacCracken, ed., *Minor Poems of John Lydgate*, part 2, 539–66).

74 *Polychronicon*, vol. I, 240, and Trevisa's translation.

75 *Fall of Princes*, book 6, lines 2885–91.

76 Pearsall, *John Lydgate (1371–1449)*, 34, and appendix 12, 58–59; Lydgate was given official permission by the prior of Hatfield to return to Bury on April 8, 1434 (see appendix 12, 58–59).

77 For an account of Humphrey's actions in the early years of the decade, which included his removal of the king's household officers shortly after Henry VI's return, and his securing of the king's signet seal in the treasury with his own, see Watts, *Henry VI and the Politics of Kingship*, 118–19, and Griffiths, *Reign of Henry VI*, 58–59. For discussion of the deterioration of the English position in France after the defeat at Orléans and Henry VI's coronations, see Griffiths, *Reign of Henry VI*, 189–200.

78 As Watts describes, during the parliament of 1433–34 it became clear that the lords "had got cold feet" about Henry VI's personal rule; in November 1433 the lords revived the council as a way of asserting that though the king ruled in his *persona publica*, his *persona privata* "still could not look after itself" (*Henry VI and the Politics of Kingship*, 120–21).

79 MacCracken argued that Lydgate supplemented Carpenter's letter with his own observations; see "Lydgate's Poem," 95. Kipling argues that Lydgate probably was not present; he gives as his reason the fact that Lydgate describes the actors in the pageants as speaking, while Carpenter does not; I discuss this change to Carpenter below. See *Enter the King*, 143, n. 59.

80 See Kipling, *Enter the King*, 143–69.

81 See Bryant, "Configurations of the Community," 21, 12.

82 The seven gifts of the Holy Ghost appear in lines 181–86 of Lydgate's verses; see MacCracken, ed., *Minor Poems of John Lydgate*, part 2, 636. Richard Osberg has argued that the four cardinal virtues – familiar from the "Disguising at London" and quintessentially political elements of good rule – form a crucial part of the city's message to its young ruler. See "Jesse Tree in the 1432 London Entry of Henry VI," 219.

83 Riley, ed., *Liber Albus*, 461.

84 Ibid., 458, 460.

85 See, for example, Carpenter's description of the seven virgins' presentation of the seven gifts of the Holy Ghost, "dicentes per rescriptum" (ibid., 459) and his later description of their presentation of sword, scepter, shield, mantel, and girdle; they provide a *written* text describing the virtues of each object – "A sinistro quoque latere septem aliae virgines lacteis liliatae vestitibus, et stellatis corporibus elucentes, septem insignia regalia rotulo pedibus carum taliter subscripto recitata praesentabant" (460).

86 See stanzas 26, 38, 54, and 55 of the verses; MacCracken, ed., *Minor Poems of John Lydgate*, part 2, 636–43.

87 *MED*, s. v. "quthen."

Bibliography

PRIMARY SOURCES

Adriaen, Marci, ed. *Moralia in Job, Libri I–X.* Corpus Christianorum Series Latina 143. Turnholt: Brepols, 1979.

Alan of Lille. *De Arte Praedicatoria. Patrologia Latina*, vol. CCX, col. 109–98.

Alighieri, Dante. *Inferno.* Trans. Charles Singleton. Princeton: Princeton University Press, 1970.

Purgatorio. Trans. Charles Singleton. Princeton: Princeton University Press, 1973.

Babington, Churchill, and Joseph R. Lumby, eds. *Polychronicon Ranulphi Higden Monachi Cestrensis: together with the English translations of John of Trevisa and of an unknown writer of the fifteenth century.* Vol. I (Babington); vol. III (Lumby). 9 vols. Rolls Series 41. London: Longman & Co., 1865–66.

Barlow, Claude W., ed. *Opera Omnia of Martin of Braga.* Papers and Monographs of the American Academy in Rome 12. New Haven, CT: Yale University Press, 1950.

Bately, Janet, ed. *The Old English Orosius.* Early English Text Society supplementary series 6. Oxford: Oxford University Press, 1980.

Bennett, J. A. W., and G. V. Smithers, eds. *Early Middle English Verse and Prose.* Oxford: Clarendon Press, 1966.

Benson, Larry D., ed. *Riverside Chaucer.* Boston: Houghton Mifflin, 1987.

Bernard of Clairvaux. *Lettere.* Ed. Ferruccio Gastaldelli. *Opere di San Bernardo*, vol. VI. Milan: Fondazione Di Studi Cistercenci, 1986.

Bertini, Ferruccio, and Vincenzo Ussani, eds. *Osberno: Derivazioni.* Spoleto: Centro Italiano di Studi Sull'alto Medioevo, 1996.

Boccaccio, Giovanni. *De Casibus Virorum Illustrium. Tutte Le Opere Di Giovanni Boccaccio*, vol. IX, ed. Vittore Branca. Milan: Arnoldo Mondadori, 1983.

Boethius. *Consolation of Philosophy.* Trans. S. J. Tester. Cambridge, MA: Harvard University Press, 1973.

Bromyard, John. *Summa Praedicantium.* Venice, 1586.

Burt, Sister Marie Anita, ed. "Jacobus de Cessolis: Libellus de Moribus Hominum et Officiis Nobilium ac Popularium super Ludo Scachorum." Ph.D. dissertation. Austin: University of Texas, 1957.

Capgrave, John. *Abbreuacioun of Cronicles.* Ed. Peter J. Lucas. Early English Text Society old series 285. Oxford: Oxford University Press, 1983.

Carnicelli, D. D. *Lord Morley's* Tryumphes of Fraunces Petrarcke: *The First English Translation of the* Trionfi. Cambridge, MA: Harvard University Press, 1971.

Charles d'Orléans. *Poésies.* Ed. Pierre Champion. Paris: Librairie Ancienne Honoré Champion, 1923.

Cicero. *De Inventione.* Trans. H. M. Hubbell. Loeb Classical Library. Cambridge, MA: Harvard University Press, 1949.

Clode, C. M. *Memorials of the Guild of Merchant Taylors of the Fraternity of John the Baptist.* London: Harrison & Sons, 1875.

Cohen, Gustave, ed. *Recueil de Farces Françaises Inédites du XVe Siècle.* Cambridge, MA: Medieval Academy of America, 1949.

Crampton, Georgia R. *The Shewings of Julian of Norwich.* Kalamazoo, MI: Medieval Institute Publications, 1994.

The Customs of London, otherwise called Arnold's Chronicle. London: F.C. and J. Rivington *et al.,* 1811.

Davidson, Clifford, ed. *A Treatise of Miraclis Pleyinge.* Kalamazoo, MI: Medieval Institute Publications, 1993.

Delpit, J. *Collection générale des documents français qui se trouvent en Angleterre recueillis et publiés.* Paris: J. B. Dumoulin, 1847.

Devlin, Sister Mary Aquinas. *The Sermons of Thomas Brinton, Bishop of Rochester (1373–1389).* Camden Society 3rd series, 85. London: Offices of the Royal Historical Society, 1954.

Dick, Wilhelm, ed. *Die Gesta Romanorum nach der Innsbrucker Handschrift vom Jahre 1342 und Vier Münchener Handschriften.* Erlangen and Leipzig: A. Deichert'sche Verlagsbuchh. Nachf. (Georg Böhme), 1890.

Douët-D'Arcq, L., ed. *La Chronique d'Enguerran de Monstrelet.* Paris: Librairie de la Société de l'Histoire de France, 1861.

Dufournet, Jean, ed. and trans. *Le Jeu de la feuillée.* Louvain: Peeters, 1991.

Erbe, Theodore, ed. *Mirk's Festial: A Collection of Homilies, by Johannes Mirkus.* Early English Text Society extra series 96. London: Kegan Paul, 1905.

Flutre, L.-F., and K. Sneyders de Vogel, eds. *Li Fet des Romains.* Paris: E. Droz, 1938.

Fowler, David C., Charles F. Briggs, and Paul Remley, eds. *The Governance of Kings and Princes: John Trevisa's Middle English Translation of the De Regimine Principum of Aegidus Romanus.* New York: Garland, 1997.

Fuller, Carol S., ed. "A Critical Edition of *Le Jeu des Eschés, Moralisé translated by Jehan de Vignay.*" Ph.D. dissertation. Catholic University of America, 1974.

Furnivall, Frederick J., ed. *Hoccleve's Works. III: The Regement of Princes, A.D. 1411–12, and Fourteen of Hoccleve's Minor Poems.* Early English Text Society extra series 72. London: Kegan Paul, Trench & Trübner, 1897; reprinted Woodbridge, Suffolk: Boydell & Brewer, 1997.

Gairdner, James, ed. *Gregory's Chronicle of London. The Historical Collections of a Citizen of London in the Fifteenth Century.* London: Camden Society, 1876.

Galbraith, V. H., ed. *Anonimalle Chronicle.* Manchester: Manchester University Press, 1927.

Gower, John. *The Complete Works of John Gower.* 4 vols. Vol. II, *English Works* and vol. IV, *Latin Works.* Ed. G. C. Macaulay. Oxford: Clarendon Press, 1899–1902.

Confessio Amantis. Ed. Russell Peck. Toronto: University of Toronto Press, 1980.

John Gower: Confessio Amantis, volume one. Ed. Russell Peck. Kalamazoo, MI: Medieval Institute Publications, 2000.

Grässe, J. G. Th., ed. *Dialogus Creaturarum. Die Beiden Ältesten Lateinischen Fabelbücher des Mittelalters.* Tübingen, 1880.

Guillaume de Lorris and Jean de Meun. *Le Roman de la Rose.* Ed. Ernest Langlois. 5 vols. Paris: Firmin-Didot, 1914–24.

Hector, L. C., and Barbara F. Harvey, ed. and trans. *The Westminster Chronicle, 1381–1394.* Oxford: Clarendon Press, 1982.

Henry, Avril, ed. *The Mirour of Mans Saluacioune.* Philadelphia: University of Pennsylvania Press, 1987.

Herrtage, Sidney. *The Early English Versions of the Gesta Romanorum.* Early English Text Society extra series 33. London: N. Trübner, 1879.

Herzstein, Salomon, ed. *Tractatus de Diversis Historiis Romanorum et Quibusdam Aliis. Erlanger Beiträge zur Englischen Philologie,* part 14. Ed. Hermann Varnhagen. Erlangen: Verlag von Fr. Junge, 1893.

Hoccleve, Thomas. *The Regiment of Princes.* Ed. Charles Blyth. Kalamazoo, MI: Medieval Institute Publications, 1999.

Holcot, Robert. *Super Libros Sapientiae.* Hagenau, 1494; reprinted Frankfurt: Minerva GmbH, 1974.

Honorius. *Speculum Ecclesiae. Patrologia Latina,* vol. CLXXII, col. 807–1107.

Isidore of Seville. *Etymologiarum sive Originum Libri xx.* Ed. W. M. Lindsay. Oxford: Clarendon Press, 1911.

Etymologiae. Patrologia Latina, vol. LXXXII, col. 73–728.

James, Bruno Scott, trans. *The Letters of Bernard of Clairvaux.* London: Burns Oates, 1953.

Jean de Thuin. *Li Hystore de Julius Cesar.* Ed. Franz Settegast. Halle: M. Niemeyer, 1881.

Ker, N. R., ed. *Facsimile of B. M. MS Harley 2253.* Oxford: Oxford University Press, 1965.

Kingsford, Charles L., ed. *Chronicles of London.* Oxford: Clarendon Press, 1905.

Langland, William. *The Vision of Piers Plowman: A Complete Edition of the B-Text.* Ed. A. V. C. Schmidt. London: J. M. Dent, 1978.

Lawlor, Traugott. *The Parisiana Poetria of John of Garland.* Appendix 2, "The Two Versions of Geoffrey of Vinsauf's *Documentum,*" 327–32. New Haven: Yale University Press, 1974.

Livy. *History of Rome Books VII–X.* Trans. B. O. Foster. Cambridge, MA: Harvard University Press, 1926.

Lucan. *The Civil War (Pharsalia).* Trans. J. D. Duff. Cambridge, MA: Harvard University Press, 1928, 1988.

Luders, A, T. Tomlins, J. France, and W. E. Taunton, eds. *Statutes of the Realm.* 11 vols. London: Eyre & Strahan, 1810–22.

Lydgate, John. *Fall of Princes.* 4 vols. Ed. Henry Bergen. Early English Text Society extra series 121, 122, 123, 124. Oxford: Oxford University Press, 1924–27, 1967.

The Life of Saint Alban and Saint Amphibal. Ed. J. E. Van Der Westhuizen. Leiden: Brill, 1974.

Lydgate's Disguising at Hertford Castle: The First Secular Comedy in the English Language. Ed. Derek Forbes. Pulborough: Blot Publishing, 1998.

The Minor Poems of John Lydgate. Part 1. Ed. Henry Noble MacCracken. Early English Text Society extra series 107. Oxford: Oxford University Press, 1911, 1962.

The Minor Poems of John Lydgate. Part 2. Ed. Henry Noble MacCracken. Early English Text Society old series 192. Oxford: Oxford University Press, 1934.

The Serpent of Division by John Lydgate the Monk of Bury. Ed. Henry Noble MacCracken. London: H. Frowde, 1911.

The Serpent of Deuision Wherein is contained the true History or Mappe of Romes ouerthrow ... Whereunto is annexed the Tragedye of Gorboduc, sometime King of this Land, and of his two Sonnes, Ferrex and Porrex. Printed by Edward Allde for Iohn Perrin, 1590. STC (2nd edn) 17029.

The Siege of Thebes. 2 vols. Ed. Axel Erdmann and Eilert Ekwall. Early English Text Society 108, 125. Oxford: Oxford University Press, 1960.

Troy Book. 4 vols. Ed. Henry Bergen. Early English Text Society extra series 97, 103, 106, 126. London: Kegan Paul, Trench & Trübner, 1906, 1908, 1910, 1935.

Troy Book: Selections. Ed. Robert Edwards. Kalamazoo, MI: Medieval Institute Publications, 1998.

Manzalaoui, M. A., ed. *Secretum Secretorum: Nine English Versions.* Early English Text Society original series 276. Oxford: Oxford University Press, 1977.

Map, Walter. *De Nugis Curialium: Courtier's Trifles.* Ed. and trans. M. R. James. Revised by C. N. L. Brooke and R. A. B. Mynors. Oxford: Clarendon Press, 1983.

Martin of Braga. *De quattuor virtutibus cardinalibus; or Des mots dorez des quatre vertus.* Paris: Pierre Le Rouge for Antoine Vérard, 1491.

Nencioni, Giovanni. *Uguccione da Pisa: Derivationes.* Florence: Academia della Crusca, 2000.

Nicolas, Sir Harris, ed. *A Chronicle of London, from 1089 to 1483.* London, 1827; reprinted Felinfach: Llanerch Publishers, 1995.

Proceedings and Ordinances of the Privy Council of England. Vol. III. London, 1834.

Norton-Smith, John. *John Lydgate: Poems.* Oxford: Clarendon Press, 1966.

Öesterley, Hermann, ed. *Gesta Romanorum.* Berlin: Weidmannsche Buchhandlung, 1872.

Ordal, Norbert d'. *Breviloqui.* Barcelona: Editorial Barcino, 1930.

Ovid. *The Art of Love and Other Poems.* Trans. J. H. Mozley. Loeb Classical Library. Cambridge, MA: Harvard University Press, 1929.

Heroides, Amores. Trans. Grant Showerman. Loeb Classical Library. Cambridge, MA: Harvard University Press, 1914, 1996.

Metamorphoses. Trans. Frank Justus Miller. Cambridge, MA: Harvard University Press, 1916.

Owst, G. R. *Literature and Pulpit in Medieval England.* Cambridge: Cambridge University Press, 1933.

Papias. *Vocabulista.* Venice, 1496; reprinted Torino: Bottega d'Erasmo, 1966.

Pliny. *Natural History.* 10 vols. Trans. H. Rackham. Loeb Classical Library. Cambridge, MA: Harvard University Press, 1952.

Rickert, Edith. "Extracts from a Fourteenth-Century Account Book." *Modern Philology* 24 (1926–27): 111–19.

Riley, H. T., ed. *Liber Albus.* London: Longman, Green, Longman, & Roberts, 1862. *Memorials of London and London Life, in the XIIIth, XIVth and XVth Centuries.* London: Longmans, Green & Co., 1868.

Ruggiers, Paul, ed. *The Facsimile Series of the Works of Geoffrey Chaucer.* Vol. v. *Manuscript Trinity R.3.19: A Facsimile.* Norman, OK: Pilgrim Books, 1987.

Rymer, Thomas, ed. *Foedera.* The Hague: Joannem Neulme, 1739–45.

Sandred, Karl Inge, ed. *A Middle English Version of the Gesta Romanorum edited from Gloucester Cathedral MS 22.* Uppsala: Acta Universitatis Upsaliensis, 1971.

Smith, Charles Roger, ed. "Concordia Facta inter Regem Riccardum II et Civitatem Londonie." Ph.D. dissertation. Princeton University, 1972. Ann Arbor: University Microfilms, 1972.

Steele, Robert, ed. *Opera Hactenus Inedita Rogeri Baconi, Fasc. V: Secretum Secretorum.* Oxford: Clarendon Press, 1920.

Three Prose Versions of the Secreta Secretorum. Early English Text Society extra series 74. London: Kegan Paul, Trench & Trübner, 1898.

Stow, John. *Survey of London.* Ed. Charles Kingsford. Oxford: Clarendon Press, 1908.

Suetonius. *Lives of the Caesars.* Trans. J. C. Rolfe. Loeb Classical Library. Cambridge, MA: Harvard University Press, 1913, revised 1998.

Tertullian. *Apologeticus and De Spectaculis.* Trans. T. R. Glover. Loeb Classical Library. Cambridge, MA: Harvard University Press, 1953.

Tolkien, J. R. R., and E. V. Gordon, eds. *Sir Gawain and the Green Knight.* 2nd edn. Rev. Norman Davis. Oxford: Clarendon Press, 1967.

Trivet, Nicholas. *Exposicio Fratris Nicolai Trevethi Anglici Ordinis Predicatorum Super Boecio de Consolacione.* Edmund Taite Silk Papers. Manuscripts and Archives. Yale University Library.

Tyrrell, Edward, and Nicholas H. Nicolas, eds. *A Chronicle of London from 1089 to 1483.* London: Longman & Green, 1827.

Uguccione da Pisa, *Derivationes: Edizione critica princeps.* Ed. Enzo Cecchini, Guido Arbizzoni, Settimio Lanciotti, Giorgio Nonni, Maria Grazia Sassi, Alba Tontini. Florence: Sismel, Edizioni de Galluzzo, 2004.

Veinant, Auguste, ed. *Sensuyt le Roman de edipus filz du roy Layus lequel Edip' tua son pere. Et depuis espousa sa mere: Et en eut quatre enfas.* Paris: Ch. Lahure, 1858.

Vincent of Beauvais. *Speculum Quadruplex; sive Speculum Maius.* 4 vols. Vol II, *Speculum Doctrinale*; vol. IV, *Speculum Historiale.* Graz: Akademische Druck-u. Verlaganstalt, 1964–65.

Virgil. *Works.* Vol. I. *Eclogues, Georgics, Aeneid* I–VI. Trans. H. Rushton Fairclough; rev. G. P. Gould. Cambridge, MA: Harvard University Press, 1999.

Bibliography

Vita S. Johannis Eleemosynarii. Patrologia Latina, vol. LXXIII, col. 337–92.

Wenzel, Siegfried. *Fasciculus Morum: A Fourteenth Century Preacher's Handbook.* University Park: Pennsylvania State University Press, 1989.

Willis, J. *Macrobius.* 2 vols. Stuttgart: B. G. Teubneri, 1963, 1994.

Wright, Thomas, ed. *Political Songs and Poems Relating to English History.* Rolls Series 14. London: Her Majesty's Stationery Office, 1859.

SECONDARY SOURCES

Aers, David. "Medievalists and Deconstruction: An Exemplum." In *From Medieval to Medievalism.* Ed. John Simons. New York: St. Martin's Press, 1992, 24–40.

"*Vox Populi* and the Literature of 1381." In *The Cambridge History of Medieval English Literature.* Ed. David Wallace. Cambridge: Cambridge University Press, 1999, 432–53.

Allen, Judson Boyce. *The Friar as Critic: Literary Attitudes in the Later Middle Ages.* Nashville: Vanderbilt University Press, 1971.

Anglo, Sidney. *Spectacle, Pageantry, and Early Tudor Policy.* Oxford: Clarendon Press, 1969, 1997.

Ashley, Kathleen, and Wim Hüsken. *Moving Subjects: Processional Performance in the Middle Ages and the Renaissance.* Amsterdam: Rodopi, 2001.

Atkins, J. W. H. "Review of *The Serpent of Division*, ed. MacCracken." *Modern Language Review* 7 (1912): 253–54.

Barini, Concetta. *Triumphalia.* Torino: Societá Editrice Internazionale, 1952.

Barnum, Priscilla Heath. *Dives and Pauper.* Early English Text Society old series 275. Oxford: Oxford University Press, 1976.

Barron, Caroline M. *The Medieval Guildhall of London.* London: Corporation of London, 1974.

"The Quarrel of Richard II with London 1392–7." In *The Reign of Richard II: Essays in Honour of May McKisack.* Ed. F. R. H. Du Boulay and C. M. Barron. London: Athlone Press, 1971, 173–201.

Baswell, Christopher. "Aeneas in 1381." *New Medieval Literatures* 5 (2002): 7–58.

Beckwith, Sarah. *Signifying God: Social Relation and Symbolic Act in the York Corpus Christi Plays.* Chicago: University of Chicago Press, 2001.

Beer, Jeannette. *A Medieval Caesar.* Geneva: Droz, 1976.

Benson, C. David. "The Ancient World in John Lydgate's *Troy Book.*" *American Benedictine Review* 24 (1973): 299–312.

"Civic Lydgate: The Poet and London." In *John Lydgate: Poetry, Culture and Lancastrian England.* Ed. Larry Scanlon and James Simpson. Notre Dame, IN: University of Notre Dame Press, 2005.

Bergeron, David. *English Civic Pageantry, 1558–1642.* Columbia: University of South Carolina Press, 1971.

Binski, Paul. *The Painted Chamber at Westminster.* London: Society of Antiquaries, 1986.

Bibliography

Bird, Ruth. *The Turbulent London of Richard II*. London: Longman's, Green & Co., 1949.

Boffey, Julia, and John J. Thompson. "Anthologies and Miscellanies: Production and Choice of Texts." In *Book Production and Publishing in Britain, 1375–1475*. Ed. Jeremy Griffiths and Derek Pearsall. Cambridge: Cambridge University Press, 1989, 279–315.

Boitani, Piero, ed. *The European Tragedy of Troilus*. Oxford: Clarendon Press, 1989.

Bowers, John. *The Politics of Pearl: Court Poetry in the Age of Richard II*. Cambridge: D. S. Brewer, 2001.

Boyle, Leonard. "The Date of the *Summa Praedicantium* of John of Bromyard." *Speculum* 48 (1973): 533–37.

Brennan, T. Corey. "Triumphus in Monte Albano." In *Transitions to Empire: Essays in Greco Roman History, 360–146 B.C., in Honor of E. Badian*. Norman: University of Oklahoma Press, 1996, 315–37.

Brewer, Derek. "Comedy and Tragedy in *Troilus and Criseyde*." In *The European Tragedy of Troilus*. Ed. Piero Boitani. Oxford: Clarendon Press, 1989, 95–109.

Brotanek, Rudolph. *Die Englischen Maskenspiele*. Leipzig: Wilhelm Braumüller, 1902.

Brusendorff, Aage. *The Chaucer Tradition*. Oxford: Clarendon Press, 1967.

Bryan, W. F., and Germaine Dempster, eds. *Sources and Analogues of Chaucer's Canterbury Tales*. Chicago: University of Chicago Press, 1941.

Bryant, Lawrence M. "Configurations of the Community in Late Medieval Spectacles: Paris and London During the Dual Monarchy." In *City and Spectacle in Medieval Europe*. Ed. Barbara A. Hanawalt and Kathryn L. Reyerson. Minneapolis: University of Minnesota Press, 1994, 3–33.

Burnley, J. D. "Curial Prose in England." *Speculum* 61.3 (1986): 593–614.

Butterfield, Ardis. *Poetry and Music in Medieval France: From Jean Renart to Guillaume de Machaut*. Cambridge: Cambridge University Press, 2002.

Camille, Michael. *Images on the Edge: The Margins of Medieval Art*. Cambridge, MA: Harvard University Press, 1992.

Cannon, Christopher. "Monastic Productions." In *The Cambridge History of Medieval English Literature*. Ed. David Wallace. Cambridge: Cambridge University Press, 1999, 316–48.

Carpenter, Christine. *The Wars of the Roses: Politics and the Constitution in England, c. 1437–1509*. Cambridge: Cambridge University Press, 1997.

Chambers, E. K. *The Mediaeval Stage*. 2 vols. Oxford: Oxford University Press, 1903.

Chickering, Howell. "Form and Interpretation in the *Envoy* to the *Clerk's Tale*." *Chaucer Review* 29 (1995): 352–72.

Chism, Christine. *Alliterative Revivals*. Philadelphia: University of Pennsylvania Press, 2002.

Christie, Mabel E. *Henry VI*. Boston: Houghton Mifflin, 1922.

Clark, J. P. H. "'Fiducia' in Julian of Norwich." *Downside Review* 100 (1982): 203–20.

Cloetta, Wilhelm. *Beiträge zur Literaturgeschichte des Mittelalters und der Renaissance*. Vol. I, *Komödie und Tragödie im Mittelalter*. Halle: Max Niemeyer, 1890.

Bibliography

Clopper, Lawrence. *Drama, Play and Game: English Festive Culture in the Medieval and Early Modern Period.* Chicago: University of Chicago Press, 2001.

"The Engaged Spectator: Langland and Chaucer on Civic Spectacle and the Theatrum." *Studies in the Age of Chaucer* 22 (2000): 115–39.

Clough, Andrea. "Medieval Tragedy and the Genre of *Troilus and Criseyde.*" *Medievalia et Humanistica* 11 (1982): 211–27.

Coldewey, John. "Plays and 'Play' in Early English Drama." *Research Opportunities in Renaissance Drama* 28 (1985): 181–88.

Coleman, Janet. *Medieval Readers and Writers: 1350–1400.* New York: Columbia University Press, 1981.

"The Science of Politics and Late Medieval Academic Debate." In *Criticism and Dissent in the Middle Ages.* Ed. Rita Copeland. Cambridge: Cambridge University Press, 1996, 181–214.

Coleman, Joyce. *Public Reading and the Reading Public in Late Medieval England and France.* Cambridge: Cambridge University Press, 1996.

Connolly, Margaret. *John Shirley: Book Production and the Noble Household in Fifteenth-Century England.* Brookfield, VT: Ashgate, 1998.

Copeland, Rita. "Lydgate, Hawes, and the Science of Rhetoric in the Late Middle Ages." *Modern Language Quarterly* 53 (March, 1992): 57–81.

Rhetoric, Hermeneutics and Translation in the Middle Ages: Academic Traditions and Vernacular Texts. Cambridge: Cambridge University Press, 1991.

Crane, Susan. *The Performance of Self: Ritual, Clothing and Identity During the Hundred Years War.* Philadelphia: University of Pennsylvania Press, 2002.

Davenport, W. A. *Fifteenth-Century English Drama: The Early Moral Plays and Their Literary Relations.* Cambridge: D. S. Brewer, 1982.

DeVries, David N. "And Away go Troubles Down the Drain: Late Medieval London and the Politics of Urban Renewal." *Exemplaria* 8.2 (1996): 401–18.

Doyle, A. I. "English Books in and out of Court from Edward III to Henry VI." In *English Court Culture in the Later Middle Ages.* Ed. V. J. Scattergood and J. W. Sherborne. New York: St. Martin's Press, 1983, 163–81.

Duffy, Eamon. *The Stripping of the Altars: Traditional Religion in England, 1400–1580.* New Haven: Yale University Press, 1992.

Ebin, Lois. *Illuminator, Makar, Vates: Visions of Poetry in the Fifteenth Century.* Lincoln: University of Nebraska Press, 1988.

John Lydgate. Boston: Twayne, 1985.

Edwards, A. S. G. "The Influence of Lydgate's *Fall of Princes c.* 1440–1559: A Survey." *Medieval Studies* 39 (1977): 424–39.

"John Shirley and the Emulation of Courtly Culture." In *The Court and Cultural Diversity.* Ed. Evelyn Mullally and John Thompson. Cambridge: D. S. Brewer, 1997, 309–17.

Edwards, J. G. "Ranulf, Monk of Chester." *English Historical Review* 47 (1932): 94.

Enciclopedia Dantesca. Rome: Istituto Della Enciclopedia Italiana.

Enders, Jody. *Rhetoric and the Origins of Medieval Drama.* Ithaca, NY: Cornell University Press, 1992.

Epstein, Robert. "Lydgate's Mummings and the Aristocratic Resistance to Drama." *Comparative Drama* 36 (2002): 337–58.

Farnham, Willard. *The Medieval Heritage of Elizabethan Tragedy.* Berkeley: University of California Press, 1936.

Fassler, Margot. "Mary's Nativity, Fulbert of Chartres, and the Stirps Jesse: Liturgical Innovation circa 1000 and its Afterlife." *Speculum* 75 (2000): 389–434.

Federico, Sylvia. "A Fourteenth-Century Erotics of Politics: London as a Feminine New Troy." *Studies in the Age of Chaucer* 19 (1997): 121–55.

Ferster, Judith. *Fictions of Advice: The Literature and Politics of Counsel in Late Medieval England.* Philadelphia: University of Pennsylvania Press, 1996.

Fisher, John. *John Gower: Moral Philosopher and Friend of Chaucer.* New York: New York University Press, 1964.

Fleming, John. *An Introduction to the Franciscan Literature of the Middle Ages.* Chicago: Franciscan Herald Press, 1977.

Fowler, Alastair. *Triumphal Forms: Structural Patterns in Elizabethan Poetry.* Cambridge: Cambridge University Press, 1970.

Fradenburg, L. O. Aranye. *Sacrifice your Love: Psychoanalysis, Historicism, Chaucer.* Minneapolis: University of Minnesota Press, 2002.

Gibson, Gail. "Bury St. Edmunds, Lydgate, and the N-Town Cycle." *Speculum* 56 (1981): 56–90.

Godefroy, Frédéric, ed. *Dictionnaire de l'ancienne langue française.* Paris: F. Vieweg, 1888.

Grady, Frank. "The Lancastrian Gower and the Limits of Exemplarity." *Speculum* 70 (1995): 552–75.

Gransden, Antonia. *Historical Writing in England. vol. II, Circa 1307 to the Early Sixteenth Century.* London: Routledge & Kegan Paul, 1982.

Green, Richard Firth. *A Crisis of Truth: Literature and Law in Ricardian England.* Philadelphia: University of Pennsylvania Press, 1999.

Poets and Princepleasers: Literature and the English Court in the Late Middle Ages. Toronto: University of Toronto Press, 1980.

"Three Fifteenth-Century Notes." *English Language Notes* 14 (1976–77): 14–17.

Griffiths, Ralph A. *The Reign of King Henry VI: The Exercise of Royal Authority, 1422–1461.* Berkeley and Los Angeles: University of California Press, 1981.

Haas, Renate. "Chaucer's *Monk's Tale*: An Ingenious Criticism of Early Humanist Conceptions of Tragedy." *Humanistica Lovaniensia* 36 (1987): 44–70.

Habermas, Jürgen. *The Structural Transformation of the Public Sphere: An Inquiry into a Category of Bourgeois Society.* Trans. Thomas Burger with the assistance of Frederick Lawrence. Cambridge, MA: MIT Press, 1989.

Hamilton, George L. "Some Sources of the Seventh Book of Gower's 'Confessio Amantis.'" *Modern Philology* 9 (1912): 323–46.

Hammond, Eleanor. *English Verse between Chaucer and Surrey.* Durham, NC: Duke University Press, 1927.

"Lydgate's Mumming at Hertford." *Anglia* 22 (1899): 364–74.

Bibliography

"Two Tapestry Poems by Lydgate: *The Life of St. George* and the *Falls of Seven Princes*." *Englische Studien* 43 (1910): 10–26.

Hanna, Ralph. "Analytical Survey 4: Middle English Manuscripts and the Study of Literature." *New Medieval Literatures* 4. Ed. Wendy Scase, Rita Copeland, and David Lawton. Oxford: Oxford University Press, 2001, 243–64.

Harris, William O. *Skelton's Magnyfycence and the Cardinal Virtue Tradition.* Chapel Hill: University of North Carolina Press, 1965.

Herbert, J. A. *Catalogue of Romances in the Department of Manuscripts in the British Museum.* 3 vols. London: Longmans & Co., 1910.

Holliday, Peter. *Origins of Roman Historical Commemoration in the Visual Arts.* Cambridge: Cambridge University Press, 2002.

Holsinger, Bruce. *Music, Body and Desire in Medieval Culture: Hildegard of Bingen to Chaucer.* Stanford: Stanford University Press, 2001.

Horrox, Rosemary. "The Urban Gentry in the Fifteenth Century." In *Towns and Townspeople in the Fifteenth Century.* Ed. John A. F. Thomson. Gloucester: Alan Sutton, 1988, 22–44.

Hunt, R. W. "The 'Lost' Preface to the *Liber Derivationum* of Osbern of Gloucester." In *The History of Grammar in the Middle Ages: Collected Papers.* Ed. G. L. Bursill-Hall. Amsterdam: John Benjamins B. V., 1980, 151–66.

Jacob, Ernest. *The Fifteenth Century: 1399–1485.* Oxford: Clarendon Press, 1961.

Jacquiot, Josèphe. "De l'entrée de César à Rome à l'entrée des Rois de France dans leurs bonnes villes." In *Italian Renaissance Festivals and their European Influence.* Ed. J. R. Mulryne and Margaret Shewring. Lewiston, NY: Mellen Press, 1992, 255–65.

Jameson, Fredric. *Marxism and Form.* Princeton: Princeton University Press, 1971.

The Political Unconscious: Narrative as a Socially Symbolic Act. Ithaca, NY: Cornell University Press, 1981.

Jennings, Margaret. "Monks and the 'Artes Praedicandi' in the Time of Ranulph Higden." *Revue Bénédictine* 86 (1976): 119–28.

Jones, Joseph R. "Isidore and the Theater." *Comparative Drama* 16 (1982): 26–48.

Jones, Marion. "Early Moral Plays and the Earliest Secular Drama." In *The Revels History of Drama in English.* Vol. 1, *Medieval Drama.* Ed. Lois Potter. New York: Methuen, 1983, 213–91.

Kantorowicz, Ernst. "The 'King's Advent' and the Enigmatic Panels in the Doors of Santa Sabina." *Art Bulletin* 26 (1944): 207–31.

The King's Two Bodies: A Study in Medieval Political Theology. Princeton: Princeton University Press, 1957.

Katzenellenbogen, Adolph. *Allegories of the Virtues and Vices in Medieval Art from Early Christian Times to the Thirteenth Century.* Studies of the Warburg Institute 10. London: Warburg Institute Press, 1939.

Kelly, Henry Ansgar. *Chaucerian Tragedy.* Cambridge: D. S. Brewer, 1997.

Ideas and Forms of Tragedy from Aristotle to the Middle Ages. Cambridge: Cambridge University Press, 1993.

Kendrick, Laura. "The *Troilus* Frontispiece and the Dramatization of Chaucer's *Troilus.*" *Chaucer Review* 22 (1987): 81–93.

Kerby-Fulton, Kathryn. "Langland and the Bibliographic Ego." In *Written Work: Langland, Labor, and Authorship.* Ed. Kathryn Kerby-Fulton and Steven Justice. Philadelphia: University of Pennsylvania Press, 1997, 67–143.

Kipling, Gordon. *Enter the King: Theatre, Liturgy and Ritual in the Medieval Civic Triumph.* Oxford: Clarendon Press, 1998.

"Lydgate: The Poet as Deviser." In *Chaucer and the Challenges of Medievalism: Studies in Honor of H. A. Kelly.* Ed. Donka Minkova and Theresa Tinkle. New York: Peter Lang, 2003, 73–101.

"Richard II's 'Sumptuous Pageants' and the Idea of the Civic Triumph." In *Pageantry in the Shakespearean Theater.* Ed. David M. Bergeron. Athens: University of Georgia Press, 1985, 83–103.

The Triumph of Honour: The Burgundian Origins of the English Renaissance. The Hague: Leiden University Press, 1977.

"Triumphal Drama: Form in English Civic Pageantry." *Renaissance Drama* 8 (1977): 37–56.

Knapp, Ethan. *The Bureaucratic Muse: Thomas Hoccleve and the Literature of Late Medieval England.* University Park: Pennsylvania State University Press, 2001.

Kozikowski, Stanley. "Lydgate, Machiavelli, and More and Skelton's *Bowge of Courte.*" *American Notes and Queries* 15 (1977): 66–67.

Künzl, Ernst. *Der Römische Triumph: Siegesfeiern im Antiken Rom.* Munich: Verlag C. H. Beck, 1988.

Lampert, Lisa. *Gender and Jewish Difference from Paul to Shakespeare.* Philadelphia: University of Pennsylvania Press, 2004.

Lancashire, Anne. *London Civic Theatre: City Drama and Pageantry from Roman Times to 1558.* Cambridge: Cambridge University Press, 2002.

Lancashire, Ian, ed. *Dramatic Texts and Records of Britain: A Chronological Topography to 1558.* Toronto: University of Toronto Press, 1984.

Lawton, David. "Dullness and the Fifteenth Century." *English Literary History* 54 (1987): 761–99.

Lerer, Seth. *Chaucer and his Readers: Imagining the Author in Late Medieval England.* Princeton: Princeton University Press, 1993.

"The Chaucerian Critique of Medieval Theatricality." In *The Performance of Middle English Culture: Essays on Chaucer and the Drama in Honor of Martin Stevens.* Ed. James J. Paxson, Lawrence M. Clopper, and Sylvia Tomasch. Cambridge: D. S. Brewer, 1996, 59–76.

Lindenbaum, Sheila. "Ceremony and Oligarchy: The London Midsummer Watch." In *City and Spectacle in Medieval Europe.* Ed. Barbara Hanawalt and Kathryn Reyerson. Minneapolis: University of Minnesota Press, 1994, 171–88.

"London Texts and Literate Practices." In *The Cambridge History of Medieval English Literature.* Ed. David Wallace. Cambridge: Cambridge University Press, 1999, 284–309.

"The Smithfield Tournament of 1390." *Journal of Medieval and Renaissance Studies* 20 (1990): 1–20.

Loomis, Roger Sherman. "Chivalric and Dramatic Imitations of Arthurian Romance." In *Medieval Studies in Memory of A. Kingsley Porter*. Ed. Wilhelm R. W. Koehler. 2 vols. Cambridge, MA: Harvard University Press, 1939, vol. I, 79–97.

Lumiansky, Robert. "The Alliterative *Morte Arthure*, the Concept of Medieval Tragedy, and the Cardinal Virtue Fortitude." In *Medieval and Renaissance Studies*. Ed. John M. Headly. Chapel Hill: University of North Carolina Press, 1968, 95–117.

MacCracken, Henry Noble. "King Henry's Triumphal Entry into London, Lydgate's Poem, and Carpenter's Letter." *Archiv* 126 (1911): 75–102.

"Response to Atkins." *Modern Language Review* 8 (1913): 103–04.

Mâle, Emile. *L'Art religieux de la fin du moyen âge*. Paris: Librairie A. Colin, 1908.

Mann, Jill. *Feminizing Chaucer*. Cambridge: D. S. Brewer, 2002.

Marigo, Aristide. *I Codici manoscritti delle 'Derivationes' di Uguccione Pisano*. Rome: Istituto di Studi Romani, 1936.

Marshall, Mary H. "Theatre in the Middle Ages: Evidence from Dictionaries and Glosses." *Symposium* 4 (1950): 1–39, 366–89.

Matheson, Lister. "Historical Prose." In *Middle English Prose: A Critical Guide to Major Authors and Genres*. Ed. A. S. G. Edwards. New Brunswick, NJ: Rutgers University Press, 1984, 209–48.

The Prose Brut: The Development of a Middle English Chronicle. Tempe, AZ: Medieval and Renaissance Texts and Studies, 1998.

Matthews, Lloyd. "Chaucer's Personification of Prudence in *Troilus* (V. 743–49): Sources in the Visual Arts and Manuscript Scholia." *English Language Notes* 13 (1976): 249–55.

"Troilus and Criseyde, V. 743–49; Another Possible Source." *Neophilologische Mitteilungen* 82 (1981): 211–13.

McCormick, Thomas. *A Partial Edition of* Les Fais des Rommains *with a Study of its Style and Syntax: A Medieval Roman History*. Lewiston, NY: Mellen Press, 1995.

McKenna, J. W. "Henry VI of England and the Dual Monarchy: Aspects of Royal Political Propaganda, 1422–1432." *Journal of the Warburg and Courtauld Institutes* 28 (1965): 145–62.

McLaren, Mary-Rose. *The London Chronicles of the Fifteenth Century: A Revolution in English Writing*. Cambridge: D. S. Brewer, 2002.

Meale, Carol. *"The Libelle of Englyshe Polycye* and Mercantile Literary Culture in Late-Medieval London." In *London and Europe in the Later Middle Ages*. Ed. Julia Boffey and Pamela King. London: University of London, 1995, 181–227.

Meiss, Millard. *French Painting in the Time of Jean de Berry: The Limbourgs and their Contemporaries (1400–1425)*. 2 vols. New York: Braziller, 1974.

Middleton, Anne. "The Idea of Public Poetry in the Reign of Richard II." *Speculum* 53 (1978): 94–114.

Miller, Anthony. *Roman Triumphs and Early Modern English Culture*. New York: Palgrave, 2001.

Minnis, Alastair J. "De Vulgari Auctoritate: Chaucer, Gower and the Men of Great Authority." In *Chaucer and Gower: Difference, Mutuality, Exchange.* Ed. R. F. Yeager. English Literary Studies. Victoria: University of Victoria Press, 1991, 36–74.

"John Gower: Sapiens in Ethics and Politics." In *Gower's Confessio Amantis: A Critical Anthology.* Ed. Peter Nicholson. Cambridge: D. S. Brewer, 1991, 158–80.

Medieval Theory of Authorship: Scholastic Literary Attitudes in the Later Middle Ages. Philadelphia: University of Pennsylvania Press, 1988.

Monfrin, J. "Sur les sources du *Secret des Secrets* de Jofroi de Waterford et Servais Copale." In *Mélanges de linguistique romane et de philologie médiévale.* Ed. M. Maurice Delbouille. Gembloux: J. Duculot, 1964, vol. II, 509–30.

Moretti, Franco. "'A Huge Eclipse': Tragic Form and the Deconsecration of Sovereignty." *Genre* 15 (1982): 7–40.

Müller, Wolfgang. *Huguccio: The Life, Works, and Thought of a Twelfth-Century Jurist.* Washington, DC: Catholic University of America Press, 1994.

Nicol, Donald M. "A Byzantine Emperor in England: Manuel II's Visit to London in 1400–1401." *University of Birmingham Historical Journal* 12.2 (1970): 204–25.

Nolcken, Christina von. "Some Alphabetical Compendia and how Preachers used Them in Fourteenth-Century England." *Viator* 12 (1981): 271–88.

Norton-Smith, John. *Geoffrey Chaucer.* London: Routledge & Kegan Paul, 1974.

Núñez, Rafael Vélez. "The Masque's Antecedents in John Lydgate's Mummings and Momeries: A Revisionist Approach." In *"Woonderous Lytterature": SELIM Studies in Medieval English Literature.* Ed. Ana Bringas López, *et al.* Vigo: Universidade de Vigo, 1999, 185–89.

Olsson, Kurt O. "Rhetoric, John Gower and the Late Medieval *Exemplum*." In *Transformation and Continuity.* Ed. Paul Maurice Clogan. Medievalia et Humanistica new series 8. Cambridge: Cambridge University Press, 1977, 185–99.

Orwen, William R. "Spenser and the Serpent of Division." *Studies in Philology* 38 (1941): 198–210.

Osberg, Richard. "The Jesse Tree in the 1432 London Entry of Henry VI: Messianic Kingship and the Rule of Justice." *Journal of Medieval and Renaissance Studies* 16 (1986): 213–32.

Parkes, Malcolm. "The Literacy of the Laity." In *Scribes, Scripts and Readers: Studies in the Communication, Presentation and Dissemination of Medieval Texts.* London: Hambledon Press, 1991, 275–98.

Patch, Howard. *The Goddess Fortuna in Mediaeval Literature.* Cambridge, MA: Harvard University Press, 1927.

Patterson, Lee. *Chaucer and the Subject of History.* Madison: University of Wisconsin Press, 1991.

"Making Identities in Fifteenth-Century England: Henry V and John Lydgate." In *New Historical Literary Study: Essays on Producing Texts, Representing History.* Ed. Jeffrey N. Cox and Larry J. Reynolds. Princeton: Princeton University Press, 1993.

Bibliography

Negotiating the Past: The Historical Understanding of Medieval Literature. Madison: University of Wisconsin Press, 1987.

Payne, Robert. *The Roman Triumph.* New York: Abelard-Schuman, 1962.

Pearsall, Derek. *John Lydgate.* London: Routledge & Kegan Paul, 1970.

John Lydgate (1371–1449): A Bio-Bibliography. English Literary Studies Monograph Series 71. Victoria: University of Victoria Press, 1997.

"The *Troilus* Frontispiece and Chaucer's Audience." *Yearbook of English Studies* 7 (1977): 68–74.

Pettit, Tom. "Early English Traditional Drama: Approaches and Perspectives." *Research Opportunities in Renaissance Drama* 25 (1982): 1–30.

"Tudor Interludes and the Winter Revels." *Medieval English Theatre* 6.1 (1984): 16–27.

Pocock, J. G. *The Ancient Constitution and Feudal Law.* Cambridge: Cambridge University Press, 1957.

Politics, Language and Time: Essays on Political Thought and History. New York: Atheneum, 1971.

Porter, Elizabeth. "Gower's Ethical Microcosm and Political Macrocosm." In *Gower's Confessio Amantis: Responses and Reassessments.* Ed. A. J. Minnis. Cambridge: D. S. Brewer, 1983, 135–62.

Powell, Edward. "After 'After McFarlane': The Poverty of Patronage and the Case for Constitutional History." In *Trade, Devotion and Governance: Papers in Later Medieval History.* Ed. Dorothy Clayton, Richard Davis, and Peter McNiven. Dover, NH: Alan Sutton, 1994, 1–16.

Pratt, Robert. "Some Latin Sources of the Nonnes Preest on Dreams." *Speculum* 52 (1977): 538–70.

Ramsay, William. "Triumphus." In *A Dictionary of Greek and Roman Antiquities.* Ed. William Smith. London: John Murray, 1875, 1163–67.

Regalado, Nancy Freeman. "Staging the *Roman de Renart*: Medieval Theater and the Diffusion of Political Concerns into Popular Culture." *Mediaevalia* 18 (1995): 111–42.

Renoir, Alan. "On the Date of John Lydgate's 'Mumming at Hertford.'" *Archiv für das Studium der Neueren Sprachen und Literaturen* 198 (1961): 32–33.

The Poetry of John Lydgate. London: Routledge & Kegan Paul, 1967.

Revard, Carter. "'Gilote and Johane': An Interlude in B.L. MS Harley 2253." *Studies in Philology* 79 (1982): 122–46.

Reyher, Paul. *Les Masques anglais.* Paris, 1909; reprinted New York: Benjamin Blom, 1964.

Riddy, Felicity. "Reading for England: Arthurian Literature and National Consciousness." *Bibliographical Bulletin of the International Arthurian Society* 43 (1991): 314–32.

Riessner, Claus. *Die "Magnae Derivationes" des Uguccione da Pisa und Ihre Bedeutung für Romanische Philologie.* Rome: Edizioni di Storia e Letteratura, 1965.

Ringler, William. "Lydgate's *Serpent of Division,* 1559, Edited by John Stow." *Studies in Bibliography* 14 (1961): 201–03.

Robins, William. "Romance, Exemplum, and the Subject of the *Confessio Amantis.*" *Studies in the Age of Chaucer* 19 (1997): 157–81.

Rowe, B. J. H. "King Henry VI's Claim to France in Picture and Poem." *Library*, 4th series, 13 (1933): 77–88.

Ruggiers, Paul. "A Vocabulary for Chaucerian Comedy: A Preliminary Sketch." In *Medieval Studies in Honor of Lillian Herlands Hornstein*. Ed. Jess B. Bessinger and Robert R. Raymo. New York: New York University Press, 1976, 193–225.

Ruggiers, Paul, ed. *Versions of Medieval Comedy*. Norman: University of Oklahoma Press, 1977.

Salter, Elizabeth, and Derek Pearsall. "Pictorial Illustration of Late Medieval Poetic Texts: The Role of the Frontispiece or Prefatory Picture." In *Medieval Iconography and Narrative: A Symposium*. Ed. Flemming G. Anderson, *et al.* Odense: Odense University Press, 1980, 100–23.

Saygin, Susanne. *Humphrey, Duke of Gloucester (1390–1447) and the Italian Humanists*. Leiden: Brill, 2002.

Scanlon, Larry. *Narrative, Authority and Power: The Medieval Exemplum and the Chaucerian Tradition*. Cambridge: Cambridge University Press, 1994.

"What's the Pope got to do with it?: Forgery, Didacticism, and Desire in the *Clerk's Tale*." *New Medieval Literatures* 6 (2003): 129–65.

Scattergood, V. J. *Politics and Poetry in the Fifteenth Century*. New York: Barnes & Noble, 1972.

Schirmer, Walter. *John Lydgate: A Study in the Culture of the XVth Century*. Trans. Ann E. Keep. London: Methuen, 1961.

Schlauch, Margaret. "Stylistic Attributes of John Lydgate's Prose." In *To Honor Roman Jakobson*. 3 vols. 1757–68. The Hague and Paris: Mouton, 1967.

Schless, Howard. *Chaucer and Dante: A Revaluation*. Norman, OK: Pilgrim Books, 1984.

Schmitt, Carl. *Political Theology: Four Chapters on the Concept of Sovereignty*. Trans. George Schwab. Cambridge, MA: MIT Press, 1985.

"The Source of the Tragic." Trans. David Pan. *Telos* 72 (1987): 133–51.

Scullard, H. H. *Festivals and Ceremonies of the Roman Republic*. Ithaca, NY: Cornell University Press, 1981.

Sharpe, Reginald R., ed. *Calendar of the Letter-Books Preserved among the Archives of the Corporation of the City of London at the Guildhall*. London: J. E. Francis, 1899–1912.

Simpson, James. " 'Dysemol Daies and Fatal Houres': Lydgate's *Destruction of Thebes* and Chaucer's *Knight's Tale*." In *The Long Fifteenth Century: Essays for Douglas Gray*. Ed. Helen Cooper and Sally Mapstone. Oxford: Clarendon Press, 1997, 15–33.

The Oxford English Literary History. Vol. II, *1350–1547: Reform and Cultural Revolution*. Oxford: Oxford University Press, 2002.

Sciences and the Self in Medieval Poetry: Alan of Lille's Anticlaudianus and John Gower's Confessio Amantis. Cambridge: Cambridge University Press, 1995.

Skinner, Quentin. *The Foundations of Modern Political Thought*. 2 vols. Cambridge: Cambridge University Press, 1978.

Smalley, Beryl. *English Friars and Antiquity in the Early XIVth Century*. Oxford: Basil Blackwell, 1960.

Bibliography

"Robert Holcot, O. P." *Archivum Fratrum Praedicatorum* 26 (1956), 5–95.

Smith, D. Vance. "Plague, Panic Space, and the Tragic Medieval Household." *South Atlantic Quarterly* 98 (1999): 367–414.

Somerset, Fiona. *Clerical Discourse and Lay Authority in Late Medieval England.* Cambridge: Cambridge University Press, 1998.

Spearing, A. C. "Renaissance Chaucer and Father Chaucer." *English: The Journal of the English Association* 33 (1984): 1–38.

Spiegel, Gabrielle. *Romancing the Past: The Rise of Vernacular Prose Historiography in Thirteenth-Century France.* Los Angeles: University of California Press, 1993.

Sponsler, Claire. "Alien Nation: London's Aliens and Lydgate's Mummings for the Mercers and Goldsmiths." In *The Postcolonial Middle Ages.* Ed. Jeffrey Jerome Cohen. New York: St. Martin's Press, 2000, 229–42.

"Drama in the Archives: Recognizing Medieval Plays." In *From Script to Stage in Early Modern England.* Ed. Peter Holland and Stephen Orgel. Houndmills, Basingstoke: Palgrave Macmillan, 2004, 111–30.

Stegmüller, Friedrich. *Repertorium Biblicum Medii Aevi.* 11 vols. Vol. v. Madrid: Consejo Superior de Investigaciones Científicas, 1949.

Steiner, Emily. *Documentary Culture and the Making of Medieval English Literature.* Cambridge: Cambridge University Press, 2003.

Straker, Scott-Morgan. "Deference and Difference: Lydgate, Chaucer, and the *Siege of Thebes*." *Review of English Studies* new series 52 (2001): 1–21.

Strohm, Paul. "Chaucer's Fifteenth-Century Audience and the Narrowing of the 'Chaucer Tradition.'" *Studies in the Age of Chaucer* 4 (1982): 3–32.

England's Empty Throne: Usurpation and the Language of Legitimation, 1399–1422. New Haven: Yale University Press, 1998.

Hochon's Arrow: The Social Imagination of Fourteenth-Century Texts. Princeton: Princeton University Press, 1992.

"Lydgate and the Emergence of Pollecie in the Mirror Tradition." In *"Politique": Language and Statecraft from Chaucer to Shakespeare.* Notre Dame, IN: University of Notre Dame Press, 2005.

"Rememorative Reconstruction." *Studies in the Ages of Chaucer* 23 (2001): 3–16.

Theory and the Premodern Text. Minneapolis: University of Minnesota Press, 2000.

Sutton, Anne, and Livia Visser-Fuchs. "The Provenance of the Manuscript." In *The Politics of Fifteenth-Century England: John Vale's Book.* Ed. Margaret Kekewich *et al.* Stroud: Alan Sutton Publishing, 1995, 73–126.

Symes, Carol. "The Appearance of Early Vernacular Plays: Forms, Functions, and the Future of Medieval Theater." *Speculum* 77 (2002): 778–831.

Taylor, John. *The Universal Chronicle of Ranulf Higden.* Oxford: Clarendon Press, 1966.

Thrupp, Sylvia. *The Merchant Class of Medieval London.* Chicago: University of Chicago Press, 1948.

Torti, Anna. "From 'History' to 'Tragedy': The Story of Troilus and Criseyde in Lydgate's *Troy Book* and Henryson's *Testament of Cresseid*." In *The European Tragedy of Troilus.* Ed. Piero Boitani. Oxford: Clarendon Press, 1989, 171–97.

Bibliography

Toynbee, Paget. "Dante's Latin Dictionary." In *Dante Studies and Researches.* 1902; reprinted Port Washington, NY: Kennikat Press, 1971.

Tubach, Frederic. *Index Exemplorum: A Handbook of Medieval Religious Tales.* Helsinki: Suomalainen Tiedeakatemia/Academia Scientiarum Fennica, 1969.

Tuve, Rosemond. *Allegorical Imagery: Some Medieval Books and their Posterity.* Princeton: Princeton University Press, 1966.

Twycross, Meg. "Some Approaches to Dramatic Festivity, Especially Processions." In *Festive Drama.* Ed. Meg Twycross. Cambridge: D. S. Brewer, 1996, 1–33.

"The Theatricality of Medieval English Plays." In *The Cambridge Companion to Middle English Theatre.* Ed. Richard Beadle. Cambridge: Cambridge University Press, 1994, 37–84.

"My Visor is Philemon's Roof." *Fifteenth-Century Studies* 13 (1988): 335–46.

Twycross, Meg, and Sarah Carpenter. *Masks and Masking in Medieval and Early Tudor England.* Burlington, VT: Ashgate, 2002.

Twyman, Susan. *Papal Ceremonial at Rome in the Twelfth Century.* London: Henry Bradshaw Society, 2002.

Tydeman, William. *The Theatre in the Middle Ages: Western European Stage Conditions, c. 800–1576.* Cambridge: Cambridge University Press, 1978.

Vale, Juliet. *Edward III and Chivalry: Chivalric Society and its Context.* Woodbridge, Suffolk: Boydell Press, 1982.

Versnel, H. S. *Triumphus: An Inquiry into the Origin, Development and Meaning of the Roman Triumph.* Leiden: Brill, 1970.

Voigts, Linda Erhsam. "A Handlist of Middle English in Harvard Manuscripts." *Harvard Library Bulletin* 33 (winter 1985): 5–96.

Wallace, David. *Chaucerian Polity: Absolutist Lineages and Associational Forms in England and Italy.* Stanford: Stanford University Press, 1997.

Warren, Larissa Bonfante. "Review of *Triumphus.*" *Gnomon* 46.6 (1974): 574–83.

Warton, Thomas. *History of English Poetry.* London: Thomas Tegg, 1824, reprinted 1840.

Watson, Nicholas. "Censorship and Cultural Change in Late Medieval England: Vernacular Theology, the Oxford Translation Debate, and Arundel's Constitutions of 1409." *Speculum* 70.4 (October 1995): 822–64.

Watts, John. *Henry VI and the Politics of Kingship.* Cambridge: Cambridge University Press, 1996.

"The Pressure of the Public on Later Medieval Politics." In *The Fifteenth Century, IV: Political Culture in Late Medieval Britain.* Ed. Linda Clark and Christine Carpenter. Woodbridge, Suffolk: Boydell Press, 2004, 159–80.

Weijers, Olga. "Lexicography in the Middle Ages." *Viator* 20 (1989): 139–53.

Weiske, Brigitte. *Gesta Romanorum.* 2 vols. Tübingen: Max Niemeyer, 1992.

"Die 'Gesta Romanorum' und das 'Solsequium' Hugos von Trimberg." In *Exempel und Exempel-sammlungen.* Ed. Walter Haug and Burghart Wachinger. Tübingen: Max Niemeyer, 1991, 173–207.

Welsford, Enid. *The Court Masque: A Study in the Relationship Between Poetry and the Revels.* Cambridge: Cambridge University Press, 1927.

Welter, J.-Th. *L'Exemplum dans la littérature religieuse et didactique du moyen âge.* Paris: Société d'Histoire Ecclésiastique de la France, 1927.

Wenzel, Siegfried. *Preachers, Poets and the Early English Lyric.* Princeton: Princeton University Press, 1986.

Verses in Sermons: Fasciculus Morum and its Middle English Poems. Cambridge, MA: Medieval Academy of America Press, 1978.

Westfall, Suzanne. *Patrons and Performance: Early Tudor Household Revels.* Oxford: Clarendon Press, 1990.

Wetherbee, Winthrop. "Latin Structure and Vernacular Space: Gower, Chaucer and the Boethian Tradition." In *Chaucer and Gower: Difference, Mutuality, Exchange.* Ed. R. F. Yeager. English Literary Studies. Victoria: University of Victoria Press, 1991.

Wickham, Glynne. *Early English Stages, 1300–1600.* 3 vols. London: Routledge & Kegan Paul, 1959.

The Medieval Theatre. Cambridge: Cambridge University Press, 1987; reprint of Weidenfeld & Nicolson, 1974.

Williams, Raymond. *Marxism and Literature.* Oxford: Oxford University Press, 1977.

Windeatt, Barry. "Classical and Medieval Elements in Chaucer's Troilus." In *The European Tragedy of Troilus.* Ed. Piero Boitani. Oxford: Clarendon Press, 1989, 111–31.

Withington, Robert. *English Pageantry: An Historical Outline.* 2 vols. Cambridge, MA: Harvard University Press, 1918; reprinted New York: Benjamin Blom, 1963.

"The Early Royal Entry." *Periodical of the Modern Language Association* 32 (1917): 616–23.

Wolffe, Bertram. *Henry VI.* London: Eyre Methuen, 1981; reprinted New Haven: Yale University Press, 2001.

Index

CAMBRIDGE STUDIES IN MEDIEVAL LITERATURE